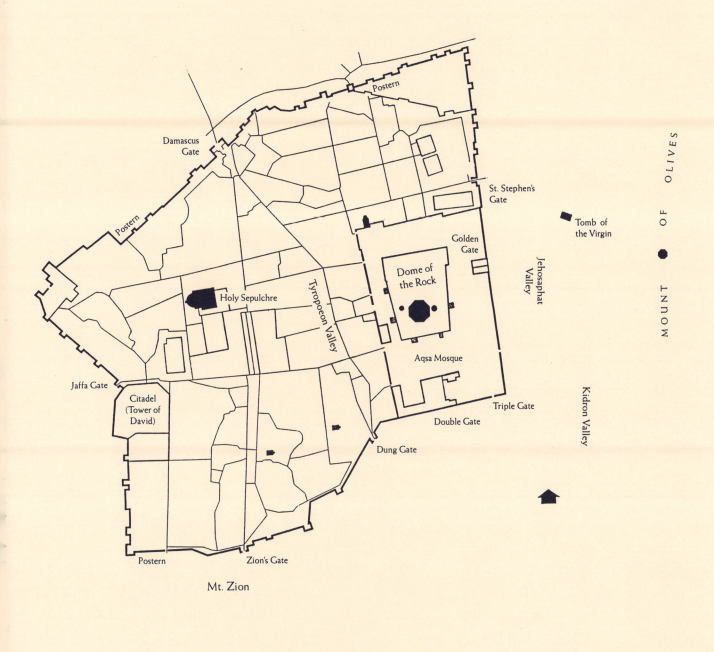

Postern

Damascus
Gate

Postern

St. Stephen's
Gate

Golden
Gate

Holy Sepulchre

Tyropoeon Valley

Dome of
the Rock

Jehosaphat
Valley

Tomb of
the Virgin

MOUNT OF OLIVES

Aqsa Mosque

Jaffa Gate

Citadel
(Tower of
David)

Triple Gate

Double Gate

Kidron Valley

Dung Gate

Postern

Zion's Gate

Mt. Zion

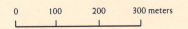

0   100   200   300 meters

The SHAPE of the HOLY

OLEG GRABAR

The
SHAPE
of the
HOLY

Early Islamic Jerusalem

With contributions by

Mohammad al-Asad

Abeer Audeh

Saïd Nuseibeh

Princeton University Press

PRINCETON, NEW JERSEY

Library of Congress Cataloging-in-Publication Data
Grabar, Oleg.
    The shape of the holy: early Islamic Jerusalem / Oleg Grabar:
  with contributions by Mohammad al-Asad, Abeer Audeh, Saïd Nuseibeh.
        p.   cm.
    Includes bibliographical references and index.
    ISBN 0-691-03653-5 (cloth: alk. paper)
    1. Jerusalem—History.   2. Qubbat al-Ṣakhrah (Mosque: Jerusalem)
  3. Temple Mount (Jerusalem)   4. Jerusalem—Antiquities.   I. Al-Asad, Mohammad.
  II. Audeh, Abeer.   III. Nuseibeh, Saïd.   IV. Title.
    DS109.916.G73   1996
    956.94′4203—dc20   95-50443

This book has been composed in 11/14 Weiss by The Composing Room of Michigan Inc.
Design by Diane Levy
All photographs of the interior of the Dome of the Rock © 1992 Saïd Nuseibeh, San Francisco
Princeton Press books are printed on acid-free paper and meet the guidelines
for permanence and durability of the Committee on Production Guidelines
for Book Longevity of the Council on Library Resources

Printed in Hong Kong

10 9 8 7 6 5 4 3 2 1

For Nicolas
WHO ALSO WAS THERE

CONTENTS

LIST OF ILLUSTRATIONS

THIS BOOK is the result of a passionate fascination with the Old City of Jerusalem which began more than forty years ago. In 1953 I was appointed Fellow of the American School of Oriental Research (now the Albright Institute) in Jerusalem. In early September of that year, my wife, Terry, and I disembarked in Beirut from the small Greek boat which had carried us across the Mediterranean. We must have arrived fairly early in the morning, since three separate taxi-services brought us that very evening to Jerusalem, via Damascus and Amman. The vision of the walls of the city unencumbered by buildings as the road turned away from Bethany is still imprinted in my memory, the Dome of the Rock is still vaguely grey and worn by age rather than shining gold like the top of a new gift box.

I was at that time working on other matters, particularly the remains from the Umayyad palace at Khirbat al-Mafjar, but, quite regularly, I began to walk through the Old City, to read about the medieval history of the city, and to accumulate data of all sorts, eventually to publish a study on the Dome of the Rock that remained for years a sort of "counter-cultural" explanation of the building. Thus my first thanks go to those who made that academic year 1953–54 possible and exhilarating: Karl Kraeling, Henry Detweiler, and James Muilenberg, long deceased by now, who accepted and encour-

aged a non-biblical student in an institution where the time of Christ was judged almost contemporary; Frank and Betty Ann Cross, who have remained close friends for all these years, who introduced me to Melville and to theology, who were always willing to discuss Dostoevski or the inevitability of biting flies on all Umayyad sites; Ivan Kaufmann, with whom we took so many trips and who liked to read contemporary poetry while burning incense; Yusuf Sa'ad, the keeper of treasures at the Palestine Archaeological Museum (now the Rockefeller Museum), who helped me find my way in the archives of the Museum during a cold winter when I learned to read and write with gloves on; Awni Dajani, a member of a huge Palestinian family with relatives from Toronto to Damascus (all acknowledged cousins), then Inspector of Antiquities in Jerusalem, with whom I explored the hidden worlds buried to the west of the Haram al-Sharif; Dorothy Garrod, the gentle and celebrated prehistorian who introduced us, poor graduate students, to the joys of Latrun sherry; the very first team of researchers on the Dead Sea scrolls led by the luminous Père Roland de Vaux; the Musa Nasser family who had just transformed their private secondary school in Bir Zeit into a junior college where my wife found a job teaching English to the first freshman class; and an assorted mosaic of people never encountered in one's usual habitat: patriarchs of many varieties of Christianity, Edmund Wilson seeking the Dead Sea scrolls, Stewart Perowne singing in the choir of St. George's cathedral, Mrs. Vester in her kingdom of the American Colony, Arthur Jeffery, Columbia's autocratic Professor of Arabic, Kathleen Kenyon and her Jericho crowd, tall and lanky G. Lankester Harding with his endless searches for thamudic or safaitic inscriptions and his picnics at the shore of the Dead Sea, Professor Frank Albright appearing for a rare visitation, Henri Seyrig, the aristocratic and genial director of the French Institute in Beirut, K.A.C. Creswell coming from Cairo, and Père Louis-Hughes Vincent withering away in the Dominican convent of St. Etienne. These people are acutely present in my memory and they are part of my fascination with a city that affected all of them.

In 1960, I was appointed director of the American School for the academic year 1960–61. Relatively prostrate after the partition of 1948, the city was now bustling with a great deal of building and other activities, but it was a frustrated and often depressed city. Old friends were still there, and there were new acquaintances: Paul and Nancy Lapp, our colleagues at the School, with their ferocious passion for archaeological learning; Peter Parr, Diane Kirkbride, and other standard bearers of British archaeology in Palestine and Transjordan; the Egyptian engineers who allowed me to roam all over their scaffolding in the Dome of the Rock they were then restoring; the United Nations teams for whom I organized occasional walking tours of the Haram; the collection of learned men, the one woman, and the assorted diplomats who supervised the operation of the Palestine Archaeological Museum and whose meetings were exemplars of studied politeness; the Supreme Muslim Council that authorized me to photograph the mosaics of the Aqsa Mosque and the perennially laughing Fred Anderegg who took the photographs; the visit of the patriarch of Moscow which taught me much about the silliness of religious politics and of the politics of religion during the Cold War; my friend and colleague Ihor Ševčenko with whom I traveled to Syria and Turkey, who read stories to our children, and who managed to get me into the United

States Air Force hospital in Adana when I was too ill to continue the annual trip of the School; Claus Brisch and Christel Kessler, with whom I took several memorable trips to the Jordanian steppe; Richard Ettinghausen gathering information for his book on Arab painting; two American divines appearing at the door of The American School and claiming to be Moses and Elijah; and so many others. Many of the acquaintances and friends from these years are still alive, although retired for the most part, and I hope that they will see this book as, among other things, a tribute to my memories of them.

Between 1961 and 1989, most of my professional and personal life led me away from Jerusalem. Here and there I gave a lecture on the medieval city, I visited it twice and recall in particular a memorable trip in 1972, when Benjamin Mazar and Meir Ben-Dov led me around the excavations they were carrying out to the south and the southwest of the Haram. Those were complicated years for the Old City of Jerusalem, as it became unified with the much larger modern capital of a young and energetic state. It acquired a relatively modern infrastructure which made it cleaner and safer than it had been. The rehabilitation of the Jewish quarter led to important and successful excavations and restorations, the citadel was transformed into a museum, the open space in front of the Western Wall became a site for national Israeli manifestations alongside traditional forms of worship, and the monuments of Mamluk Jerusalem were surveyed and eventually published by the British School in the city. The political and human tensions were often overwhelming, but the Old City survived even the massive building programs around it. I kept on reading and teaching about Jerusalem, maintaining bibliographical files and notes. Once or twice I gave a seminar on it and one in particular, around 1985, rekindled my interest in its character within the broader spectrum of urban history throughout the Islamic world and even elsewhere. Gradually I became more concerned with comparative ways of looking at history and at architectural processes than I had been during my formative years as a scholar, and, during my many years on the Steering

Committee of the Aga Khan Award for Architecture, I began to see cities as spaces for human behavior and not simply as collections of constructions and of monuments.

When I left Harvard in 1989, after thirty-four years of teaching there and at the University of Michigan, I decided to devote my first years at the Institute for Advanced Study to the many folders of notes and to the various interpretations I had accumulated on Jerusalem in order to write this book. By a stroke of good fortune, this decision led to new and fruitful associations. I had asked Mohammad al-Asad, a Jordanian architect who had completed his doctorate in Harvard's Department of Fine Arts, to help me with drawings for the book. He suggested investigating the relatively new technology of computer drawing and, together with Abeer Audeh, a young Palestinian architect, he then spent two years preparing a series of computer images of the early medieval city. The problems and limitations involved in using this new technology for reconstructing older cities are described in an appendix of this book. The possibility of manipulating a single image and eventually animating it modified and rationalized my whole conception of the city. The three of us spent many hours simply waiting for images to emerge on the computer screen, and the conversation during these intervals established a bond between us and the city and between us as individuals, one of the brightest memories I have of the whole project. Through Mohammad al-Asad, I was introduced to the Center for Interactive Computer Design at Princeton University and to Kirk Alexander, whose enthusiasm was only occasionally overwhelmed by his responsibilities. The final rendering of the drawings by Mohammad al-Asad and Abeer Audeh was done in the Center for Interactive Computer Design, and a videotape introducing our work was made possible through a grant from the Gladys K. Delmas Foundation. The files on Autocad and this video are available to all who are interested in the subject. I decided to limit most of the architectural illustrations and reconstructions of the city to the outcome of these computer-drawn techniques, inasmuch as new drawings of the traditional variety are worthwhile only if new and accurate measurements are taken.

A second encounter was with Saïd Nuseibeh, a member of a prominent Palestinian family in Jerusalem and professionally a young photographer from San Francisco. Without being aware of my interest in medieval Jerusalem, he had written to volunteer his service for whatever architectural project I had in mind. Thanks to the cooperation of the Supreme Muslim Council in Jerusalem presided over by the Honorable Hasan Talakub and of Dr. Issam Awwad, the efficient chief engineer of the Haram, Saïd Nuseibeh was given permission to photograph, for the first time in color and with all necessary scaffolding and lights, the mosaics of the Dome of the Rock. The results are spectacular, and I have profited much from the enthusiastic insights of Saïd's artistic temperament. His work was made possible by generous grants from the Palestinian Welfare Association, the Gladys K. Delmas Foundation, and the Institute for Advanced Study. I hope that the eight assemblages of the mosaics on the inner face of the octagon (figs. 42–49) will give a sense not only of Saïd Nuseibeh's talent but also of the astounding quality of mosaics which can finally be studied as they deserve to be. A more complete set of photographs is available in a book by Saïd Nuseibeh entitled *The Dome of the Rock* (forthcoming Rizzoli 1996) to which I wrote an introduction.

I am most grateful for the help of all these individuals and institutions. I hope that they will feel properly rewarded by their having made possible the wider knowledge of monuments hitherto poorly available or restricted to a few travelers with proper connections. And, although I am strongly committed to the principle that all monuments belong equally to all men and women, I acknowledge the special relationship to the Haram al-Sharif which has grown for Muslims from Palestine and neighboring lands. I am glad that young Muslims from Jordan and Palestine were so prominent in the task of presenting Jerusalem. In part, this book reflects my own gratitude for the wonderful ways in which, over four decades, I have been welcomed in Arab and Muslim lands and by colleagues and students, Muslim or Christian, from the Arab world.

For the last stages of this work, I was helped by Joanna Spurza, who took time away from finishing her own thesis to deal with my notes and photographs with energetic efficiency; Suki Lewin and Martha Mulkiewicz who, always with good humor, typed and retyped, printed and collated so many pages with obscure references; the staff of the Library at the Institute for Advanced Study whose genius for finding books and articles is unmatched anywhere except for Solomon's fabled jinns. Jeff Spurr, the learned slide librarian in the Aga Khan Program at Harvard University was instrumental in finding two photographs with astounding efficiency and rapidity, and this is as good a place as any to thank him and his colleague, Andras Riedlmayer, for many years of intelligent and good-natured help. And I cannot even recall how often conversations with colleagues or visitors in Princeton helped in shaping details or whole interpretations elaborated in this book, but important among them were Glen Bowersock, Muhammad Arkoun, Michael Cook, Mark Cohen, Shaun Marmon, Avrom Udovich, Irving Lavin, Slobodan Čurčić, and Giles Constable. I am also grateful to Lucette Valensi, at the École des Hautes Études in Sciences Sociales in Paris, Anthony Welch at the University of Victoria, Jean-Marie Spieser at the University of Strasbourg, Robert Ilbert at the University of Aix-Provence, Lisa Golombek at the Royal Ontario Museum, Gilbert Dagron and Mark Fumaroli at the Collège de France, all of whom invited me to give lectures and seminars on Jerusalem during which I learned much from very different participants. Special thanks are owed to Renata Holod, who, once again, read one of the drafts of this book, and to my friend Miriam Rosen-Ayalon, who has spent many decades meditating on the monuments of Jerusalem.

I have not profited as much as I could have from the recent Israeli scholarship on early Islamic Jerusalem developed in particular among the philologists and historians at the Hebrew University. Our points of departure and basic concerns are somewhat different, but I might have made better use of Amikan Elad's *Medieval Jerusalem and Islamic Worship* (Leiden, 1995), had it come out earlier. I am particularly grateful to Julian Raby for having shown me two unpublished papers of his, which include a lot of information from Jerusalem archives that I thought were unknown except to me, and to Michael McCormick for sharing with me some of his work on Western pilgrims.

In the final analysis, I owe most to the Holy City itself and to Terry Harris Grabar, who shared with me my first enthusiasm for that city and bore most of the practical difficulties of our second stay there with unflinching dedication to her official and family responsibilities. In 1993 when we returned together to the American School, as I still prefer to call it, we took many walks, almost exclusively in the Old City, remembering together how much of what we are now was shaped by these two years in Jerusalem. The city has still a striking mix of holiness among many more sects than before, greed, generosity, hypocrisy, candor, power struggles, images and inscriptions spelling out hate and love, hope and despair, local provincialism and universal presence. It will probably be so till the end of time, as man will always go on shaping the holy to his own level of imperfection.

As usual, a few practical warnings are necessary. Diacritical marks have been avoided except when needed for the transliteration of single words, or for the clarity of an argument. The system of transliteration used is a simplified version of the one used by the Journal of the Middle East Studies Association. Major Koranic quotations in inscriptions are in capital letters, in order to distinguish them from occasional insertions in the midst of them. The large esplanade in the southwestern sector of the Old City in Jerusalem has been more or less indiscriminately called the Haram al-Sharif (its official contemporary appellation), or simply the Haram, Mount Moriah, or the Temple area. The complicated history of each of these terms was and still is beyond my concern. The word "mihrab" is throughout spelled without diacritical marks, as it occurs frequently and with several different meanings.

Finally this book owes a great deal to the gentle and yet firm prodding of Elizabeth Powers and to the patient efforts of Elizabeth Johnson and Carol Cates of Princeton University Press.

The SHAPE of the HOLY

The Period and Its Sources

IN JULY 1099 Jerusalem was in ruins. The devastation was only partly physical: a few towers and segments of walls were destroyed, a number of houses broken into and demolished, perhaps a few public or restricted buildings like markets, mosques, and synagogues damaged or annihilated by fire, and the sanctuaries of the Haram al-Sharif looted by the warriors from the West. It was mostly a human devastation. Already before the arrival of the Crusaders, the Cairo-appointed governor of the city, Iftikhar al-Dawlah, is alleged to have sent all Christian inhabitants out of the city because he feared a siege and was not sure of their allegiance, not to speak of the food and water needed to keep them alive. After the capture of Jerusalem, nearly all of its Jews and Muslims were killed, and the survivors lay prostrate in their fears. A totally alien band of knights, monks, priests, and commoners from afar were about to settle in the city they considered to be a reward for their militant faith.[1]

What happened over the following years is not the concern of this book. That story belongs to another narrative, the history of an expanding Western Christian world, a history with its own dreams, fascination, greatness, and at times criminal follies.

Direct rule by Crusaders lasted only three generations, as Saladin reestablished Muslim authority over the city in 1183. By the end of the following century, Western European Latin Christians had disappeared from the Holy Land and its adjoining territories. The exceptions were the Franciscan monks holding on to the Holy Places and occasional pilgrims who braved increasingly difficult circumstances to reach these hallowed sites. Orthodox Christians, mostly Arabs with a predominantly Greek clergy, and smaller Eastern Christian communities, usually Monophysite, maintained a segregated life in the western half of the city.

Yet Jerusalem did not simply return to whatever it had been before the arrival of the Crusaders. It was not for want of trying, however, as inscriptions from the city as well as numerous accounts in chronicles present a fascinating picture of the rulers from the victorious Ayyubid dynasty and the religious leaders who accompanied them purifying a city wrested from Latin rule. Their aim was to ensure that holy personages or prophets and holy events from history and from religious lore found their proper place in the holy city. Their efforts were, at times, incongruous, as when they

Figure 1. Jerusalem from the Mount of Olives, Bonfils photograph taken ca. 1860. The Haram is clearly visible in the center with the high Dome of the Rock to the right of center and the elongated Aqsa Mosque to the left. The rest of the city bears no other clearly visible monuments nor significant topographic features. In fact the domed synagogue to the left of center is more visible than the Holy Sepulchre more or less in the middle. The only constructions visible outside of the walled city are the Mount Zion ensemble to the upper left.

identified an old and sacred past in the forms of the Western architecture imported by the Crusaders. The Haram al-Sharif, the huge Muslim sanctuary in the eastern half of the city, preserves several examples of small edifices, mostly cupolas with Romanesque or Gothic elements, rebuilt in the thirteenth century or even as late as the seventeenth, which serve to commemorate some pious patron and a holy memory, that of the Prophet Muhammad or the biblical Joseph, allegedly associated with some particular place in the sanctuary whose exact location had been lost.[2]

Two features characterize these accounts and the mostly thirteenth-century events they depict. One is the passionate search for meanings for all man-made forms and built places, to be drawn from the rich memories of Jerusalem; in a city bathed in holiness, no physical remain can be without a sacred meaning. Contrasting with this search for significance is the fact that the religious or political ideas and the pious functions that emerged within the Muslim world during the short century of Crusader occupation were, for the most part, absent in earlier centuries or, at the very least, less consistently present. A strict and rational legal system now propounded in new institutions like the madrasah, and a rigorous and sometimes narrow-minded orthodoxy replaced what had been a richly textured variety in the life of the faithful. The new synthesis elaborated in the thirteenth century and the forms associated with it transformed the city of Jerusalem into a unique masterpiece of medieval Islamic urbanism in which, for reasons peculiar to that city, the building of monuments seemed to predominate over other human activity. This late medieval, essentially Mamluk, city was, in the sixteenth century, enshrined within strikingly rebuilt walls. The patron and sponsor of these walls was the new Solomon, the Ottoman sultan Suleyman the Magnificent, or the Law-giver as he was known in the Muslim world, who had fostered major restorations in Mekkah and Madinah as well as in Jerusalem, not to speak of his impact on the capital, Istanbul.

The transformation of the city after the end of the Crusades was an act of cleansing from supposedly alien intrusions as well as the establishment in Jerusalem of a new type of late medieval city that was then spreading over those parts of the Muslim world that had escaped the Mongol onslaught.[3] This transformation acquired in Jerusalem a character that issued from the city's store of sacred memories which is absent elsewhere: the emotional and visual power of a permanent setting with changing meanings behind or alongside whatever the taste and needs of different times might dictate. Even today the relatively modern metropolis that surrounds the walled city does not vitiate the certitude that whatever exists behind its grandiose and anachronistic walls belongs (or should belong) to an age other than the contemporary one—perhaps, more accurately, to something timeless, inaccessible without a special physical and spiritual effort. In old photographs of over a century ago (see fig. 1), as in even earlier drawings (fig. 2), the walled city

Figure 2. Louis-François Cassas, Vue de Jérusalem, *ca. 1800, watercolor (130 × 100 cm.). Another traditional view of the city from the Mount of Olives based on sketches made in 1785. In the back of the city, the citadel looms particularly tall, as do the minarets framing the Holy Sepulchre to the right of center. The crowd in foreground belongs to standard groupings of witnesses.*

appears as it no doubt had done for centuries: a lonely and unexpected rectangular space awkwardly set on nearly barren hills, with a few roads and houses in the treeless and rocky landscape outside the walls of the city. There is almost nothing in the city visible in the 1860 photograph that was not there in 1558. At the same time, there is almost nothing visible in it that is earlier than the first century. Although covering much that is older, some of which has been revealed by archaeology, the Old City of Jerusalem is a Late Antique and medieval town.

This book is devoted to one segment of this long Late Antique and medieval history of Jerusalem. Just as it ended in 1099 with a massacre, this particular segment of history also began with destruction, as the old Jewish Jerusalem, spectacularly rebuilt by Herod the Great towards the end of the first century before the common era, was twice utterly destroyed, in 70 and in 132. Maintained and partly rebuilt as a provincial Roman garrison town, the city acquired a new significance with the building up of the holy places associated with Christ soon after Constantine's conversion to the new faith in 325. Christian significance swept over the whole of a Palestine eventually to be anointed as the Holy Land[4] and blossomed, especially in Jerusalem, with monumental constructions during the rule of the Byzantine emperor Justinian in the sixth century. Much has been written about Christian Jerusalem, ranging from learned studies to acrimonious debates, and now to popular maps and drawings for today's tourists, holy or not. This book begins with an attempt to reconstruct the rough outline of Christian Jerusalem, as it would have appeared by the end of the sixth century. For one of the arguments of this book is that the Christianization of the Roman overhaul of the Herodian city fixed the monumental foci of Jerusalem until the massive rebuilding within the walls and the expansion beyond the walls which began in the nineteenth century.

What is commonly known as the Byzantine period in Palestinian history ended twice. In 614 an invading Persian army destroyed the city and took many of its Christian inhabitants, including the pa-triarch, captive. Even worse than physical destruction of buildings and men was the emotional shock of an enemy from far away removing the relic of the Holy Cross from the center of Christendom. And then, shortly after the restoration of Byzantine rule and the return of the Holy Cross in 628, a more momentous transformation occurred. According to the commonly accepted version of the actual events, in 636 or 638 the Arab Muslim caliph Umar ibn al-Khattab accepted the surrender of the Christian patriarch Sophronius, and Islam, the last version of the great monotheistic revelation which began with Judaism, became the dominant power in the city. With the exception of the one hundred and fifty years of Crusader presence, this domination remained until 1917 and the ensuing treaties that ended World War I.

This book ends with the interruption in Muslim rule brought about by the Crusaders. Although this decision may seem paradoxical since the vast majority of the physical and monumental remains of Jerusalem date from the second, Mamluk, period of Muslim rule, which began in the middle of the thirteenth century and ended with the Ottoman takeover of the early sixteenth, two reasons justify it. First, Mamluk Jerusalem has been the subject of an exhaustive survey by the British School of Archaeology in Jerusalem, which provides a unique catalogue, thoroughly documented with drawings, descriptions, and photographs, of all the monuments of the city erected during nearly three centuries of its history.[5] Second, any understanding of the period after 1100 requires a full awareness of Mamluk architecture, history, and culture in Cairo, Damascus, Aleppo, and many smaller cities of Egypt and the Levant.[6] Many scholars and teams of researchers are engaged in the study of the regional architecture and culture of Mamluk times and, with the major exception of the Dome of the Rock, what happened in Jerusalem in terms of buildings and urban development is not essentially different from what happened in Cairo or in Gaza, to take two extreme examples, one of a huge metropolis constantly studied and surveyed and the other of a small provincial town whose Mamluk monuments were recently published in exemplary form.[7] In those areas where Jerusalem is different and even unique, the reasons for the differences were laid out in the first period of Muslim rule, between 636 or 638 and 1099. These were the centuries that elaborated the mutation of a Christian town into a Muslim one and thus created the physical and, in many ways, the mental paradigms of the city that have remained until the late twentieth century.

The central issues are deceptively simple: how did a particular type of organism, a city, or the specific example known as Jerusalem, change its religion? How were the architectural and liturgical forms of the city and the behavior compelled or inspired by these forms modified by a new faith and by new relationships between communities still attached to other faiths? Did forms change? Or the meanings attached to them and, as a result, the attitudes of people to forms? If changes in meaning and behavior occurred, how did they change the city? Or, being as charged with meanings as Jerusalem was, did the city itself compel changes in behavior and contribute meanings to the culture that ruled it?

The broad methodological and intellectual implications of these simple questions are numerous and possibly of greater importance than the specifics of one place on earth at a precise time, however meaningful that particular city may be to many people. One implication is that of the continuing significance of architectural forms, even when uses and functions change. Another is that of the continuity of religious associations and modes of pious behavior, regardless of their relationship to new tastes or new obligations. A third is the maintenance, regardless of political and cultural changes, of certain dominant modes of life or types of activity—piety in the case of Jerusalem, but trade, industry, or power in other instances. In the broadest possible sense, major cultural and political modifications imposed on but not generated by existing spaces raise all sorts of questions about the relationship of the new to the old, of the present to the past, about the functions of spaces after their initial purposes are half or totally forgotten, about the memories of men and women, but also the res-onances of stones and sacred spots. There are cultural regions, much of the Iranian world for instance, where the new tends to settle next to the old and where the focus of power, belief, or importance shifts, usually fairly slowly, from one space to the other within a large geographic area. Such was the pattern of growth in Isfahan, Herat, and Samarqand. In other areas, at times for practical reasons such as the presence or absence of easy access to water (Damascus in Syria, for example), at other times because of habit and tradition (Rome, or Konya-Iconium in Anatolia), the same space is used by successive cultures. Can one propose generalized models of development for different parts of the world? Or is each instance unique?

Before dealing with such wide-ranging issues, it is, however, essential to understand as fully as possible what gives a holy city its special character within a specific period. The contention of this book is that medieval Jerusalem was an Islamic city, dominated by Islamic monuments of which the Dome of the Rock was meant to be and still is the most prominent. It is a further contention that the stunning quality of that building has helped preserve it in approximately the shape it had originally, even as the meanings associated with it have changed over the centuries, affecting or reflecting the evolution of the city itself.

We do not possess for Jerusalem, nor for that matter for any city of the Muslim world, the density and variety of sources available, for instance, for Rome and even for Constantinople whose histories have been eloquently reconstructed over the past decades.[8] Jerusalem was not a capital and therefore was not automatically described for the benefit of a whole empire, as was Baghdad where urban histories and references in more or less official chronicles made possible reconstructions of the city by scholars, even though nothing remains of the Abbasid capital.[9] Nor was Jerusalem ever a pan-Islamic pilgrimage city like Mekkah. For the latter, numerous and complex memories from pre-Islamic times and the first Muslim centuries are well documented and can be retrieved thanks to an elaborate early ninth-century history with careful descriptions accompanied by a few drawings.[10] In the very early sixteenth century, when antiquarian concerns dominated Muslim historiography, Mujir al-Din, a native of Jerusalem, wrote a complete holy history combined with a pilgrim's guide for his city.[11] But his vision, his perceptions, and his knowledge were colored by the evolution of medieval religious culture and, even if many details can profitably be used for earlier times, the value of his account is primarily for the period during which he wrote, essentially the pre-modern era of Muslim history. It is possible, although I believe unlikely, that city histories existed for Jerusalem before the eleventh century and especially before the Crusades, but none has been preserved and we do not, therefore, have a single basic written source around which the story of early medieval Jerusalem could be woven, as we do have for Baghdad, Cairo, Damascus, or Bukhara.

This is not to say that there are no sources on Jerusalem. Quite the contrary. For the early centuries of Islamic urban history Jerusalem is provided with a greater wealth of information than Damascus, Cordova, Isfahan, or Nishapur. But the sources available for the city consist of very different kinds, each one with its own strengths and limitations, prejudices and objectives: documentary materials as well as visual observations and archaeological reconstructions, and even contemporaneous discourses which affected any thinking about Jerusalem in the Middle Ages.

Six kinds of resources can be identified: external and remote written sources, Jerusalem-centered written sources, local documents, archaeology, visual reconstruction, and scholarship on medieval Jerusalem. The extent and reliability of the sources have determined the shape of this history.

"Remote" Written Sources

This category includes, first of all, the more or less pan-Islamic chronicles from Ya'qubi (late ninth century) to Tabari (tenth century) and Ibn al-Athir (twelfth century) composed with a variety of purposes and points of view in or around the court and administration of the caliphate in Baghdad.

Most of these chroniclers use each other's information and identify their own sources, although some tend to be more literary and biased than others, transforming their histories into works of belles-lettres, sometimes with obvious or hidden ideological programs.[12] Much has been written recently about the expository procedures of these historians, especially insofar as they formulate a vision of the early and formative Muslim world.[13] Less effort has been applied to explaining their attitudes toward the empires of the Umayyads or the Abbasids and, on the whole, it is nearly impossible in the absence of true archival documents to evaluate the veracity of their statements about a place like Jerusalem, remote and secondary from this perspective. The historian of a specific place rather than of a political entity is faced with a dilemma in accepting or rejecting these accounts, which can only rarely be confirmed by inscriptions or archaeological remains. He can reject them unless they are corroborated by other evidence or he can accept them provisionally. In this book I tended to the former rather than the latter.

Next to chroniclers are the geographers, usually also sponsored by the imperial capital, who fitted Jerusalem within a variety of standard schemes describing the Muslim world. Taxation or roads for trade and for the pilgrimage are the main incentives for these works, but educated curiosity and the expository talents of some of the geographers, who spice standard narrative descriptions with local flavors, have made them invaluable for information on cities. Two of them, Ibn al-Faqih (fl. ca. 903) and Muqaddasi (after 985), wrote extensive descriptions of Jerusalem.[14] Al-Muqaddasi was a native of Jerusalem and therefore not quite a "remote" source, but his audience was not composed of his compatriots. Most of the other geographers report on places removed from their experience rather than those well known to them. They follow, often quite closely, reports from others, and the city is to them a "thing" which may embody wondrous myths. In this sense, more often than chroniclers, they reflect subjective and folk opinions in addition to repeating standard descriptive information.

Another genre of remote sources which has

yielded interesting information about the city, especially in its pious aspects, is the religious literature of *hadith*, the Traditions about the life of the Prophet, and of *tafsir*, the interpretations of the Koran. Both these sources have undergone and continue to undergo a fascinating new examination and, as a result, information about the appearance of the city has emerged in a most unexpected way.[15] Traditions and commentaries on the Holy Writ are no longer seen simply as documents for the time of the Prophet to be accepted or rejected as interpretations of the Koran. It is argued now that all accounts of the Prophet's life, however unacceptable to scholarly and religious judgment, and all types of exegesis, however erroneous, are statements of views and opinions that existed when the statements were made. They are valid indicators of the *mentalité* prevalent at the time and place of their appearance, even though not necessarily an accurate reporting of events or opinions.[16]

A fourth type of remote source derives from *adab* literature, the body of writing in Arabic that describes those things a cultivated person was supposed to know. One example of *adab* contains a description of Jerusalem. It is Ibn Abd al-Rabbih *al-'Iqd al-Farid* ("The Unique Necklace of Precious Stones"), written in Spain before 940, which describes an image of the city appropriate for a cultivated sunni from al-Andalus. It was written as far from Jerusalem as was possible in the tenth century, but it reflects what may have been the account of an eyewitness or simply the writing of one of the early geographers, possibly Ibn al-Faqih, as suggested by some scholars.[17]

Two other remote sources must be added to the Arabic and Muslim chronological, descriptive, historical, and pious sources that are the normal resource of the medievalist. Greek and even Latin chronicles occasionally echo reports from the distant Holy Land. Such reports, however, are frequently mentioned in Eastern Christian chronicles depicting the history and the life of orthodox or heterodox communities that are usually fiercely independent and maintain their distance from mainstream establishments. In the often contentious ecclesiastical histories of Copts, Armenians, Geor-

gians, Syrian Jacobites, or Nestorians, Jerusalem appears occasionally, but with sectarian variations that still need investigation. A different kind of complexity exists within the many Jewish sources dealing with Jerusalem. First of all, historical sources and actual documents about life are much more common for the eleventh century than for earlier centuries. It is easy but dangerous to project back to earlier times the rich Jewish life of the Fatimid period. And then, with Jewish sources, as with those of other religious communities, the concern for Jerusalem was often expressed far from the city and not always with full awareness of what actually happened in it.[18]

Finally, it is probably in the category of "remote" sources that one should put a very remarkable series of primarily Jewish and Christian texts, mostly from the seventh century, in which Jerusalem plays a part either because its actual affairs are reflected in these texts or because the city has an eschatological role in the message of the texts. The messianic proclamations that were so important in those turbulent times may well have been directly affected by momentous events in Jerusalem, such as the taking of the city by the Persians in 614 (with diametrically opposed Jewish and Christian reactions), the Arab conquest, and the establishment of the Umayyad dynasty.[19] These eschatological sources have been recently characterized as projecting a double distortion, a distortion of historical events to make them fit the fixed scenario of the end of the world and the scenario itself modified to be adapted to different historical situations.[20] In the peculiar ebb and flow of messianic passions, concrete predictions about the future of Jerusalem change in character after the early decades of the eighth century, as the medieval vision of a bejewelled celestial Jerusalem transforms many an account of the earthly city.[21]

Remote sources are the obligatory companions of the historian of Jerusalem, because they alone show how the city appeared in the imagination and in the memory of the several cultural spheres to which it belonged and because they connect its real or assumed events with whatever was happening elsewhere. The problem with these sources is that they hardly ever considered the physical setting of Jerusalem, since it was rarely experienced by their authors. There is, therefore, an unreal and abstract quality about many of these accounts, and their utilization for the purpose of imagining the early medieval city is problematic. This is especially so for the Justinianic period in the sixth century or the high Abbasid one in the ninth, when a strong imperial power, seeking to demonstrate in the written record its concerns for the whole empire, rarely described local circumstances.

Jerusalem-Centered Sources

For a variety of reasons related to the holiness associated with Jerusalem, the city was commemorated quite early in the Middle Ages through accounts meant to re-create it or its qualities for an audience located elsewhere. Furthermore, whatever happened there was more abundantly recorded by its own inhabitants than was usual for urban centers of comparable size during the early Middle Ages of the Christian and Muslim worlds. Most of these sources deserve a monographic treatment and repeated reappraisal, because nearly all of them are the product of a very particular experience, event, opportunity, or cultural practice, unlike remote chronicles and geographical descriptions, and they do not lend themselves to easy generalization. A few have been studied in some detail or have been used more frequently than others in secondary literature. In contrast to remote sources, the local ones are like sudden spotlights on specific places, events, or moments, illuminating them but leaving enormous areas and periods in shadows. They are often more tantalizing than enlightening, but serve as convenient landmarks to be connected by hypothetical reconstructions.

The main Jerusalem-centered documents pertinent to the period covered by this book are five. First, there is the Madaba map (figs. 9–10), a unique mid-to-late-sixth-century mosaic depiction of the biblical Holy Land found in a small church in Transjordan. Technically, the map belongs to a striking group of Transjordanian Christian mosaics whose number increases every year and whose understanding is being revolutionized by recent discoveries.[22] The exact purpose and the associations of this large panel (around six by twenty-four meters) depicting the Holy Land still elude us. But for our purposes, what is important is that the largest unit in the map is a cartographic representation of the city of Jerusalem. This representation, about which much has been written, is unique in that it provides an image of the city, rather than a text about it, less than a century before the Muslim conquest of the city. It is an image distorted both by the technology of its design and by the ideology that underlies it, but it is a fascinating vision from which a schematic reconstruction of the city can be proposed.[23]

A second group of Jerusalem-centered sources are the accounts by Christian pilgrims and officials from the time of Procopius of Caesarea in the early sixth century, when Justinian was actively involved in Jerusalem, until the time of Bernard the Monk, who was there in 830 and seems to have been the last Western pilgrim before the Crusades to leave a lengthy written statement about the city. These accounts are now conveniently available in a book edited by John Wilkinson. Their value and reliability vary, and each of them deserves, and some have received, a study of its own. It is curious that, even though pilgrimages from the West continued almost uninterruptedly until the Crusades, accounts by pilgrims seem to disappear as a literary genre during the late Carolingian period. One of the early pilgrims, Arculf, who was there in 670 and left drawings of the Christian holy places that have been the subject of some discussion, is the only one to mention Muslim buildings.[24]

The third source of this type is the long text left by the geographer Muqaddasi. Born in Jerusalem around 945 of a noted family of business people, he put together, around 985, a wonderful description of the whole Muslim world. As amply demonstrated by André Miquel in his recent volumes on Arab geographers as well as his translation of Muqaddasi's chapter on Syria and Palestine, Muqaddasi was an astute observer of his surroundings and a fervent patriot of his native city. The fact that he was so knowledgeable about the rest of the Muslim world gives particular authority to his descriptions and value to his judgments. He witnessed the first and most brilliant decades of Fatimid rule from Egypt and became an enthusiastic, if hardly fanatic, supporter of the new regime. His account is one of the two main written sources for our reconstruction of Jerusalem before the Crusades.[25]

A particularly original primary source for the Fatimid period is contained in Nasir-i Khosraw's travel account from 1047. The author, a remarkable religious thinker and poet from Iran, became what we would call today a "government sponsored" tourist to Jerusalem after it was refurbished by the Fatimid dynasty in Cairo.[26] He recalls in sequence his walks in the city and especially in its sanctuaries. Like a trained anthropologist, he took notes and made drawings of what he saw, and it seems clear that he wanted the readers of his text, far away in northeastern Iran, to visualize what he described. Neither his notes nor his drawings have been preserved, but the precision of his descriptions is quite remarkable.

Finally, in this group of Jerusalem-centered sources, there are several texts, all datable before 1100, which are early versions of a genre just beginning then to develop within Islamic society— the fada'il ("virtues" or "praises"), books devoted to the mostly religious uniqueness of a city.[27] These documents are most useful in demonstrating the climate of pious beliefs that distinguishes a city and in retelling the religious legends attached to it, in general or through specific monuments. They rarely describe a city, and such information as they provide about the visible world is usually incidental. Many were probably written without a physical knowledge of the cities they describe, but they are important in identifying the memories attached to a city. They are more useful for the time in which they were written than as historical documents for the past. Three different texts have been preserved for Jerusalem, but they are not all easily available. The most accessible is al-Wasiti's Fada'il al-Bayt al-Muqaddas, written apparently before 1019 in Jerusalem itself and published with an excellent introduction.[28] The second one, al-Musharraf's Fada'il Bayt al-Muqaddis wa al-Khalil wa Fada'il al-Sham ("The Merits of Jerusalem and Hebron and the Merits of Syria"), written by a resident of Jerusalem in the middle of the eleventh century, is preserved as a late manuscript in Tübingen and is still unedited.[29] A more complicated problem is posed by a fragment preserved from al-Muhallabi's geographical manual written before 990 and published in part by Salah al-Din al-Munajjad. The whole text, if it ever becomes known, will probably belong to my first group of "remote" sources, but the section on Jerusalem, which has been published, is so full of the kind of biblical and pseudo-biblical stories found in the slightly later fada'il that it is proper, at this stage, to consider them all together.[30] The critical evaluation of these texts has not yet been attempted, but it is clear that they served primarily to feed the collective memory of believers by stressing various forms of Israiliyat (i.e., Judaic memories within Islam) and to explain standard accounts of a type of piety prevalent in the eleventh century.[31]

Local Documents

These are documents found in Jerusalem or which deal directly with the city, documents that are uniquely connected with it and whose authenticity cannot be questioned. The fourteenth-century juridical documents discovered in a storeroom of the Haram and the numerous waqfiyahs or endowments from Mamluk and Ottoman times afford a rich local documentary source on the activities and life of the city,[32] but the earlier periods are less well covered and I can identify only four groups of comparably localized authentic sources.

The richest group consists of some sixty-six Arabic inscriptions, ranging from a few words to the one 240 meters long in the Dome of the Rock. The vast majority of these were published many decades ago by Max van Berchem; they are included in the systematic Répertoire Chronologique d'Epigraphie Arabe.[33] It is rather curious that so few pre-1100 inscriptions (including graffiti) have been discovered since the first decade of the twentieth century, in spite of several excavations and many surveys.[34] The early inscriptions are all very different from each other and often from the norms established elsewhere. They include the very official milestones of Abd al-Malik, unique in Islamic archaeology, as well as a few highly idiosyncratic funerary inscriptions whose texts curse all those who would dare to jump over the tomb or otherwise to profane the deceased.[35] It is difficult to know whether the variety of inscriptions is the result of their early date or of the peculiarities of Jerusalem specifically. Nearly all of them provoke important observations or queries and they often open up more intriguing speculations than other written texts.

A relatively small number of Greek papyri from Aphrodito in Egypt mention a mosque in Jerusalem and a second structure, possibly a royal one, in the same city. They refer to a few workers and to a certain amount of money from taxes. They are clearly dated between 709 and 714,[36] attested by the dates of Qurra ibn Sharik, the governor of Egypt mentioned in them.

A very large number of Geniza documents, the fabulous fragments from the Jewish community in Cairo that have revolutionized so much of Mediterranean history before 1200, deal concretely with the city of Jerusalem rather than simply mention it in passing.[37] Within the purview of this book, these documents are operative only for the eleventh century, with occasional implications for earlier times. They deal, for the most part, with the daily life of the Jewish community, not with deep theological or historical issues, nor with physical surroundings.

Finally, numismatic evidence is usually important in determining the place of a city in the contemporary hierarchy of power and occasionally useful for the establishment of chronologies. There are several early Islamic coins with the mint names of *Iliya* or of *Iliya Filastin*, both references to Jerusalem, issued under its Roman name of *Aelia Capitolina*. Quite recently it has been proposed that a coin with the Greek *IERO* on the obverse be attributed to Jerusalem after the Muslim conquest, but the assumption that the Greek word for Jerusalem would

have been used after the Muslim conquest when it had not been used before seems an odd one.[38] Relatively few coins were minted in Jerusalem after the foundation of Ramlah as the capital of Palestine in 708 and some confusion remains about the exact sequence of coinage in the first eight decades of Muslim rule.[39] The existence of coins attributable to Jerusalem before and after the coinage reform instituted by Abd al-Malik in 692 argues, however, for some administrative or symbolic significance to the city before a new pattern of organization took over.

Archaeology

Two types of archaeological activity affecting Jerusalem have created two different kinds of sources. One can be called intrusive archaeology, as it modifies whatever it explores. Excavations or soundings carried out as part of large-scale archaeological enterprises or of restoration and maintenance requirements, even if they were not intended to do so, have often, over the past century and a half, provided information for the medieval period. The interpretation of individual finds can be controversial, especially because precise dating is usually difficult when one considers the randomness of large-scale surveys and engineering operations necessary for excavation in any urban context. Few excavations were carried out in ways that meet even minimal standards of archaeological practice. In fact, the archaeology of large urban centers cannot yet be accomplished with the thoroughness and precision required for a refined re-creation of the past. Anything discovered by archaeological means is an authentic document, but too often removed from its context and, therefore, difficult to interpret.

The major excavation undertaken in the 1960s by Kathleen Kenyon and Father Roland de Vaux did not, with a few minor exceptions, involve the areas of early medieval Jerusalem, and such data as may have come to light have not yet been published.[40] The following list of archaeological enterprises is limited to those with sufficiently significant and accessible results to have been included among the sources used in this book.

Controlled archaeological investigations carried out in and around the Aqsa Mosque several times during this century have been summarized and analyzed by Robert Hamilton. His book, though difficult to find and unduly detailed, provides something rare in the archaeology of Islamic monuments: the clear evolution of a building's structural history. What turned out to be more complicated is the chronological interpretation of the evidence, and divergent views have appeared. Hamilton's presentation remains, however, a model explication of a building.[41] Additional records exist both in the Haram itself and in the Palestine Archaeological Museum, now the Rockefeller Museum. To my knowledge these records have not been published or used in any significant way since 1949.[42] Like the Aqsa Mosque, the complex of the Holy Sepulchre has been studied with some care during various repairs. The results have been incorporated in part in the summary but clearly written works of Father Charles Couäsnon, and in the more thorough but less readable volumes of Father Virgilio Corbo. Alternate interpretations on the findings of these two local archaeologists have been published.[43]

Systematic excavations have been carried out to the south and southwest of the Haram al-Sharif under the direction of the late Professor Benjamin Mazar. Whatever reasons led to the excavations and despite the criticism that can be leveled against the way in which they were carried out, they uncovered spectacular courses of masonry on the Herodian wall of the Haram and an elegantly structured approach of steps leading to the southern entrances into the Jewish sanctuary. The unexpected results of these excavations for the early Middle Ages consist of several buildings from early Islamic times which are discussed below. Meyer Ben-Dov has proposed several very imaginative reconstructions of these and other buildings, but there are no published reports of the excavations nor of the finds that may be pertinent to early medieval times.[44] The excavations carried out by the late Nahman Avigad in the Jewish quarter, published in archaeological journals and in a book for the general public,[45] have resulted in reconstructions which have been incorporated in the rebuilding of the Jewish quarter. This incorporation of ancient remains into contemporary living has been successful visually, but leaves much to be desired socially and culturally, and in a sense fails to explain the past, while absorbing it quite successfully.[46]

Information about the early medieval period is also provided by accidental discoveries and by archaeological investigations concerned with other periods. Examples include a wall ten meters long discovered east of the Golden Gate, several strata of medieval use near the Damascus Gate, much in the citadel area, medieval finds in the excavations near the Lutheran church in the center of the city. All of these instances have yielded minute fragments of a huge puzzle but are unfortunately difficult to piece together for a coherent vision of the city.[47]

The second type of archaeological information for the early medieval period consists of reading the existing fabric of the city and its monuments. The methodological problems in this kind of archaeological work are quite different from excavation. For instance, it is not always easy to distinguish between what is old and what looks old, or to agree that something new is but a reinterpretation of something old and therefore a valid document for a time which precedes its creation. The permanence of trading areas and bazaars is often exemplified by the presence now of modern shopping ways in places formerly used for these purposes. But a quaint street may be a manifestation of contemporary economic and social distress rather than an illustration of the ways of the past. There is thus something slightly arbitrary in choosing the elements of the contemporary city for reconstructions of the past.

Four such elements can, however, be identified. There are, first of all, the walls and gates of the city, including the eastern and southern walls of the Haram al-Sharif, which are the most spectacular and immediately visible features of the city. I share without argument the assumption that the present walls more or less coincide (except to the south) with the walls of the early medieval city. But many different techniques of masonry are clearly apparent and they correspond to different periods of construction and repair. These variations are most telling on the southern and southeastern sections of the walls. The mapping of the existing kinds of masonry and their eventual analysis should bring about an interesting chronology of construction techniques that could be used for a history of the city.[48]

The analysis of the present urban fabric of streets, pools, water channels, houses, and public and private buildings is more complicated. There is general agreement based on solid archaeological or other evidence that the main urban axes of streets and the reservoirs of water have not changed significantly since the Roman rebuilding of the second century and that some elements are even earlier. It is also reasonable that the place of power was already in the area of the present citadel on the western wall of the city and it is probable that there was a city market somewhere south of the complex of the Holy Sepulchre, just as there was a column ('amud in Arabic) by the Damascus Gate which led to the modern name of the gate as *Bab al-'Amud*, "gate of the column." As to smaller streets, houses, open spaces, accumulations of debris, their location in the past is unclear. It is tempting to assume that the nineteenth-century city was a continuation of an earlier one and the argument may be valid, if one imagines the model as the fairly well-known Mamluk town of the fifteenth century, but it is not *a priori* acceptable for the period before the Crusades because of the rapid succession of destruction and construction that took place between 1100 and 1300. There is no justification for reconstructing the early medieval city based on the reasonably preserved late medieval one, always excepting a few major arteries already developed in Roman times. The traditional way of using the existing city as a resource is to assume permanence and continuity unless it can be disproved,[49] but this assumption is a questionable one for Jerusalem.

The Dome of the Rock is remarkable in that there is no significant archaeological intrusive evidence regarding it. It dominates the city now as it did in the past. The understanding of the building relies on internal evidence that does not require excavations or intrusions except to answer relatively minor technical questions involving construction and decoration. At the same time, much information must have been revealed in 1960 and 1961 when its foundations were uncovered in order to be strengthened, and when the surroundings of the rock itself were partly cleared.[50]

The buildings on the Haram other than the Aqsa Mosque and the Dome of the Rock, as well as those at the western and northern boundaries of the sanctuary's space form a catch-all category of constructions from many different periods for most of which it is reasonable to assume an early use. The principle I have followed in dealing with them is to discuss only features that are dated or mentioned in texts before 1100 or that, for logical reasons, had to have been there—for instance, the gates and passageways under the Aqsa mosque that are required for the mosque above them. But it is possible to imagine an intrusive archaeological investigation of the Haram that would illuminate the earlier centuries, even after the massive reorganization of Mamluk and Ottoman times.

Visual Evidence

However defined and refined, the sources mentioned so far are all traditional means for the reconstruction of a city's history. What I call "visual evidence" has acquired a new dimension thanks to contemporary technology. One's ability to look at whole cities has been significantly sharpened by new sophistication in the field of urban planning within schools of architecture.[51] This technological approach, available for all cities, derives from the obvious fact that the natural or man-made fabric of any place imposes on those who live in it a set of visual impressions that identify and explain what was built, how it was built, what was remembered and transformed into symbols, and especially what settings were provided for life, for behavior, or for spiritual enlightenment. Typical examples of components in the definition of this approach are the seven hills of Rome, the Eiffel Tower and Hauss-man's boulevards in Paris, the hills surrounding Mekkah and the Ka'bah inside the city, the Ring in Vienna, the canals of Venice or of St. Petersburg, and so on. Even more important than the identification of such fixed constraints on a city's shape are the relationships between them: the appearance and disappearance of obelisks in the streets of Rome, the star-like explosion of streets from the Arch of Triumph in Paris, the contrast between upper and lower cities in Quebec, and so on. Visual evidence consists of those places and their relationships, whose perception shapes functional behavior and channels emotional or ideological attitudes along certain paths. Attitudes can be positive in accepting the objectives of the space created in the city or negative in rejecting them. We shall see in Jerusalem examples of both.

The unusual topography and the long and complicated history of Jerusalem had created by the early Middle Ages a web of visual associations and spiritual memories that was as much a part of the city as anything built in it. Or rather, everything built had to fit within an existing system of visually understood features, whether it sought to alter that system or to acknowledge its power and its meanings. The operative signs of the city are thus constantly changing, but the reasons why they are needed may well extend over longer periods of time, may even be integral to the city. Like particles in the quantum universe formulated by physicists, this ever-changing web is an elusive but real component of the city and, again as in physics, the observer is a part of what is observed. One of the aims of this book is to identify this visual component of Jerusalem and to describe the peculiar mix of physical forms, written documents, and imaginative assumptions that helped to define it many centuries ago and that may still be observed today.

To illustrate this visual evidence, a new technology of computer-aided design was used. An appendix by Dr. Mohammad al-Asad, who with Ms. Abeer Audeh spent two years preparing the documentation which led to many of this book's illustrations, explains how these new images were created. Although computer-generated imagery loses some

of its impact when transformed into static images, this imagery introduces a different kind of analytical abstraction from the rendering of urban forms into words, the abstraction of raw urban shapes before they acquire their actual, often modified, texture. The theoretical implications of this new kind of abstraction are much beyond the ambition of this book.

Scholarship

Although much has been written about Jerusalem, the medieval and especially the early medieval city is often squeezed between the David-to-Herod Jewish history of the city destroyed early in our era, and the late Ottoman city of the nineteenth century. Many of the almost innumerable books on Jerusalem—in at least twenty languages—are destined for the most part to remain unread and unused,[52] but there are exceptions. Perhaps the most remarkable consists of the three volumes on the buildings of Jerusalem since Chalcolithic times published by Klaus Bieberstein and Hanswulf Bloedhorn in connection with the equally outstanding three maps of the city, in chronological sequence, put together by the *Tübinger Atlas des Vorderen Orients (TAVO)*. These all came too late for me to make extensive use of them. Future work on Jerusalem will have to begin with their seventy pages of bibliography and references to buildings, things, and accounts about buildings and things.[53]

The purpose of the pages that follow is, then, to present those writings that have helped to shape the approaches and evidence discussed in this book, and especially to situate what I hope will be its own particular contribution within a long history of concerns for Jerusalem. This presentation follows an order in which chronological historiography and thematic methodology overlap. This is so in part because, unlike physics, history does not grow as a rigid sequence of experiments and theories building on each other, but as a river meandering between read and unread research, acknowledged and ignored information, known and unknown languages. This book is in a sense a reconstruction of my own searches for Jerusalem's past, but it is also an essay on the rather unusual range of ways in which the city has been and can be interpreted.

The city's striking and unusual terrain—a set of hills separated by deep valleys—was geographically and scientifically expressed in the surveys carried out by British army engineers for the Palestine Oriental Society in the 1850s and 1860s. A mixture of imperial ambitions, Christian belief, scientific aims, and human spiritual and bodily weaknesses pervades the accounts of the work by Charles Warren and Charles Wilson over many seasons. The beautiful large maps of the *Survey of Western Palestine* as well as the many drawings in all of their books are the exemplary and, at times, touching results of their efforts.[54] They were not alone in the middle of the nineteenth century in their efforts to measure, draw, and capture every part of the Holy City for Christian and Jewish believers or for antiquarians and historians in search of the settings for biblical events. Their images and measurements were the most accurate ones and they have been the basis for most of the city's reconstructions. As one peruses the nineteenth-century books, it is difficult not to be affected by the images of women in long heavy robes being lowered in baskets to see the Roman streets on the Western side of the Haram or to be struck by the courage of underpaid British non-commissioned officers enduring hardship and dying of fever while recording the Holy City.

There was, to my knowledge, no comparable concern for the physical shape of Jerusalem on the part of Muslims, although I expect that the Ottoman army made surveys for maps.[55] Yet the first major work devoted to Islamic Jerusalem was published in 1922 and 1927, the three tomes of the *Matériaux pour un Corpus Inscriptionum Arabicarum* devoted to Jerusalem under Muslim rule, in the prestigious oversize series of the French Institute in Cairo. The publication of inscriptions in the *Matériaux* was the brainchild of the Swiss aristocrat and scholar Max van Berchem. His volumes on Jerusalem, completed after his death, are models of deductive and imaginative scholarship, as the reading

of inscriptions, truly authentic documents in their time, serves as the spindle around which written histories, archaeological information, ethnographic documents, personal observations, and art historical judgments are spun into a sequence of explorations into the character of the medieval city.[56] To Max van Berchem, these were but preliminary studies leading to a full history. Such a history did not appear, just as the full and excellent catalogue of all Mamluk buildings in the city put together by the British School of Archaeology in the 1970s and 1980s did not produce an interpretation or explanation of the city that could be used by historians of all persuasions or by contemporary architects and planners.

The latter have produced wonderful books of photographs with occasional imaginative plans and sketches. Their more interesting contribution to the historian lies in the identification and highlighting of the structural components such as streets or vistas on the uneven terrain of Jerusalem. Too many of their reconstructions belong to the realm of fantasy and show great disregard of the city's past.[57]

On a completely different level because rarely connected with visual impressions, we also have, in several languages (Russian, English, French, Arabic, and Hebrew), with or without interpretations, anthologies of texts dealing with Jerusalem, at times included in written surveys of the whole of Palestine. Some are compendia without much commentary. Others are limited to particular interpretations of history or are concerned with a single space. But nearly all present texts in chronological order and, what is especially interesting for our purposes, most of them assume that the history of the city can be understood without its being seen. It is as though Jerusalem, far more than Cairo or even Constantinople, could, like Rome, be understood in the context of one's own life, wherever it occurs.[58]

Among these books, two deserve to be singled out. One is Guy Le Strange's *Palestine under the Moslems,* the first book to pay particular attention to major and minor monuments and to propose reconstructions of buildings based on texts as much as on the available archaeological information. Le Strange's book has been reedited and is easily accessible. The other book, unique in being focused on Palestine between the Arab conquest and the Crusades, the exact period covered by this book, is a bibliographical rarity. Published in 1902—Le Strange's book came out in 1892—Mednikoff's 1700 pages of Arabic texts, translated into Russian and interpreted according to the exacting canons of scholarship around 1900, are a true masterpiece of learning.[59]

Even when inspired by ideological and religious motives, most of these books provide no interpretations and draw no conclusions but give only factual explanations of texts and occasionally of other artifacts. The fear of overt hypotheses so deeply rooted in positivist scholarship, however, does not extend to one topic associated with Jerusalem: its holy sites and the relationship between the city as it is now and its Christian and Jewish pasts. Leaving aside a fair number of views that are pure fantasy, several major studies dedicated to the elucidation of holy places and holy history, contributed nonetheless to an understanding of the city beyond the development, construction, or use of sanctuaries. Such are the great undertakings of Fathers Louis Hugues Vincent, F. M. Abel, and Jan Simon, or of Theodore Busink, not to speak of occasional articles in the semi-popular press devoted to biblical studies.[60] The objective of all those studies was to imagine and reconstruct as accurately as possible the ancient Jerusalem of the Temple of Solomon, the "Hellenistic" city of Herod in which Christ's life and Passion took place, and the creation and development of a Christian city in the period from Constantine to Justinian. The enormous literature on Jerusalem, augmented every year, is almost exclusively connected to these three topics, as each generation of believers, Jews or Christians, seeks its own image of the spaces in which key moments of their faith were enacted, in whatever language or style of expression is fashionable. The seventeenth-century Baroque reconstructions of the Temple of Solomon and the ponderously elaborate Beaux-Arts projections of the nineteenth century have been followed by today's computer-generated abstractions, but the objective is always to evoke in a currently meaningful fashion the places of the Revelation.

And it is almost exclusively in these Jewish and Christian contexts that Muslim Jerusalem has appeared and been analyzed. The location of two or three successive Jewish Temples is the space of the Haram al-Sharif, and the very Islamic Mamluk city has dictated the contemporary shape of and the access to almost all Christian sanctuaries, especially the Holy Sepulchre, as well as the areas in which all non-Muslims live. Thus scholarly searches for the Christian and Jewish pasts have usually led to what seemed to be the Muslim present, and the Muslim past was often occluded by being confused with the present in the "orientalist" minds of many generations of scholars.[61] Christian and, more especially, Jewish associations are unavoidable in Jerusalem, forming the very foundation on which the medieval city was built. But what was built in the Middle Ages is a result of Muslim initiative and belongs to a different, albeit related, religious and emotional experience in the history of Jerusalem and of western Asia and the eastern Mediterranean as a whole.

In fact, new concern for medieval, and more specifically early medieval, Jerusalem has arisen over the past fifteen to twenty years for reasons both political, in a broad and generally very favorable sense of the word, and scholarly. Since the Festival of Islam in England in 1972 and the Aga Khan Awards for Architecture in 1977 (the date of the first Aga Khan Seminar on Architecture), the artistic and architectural heritage of the Muslim world has become the focus of increasing academic and cultural attention, which has been directed especially to places like Jerusalem where there was political conflict. For Jerusalem itself, there are relatively few tangible results from these concerns.[62] The psychological setting of the city was transformed after the war of 1967, which led to national and international commissions and surveys, to architectural plans and designs, to a spate of guidebooks for a suddenly multiplied influx of tourists seeking information about what they saw, to multiconfessional conferences with publications of proceedings and complaints to UNESCO and other international bodies about true, alleged, or threatened circumventions of law, justice, or propriety. Leaving aside the more superficial meetings and the useful but thoughtless albums of photographs and drawings which have emerged over the past decades, many of the studies that came out of these new opportunities still concentrate on those theological or historical features that relate the Muslim city to the memories of Christian or Jewish presence and rule.[63]

Scholarly motivation is less flamboyant than political or promotional but more fruitful for our purposes. After several decades of wrestling with a universal "Islamic" art largely independent of political considerations, scholarship in Islamic art turned its attention to individual periods and to specific works of art, even to parts of monuments, in the unacknowledged belief that immediate resolutions of concrete problems are more productive than grandiose generalities. As a result, a monument like the Dome of the Rock suddenly received more attention than it had for years, often with very interesting consequences.[64]

→ ✦ ←

THERE IS no simple way to summarize the immense variety of sources available for the study of medieval Jerusalem or the exact state of the knowledge we have of it. Both are remarkably uneven. Thus, whereas the Dome of the Rock is provided with enough documents and studies to allow a full contextual explanation, any knowledge of the Holy Sepulchre is destined to remain fragmentary and contentious. Most sources are at least once removed from actual experience of the physical city and, rather than providing visual description, they reflect imperial or ecclesiastical, political or ideological, sentimental or rationally descriptive concerns. The objective of this book is to elucidate the shape of the city not according to any faith or to any written text or belief, but as a visual perception of a unique urban order.

The sources available for Jerusalem and the scholarship about the city explain why visually centered

interpretations do not exist and also why they are possible. Interest in Jerusalem has focused on separate religious issues because of the character of the written sources, the confessional allegiances of scholars in the past generation, and the nature of political and national associations supporting research. The last is not yet pertinent to the early middle ages; religious motivation is paramount. Even though all three systems of faith—Judaism, Christianity, and Islam—proclaim the physical importance of the city in their own version of the Revelation, that expression has, most of the time, been translated into a set of statements in which the real city has been curiously absent. The Jerusalem of Protestant hymns or of Catholic and Orthodox Christian liturgies (especially at Easter) is an imaginary city, often celebrated in northern climes, its desert setting ignored. The Jewish liturgical expectation to be "next year in Jerusalem" is a messianic rendezvous rather than anticipation of a physical connection with a real city. And the Muslim's first *qiblah* or direction to prayer as well as the association of Jerusalem with the Prophet's Nocturnal Voyage are sacred memories which do not require the knowledge of a concretely shaped space. The key premise with which I begin is that, since most of the recording of knowledge took place through words, written texts have defined the past and the means through which we understand beliefs and pious behavior. The physical piety of pilgrims, their emotional relationship to spaces and places, occasionally detected in theological discourse, and the daily experience of the local believer, all these have been thought to be irretrievable or irrelevant to the deeper issues of religious thought and history.

But this is precisely where the peculiarity of Jerusalem's topographic history can be of use. That the religious and secular spaces of the whole city hardly changed between the first and the nineteenth centuries and that much of that city has been surrounded but not replaced by a new city make it possible, both logically and practically, to remove successive accretions and to retrieve stages, currently invisible, in the city's development. Even today, only the most jaded or the most boorish visitor fails to feel, when he first *sees* the walls of the "Old City" and then *crosses* them to enter into the historic city, that he is entering another time and, almost automatically, the visitor adjusts his perceptions to his memories or knowledge of the past. The judgments may be flawed, but the possibility exists of capturing fragments of several different pasts because of the constrictions imposed in Jerusalem by nature's space and by man's activities.

Logically, the reconstruction of the stages involved in the history of the city could be accomplished archaeologically, by the systematic removal of discrete layers of spatial order, probably not impossible with contemporary techniques for the computerized storing of visual information, but beyond the competencies and funds available to me. What was done instead was to reconstruct images of the city at certain moments of its history by using computer-based technology to store and manipulate information provided by traditional written or archaeological sources. A series of reconstructions is proposed that seems to make sense, given what we know now, and that can be refined as more data become available and are added to the files.

Four moments in the history of Jerusalem have been selected. The first shows the Christian city that would have existed around 600 on the eve of the Persian invasion of 614. This date was chosen in part because of the existence of a lot of data from the sixth century like the Madaba map. The date is also significant because, regardless of the destructions carried out in 614, the memory of the earlier city still existed at the time of the Muslim conquest. This reconstruction of the Christian city was primarily to establish the basis for what follows.

The second moment extends from the time of the Muslim takeover in 637 until the construction of the Dome of the Rock in 692. It includes the rule of governors appointed from Madinah in Arabia until 661 and the first thirty odd years of the Umayyad caliphate. It is a period of extraordinary importance for the establishment of the spiritual and ritual categories of Muslim Jerusalem, but it has left practically no physical remains and it does not appear as a separate moment in the computer-generated reconstructions.

The third moment is the imperial Umayyad one, between 692 and the end of the dynasty in 750. It is a strikingly well-documented period and the lengthy discussion of its evidence establishes, I hope, the profound alteration to everything in the city which came out of the extraordinary activities of the Umayyad princes themselves and of practically every social or religious group present in Western Asia at the time. Nearly half of the book is devoted to one building, the Dome of the Rock, which dominates the Umayyad period. There are three reasons for the attention given to this building. First, the Dome of the Rock is documented by more contemporary and authentic documents than any other part of the city. As a result, it is not only possible to explain a great deal about what it was meant to be, but also to discuss its importance for the history of architecture in general. For—and this is my second reason—the Dome of the Rock is a masterpiece of world art in its form as well as in the meanings that have been given to it. And, finally, as is demonstrated by tourist advertisements, it still dominates the city that defines itself around it. I shall argue that its existence was an enduring visual magnet around which the rest of the city must be understood.

Initially, I felt that an Abbasid moment (750–970) could clearly be separated from the Umayyad period, as much evidence exists in the late eighth and ninth centuries of significant building activities and of formal interventions into the life of the city by the caliphs in Iraq. But as the evidence mounted regarding the momentous changes of the earlier Umayyad period and the novelties introduced by the Fatimids who took over the rule of the city around 970, Abbasid changes appeared to be visually inconsequential, even though their religious and cultural meanings were considerable. They will be described as having affected the changes brought to the whole city by the Fatimids. It is the Fatimid city that fell into the hands of the Crusaders and this is why the last chapter concentrates on the Jerusalem that can be imagined around 1060 rather than attempts to trace an evolution from the eighth to the eleventh centuries.

One last point of methodological clarification

needs to be made. One of the difficulties encountered in the writing of this book was to maintain consistency in the vocabulary of description and interpretation and in the coherence of the narrative being told. This is so because an uneasy equilibrium exists in the pages which follow between extreme precision of descriptive detail and fixation on very specific dates on the one hand and, on the other, very abstract reconstructions of shapes in an urban landscape defined by perceptions by people long dead.

I have picked up from the jargon of architectural criticism the words "intervention" and "event," used almost interchangeably, to identify either a work accomplished or a contextual change that affects the city (or any artefact) in an irreversible way. The building of the Dome of the Rock, the shortening of the walls, the earthquake of 746 (or 749) are such "events" or "interventions." But very precise pieces of the puzzle can only be understood in the light of two much broader characteristics of the city which are created or modified by "events": the physical shape, a minuscule fragment of the earth's surface transformed by man into walls, streets,

buildings, vistas, and all the activities of life; and especially, the profound reenactment of beliefs which transform sacred places into holy ones by providing them with a cult. As Maurice Halbwachs has shown half a century ago in dealing with the Gospels, beliefs themselves change with time, even when the people and events which shaped them are still the same, or are believed to be such.[65] It is not always easy to distinguish from each other the several layers of memory within belief which exist at any one time. Nor is it simple to relate them to the physical or archaeological layers of the spaces in or on which they were expressed. And the problem is compounded when the history of some four hundred years is woven onto the canvas of material remains and human memories.

This book attempts to make sense out of disparate sources and different early medieval urban forms. Its warp is history, a chronological sequence of events. Its weft consists in the physical shape and perceptions of the city. It is then embroidered with the memories of men and women from different times and cultures.

CHAPTER ONE

The Formation of an Islamic City

The Legacy of the Christian City

By 600 C.E. the disputes among ecclesiastical authorities about the value and justification of developing Jerusalem as a Christian city were probably for the most part forgotten. But the arguments used by an opponent, the bishop of Caesarea Eusebius (260–336), a contemporary of Constantine's conversion, or by an enthusiastic proponent like Cyril (320–385), bishop of Jerusalem from 346 onward, are a convenient way of introducing the city itself and especially the web of practices, beliefs, and emotions which surrounded and protected it, like so many layers of cloth preserving and nurturing a living treasure, and which inspired or were inspired by the specifics of its physical shape.[1]

Four themes underlie most of the arguments used by the literate bishops of Hellenized Late Antiquity and define the spaces with which they dealt. There is the landscape of Jerusalem—the hills, valleys, and peaks with sacred names like Sion, Golgotha, Moriah, or Eleona (the Mount of Olives). It also includes the walls and streets adapted to an uneven landscape and, since Roman imperial times, forming the skeletal fixtures of the city. There is the faith of

the Holy City. Around 600 that faith was overwhelmingly Christian, especially if one restricts one's concerns, as I do in this book, to the visual expression of faith. But, in peculiar and special ways, both paganism and Judaism were very much part in the religious profile of the city. A third theme is the life of Jerusalem, the routine daily activities of men, women, and children as well as the religious or secular festivals, and imperial interventions through building contracts, taxation, and civil control. And, finally, there is the vision of Jerusalem which ranges from those based on an immediate experience of the city to imaginary constructs found all over the Christian world.[2]

It is through its landscape, faith, life, and vision, then, that Jerusalem can be reconstructed as it would have existed around 600 C.E. and, in many ways, continues to exist even until our own time. I shall deal with these aspects without trying to provide a large number of examples and without taking part in often complicated debates about texts and archaeological finds or about the reconstruction of monuments and events derived from them. It is not that I try to avoid the search for complete truth and accuracy, but rather that the primary objective of this chapter is to set the stage for what happened after 600, not to provide a synthesis of the scholarship and documents that have so enriched our knowledge and understanding of the early centuries of medieval Jerusalem. The setting of the city contained a number of well defined and hardly controversial spaces, monuments, and memories, and these are the focus of this discussion, but they exist in a context fraught with uncertainties.

Landscape

The city of Jerusalem (fig. 7) grew around rocky ridges and deep gullies between 700 and 800 meters above sea level at the edge of the nearly waterless Judaean wilderness to the east and south and beyond old cultivated terraces (today covered with houses and largely reforested) to the north and the west. Two major and clearly perceptible spurs dominate the terrain (fig. 8): the western hill culminating in Mount Zion, the highest point in the landscape of the city, now just outside of the medieval walls; and the considerably lower eastern hill known as Mount Moriah, which is today incorporated in the Haram al-Sharif. Between the two ridges lies the Tyropoeon valley, now partly filled with debris from centuries of occupation, but still striking as one looks westward or northward from the western wall of the Herodian Temple (the Wailing Wall of Jewish pious practice) or as one contemplates the southwestern corner of the Haram, so spectacularly poised over the valley. The western ridge merges relatively gradually with the rolling terrain to the west of it, while the eastern ridge descends abruptly toward the deep, long, and narrow Kidron valley, which separates it from the high ridges of the Mount of Olives. The Tyropoeon and Kidron valleys eventually meet south of the city with the Hinnom valley, which surrounds the area from the west and the south. It is on the southern continuation of the eastern ridge, roughly at the juncture of the valleys, that the first settlements of Jerusalem were located, known not quite accurately as the "City of David." Both the western and the eastern ridges continue northward. The western one has an undulating pro-file and contains the high point of Golgotha, some four hundred meters north of Mount Zion. The eastern one rises first quite steeply and then beyond the edges of the city becomes an uneven succession of ascents and descents that extends for miles toward modern Ramallah.

The significant or active terrain of late sixth-century Jerusalem consisted of two high points to the west, Zion and Golgotha, one high point to the east, Moriah, a deep valley, the Tyropoeon, between the two, a much deeper valley, the Kidron, to the east, and the higher Mount of Olives farther eastward. The human and, as we shall see, visual story of the city was enacted in the spaces outlined by these poles. But there is another way of defining this physical setting. Whatever meanings were given to its high points or to its low-lying valleys, the setting itself can be defined in terms of degrees of accessibility and, consequently, of vulnerability. It is most easily approached from the north, especially the northeast, least so from the south and especially the southeast. Eventually, this last topographic characteristic acquired a mythical value as it separated the higher world of the living from the lower one of the dead and especially from the much higher expectation of a world to come. Such mythical values were made possible, perhaps even invited, because visual accessibility is exactly opposite to physical accessibility: Jerusalem is relatively easy to reach from the north, but difficult to perceive as a city except from one site several miles away, a site associated now with the tomb of the prophet Samuel and known during the Crusades as Montjoie as it was the first spot from which the Holy City could be seen by the European invaders. The city can easily be seen wherever you come from the southeast, while access to it is physically arduous.

We shall often return to these two ways of approaching a space, with one's feet or with one's eyes. At this stage, what matters is the unfriendly, rugged terrain, one provided with strongly identifiable features and, as a result, with a strong mythopoeic potential in the sense that a man's practice of the terrain easily leads to the transformation of its features into agents or recipients of man's beliefs.

Figure 7. Jerusalem, air view of the city from the west. The slope of the Mount of Olives appears above and behind the platform of the Haram with the Dome of the Rock isolated and parts of the western wall of Herod's Temple barely visible. The dome of the Holy Sepulchre is more or less in the center of the picture, and the western walls are visible in the middle with parts of the citadel at the right edge. The whole city seems deceptively even and its hilly setting is hidden by constructions built over centuries of debris.

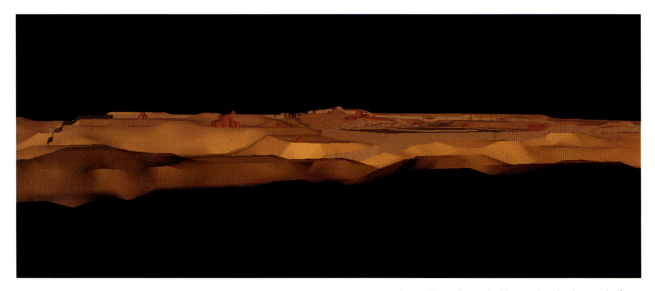

Figure 8. Schematic view of Jerusalem ca. 600 from the southeast. Mt. Moriah, to the right, is hidden under the large platform of Herod's Temple which was left unoccupied at the time. To the east (right) of the platform the slope descends rapidly into the Kidron Valley. The Tyropocon Valley is visible as a depression to the left of the platform. On the left rises Mt. Zion punctuated by two churches (the Nea and the Church of Zion). In the middle of the drawing the built ensemble of the Holy Sepulchre identifies Mt. Golgotha. The western walls of the city are in the background. Note the relatively even terrain to the north (on the right) and the very tortuous one to the south.

By 600 C.E. the original landscape of Jerusalem had been transformed by some twelve centuries of occupation. Truly radical changes took place during the centuries of Roman hegemony in Jerusalem. The control was indirect through Herod the Great (37–4 B.C.E.), then more or less direct under proconsuls like Pontius Pilate, until Jerusalem became a military colony after the last Jewish revolt was put down in 135. Under the name of *Aelia Capitolina* the Roman military settlement incorporated what was left of the city into a new, relatively standardized, urban setting. The latter survived for nearly two centuries, until 326, when Constantine's mother, Helena, visited Jerusalem and uncovered the area believed to have been hallowed by Christ's Passion. After some uncertainty about the necessity of a Christian Jerusalem, a new Christian identity was eventually fitted onto the pagan Roman city and remained until the momentous changes of the seventh century.

The Roman military city created a structure that still exists in the Old City. It is, in the fashion of so many Roman military cities, an adaptation of standard planning to the idiosyncrasies of a terrain. Its main permanent features, identified by a different color on the computer-generated drawings (fig. 8), are walls with gates and streets. The vaguely square shape of the city was dictated by walls that incorporate the totally artificial platform of the Herodian Temple to the southwest, exclude the top of Mount Zion although it is the highest point in the city, and cut across the highly uneven terrain everywhere. Very much redone over time, especially in the sixteenth century, and shifted slightly in a few places, these are still the walls of the contemporary city. The walls draw attention to a fascinating contrast between two phenomena. On one side there is a land whose geological logic can in many places be seen in the grotesque appearance of twisted layers of rocks and sediments. And then there is the absurdity of putting on top of the land an arbitrary walled structure that contradicts the shape of the land, yet introduces a rational order of human—in this particular case, imperial—power.

It was a flexible enclosure that could be enlarged, as it was probably twice in the period between 135 and 600. One enlargement included Mount Zion within the walled city, as is acknowledged by a visitor, Eucherius, the bishop of Lyon between 434 and 449, when he writes that the city was "enclosed by a lengthy wall, that now embraces Mount Zion, though the latter was once just outside."[3] This change, otherwise undated, would have preceded a second increase in the size of the city sponsored by Eudocia, the wife of the emperor Theodosius II, who, partly for political reasons, spent a lot of time and money in and on Jerusalem; in fact, the fifth century had been proclaimed by Fathers Vincent and Abel as "le siècle d'Eudocie."[4] Her wall, fragments of which remain at the southeastern corner of today's city, included a large new arca to the south, primarily to enclose churches and service buildings for pilgrims.

Eudocia's wall, if its remaining sections have been correctly identified as such, was a rather simple enclosure wall without, for instance, an easily accessible walk or towers. The exact width, height, and shape of the Roman wall are known only in places, as in the area of the Damascus Gate, the principal northern entry into the city. It was certainly a very imposing construction, as is the sixteenth-century reconstruction sponsored by Suleyman the Magnificent that stands today. It is reasonable to assume the same powerful impact of the enclosure built fifteen centuries earlier. In Jerusalem, as elsewhere in the Roman Levant, the walls fulfilled three purposes simultaneously. One was defense, as this particular city, more than any other city of Syria and Palestine, possibly than any city anywhere, had been attacked and defended with equally passionate vigor. The second purpose was protection. On a mundane level, walls were to protect the city's treasures against the casual banditry prevailing in the area since time immemorial. But they also delineated and protected a space that had been consecrated, whose values were not those of its surrounding terrain and whose qualities could be felt without necessarily being seen.[5] And the third purpose of these walls was to proclaim power, the power of an empire controlling cities and all accesses to them.

The pattern of streets in Jerusalem was also cre-

ated by the Roman empire, and the main arteries are easily visible on the Madaba map (figs. 9, 10). Two southbound streets were laid out from the Damascus Gate. One, usually called the *cardo*, follows the higher ground and ends at the Zion Gate, the main southern entry into the city, and remains of its arcades are still found in the city. A second street veers eastward first before turning south; it follows the low ground of the Tyropoeon valley and its southernmost end has been obliterated by later medieval transformations. The Madaba map shows it also with a single row of columns, as though only one side of the street was provided with an arcade. An east-west street, the *decumanus* of a Roman camp, went from the present Jaffa Gate on the west side, where the citadel is now and where a major Herodian building stood in the past, to the large platform of the Temple on the east side of the city. A shorter east-west street, with fragments of an archway still remaining, connected the "colonnaded" street to the only operating gate on the east side, today's Gate of St. Stephen.

Almost nothing is known of the small streets and connecting passages that covered the rest of the city, but the main axes of the Roman military creation are, like the walls, the permanent skeletal structure around which Jerusalem is organized even now. It is also reasonable to assume that the Romans maintained, repaired, or rebuilt most of the cisterns and the so-called "pools" or basins that held rain water or that could be filled by aqueducts or other means for the population of a city without wells. The last of these pools to have been more or less operational is located to the northeast of the Haram; it is now being transformed into a parking lot.

Walls and streets, the two principal man-made elements in the landscape of Jerusalem, contributed contradictory, or at least sharply contrasting, features to that landscape. Here was a highly uninviting nature, treeless and waterless, so uneven as to defy development, and with only the easy availability of good stone for building to its advantage. On it the Roman imperial system imposed a structure of walls, gates, and streets, which sometimes followed the terrain and at other times challenged its

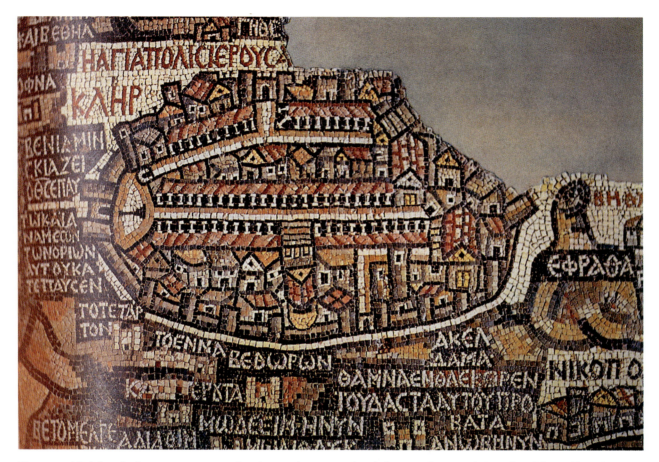

Figure 9. Madaba, Jordan, mosaic map, mid or late sixth century; detail showing the city of Jerusalem. The walls with towers and the colonnaded streets are easily distinguished. The Damascus Gate with its column is to the left, and the Gate of St. Stephen on the east wall is more or less top center; the Holy Sepulchre is the large building seen upside down in the lower center; while the large building to the right is the Zion church with the Nea just above. The identification of the remaining buildings is less certain.

constraints, but always compelled a shape that has functioned until the nineteenth century, if not until today. The Roman empire made that effort in a place without economic or administrative significance because of the long history of a faith attached to it already in 135 C.E. It was also a faith that gave a new flesh and a new skin to the skeleton built on a hallowed terrain by the engineers of the imperial army.

Faith

The faith overcome by the Roman empire was Judaism. Its monumental expression, early in the first century, was the Temple planned and built by Herod the Great. The setting of the Temple was an immense quadrilateral platform, 310 meters on the north, 488 meters on the west, 281 meters on the south, and 466 meters on the east, which covered nearly one sixth of the whole surface of the city. Even more remarkable than its size is its utter artificiality: its more or less even surface required cutting into the natural rock on the northwest and building supporting walls, up to fifty meters high, from the low terrain to the south. These walls are still, even with their later medieval and early modern additions, among the most spectacular and the most sensuously powerful stone masonries in existence anywhere. A portico of 162 enormous columns arranged in four rows made up the *Stoa* of

Herod's Temple across the whole southern end of the sanctuary. Nine entrances led to the platform, four of which, to the south and to the west, consisted of underground passages below the surface of the platform. The western ones are connected with the largely inaccessible Barclay's Gate below the surface of the Haram al-Sharif or with the monumental staircase or bridge whose standing remains constitute Robinson's Arch, a striking masonry outcrop near the southwestern corner of the platform. The southern gates were on the sites of the present Double and Triple Gates. A single northern gate, the Gate of Darkness, may have been on the site of one of the present gates. There were two western gates on the northern end of the enclosure that probably were among the medieval entries into the Haram. The eastern gate was at the same place as the present Golden Gate. Like the platform on

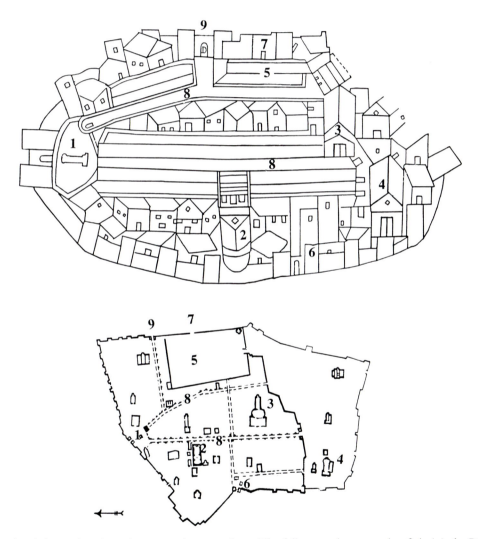

Figure 10. The plan below is based on the mosaic drawing above. The following places are identified: (1) the Damascus Gate, the main northern gate; (2) the Holy Sepulchre; (3) the Nea church; (4) the church on Mt. Zion; (5) the area of Herod's Temple (the Haram al-Sharif); (6) the Citadel and main western gate (today's Jaffa Gate); (7) Golden Gate; (8) the cardo running north-south through the whole city, with its two branches; (9) St. Stephen's Gate, the main eastern gate. The extension of the wall to the south is usually interpreted as a depiction of Eudocia's wall.

which it stood, the gates of the Herodian Temple remained as more or less permanent fixtures of the topography of Jerusalem.[6]

Nothing remains now of the Temple constructions themselves nor does one even know for certain where they were. But it is unlikely that all of what must have been an immense complex of holy as well as service buildings disappeared in the systematic destructions by the Roman army. There must have been debris—fallen walls, roofs, columns, piers, and other architectural components— and at least parts of the *Stoa* were still standing when the emperor Hadrian took formal possession of the hallowed area, building a pagan temple and erecting a statue of Jupiter there. The visual preeminence of the Roman creation may be indicated by the fact that seventh-century sources still referred to it as the *kapitolion*, the "Capitol." Fragments of the dedicatory inscription were found reused in the later masonry of the Haram's walls. Hadrian's monuments were abandoned and possibly dismantled some time after the Christianization of the empire. Even if they remained throughout the Christian centuries much better preserved than has been imagined, they gradually became, along with the ruins of the Temple, a quarry for the building of Christian and later Muslim Jerusalem.[7]

It is difficult enough to imagine one sixth of a city as an immense depot of ruins available for pilfering for the new constructions sponsored by the Christian emperors, the Church, and a wide range of lesser pious patrons, it is especially remarkable to recall that this area was not left in its sorry state accidentally, but as a willed demonstration of the prophecy of the Gospels regarding the Temple: "there shall not be left one stone upon another that shall not be thrown down" (Mark 13:2). The ruined area of the Jewish Temple, even if it consisted mostly of pagan Roman imperial buildings, was a sign of the defeat of the old Revelation and the victory of the new one. Still, its holiness could not be altogether ignored and the place became the repository of moments in the sacred narrative of Christianity: Zechariah—not the father of John the Baptist with whom he was often confused, but the wrongly stoned visionary of II Chronicles 24: 20–

21—was said to have been slain there and traces of his blood were visible; the chambers of Solomon were shown to pious tourists and the "pinnacle of the Temple," the southeastern corner that remained standing above the damaged walls on either side, was thought to have been the site of the martyrdoms of St. James and St. Stephen, and the location of one of the Temptations of Christ (Matthew 4:5, Luke 4:9); the Golden Gate became associated with the meeting of Joachim and Anna, if not the Entry into Jerusalem.[8] Whatever the chronology and interplay of these associations, which often contradict one another, the maintenance of the eastern half of Jerusalem as a huge ruined space full of architectural debris carried a message, religious no doubt, but also socio-political.

The message may have been primarily for Christians, but it was also addressed to Jews. The story of Jewish presence in or, more accurately, absence from Jerusalem during the centuries following the defeat of Bar Kokhba in 132 is a sad and depressing one, made all the more tragic by occasional mention of Jewish activity in the city which, usually as after the reign of the emperor Julian (361– 363), resulted in further humiliation.[9] Whether or not there were Jews settled in Jerusalem during this period, they played a minimal role in the life of the city. But their sacred memory of Mount Moriah remained, alongside the new one being fashioned by Christians; it was the place of the Temple and, as early as 333, according to a celebrated statement by an anonymous pilgrim from Bordeaux, Jews came once a year to anoint the *lapis pertusus* or "pierced stone" as a trace of the Temple, and then to mourn visibly and vigorously. There are indications that such penitential rites were occasionally celebrated in the fifth century, but appear to have been particularly restricted in the next century. What is constant is the mournful mood of Jewish piety in Jerusalem at that time. St. Jerome described in moving terms processions of Jews, and a certain rabbi wrote with heart-felt emotion that "they come silently and they go silently, they come weeping and they go weeping, they come in the darkness of night, and they depart in darkness."[10]

The "pierced stone" mentioned by the pilgrim

from Bordeaux has always been identified as the large rocky formation on which the Dome of the Rock would be built later. That formation has on its very top a fairly large artificial opening into a cave below. As there was no ritual or historical reason for Muslims to cut such an opening, we must assume, as everyone has, that it belonged to an early, probably Jewish—although possibly even earlier—religious practice. The initial use of the rock and the time of its piercing will probably never be known and there may be no reason to dispute the association made between the rock under the Dome of the Rock and the stone mentioned by the pilgrim from Bordeaux. But the absence, to my knowledge, of any other earlier reference, Christian or Jewish, to what must have been a very prominent feature of the area remains puzzling. Perhaps it was so surrounded by ruins that it was not easily visible; it would have been cleared only *after* the Muslim conquest, and the dimensions as well as the height of the later platform of the Haram would probably have been determined by the volume of ruins accumulated around it. Or, perhaps, the pilgrim from Bordeaux refers to something different and now gone, as Jewish rituals would not normally allow for worship in the area of the destroyed Holy of Holies. It is also possible that Jewish practices during these obscure centuries were different from those normal later, but, while the sorrowful visits of exiled believers sound true, the anointment of a holy place, as described by the pilgrim from afar, sounds more like a Christian practice than a Jewish one and, therefore, throws some doubt on the accepted identification.[11] I mention this doubt with some reluctance, because it fails to explain either the physical object, the rock, or the pious practice of mourning. It is necessary, however, to point out the precariousness of so many of our documents and the ease with which conclusions have been drawn from them.

Although questions concerning the location of the Temple must remain until the area can be studied archaeologically,[12] the important point is that, even if there were a specific spot within the large area that was identified by Jews as a trace of the Temple or some other hallowed event, Jewish be-

liefs in or about Jerusalem were channeled into the creative cultivation of myths that did not require a physical space or specific location. Memories of the past consecrated by holy texts and messianic visions for a time to come did not depend on an exact place except that they involved the whole city of Jerusalem and its immediate surroundings.[13]

Christianity, on the other hand, because of its status as the faith of the empire, transformed its memories and its myths into spaces, monuments, institutions, images, momentos, liturgies, and various kinds of ritualized or individual pious behavior. The complex mingling of holy places, sacred memories, physical actions, and objects seen or touched is well exemplified by the account left by an anonymous pilgrim from Piacenza some time around 570. He reached the city coming from the east and the Mount of Olives and eventually "climbed by many steps from Gethsemane to the gate of Jerusalem. There is an olive grove on the right of the gate; in it is the fig-tree from which Judas hanged himself. Its trunk still stands there, protected by stones. This gate of the city is north of the Gate Beautiful that was part of the Temple, and its threshold and entablature are still in position there." He then went to the Holy Sepulchre and describes the mass of objects, including crowns and other kinds of jewels, suspended around the Tomb of Christ. Elsewhere in the Holy Sepulchre he saw the altar of Melchizedech on which Abraham had intended to sacrifice Isaac and, next to it, a crack in the ground where water could be heard and, if you threw in an apple, the apple came out in the pool of Siloam, a mile or so to the south. Miraculous daily events like the bubbles that appeared in little flasks of oil the moment the flask touched the wood of the Holy Cross, the reading of Christian and Old Testament narratives, proclamations of divine mysteries like the onyx cup blessed at the Last Supper, all these were accompanied by gestures of worship, mostly kissing and praying. Although each one of this pilgrim's statements requires its own commentary about meaning or implications, the point here is the wealth of written testimony that was transmitted by pilgrim accounts to believers all over the Christian world. This testimony went hand in hand with sacred objects, like the celebrated silver ampullae or phials for oil or water preserved in Monza and elsewhere with souvenir images of the Holy Land.[14] Memories, written accounts, and objects led in turn to commemorative monumental mosaics in the great churches of Rome as well as small towns like Madaba, and to their preservation in certain manuscripts.[15]

For the city itself and our attempt to understand how it functioned and how it was perceived, the role of this vast documentation can be summarized by a few comments on the mosaic map in Madaba (figs. 9–10), whose likely date (ca. 560–565) is only a generation or two away from our target date of 600. The relative proximity of Madaba to Jerusalem, only a few days away, implies some verification from eyewitnesses able to recognize the map's components from their own experience.[16] Three observations about the map are pertinent to our purposes: the layout of the city, its three large

Figure 11. Schematic plan of Jerusalem around 600. The large red complex on the lower left is the Holy Sepulchre; the large red building on the right is the Nea church; Mt. Zion is at the lower right (southwest); the large empty space above (or east) is the Temple area on Mt. Moriah. The walls and main streets are those of the Roman period and the southern extension of the wall is approximately the one sponsored by the Byzantine empress Eudocia.

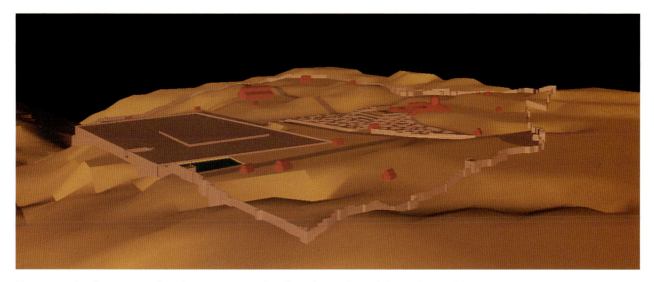

Figure 12. Bird's-eye view of sixth-century Jerusalem from the northeast. The Holy Sepulchre is to the right and the church of the Nea is in the middle; the empty area to the left with a pool in front of it marks the location of the Temple.

sanctuaries, and other, mostly ecclesiastical, buildings.[17]

The layout of Jerusalem in the Madaba map is important not for the shape of the city, which bears little relationship to reality, but for its components (figs. 11–12). There are mighty walls with twenty-six towers and six gates, of which the main northern one, today's Damascus Gate, is particularly striking by its size, by a plot of open space just after one enters the city, and by the single column whose memory is still preserved in the traditional Arabic name of the gate, *bab al-'amud*, the "gate of the column." A secondary group of two towers is found just to the south of the western gate, today's Jaffa Gate, and it is reasonable to suggest that they mark the area occupied now by the citadel on remains of major Herodian buildings, probably some of Herod's palaces. It is possible that these were the buildings used and inhabited by representatives of imperial power, but I do not know of anything to prove the point other than the fact that, much later, secular power would again be located there.[18] The Golden Gate is indicated on the mosaic map as are two southern gates on the original Roman wall—more or less equivalent to the modern Zion and Dung gates—but no

gate is apparent on the fairly clearly marked enclosure wall sponsored by Eudocia.

The major streets are clearly depicted, the *cardo* with its two arcades straight from the Damascus Gate to the Zion Gate, and its eastern offshoot, the "colonnaded street," apparently with only one row of columns, following the low road into the Tyropoeon valley and the Dung Gate of today. A short northern street joins the citadel to Mt. Zion. The east-west thoroughfares are less well identified on the map, just as they are less obvious today. One is parallel to the northern edge of the Haram and the other one, least clearly indicated on the Madaba map, was the *decumanus* which connected the two north-south roads to the western gate and to the putative administrative or political center of the city. It clearly played a lesser role in Christian Jerusalem. There is no information on secondary streets, but the emphasis given to the two branches of the *cardo* and to the east-west segment leading from the eastern gate are clear indications that these were the main streets, the ones around which the religious and presumably economic life of the city as well as its symbolic meaning actually revolved.

Protected like a fortress, Jerusalem is shown as

an irregular network of streets on which treasured holy buildings were strung. It is an image that is further developed, for example, in the Roman and Ravenna mosaics of the sixth century, where ornamental buildings are glimpsed behind frequently bejeweled walls. But in the Madaba map, the conventions for representation belong to a generally accepted and fairly common typology for depiction of cities.[19] Only differences in details and occasional deviations from standard types are sufficiently telling to justify an interpretation of Jerusalem as an enclosed city-sanctuary, not easily accessible but with an inner structure and treasures known to or imagined by those who never visited it.

The three major sanctuaries are the complex of the Holy Sepulchre, the New Church of the Virgin Mary known as the *Nea*, and the "Mother" of all churches, the church on Mt. Zion. The complex of the Holy Sepulchre (fig. 13) is the only one to have had a continuous history of use from the first Constantinian constructions of the second quarter of the third century until today. By 600 C.E., it was reached from an opening in the colonnade of the *cardo* by a set of steps. There was then a courtyard that channeled the faithful to a variety of places commemorating moments in the death, burial, and resurrection of Christ, to the great five-aisled basilica of Constantine, and to a number of service areas reserved by and for ecclesiastical and maintenance purposes. The details of most reconstructions are controversial, as literary, archaeological, and liturgical sources are insufficient and lend themselves to different explanations. There probably never will be a truly accurate depiction of the sixth-century building,[20] as there never has been a single understanding of it. The unwritten purpose of the complex was and is now to make many reactions possible, provided they derive from true faith and from correct liturgical behavior.

Two features of the late sixth-century complex are pertinent here. One is its setting: this monumental composition, from the steps of its entrance, faced and contemplated the barren space of the Jewish Temple on the other side of the town (fig. 14), a permanent reminder of the Church's victory over the Synagogue, as later western theologians

would put it. A large basilical hall with five naves,[21] was approached through an atrium, and led to a courtyard and the rotunda with a high dome some twenty meters in diameter over the Holy Sepulchre itself. On the south side there were additional sanctuaries, most particularly the Church of Golgotha, a baptistery, and the shrine of the Cross. On the north side there were commons. In short, a sequence is provided of an elaborate entrance, a long congregational hall, and a centrally planned shrine. The sequence has a longitudinal axis and a direction for movement. Its dominant feature is the dome of the Anastasis, as is clear from the late seventh-century drawings inspired by Arculf,[22] although the Madaba map gives equal prominence to all these features. The complex of the Holy Sepulchre dominated the city physically, as it rose above the arcade of the street, facing eastward toward the area of the Temple and, beyond it, toward the Mount of Olives and the Church of the Ascension, a tall tower recalling the hallowed event of Christ's Ascension into Heaven and forecasting His eventual return on the Last Day.

It is important to point out that the Holy Sepulchre had acquired over the centuries many meanings besides the commemoration of the death, burial, and resurrection of Christ. There were the implements and signs of the Passion and other memorabilia: the three crosses under an altar of silver and gold on nine columns, the twelve silver bowls in which Solomon caught the demons, and the ring with which he sealed them, the Lance with which Christ was pierced, the plate on which the head of John the Baptist was carried, the horn with which David was anointed, the place where Adam was formed, the altar on which Zechariah was killed, the altar of Abraham and Melchizedech, an icon of Mary, and so on.[23] All these consecrated places and objects were, in all likelihood, responses to the queries of pilgrims, as a long history, itself a compilation of sacred texts and of pious legends, was made visible through architectural spaces, representations, memorabilia of events, and manufactured objects associated with those events and with the heroes of the history. Ecclesiastical authorities, conscious no doubt of the income generated by

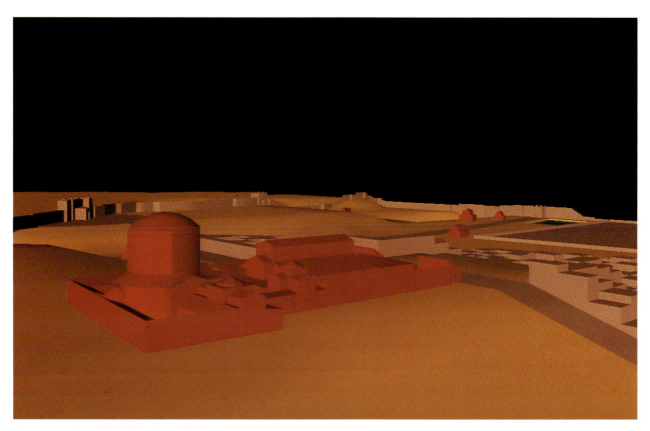

Figure 13. The Holy Sepulchre, schematic reconstruction from the southwest. The northwest corner of the Temple area is visible to the right. These drawings are all based on reconstructions, mostly by Ch. Couäsnon, and they are only hypothetical schemes for the building. The dark path on the right is the cardo leading to the Damascus Gate to the left. The high cylinder is the Rotunda of the Holy Sepulchre complex, while the basilical hall to the right is the congregational part of the ensemble. The colonnade of the cardo was not drawn on the computer.

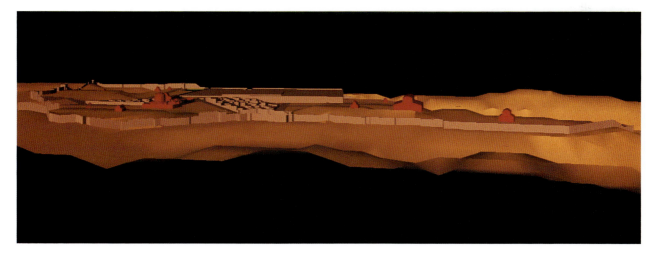

Figure 14. Christian Jerusalem from the west. The Temple mount is in the center and the two main Christian sanctuaries appear to frame it, one with its facade facing the ruined Temple and the other facing in the opposite direction. The Church of Zion is at the extreme right. The apse of the church and its overall dimensions have been retrieved archaeologically. The rest is conjectural.

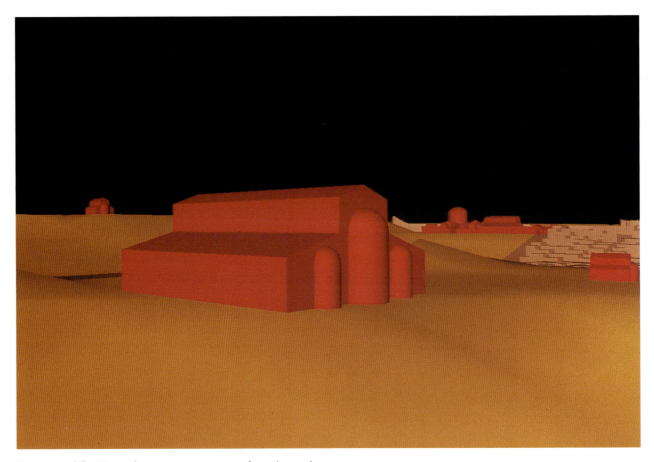

Figure 15. The Nea, schematic reconstruction, from the southeast.

pious tourism, were apparently quite willing to accept all these associations—real, imaginary, or fraudulent—and ways of expressing the faith. But the more important point is the coexistence in this shrine, uniquely central for all Christians, of an authorized piety—expressed, for instance, in the classical poetry of Sophronius, the patriarch at the time of the Muslim takeover[24]—and of more popular beliefs. Sophronius writes of the Passion and, elsewhere in the city, of the Virgin, while the Piacenza pilgrim witnesses minor miracles wherever he goes. In the pre-Iconoclastic world of Late Antiquity, both levels of piety found visual expression in architecture, objects, and images.

Much less can be said about the other two major Christian monuments of Jerusalem, although both are prominent on the Madaba map. In about 543 a New Church of the Virgin Mary ordered by the emperor Justinian was dedicated.[25] Its remains were recovered during the rehabilitation and restoration of the Jewish Quarter in 1969–1976 and it is now possible to reconstruct it in its schematic form (fig. 15). Procopius of Caesarea, the chronicler of Justinian's reign, left a description of what it was and how it was built, reflecting, as he often does, what would be called today the "budgetary implications" of the job. The church was handsomely endowed and was preceded by semicircular spaces with two hospices intended for foreign visitors and for the poor respectively. It thus introduces into our image of the city of Jerusalem the sponsorship of welfare needs, an activity that would sporadically continue throughout the Middle Ages and that would find its most spectacular culmination in the Mamluk buildings of the fourteenth and fifteenth centuries.

Since excavations have only uncovered the foundations and basic plan of the church, the main source for its interpretation is Procopius' panegyric on the buildings of Justinian, a Byzantine remote source that shares many structural and ideological parallels with Islamic Abbasid sources of the ninth and tenth centuries with which I shall deal in the next two chapters. For the construction of the church, Procopius recorded two features pertinent to the whole city. One is in part a cliché affecting pre-industrial monumental construction from the tower of Babel to Suger's St. Denis or Louis XIV's palaces, the extraordinary effort of funding the building; the other one is the technical inventiveness needed to build the church on the rocky slope of a hill. Tall vaulted substructures, partly uncovered by recent excavations, created a flat platform on which the church was built. Such an effort was certainly necessary on the sharp rise of Mt. Sion, but why was the church built on such an inhospitable and inconvenient space? The reason is probably that it could then compete visually and conceptually with the stupendous constructions ordered by Herod for the Temple across the Tyropoeon valley. Furthermore, while the entrance of the Holy

Sepulchre established in Constantine's times faced the deserted surface of the Temple area, the Nea church followed the new pattern of an eastern orientation for churches and, as a result, made that surface invisible to those who came in and out of the Christian building by turning its back to the Temple (fig. 16), while from the valley itself or from anywhere in the southern half of the city, Justinian's patronage in the Holy City was meant to overshadow that of Herod by towering over it. And it is just possible that the emperor who, according to his own words, competed with Solomon in sponsoring Hagia Sophia in Constantinople, was in Jerusalem following once again in the footsteps of the partly mythic builder-king and builder-prophet of revealed history.[26]

Except for standard statements about stateliness, wondrousness, or about the unusual size of the entrance complex, Procopius does not describe the interior of the church nor does he say anything about its decoration. It is possible that there was not much of the latter, although major Justinianic

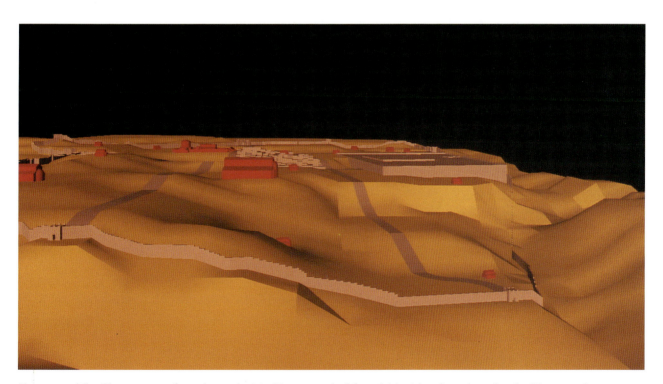

Figure 16. The Christian city from the south. Mt. Zion is to the left and Mt. Moriah to the right; the Nea is in the center and the Holy Sepulchre in the background.

churches like that of the monastery of St. Catherine on Mt. Sinai are usually provided with one or more expensive mosaic panels pertinent to their holiness, and something even more spectacular would have been expected in Jerusalem. Perhaps, in a fashion we will see repeated with the Dome of the Rock, there was something unfinished or misunderstood about Justinian's church in the Holy City. Procopius notes, with a tinge of the supercilious attitude of a Constantinopolitan toward provincials, that the incomparable church dedicated to the Mother of God, the *Theotokos*, was called the "New Church" (the *Nea*, as it has been known almost ever since) by the natives (*oi epikhoioi*). It is as though the very sensible idea of matching the celebration of the theophany of Christ's birth with His death and ascension, the latter two being already established by sanctuaries, was an intrusion, a novelty, in a well established local pious hierarchy. The latter, as emerges so clearly from the Piacenza pilgrim, celebrated Mary elsewhere in Jerusalem, in the "basilica" in the Kidron valley to the east of the walled city, where her house was alleged to have been, where she died and was buried in an octagonal building.[27] Once more, we see at work two parallel strands in the functioning of the city and in the ways in which this functioning was reflected in major buildings. One reflects the values of the ruling power, in this case imperial and remote, in providing for piety, the other reflects an actual practice of the faithful more difficult to assign to a social or ethnic source.

The third major Christian monument in Jerusalem was the church on Mt. Zion, also identified as a particularly large building on the Madaba map. The complexity, variety, and confusion of Christian associations with the highest point in Jerusalem has been pointed out many times.[28] By 600, the basilica of Holy Zion "contained many remarkable things," according to the Piacenza pilgrim, among which he lists: a stone allegedly used by Jesus and possessing miraculous properties, the column at which Jesus was scourged and which had medicinal properties if one touched it, the horn from which Israelite kings were anointed, the stones used for St. Stephen's martyrdom. They are, with one exception, items of relatively minor importance, a sort of catchall for the gullible pious tourists to the Holy City. The exception is the commemoration, through the cup of the Apostles, of the Last Supper and of the Pentecost, and it is for this recollection that the basilica built there was called the "Mother" of all churches and that the Zion church became the episcopal see of Jerusalem. It is nearly impossible to reconstruct what must have been a sanctuary comparable in type and size to the Holy Sepulchre and which included the following: a large congregational hall, separate chapels or simply places dedicated to a holy event or person, the house of Caiphas transformed into a church, the "upper room" where the Last Supper took place, monastic lodgings, commons. It was an important stopping place for pilgrims, but, in spite of its doment location, it never acquired in the early Middle Ages the spiritual and/or ideological importance associated with the other two sanctuaries, nor was its visual effect particularly noted. Even today, the sanctuaries of Mt. Zion may dominate the city of Jerusalem but they do not have an impact commensurate to their dimensions, their location, and the liturgical meaning associated with them. It is as though the human uncertainty and confusion about the significance of that space diminished its potential in the visual construction of the city.

There have been many attempts to identify other Christian buildings that appear in the Madaba map, the exact location of churches and other establishments mentioned by pilgrims, and the list of sanctuaries where it is alleged that the faithful massacred by the Persians in 614 were buried. In addition, fragments of Christian buildings found during formal and informal excavations and several mosaic floors without preserved architectural context must have been parts of churches.[29]

From all the sources, nearly fifty Christian buildings can be listed for the city of Jerusalem and its immediate surroundings, in addition to the three major sanctuaries, as well as a dozen chapels hewn from caves or caverns that, although they hardly count as building, became holy places or dwellings for holy men and women. Seventeen to twenty-one of these buildings were inside the walled city and its southern extension. The exact location of many of them is unknown or controversial and their distribution over our reconstructed sketches is partly arbitrary (figs. 11–12). But it is only so from the point of view of archaeological accuracy. For, in another sense, it was true that sanctuaries commemorating the narrative of the Gospels and the presence of saints and of holy men and women in Jerusalem were everywhere and gave a special cachet of piety and spiritual wealth to the entire city. It was not, as in fourteenth- and fifteenth-century Mamluk Jerusalem, restricted to the specific area to the west and north of the Haram. Mamluk Jerusalem exhibited the peculiarly late medieval Muslim emphasis on retreats for learning and training and on functions useful to the faithful, while proclaiming the wealth and importance of patrons through elaborate portals and grand inscriptions. In Late Antiquity the Christians multiplied holy places around past events and deceased saints and provided them occasionally with mosaic decoration, thereby emphasizing the commemorative character of Christian piety and the wealth of some of its patrons.

But wealth, commemoration, and power were not the main motives behind Christian religious buildings. The accounts of pilgrims are full of encounters with poor men and women who lived in caves and awaited the "dread judgement of God." This was particularly true in the Kidron valley to the east of the walled city and on the slope and top of the Mount of Olives. The Piacenza pilgrim talks of "vast numbers" of monks and nuns in religious establishments that seem to have overlooked the city from the east.[30] Very little is left of whatever was there around 600, and it is only with a great deal of imagination that one can conjure up the Constantinian Church of the Eleona or the Church of the Ascension. The former was probably a standard congregational hall with three or five naves, while the latter was a high octagonal or circular building, open to the sky and, according to Arculf in 670, with a circular bronze railing around some dust displaying Christ's footprints. On the western side of the building there were

eight upper windows paned with glass. Inside the windows, and in corresponding positions, are eight lamps. Positioned so that each one of them seems to hang neither above nor below its window, but just inside it. These lamps shine out . . . with such brilliance that they light up . . . also the steps leading all the way up from the Valley of Jehosaphat to the city of Jerusalem, which are lighted, however dark the night. Most of the nearer part of the city is lighted as well. The remarkable brilliance of these eight lamps shining out by night from the holy Mount and the place of the Lord's Ascension brings to believing hearts a readiness for the love of God, and brings awe to their mind and deep reverence to their soul.[31]

This account is all the more remarkable since it was written two generations after the Muslim conquest, but before the major program of constructions carried out by the Umayyads on the Haram. It illustrates quite strikingly the maintenance of high ceremonial visibility for Christian practices *after* the new rule was established and explains in part the Muslim reaction by the end of the seventh century.

Furthermore, the Ascension of Christ commemorated through footprints, the circular or octagonal forms, and the relationship of the Church of the Ascension to a congregational church nearby (possibly no longer functioning at the time of Arculfus), are remarkably akin to characteristics of buildings found on the Haram that were soon to be rebuilt and were probably already in some stage of conceptualization. Furthermore, the visual expression of the building's association with Jerusalem is made through light, lamps which are *seen* from the city, shining somewhat miraculously and illuminating the way to the city. The point becomes particularly powerful once we realize that the path to the city passed through places of burial and a number of sanctuaries or dwellings connected to the holiness of the dead. As we know from a celebrated miniature in the sixth-century Syriac Rabbula Gospel book, Christ's return was to occur at the place from which He departed from earth. Thus, the sanctuary of the Ascension was more than the commemoration of an event in the holy narrative of Christianity, it was also the beacon announcing eternal life. In the eschatologically charged atmosphere of the seventh century, such an emphasis seems appropriate. Whether it was already so powerfully felt in 600 is not clear from the written disquisitions of the learned or the reports of pious pilgrims that have been preserved. But it may well be the reason why so many simple people, relatively or totally unknown to mainstream Christian history, chose to be buried there. The architectural setting and the psychological stage for eschatological interpretations had been set by the buildings that were on the Mount of Olives by the end of the sixth century.

Strictly religious aims dominated the architecture of Jerusalem. We know much less about the hostels, hospitals, and monasteries that served the pious or the needs of pilgrims and visitors. There were establishments connected with a broader network that extended to monasteries like St. Saba's in the Judaean wilderness and included roads and inns or dormitories.[32] This network is not directly pertinent to my investigations but, in a land where banditry was endemic, Jerusalem, surrounded by walls and with gates easy to close, was in time of insecurity the protector and refuge for the pious.

In dealing with the faith of medieval Jerusalem, a few words are necessary about beliefs that played a part in the city even though they were not officially sanctioned. One of these is paganism. By 600 it was only a memory insofar as the spiritual and intellectual life of the city was concerned—an evil occasionally invoked by preachers recalling the temple of Venus on the Golgotha or the statue of Hadrian where the Jewish Temple had been. But its presence was witnessed by the streets and gates of the city built by the Romans and the imperial debris—capitals, columns, and stones, sometimes with inscriptions, which were endlessly reused. In addition, Greek remained the dominant language of literate expression, still unchallenged by the Semitic languages of most of the native population and by the Armenian and Georgian of a growing number of inhabitants.[33]

More complex and far more profound is the presence of Judaism. On a human level, it was minimal; the banning of Jews from Jerusalem was one of the few fairly consistent policies of Byzantine and ecclesiastical authorities, even if subtle exceptions, as during the time of Eudocia, have been duly noted by scholars. One synagogue still functioned in the fourth century, but apparently not later, and there were a few references to Jews mourning the destruction of the Temple. It is likely that individual Jews visited the city for pious or other purposes, but officially the community was not there during three hundred years of Christian rule. Yet Jerusalem was permeated with Jewish historical memory even in the absence of liturgical and ritual practices. Adam, Abraham, Isaac, Jacob, Joseph, David, and Solomon are only the major figures of a narrative that continued to unfold in Jerusalem in such a way that all spaces were affected by it and there was a place identified for everything that was hallowed in it.[34] The intensity of Jewish holiness may not have been what it was at the time of Josephus or what it would become in later medieval times, but that earlier intensity was constantly recalled or recapitulated by generations of believers outside Jerusalem.[35] Jewish Jerusalem was, in some fashion or other, wherever Jews were living.

As always in Jerusalem, more than one layer of holiness was present in the Christian city. Certain Christian practices adopted pagan forms and took over a Jewish layer of memories. They christianized these memories by adapting their meaning to the new Jerusalem of Christ. Even if one does not accept all the relationships that can be made between the new Christian holy places and the Jewish past in the city—churches on the Mount of Olives or on Golgotha designed so as to include the view of the destruction of old Jerusalem, the church of Zion built to glorify the new chosen people, churches dedicated to St. James and St. Stephen to commemorate Christians killed by Jews, transfer of the vessels allegedly found in the Temple to the Nea of Justinian and other major Christian sanctuaries—it is certain that Christian ideology transformed every Christian activity into a proclamation of victory over Judaism.[36] Or, to put it in the terms used by Cyril of Jerusalem in the fourth century: "Jerusalem crucified Christ, but that which now is worships him."[37]

Life of the City

From all that can be known about the sanctuaries, churches, monasteries, and chapels of Jerusalem, it is easy to imagine the life of the city entirely regulated by the Christian liturgical calendar with its daily and annual order of feasts, fasts, and rites. Recent studies have given considerable emphasis to the visibility of the liturgy, as processions with repeating sequences of chants, recitations, and prayers created what has been called a "stational" pattern of the liturgy throughout the city, and as the chants of Jerusalem were copied in Georgia and in the West.[38]

A distinction can probably be made, on the one hand, between the official liturgical life of the Church and the state that supported it and, on the other, the private piety of individual believers. When Paula, a noblewoman from Rome, visited Jerusalem with St. Jerome, she was offered hospitality at the *praetorium* or place of government by a local proconsul who was a friend of the family, but "she chose a humble cell and started to go round visiting all the places with such burning enthusiasm that there was no taking her away from one unless she was hurrying on to another."[39] She goes everywhere, prays, kisses stones, has visions, and falls on her knees but, apparently, does not attend a religious service and does not take communion. She may have done both of these things, of course, but this is not the story St. Jerome wishes to report. In fact, few of the pilgrims who left accounts of their visits to Jerusalem mention religious services and a local clergy. Yet the chronicles, especially of the ecclesiastical variety, are full of tales of episcopal strife, imperial battles with the clergy, theological disputes around conciliar decisions, and other vicissitudes of a Church rich in ideological concerns and political ambitions.

It will be implicit in the pages to follow that we encounter in Jerusalem two ways of professing one's faith, an organized, formal, and official one (whatever its ecclesiastical allegiances) and a personal, private one, nearly independent of a clergy. The former is evidenced in buildings, liturgical texts, and recorded history. The latter appears between the lines of records and documents, and we shall see shortly how it expanded after the Persian invasion. The buildings dedicated to Christianity cannot always be recognized in the ruins of the past, but the Christian "places" (*loca*), the very term used by St. Jerome in recounting Paula's visit, can be imagined. The slopes of the Mount of Olives in particular were the favorite locale for private piety.[40]

Both formal and informal religious practice require maintenance. We know something about the location of hostels and other buildings for pilgrims, but almost nothing about how they functioned. Food and water must have been available, and a large market existed south of the Holy Sepulchre in the area known now as the *muristan*, for centuries the commercial hub of the city. Then as now, farmers must have brought their goods to shops or stalls near the gates of the city. It should eventually be possible to know whether most goods came from the north, as they do now, and the location of markets could alone provide a dimension missing so far in the reconstructions of the city—human and animal traffic. Because of its location away from major trade routes, Jerusalem was not a major communication center, but it had to deal with a fluctuating population which could be large during major religious feasts—Easter, for instance. Municipal authorities must have supervised tax collection and health control. The latter was addressed in part by public baths, several of which are known inside the walled city, although their access to water may well have been a problem in a city without a constant supply.

Two aspects of life other than the religious deserve mention: private housing and government buildings. We have very little information about the first. A small number of so-called "Byzantine" houses have been identified on implicit archaeological grounds, and fragments of a bath were discovered during the excavations carried out south and southwest of the Haram. The hypothetical reconstruction of the houses shows rather large establishments with rooms on two floors around a courtyard set in clusters, presumably reachable by way of paved streets and passageways.[41] These reconstructions appear reasonable but, as they are located in the lower part of the city, farthest away from major Christian places of worship and commemoration, they suggest that Jerusalem was a city of relatively large means, without a class of urban poor, a misleading or even dubious suggestion. Yet it is supported by another paradox, valid today as it probably was in the past: even though Jerusalem had no economic or political importance, it was favored by many wealthy people from elsewhere because of its spiritual and emotional values. It was also used occasionally as a place of exile for the rich and famous. Theodotus, the Count of the East, Photius, the son of Belisarius, Anastasia, the wife of an executed leader of the 532 revolt in Constantinople, the sister and daughter of the emperor Maurice, these were among the "important" people sent to Jerusalem for political and personal reasons during the course of the sixth century.[42] While exiled priests or monks had to live in monasteries, assistants and members of the imperial family were not restricted to spartan surroundings.

The other aspect of Jerusalem that deserves mention is the gradual disappearance of imperial authority, of a secular institution to enforce laws. There is no identifiable space for a governor, and I do not know where to place the *praetorium* in which Paula was invited to stay in the late fourth century. Perhaps the Tower of David, eventually to become the citadel of Jerusalem, contained space for imperial officials, a jail, and some sort of police or military force, but it is curious that, in the fifth and sixth centuries, recorded negotiations about everything were handled by the patriarch and his office was located in the vicinity of the Holy Sepulchre complex. This conclusion may, however, be modified eventually through the systematic culling of hagiographic rather than historical sources, because lives of saints are especially useful in describing tax collectors, price inspectors, and venal policemen.[43]

Vision of Jerusalem

The *Book of Revelation* contains a vivid description of "the holy Jerusalem, descending out of heaven from God" (Revelation 22:10ff.). It was a bejewelled city

of gold appearing in the fullness of time with night and day melting into permanent light, and it was both a city and a temple. In the fourth century St. Jerome alluded to Jewish messianic hopes for a "Jerusalem of gold and precious stones, which shall descend for them from heaven."[44] Such eschatological expectations were common both in Judaism and in early Christianity, as the end of time was the moment of the dreaded Judgment for the latter and the reestablishment of divine favor for the former. While identified with the specific Jerusalem constructed around Christian memories and practices, a messianic vision of Jerusalem existed wherever there were Christians or Jews. Mosaics in half a dozen Italian churches, mostly in Rome (San Giovanni in Laterano, San Lorenzo, Santa Prudenziana, Santa Maria Maggiore, and San Vitale in Ravenna) depict a bejewelled walled city with large buildings inside, among which the Rotunda of the Anastasis is usually recognizable. In the Santa Maria Maggiore mosaic, the colonnade in the doorway reflects the colonnaded street found also in the Madaba map. Thus the celestial Jerusalem to come and the actual city visited by pilgrims have become, deliberately or not, mixed up.[45]

The classical poetry of Sophronius, written around 730, echoes the same dichotomy, as the poet-patriarch simultaneously hails "Sion, radiant Sion of the Universe" for which he "longs and yearns" and describes specific holy places with individual buildings commemorating sacred events.[46] And the very same mix of physical concreteness and eschatological promise can be discerned in the decorated phials for holy water or oil from Palestine, preserved in Monza, Bobbio, and a few other places. The tomb of Christ is realistically represented, the Crucifixion is presented in a simple narrative way with minimal symbolic additions, but the Ascension appears as a forecast of the Second Coming as well as an account of a narrative from the *Book of Acts*. These phials were souvenirs reflecting the sacred memories of Jerusalem and, at the same time, a worldly taste for elaborately decorated objects that developed around imperial courts.[47] In short, at different levels and for different purposes, through images and through words, an imaginary Jerusalem was being created that could be an apocalyptic vision or the transformation of the real city into a mythical place.

The meanings associated with mythic Jerusalem appear most forcefully in connection with the Persian conquest of the city in 614 and its aftermath. The importance attributed to the conquest is puzzling and difficult to recapture. Nearly all the sources about it are Christian and describe one or both of two events. There is the conquest itself by an alien army, the removal of the Holy Cross, and the subsequent or concomitant massacres and destructions. Alternately the triumphant return of Heraclius with the Holy Cross in 630 is described; shortly thereafter, in 633, Heraclius himself is alleged to have ordered the removal of the Cross to Constantinople after the first victories of the Arabs in Palestine and Syria. All the pertinent documents dealing with these events are of ecclesiastical or monastic and usually hagiographic origin and represent a variety of ideological and pious purposes, in which the establishment of historical truth plays almost no part.[48] No known source provides a Persian view of the events. Jewish reactions are only inferred from the messianic *Book of Zerubbabel* already mentioned, while Christian sources usually argue (or so it seems) that the Jewish takeover of the city after the conquest was short-lived. Reflecting on these sources, a scholar has written recently that the key Christian text of Antiochus Strategios is "a history in which a politically realized Christendom, headed by the ideal emperor as protector of the Holy Cross, provides a significant place for his fellow Christians," while "the author of the *Zerubbabel* narrates a history in which God has reestablished Himself in His Temple as the center of the Jewish cult and, indeed, of the earth."[49] Such judgments of the main sources are appropriate and accurate, but they make it no less difficult to reconstruct what happened and what effects whatever happened had on the city.

The following attempt at a reconstruction is also hypothetical, but seems to me to harmonize written evidence and the possibilities of the spaces in which the conquest and subsequent occupation are alleged to have taken place, and especially to take into consideration the later transformations of the city. The event itself was probably, from the point of view of the Sasanian emperor and other Iranian political and military authorities, not much more than a brutal police action during continuing wars and raids into the territory of the "hereditary enemy," to use late nineteenth-century European terminology. There may have been deeper ideological or economic struggles involved, but the sources do not make any of them particularly obvious. Nor do a massacre and major destructions, which are central to nearly all Christian accounts, make sense within the context of Irano-Byzantine relations and conflicts.

For the construction of the history and shape of the city of Jerusalem, the events of the early seventh century must be seen simultaneously as the history of what happened and as the myth of what was thought to have happened.[50] The Christian accounts with their lurid descriptions of the masses of dead left unattended in churches and other religious establishments and the destruction of holy places actually suggest a chronology of events with possible implications for the physical history of the city in something like the following sequence. After the massacres and the burial of the dead there would have been direct Jewish rule until 617, perhaps with some clearing or building on the Temple area. Sources relate that the work on the Temple stopped miraculously, as God did not want the Temple to be restored. In fact, in ways and for reasons that are quite unclear, Jewish authority decreased or disappeared altogether to be replaced by Christian authority and rebuilding until 630 and the triumphal return of Heraclius with the Holy Cross still in its original container. There is hardly a trace of a Persian authority present after the initial conquest, while such presence remains in Egypt and in the coastal cities which were far more important for strategic and economic purposes.

The rebuilding that would have taken place is usually associated with the name of Modestus, a local abbot who was eventually appointed as patriarch by Heraclius and who died in 631. While sources are eloquent on the massacre of the Christian faithful, there is no report on how badly damaged the churches were or how extensive the looting, which was and is a normal side effect of war. Fires, on the other hand, which are mentioned by most sources, are not in Jerusalem a common or effective means for destruction and strike one as a cliché in a description of war rather than an account of what happened. In short, we do not really know what was destroyed. The absence of unambiguous documents makes it equally difficult to evaluate what was really accomplished by Modestus. It is reasonable to assume that all churches with a clergy or with a monastic population functioned again quite soon. None of the sources mention the destruction of walls or other defensive features nor the maintenance of a garrison. It is as though accounts of destruction and especially the profanation of churches and the massacre of holy people were to serve other purposes.

One major monument that has often been attributed to the reconstruction of the city under Modestus' leadership is the Golden Gate, the impressively decorated building on the eastern wall of the Haram (fig. 17).[51] As we shall see later, my own preference is to consider it as the Umayyad restoration of a Herodian gate, but I admit that a reconstruction of a ruined gate for Heraclius' triumphal entry into Jerusalem with the Holy Cross makes practical and ideological sense, especially if one assumes even a short-lived Jewish activity on the Temple platform. There would have been a need to reassert Christian preeminence in a space with layers of spiritual and commemorative associations that had been profaned.

The discussion of all these archaeological possibilities is unfortunately founded on such uncertain and fragile assumptions that, at this stage, no reasonable conclusions can be drawn about the extent of the destruction or about the magnitude and quality of the reconstructions. The former was probably exaggerated by the ecclesiastical and especially the eschatological writers of the seventh century, shocked by the momentous political and religious changes that occurred later with the takeover of the whole area by Muslim Arabs. The quality and quantity of the restorations, on the other hand, have been magnified by modern historians

who could not imagine a Muslim sponsorship for works with a Late Antique flavor.

On the mythical level, however, the story of the Persian invasion is much more rewarding and much more original than the historical account. The instance of Saint Athanasius the Persian will serve to make the point. About 615, a young Persian by the name of Magoundat, born in Rayy in northern Iran, from a family of Magi (i.e., priests), carefully educated as a Zoroastrian, joined the army of the Sasanian king and was stationed in various garrisons. While at Hierapolis (present Mabbug in the middle Tigris valley in Iraq), he witnessed the arrival of the Holy Cross in Mesopotamia, became interested in Christianity, and left the army, probably but not certainly by deserting. He lived for a while with a silversmith, possibly as an apprentice, and then decided to convert to the Christian faith. He went to Jerusalem, where he was baptized and entered a monastery associated with the monastic establishment of St. Saba. He spent seven years there in prayer and meditation, until 627. Then, for psychological and religious reasons (or simply for the needs of the story), he decided to become a martyr for the faith. He went to Caesarea, where official Persian authorities were located, and desecrated a Zoroastrian sanctuary. He was arrested and subjected to several trials during which every effort was made to spare him and provide ways out of his legal predicament. He withstood all these blandishments and was eventually transferred to Dastagird, the residence of Khosro II northeast of present day Baghdad. Another trial followed, accompanied this time by torture, and he was eventually executed on 22 January 628, a martyr to his new faith. Shortly thereafter Khosro II died as well, presumably as a punishment from heaven for having allowed the execution of the saint. Several accounts exist of the miracles accomplished by Athanasius, in Jerusalem and Caesarea in Palestine as well as in Mesopotamia and during the travails of his martyrdom. Recent investigation of these miracle stories has shown that they were written in different places, including Jerusalem, and that they were apparently created very soon after the alleged events of 628.[52]

The story of Athanasius, the Persian convert and

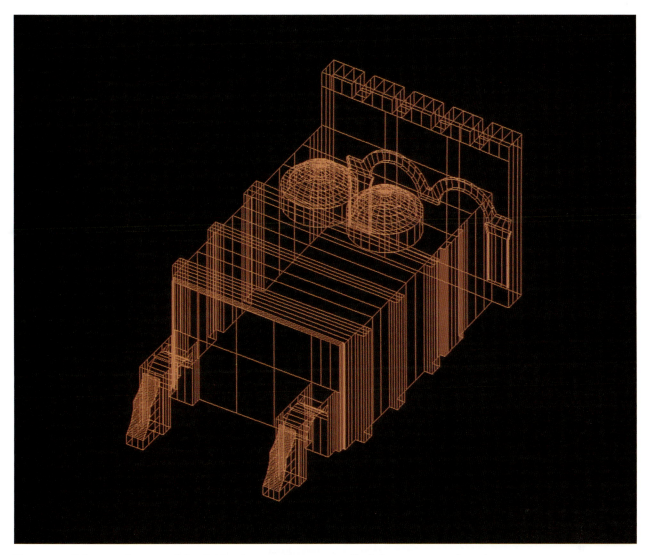

Figure 17. Schematic drawing of the Golden Gate on the eastern wall of the city as seen from the west.

martyr, is interesting for our purposes of defining the visionary mythology associated with Jerusalem for two reasons. First, major policies and imperial activities which hardly involved Palestine were accompanied by a "Jerusalem component," a justification through association with the Holy City. For instance, the story of a Persian convert who performed miracles was a narrative vehicle for expressing the Christian mission of converting the Persian empire, and the ideological ambitions of the emperor Heraclius. Or again, the eventual defeat of the Persians was transformed into a triumphal and dramatic return of the True Cross, still celebrated

in the Christian liturgy, by an emperor whose personal life and theological preferences were in fact hardly acceptable to the Church. The specifics of the city no longer matter, as confusions of cities abound in hagiographic stories and even in the account of the exile and return of the Cross. And this is precisely the place where the other reason intervenes. After the Arab Muslim takeover began to be seen by Christians as the permanent loss of the site of Christ's Passion, this traumatic event, which had taken place relatively peacefully, almost naturally, required a dramatic and violent prologue or portent. The Persian invasion, at best a "search and loot" operation with minimal objectives, was transformed into a story of the massacre of innocent Christians, the suffering and exile of a weeping patriarch, the destruction by fire of the holy places, the wickedness of the Jews, and the loss of the most vivid relic of Christ's death. All of this was followed by the triumphal Return of the Cross, forecasting the Return of Christ on the day of Judgment. A sequence of events was made to recapture the divine order of time, and Jerusalem was the locus of those events.[53]

Thus events in Jerusalem were transformed into myth, and the myths of Christianity required a setting in Jerusalem. It is this psychological and emotional climate of myth and reality that the new Muslim world, in the process of shaping itself, entered, inheriting a city full of resonance and of meanings, beliefs, and narratives constantly seeking a space to land and become monumental. It also inherited a climate of confusion, in which pious, political, and possibly mercantile purposes were inextricably mixed, even though any one believer or participant would never be aware of the complexities involved.[54] The confusion may have been temporary, but the stones, spaces, meanings, beliefs, and narratives were there awaiting an impetus to put them in place, to construct and shape with them a new holy space.

The First Decades of Muslim Rule

The ninety-odd years of Umayyad rule (661-750) were momentous in the history of mankind. They saw Muslim presence established from southern France to India and the frontiers of China and thereby a change in the equilibrium between old centers of power and civilization like China, Iran, and the Mediterranean. They witnessed a modification in the commercial, military and cultural relations between these ancient centers and the establishment of new ones in Egypt, southern Spain, and the Fertile Crescent. One small result of Muslim presence was the transformation of the battered Christian city of Jerusalem, barely revived after half a generation of indirect Persian rule, into

a city controlled, or at least dominated, by the new faith. The physical and visual core of what is known as the Old City is still in our times affected by what happened during a couple of decades of this Umayyad century.

The evidence for major changes is easy to spot. The area of Herod's Temple became the *Haram al-Sharif*, the "Noble Sanctuary," of Muslim tradition, even if several centuries were to elapse before that formal appellation was actually used. The Dome of the Rock and the Aqsa Mosque were built, dominating the visual profile of the city, and still stand today, even though the Mosque itself has been much redone. And, as recent excavations have shown, other constructions of significant size were built as well, even though their impact on the continuing life of the city is more difficult to determine. Numerous written references to Umayyad Jerusalem exist in Arabic and Hebrew, and in the languages of several Christian communities.

I thought it possible, at first, to establish a chronology of the events pertaining to building recorded in written, material or visual form. But too many uncertainties remained and a chronology would have been full of conditional verbs and question marks. Nevertheless, I shall propose below a possible sequence of events in the transformation of Jerusalem that takes into consideration simultaneously the actual buildings, the conceptual imagination affecting the city, and significant events within the Muslim world. Since direct dated evidence is inadequate, this sequence depends on the study of each component in terms of its own internal evidence and its merits. I shall argue that a reasonable and probable chronology does emerge once the functions of newly erected buildings have been understood and a small number of events, in Jerusalem or elsewhere, have been clarified with respect to their effect on the character and mood of the city. For a primary thesis of this book is that, as some and perhaps even all cities are charged with emotional and ideological values attached to their physical components, changes in values *as well as* new monumental ensembles affect the perception and interpretation of a city at any one time.

A small number of major architectural creations

are the principal agents in the city's transformation during the ninety some years of Umayyad rule. The most important one and the one provided with the richest documentation is the Dome of the Rock to which the following chapter is devoted. The Aqsa Mosque, the platform of the Haram al-Sharif, the settlements to the south of the former Temple area, and fragmentary bits of evidence elsewhere provide additional, if less clearly focused, information. They will be discussed in yet another chapter, together with the little that can be surmised about the changes in population that occurred in the seventh and eighth centuries. All these visible and often impressive architectural "events," were triggered by whatever happened during the twenty-five years between the appearance in 637 of Arab Muslims in Jerusalem and the establishment in 661 of the Umayyad caliphate. In many ways like the Christian city it was built upon, the first Muslim Jerusalem created a legacy for later times that was more mythical than visible, and yet inescapable. An awareness of its main features is essential to understand the revolutionary changes that took place after 691 and the full establishment of the Umayyad dynasty.

Medieval Muslim sources of the remote variety, local pious treatises, and Christian chronicles in Greek, Arabic, and Syriac provide many accounts of the transfer of Jerusalem from Christian to Muslim hands, and of events in the Holy City before the building of the Dome of the Rock around 692. Earlier scholars like de Goeje, Mednikoff, and Caetani tried to squeeze a coherent and sequential synoptic narrative out of the numerous surviving stories, and so have contemporary historians like Goitein, Gil, and Mahmud, even though, unlike their predecessors, they no longer publish thick volumes of commentaries on each separate source.[55] In spite of all these efforts, it is impossible to reconstruct what actually happened, since genuine contemporaneous documents are entirely lacking and even the few Arab-Byzantine coins minted in Jerusalem are now considered to be later than the time of Abd al-Malik's reforms late in the century.[56] The only authentic eyewitness account of the new Muslim Jerusalem was recorded in the

British isles by a Gallic bishop who had been there, although a few eastern Christian ecclesiastical and hagiographic sources reflect genuine occurrences at the time of the conquest or shortly thereafter. Even the exact date of the takeover, 636 or 638, is not certain, and the clinching arguments for the later date, which I believe to be the correct one, are based primarily on the little that is known about the life of Sophronius, then patriarch of the Holy City.[57] The reasons for uncertainty about as simple a matter as the date of the takeover follow from the nature of the sources. All the Christian sources are relatively remote from Jerusalem, and the Muslim ones are quite remote geographically and temporally.[58] Furthermore, their relationship to Jerusalem was determined by beliefs, practices, and expectations which made their accounts more or less overt ideological statements, justifying or condemning the ways in which the beginning of the Muslim presence was understood.[59]

One way to proceed is to admit that the exact truth cannot be known and simply to record a few events like the death of the patriarch Sophronius, the adventures of a priest who opposed his superiors, a caliph's visits to the city, the brief description by Arculf some time around 670. These events are small pieces of a story played out against a transfer of authority whose specifics were unimportant to remote writers because the economic and political values of Jerusalem were insignificant. The one exception to this attitude lay in the control of holy places. The Christians held on to the properties of their churches and the Muslims took over the empty, if not necessarily desecrated, area of the Jewish Temple. Once these limited and almost randomly available details are established, we can proceed to the last decade of the century when documents begin to appear.

The second choice for proceeding is to accept one of the available harmonizations of various sources or to make one's own, in order to provide support for later interpretations of Jerusalem based on more numerous and at times more reliable sources and documents. This option seemed preferable to me, inasmuch as it corresponds to the way of my own understanding of medieval Jerusalem evolved, from a fascination with the Dome of the Rock and early Islamic monuments to the conception of a Jerusalem on the eve of the Crusades quite different from the one the Muslims found and certainly from the city of today. For either to be understood, an early history had to exist with characteristics that condition and even make inevitable what happened later. This procedure of outlining a past on the basis of the present may be a dubious route for a historian to take, but in the absence of sufficient sources for the reconstruction of events of considerable importance for the present, it has the advantage, when properly understood, of proposing a setting into which later and better documented monuments and events can be fitted with relative ease. Here, then, is the speculative story of how a Christian Jerusalem was transformed into a city controlled by Muslim Arabs.

Khalid ibn al-Walid, the great military commander of tribal armies from Arabia, had taken the southern Syrian city of Bosra in May 635, and after the battle of Ajnadayn in central Palestine, the cities of the Palestinian coast and the hills of northern Palestine one by one accepted Muslim sovereignty. Late in 636, after the Byzantine defeat at the battle of Yarmuk, the roads leading in and out of the city of Jerusalem become unsafe, and some plundering of isolated monasteries seems to have taken place. This may have been caused by the presence of Muslim Arabs engaged in taking control of towns and villages, or by the collapse of Byzantine military power leading to generalized lawlessness which permitted bandits to thrive. Until the nineteenth century, bandits controlled the roads of Palestine, especially in hilly and deserted areas, whenever central police forces were weak. Jerusalem, however, remained safe in the midst of this turmoil, protected as it was by high walls and six easily defended gates. There must have been some organized military or police force in the city or else its inhabitants were able, under the leadership of the elderly and venerable patriarch Sophronius,[60] to offer enough show of force that the Muslim tribal armies were unable or unwilling to compel the city's acceptance of Muslim rule.

Something happened late in 637 or early in 638 to change the situation and to lead to the most extraordinary event depicted in Muslim and Christian sources, the arrival of the caliph Umar to accept the surrender of Jerusalem.[61] Sophronius, who had lost contact with the coastal cities as well as with the Transjordanian ones and who had probably heard of the terms favorable to Christians in the treaties with Muslims signed in Damascus and Hims, decided it was useless to continue resisting and reasonable to accept Muslim sovereignty. The safety of Christian lives and property and the preservation of religious spaces had been maintained in every known truce or peace agreements.[62] Several later accounts relate that Sophronius himself demanded the physical presence of the caliph in Jerusalem and that the latter acceded to the request. Other accounts relate that Umar had come to Syria anyway to settle some internal Muslim matters and a side visit to Jerusalem could easily be accommodated.[63]

A number of events connected with the presumed presence of Umar in Jerusalem illustrate distinctive themes of the Muslim city, even if later accounts enlivened them and added all sorts of improbable details. The narrow boundary between something that happened (someone did arrange for a change in sovereignty) and the ways in which it has been reported can be discerned in small details surrounding Umar's actions before and after the formal surrender of the city: he changed from a horse to a camel and then to a donkey or mule; he could not enter the city without having his clothes washed, but since he only had one set of clothes, he had to borrow temporary vestments from the Christian patriarch. These are embellishments serving to emphasize the simplicity of the second caliph and to contrast it with the ornate accoutrements of the Christian clergy and even with the ambitions of other Muslim leaders easily attracted by rich clothes and elaborate ceremonies.

The narrative of Umar's stay inside the city was to have significant consequences for the development of the city, as it was meant to presage what happened later. Sophronius takes Umar on a tour of Jerusalem. They stop at the Church of the Holy Sepulchre, where Umar refuses to pray in spite of

Sophronius' invitation, because he does not want to create a precedent that would establish a Muslim right to pray there. It is, of course, most unlikely that such would have been his reasoning, but Sophronius' invitation to pray in the world's principal Christian sanctuary is a reasonable and normal procedure in Christian Byzantine practice. It was an attempt to attract, if not to seduce, the Muslim leader(s) to recognize, through the beauty of the church, the true version of the Revelation. At this early date, Muslim Arabs were neither adversaries nor rivals to the Christians, but mostly a nuisance that the Christians expected would leave or be converted and get enlightened.[64]

Umar (on his own, led by Sophronius, or inspired by Jewish converts or by other companions, all these variations occur in later accounts) toured the city and eventually reached the place formerly occupied by the Jewish Temple, an area covered with refuse and architectural debris—columns, piers, cut and carved stones, fragments of arches and architraves—and possibly some standing remains from the Roman temple and the old Herodian Temple. There Umar, alone or with the patriarch, "discovered" the rock supposedly connected with the memories of the Temple whose exact significance to Umar is never mentioned. And then, in a manner reminiscent of an official today posing in a hard hat with a shovel on a future building site, Umar began to clear the area of its refuse; having done so, he prayed there alone.

Busse has argued recently that, after seeing the Temple area, Umar went to the "citadel" at the Western Wall of the city and identified it as a Muslim holy place. The arguments, to some of which I shall return, are not entirely convincing and it seems more reasonable to me that he ended his visit in what is now the Haram al-Sharif. That this vast area had been the site of the Jewish Temple was known to all concerned, and one can easily imagine that Christian authorities were quite willing to have the newcomers take over a space for which the Christians had no use. Even the point that the Christian message was victorious over the Jewish one was no longer that important to maintain, since the Jews were no longer found in Jeru-

salem (all sources agree to that), and a Jewish attempt to assert their presence under Persian rule had met with tragic failure. But what did Umar and his Muslim companions see in this particular space in Jerusalem? And did they do anything to indicate the specificity of their beliefs that conformed with the space or their acceptance of the belief of others?

All later statements imply or explicitly assert that Jerusalem witnessed a legitimizing of power in psychological and spiritual ways unavailable in Damascus, Alexandria, Hims, or even Cesarea, all far more important urban centers taken by Muslim forces around the same time. Only in Jerusalem is the caliph present, and he formally and forcefully exhibits the pious Muslim simplicity in garb and mount in contrast to Christian ecclesiastical wealth. Muslim power is also evidenced in many details of the surrender agreements, such as granting permission to Christians to show the Cross and maintain their rituals, or the limitation on the number of Jews allowed in the city. Even in eschatological terms Umar's arrival is said to have been predicted by sages of old, and by a Jew from Damascus who saluted him as "master of Jerusalem" even before he got there.[65]

Next to the probable knowledge by Muslims of the symbolic power and physical position of the Jewish Temple area, a second theme in Muslim occupation of Jerusalem was the identification of the first *qiblah* or direction of prayer in the rock on the Haram. The Revelation establishing the change in direction (K 2:136ff.) does not mention Jerusalem as the first *qiblah*, although the assumption that it was so is justified by the later Traditions and the even later commentaries on the Scripture. The divine order itself had come a bare sixteen years before 638 and quite a few witnesses to it were probably still alive. It is, however, psychologically most unlikely that the spot of the original *qiblah* would have been commemorated, were it not for one detail which appears in most later stories: the celebrated Jewish convert Ka'b al-Ahbar[66] proposed to Umar that he pray north of the rock facing southward, so that both *qiblahs*, the old and the new, be in front of him; Umar refused, upbraiding

Ka'b for trying to force a Jewish practice on him, and prayed to the south of the rock, where he eventually ordered the building of a *masjid* or mosque for the faithful. The point of the story clearly is to indicate how Umar resisted pressures to make a symbolic gesture that could be interpreted as Jewish, just as he refused to pray in the Holy Sepulchre like a Christian. These symbolic actions stressing Muslim uniqueness were an essential element in the memories of medieval Jerusalem, regardless of the likelihood of the events.

Another story involving the Haram is far less precise and, therefore, more likely to reflect a real feeling on the part of Umar or of the first Muslims in Jerusalem, whoever they were: when Umar came to the Haram area, he recognized something the Prophet had mentioned to him. The statement is usually sufficiently vague that it cannot be easily related to a specific spot on the Haram or elsewhere in Jerusalem. It could, of course, refer to the place of the original *qiblah*, but, as we have just seen, the recollection of an abandoned object is hardly the stuff of religious lore. It is perhaps more likely that it was already a reference to the *isra'*, the Night-Journey of the Prophet, which plays such an important part in the later history of the Haram and to which I shall return more than once.[67] Without assuming the existence as early as 638 of all the details that will be woven around that extraordinary event, it is reasonable that a very important aspect of the Prophet's Revelation—his real and physical or spiritual and mystical journey to cosmic boundaries—was a major part of the collective memory carried by the faithful. Anticipating the later names of gates to the Haram, many stories relate that the caliph Umar entered the sacred precinct through the southern *Bab al-Nabi* or "Gate of the Prophet," which would have been the gate through which the Prophet came on his mystical journey.[68]

The theme of the *isra'* could easily be connected with another aspect of Jerusalem, the end of time and the Last Judgment, of which the first Muslims to come there were aware. Jerusalem was the main locus for events preparing the establishment of divine rule on earth,[69] just as it was the place of Christ's Ascension, His last theophany before the triumphant return. The two themes, it will be recalled, were depicted in a splendid mosaic reproduced in the sixth-century Syriac Gospel book known as the Rabbula Gospel. The fearful judgment and the reward or punishment that followed were sufficiently part of the Muslim Revelation to justify a connection between pan-Abrahamic theophanies and their latest, Arab and Muslim, version. It is doubtful that much more was involved at the time of the conquest itself, but it is easy to imagine that the Muslims answered Christian visions of the future with the argument that their Prophet had already seen it. A curious side story found in an early "remote" source may confirm the point that an extraterrestrial connection was available in the city: it tells of a man who fell into a well somewhere near Jerusalem just before the Muslim conquest and got to Paradise, from whence he brought back a single leaf (*waraqah*), of a tree or of parchment, which was eventually kept in the Treasury of the Muslims, presumably as a "sign" of Paradise.[70]

And there was a final Muslim theme that could be associated with Jerusalem, the *mihrab Da'ud*, the place in which God forgave David for his sins. The story itself (K 38:21–25) is a strange and complicated one, with references and allusions that may have been clearer to contemporaries than they were to later commentators. What is important for Jerusalem is the mention of a specific built space called a *mihrab*, a throne-room or simply a richly decorated private room, in which David makes a dubious judgment, turns to God in repentance, is forgiven and made a *khalifah* (or "representative") of God on earth to establish justice everywhere.[71] In addition to themes of judgment and royal power already described in early Muslim attitudes toward Jerusalem, this story introduces an actual place that existed in that city. Later on, after the Crusades, the *mihrab Da'ud* was located in the citadel on the western side of the medieval city, as is reasonable given its association with royal power, but early accounts that mention the story locate the *mihrab* somewhere on the Temple platform, also reasonable if one considers the memories of Solomon and David associated with that space. I remain skeptical about the recent attempt by Busse to turn to early Islam for the association between the Koranic reference and the citadel, if for no other reason than that it is contradicted by what happened during the subsequent three centuries. On the other hand, it is impossible to determine the spot on the Haram that would have been identified as the *mih-rab Da'ud*. Curiously, as we shall see, this particular reference in the Koran, which appears to be so clear and so necessary to the religious sense of the city, played only a small part in the development of Muslim Jerusalem, as though the number of sacred meanings is sometimes in reverse proportion to the specificity of the memory associated with them.

In the interpretation I am proposing, the first Muslims in Jerusalem, whether or not the caliph Umar was among them, were affected and motivated by five associations with the city: the authority and almost moral quality of what happened in it, the *isra'*, the first *qiblah*, eschatology, and the place where David repented and was rewarded by God. The only one of these involving a specific space was the least significant action taken by the first Muslims—the appropriation of the huge area defined by the Herodian Temple. Rather than view this decision as the concerted result of a pious or doctrinal position, I prefer to understand it as a convenient solution to the practical problem of controlling the city. A vast space with many associations was taken over and each religious group could interpret that fact differently. The Christians saw the Muslim takeover of the Temple Mount as a way to keep Jews out of an area they had twice (under Julian the Apostate and briefly during the Persian invasion) wanted to restore as the Temple. To Jews, it was the rehabilitation of a holy place by a religious movement whose exact nature was not very clear at the time, but whose conceptual and historic ties to Judaism were numerous and obvious.[72] To Arab Muslims, the taking of Jerusalem and the possession of the Haram legitimized their presence and successes in Arabia, Syria, Transjordan, and Palestine. Furthermore, while negotiating an apparently very generous agreement with the Christians led by their ecclesiastical, not political,

head, they gained a sacred space larger than any known in Arabia (or, for that matter, anywhere else), a space with its own sacred memories, somewhat subdued at the time, but fully partaking of the more general memories associated with Jerusalem as a whole. Several Muslim themes could easily be reconciled with these holy memories, because Islam already had, through Judaism, a relationship to Jerusalem, or because the new Muslim associations belonged typologically to the holy memories and holy practices of the city involving spaces with the remains of buildings, a large rock for focus and direction, and the potential for pilgrimages.

Such is the reconstruction I am proposing for the fateful events of 638. It can be argued that this reconstruction is just one more imaginary narrative shaped by the interpretations given to later, more clearly documented events and buildings. To a degree this criticism is valid, but the reconstruction has, I hope, one advantage over the medieval Muslim stories or the contemporary transformations of these stories: it seeks to take into account mental attitudes, rather than to describe events. It is therefore unnecessary to know whether Umar was present in Jerusalem or not, or what words were exchanged between protagonists. A certain mood for holy and other associations, I argue, was set, and that became a new factor in the growth of the city.

A number of documented events did, however, follow the transformation of Jerusalem into a city ruled by Muslims; evidence exists for three between 638 and the major changes which began around 692. The first, involving the Haram itself, derives from the eyewitness testimony of the Gallic Bishop Arculf as reported by the Irish abbot Adomanus. The bishop visited Jerusalem about 670 and left drawings, copied by Adomanus, that are important documents for the Christian sanctuaries in the city.[73] He also noted that "near the wall [of the city] on the east . . . where once stood the magnificent Temple, the Saracens have now built an oblong house of prayer, which they pieced together with upright planks (*subrectis tabulis*) and large beams (*magnis trabibus*) over some ruined remains and it is of poor quality (*vili fabricati sunt opere*). This they attend and it is said that this building can hold three thousand people."[74] This mosque was a simple rectangular, trabeated building, probably with a wooden ceiling resting on stone supports, which were most likely columns found in the area. The exact location of the building is not mentioned, but it is reasonable to suppose that it was on the southern edge of the Haram more or less where the present Aqsa Mosque stands. The ruins over which (*super quaedam*) it was built must have been the remains of the monumental arcades and gateways that had been ordered by Herod for raising his platform.[75]

The building of this mosque began shortly after the conquest, as can be deduced from two different sources. A nearly contemporary Georgian source relates that an archdeacon by the name of John, from the church of St. Theodore, volunteered to work on the construction, in spite of the urging of the patriarch Sophronius who eventually excommunicated him. The poor archdeacon, who may have worked on the mosque simply as a way to earn a living, died shortly thereafter from an accident on the Mount of Olives but not before repenting his sin of disobedience.[76] The other source, less precise, consisting of several references found in later Karaite documents and confirmed by Muslim accounts, notes that Jews were involved in the cleaning of the Haram until 717–720, when slaves from the Muslim treasury were given that task.[77] It is reasonable to conclude that the Muslims began, almost immediately after the conquest, the huge job of clearing and fixing up the enormous area they had inherited so unexpectedly, probably for no reason other than a practical one. We have seen that pious Muslim associations were still very vague and unfocused, and non-Muslim ones were either banned, like the expressions of Jewish piety, or no longer practical, like the Christian maintenance of a desecrated space for symbolic reasons. On a totally different level, something much more fruitful took place: a major project of public works that employed anyone who wanted to participate, recently arrived Jews or disgruntled archdeacons.

The second event of these decades, just as important as the creation of a Jerusalem-based work force, poses difficult problems of interpretation. In 661, the head of the Umayyad clan, Mu'awiyah ibn abi Sufyan, governor of Syria and one of the truly brilliant Arab leaders of that century, was elected to the caliphate and received *in Jerusalem* the homage of Arab Muslim leaders. On that occasion, Mu'awiyah is said to have visited the Church of the Holy Sepulchre, the Church of the Ascension on the Mount of Olives, and the tomb of the Virgin in Gethsemane. No mention is made of a visit to the mosque on the Haram, presumably built by then, but it can hardly be imagined that whatever ceremony was involved did not take place on the platform, by then more or less cleared, if not formally organized. When the late S. D. Goitein suggested Mu'awiah's involvement in the building of a Muslim Jerusalem,[78] historical logic rather than specific documents had led him in the right direction. His views were not really accepted then, but recently several scholars dealing with Jerusalem from very different points of view have focused again on the rule of Mu'awiyah as a crucial one in the Islamization of the city as well as governance of a non-Muslim population.[79] Whatever his plans for the city may have been, he established the precedent of identifying Jerusalem with the legitimization of authority, above and beyond whatever pious meanings were involved in the city. Mu'awiyah's son, Yazid, also received the homage of Muslim leaders there, but his reign was short (680-683) and from the very beginning shaken by revolts and internecine struggle.

The third event is the changing character of Jerusalem's population and probably its wealth, although the latter is difficult to judge with the evidence we possess. Christian churches and monasteries continued to function in the seventh century as before, and there is evidence of new institutions, in particular as heterodox communities profited from the absence of Byzantine power to establish themselves in the Holy City, but the exact chronology of their arrival is uncertain. Jews moved back into the city, although there probably were not very many at the beginning, and the later accounts are full of arguments between authorities of the three religions about the number of Jews who would be permitted. Because the Karaites (who did not exist in the seventh century) would become such vocal members of the Jewish community after the end of the eighth century, it is possible that sectarian Jewish groups came first in larger numbers than the more traditional rabbinic Jews, but this is purely hypothetical. In all likelihood the Jews settled north or northeast of the Haram, although the only thing attested is that they were not very far from the Temple area.[80] Then Muslim Arabs settled in the city. Arculf's estimate of three thousand faithful in the mosque is difficult to extrapolate for population figures. It is almost certain that they settled first south of the Haram. Although one does not know much about how many came and from where, Medinese and Yemeni families seem to have predominated.[81] The saying was current that "the building of Jerusalem is the destruction of Medina," to which was sometimes added, "and the destruction of Medina is the beginning of the war at the end of times," thus once again returning to the eschatological mission of the city.

It is possible that the large structures excavated south of the Haram belong to these decades, and perhaps that the Dome of the Chain, that strange small building to the east of the Dome of the Rock, is earlier than the other buildings on the Haram because it is located on the exact geographical center of the platform.[82] But these buildings can be discussed more easily after dealing with the larger standing monuments—the Haram, the Dome of the Rock, and the Aqsa Mosque. They contain no intrinsic evidence dating them to the first decades of Muslim presence in Jerusalem, and to give them such an early date requires the existence, almost from the beginning, of a sort of visual and religious Muslim master plan for the Haram. The existence of such a plan, even an inchoate one, is hardly likely, but this argument can better be developed in relation to clearly datable monuments.

The simpler conclusion I prefer to propose is that, around 660 or so, a large area of the Jewish Temple had been cleared, a rude mosque had been built on its southern end, one or more teams of laborers were available to build and repair, and several new groups of people had come to settle in the city. Along with physical and human changes in the city and its population, there were new ideological and spiritual connections in Jerusalem: their specific purpose was to legitimize Umayyad princes and pious associations, which were becoming less vague as eyewitness accounts of local stones or the Prophet's utterances were changed into memories sacred for all believers.

CHAPTER TWO

The Dome of the Rock

THE DOME OF THE ROCK (figs. 18–19) is the earliest work of Islamic architecture still standing in more or less its original shape and with much of its original decoration. Even in the contemporary setting of a modern city with its tall, massive buildings all over the hilly landscape, the Dome of the Rock still dominates much of the Old City of Jerusalem, the magnet of advertisements for tourism and the state of Israel and the central image of posters in Palestinian-owned shops shops all over the world.

It is a deceptively simple building (figs. 20–21) located on a high platform that was erected at some indeterminate time on the large esplanade in the southeastern corner of the city. Its wooden gilt dome is slightly over twenty meters in diameter and rises like a tall cylinder to a height of some thirty meters over the surrounding stone-paved platform. It is supported by a circular arcade of four piers and twelve columns. An octagon of two ambulatories on eight piers and sixteen columns holds the cylinder tightly, as in a ring. The ambulatory is fourteen meters deep, thus giving to the whole building a diameter of forty-eight meters; it

rises to only eleven meters inside and thirteen outside, thus strengthening the impact of the cupola, especially from afar. There are four doors, one at each of the cardinal points corresponding only approximately to the main axes of the Haram al-Sharif, even less so to those of the higher platform on which the Dome of the Rock stands. An extensive decoration of mosaics, painted wood, marble, multi-colored tiles, carpets, and carved stone covers most of the building, inside and outside. This decoration comes from many different periods and has often been repaired with varying success, as the ravages of time and changes in taste affected the maintenance of the building.

It is important to recall that, in addition to its continuing forceful presence, the Dome of the Rock was the first monument sponsored by a Muslim ruler that was conceived as a work of art, a monument deliberately transcending its function by the quality of its forms and expression. An often quoted later text by Muqaddasi, a native of Jerusalem, acknowledges with pride the aesthetic ambition of the building and thereby identifies one of the possible reasons for its construction. Muqad-

Figure 18. The Haram al-Sharif today, airview. Airviews are always misleading as historical documents; they may overemphasize the starkness of the spaces around the Dome of the Rock, which have recently been covered with trees. One should note how the bright colors of the Dome of the Rock contrast with the yellow stone of Palestine.

dasi's story deserves to be given in full, as it signals many of the themes that will recur more than once in what follows.

Now one day I said, speaking to my father's brother: "O my uncle, verily it was not well of the caliph al-Walid [Abd al-Malik's successor who ruled from 705 to 715 and who ordered the building of the Great Mosque of Damascus] to expend so much of the wealth of the Muslims on the Mosque of Damascus. Had he expended the same on making roads, or in caravanserais, or in the restoration of the frontier fortresses, it would have been more fitting and more excellent of him." But my uncle said to me in answer: "O my little son, you have no understanding. Verily al-Walid was right and he *was prompted to a worthy work. For he beheld Syria to be a country that had long been occupied by the Christians, and he noted there the beautiful churches still belonging to them, so enchantingly fair and so renowned for their splendor, as are the Qumamah [refuse, a vulgar pun on qiyamah or resurrection, the Arabic term for the church of the Holy Sepulchre in Jerusalem] and the churches of Lydda and Edessa. So he sought to build for the Muslims a mosque that should prevent their gazing at these [i.e., the Christian churches] and that should be unique and a wonder to the world. And in this manner is it not evident how the caliph Abd al-Malik, noting the greatness of the dome of the Qumamah and its magnificence, was moved, lest it should dazzle the minds of the Muslims, and hence erected above the Rock the Dome which is seen there?* [1]

Figure 19. The Dome of the Rock today, as seen from the east through the artifice of long distance-photography.

Without excluding other interpretations, Muqaddasi puts the Dome of the Rock in the thick of a competition, almost a confrontation, between Christianity and Islam or, perhaps more accurately, between Christians and Muslims. The question for the historian is whether a judgment expressed in the latter part of the tenth century which can easily be explained by the specific conditions of that time, should legitimately be extended to the time of the Dome's construction. Outside of the building itself, there is no more or less contemporary document from a Muslim source that could confirm or contradict Muqaddasi's assertions.

There are, on the other hand, a few Christian and Jewish sources, some somewhat later than the event and others nearly contemporary, that testify to the importance of the new building within the consciousness and the memory of the non-Muslim population. Sa'id ibn Bitriq, a later Christian source, relates that the cupola of the Dome of the Rock (whose construction he attributes to al-Walid, 'Abd al-Malik's son) was taken from a Christian church in Baalbek in Lebanon and removed to Jerusalem.[2] Within a group of moralizing stories written in Greek around 680, one Anastasius of Sinai, a Christian monk, writes that he witnessed in Jerusalem the "clearing of the high place [most likely the area of the Haram today] by Egyptians helped by demons at night. Now, the rumor is that the Temple of God [i.e., the Jewish Temple] is being built there."[3] A Syriac chronicle dated in 716 relates that al-Walid "assembled all the treasures of the Saracens, . . . putting them into a single treasury in Jerusalem." The latest student of this text argues, quite reasonably, that the treasury is a reference to the Dome of the Rock completed some twenty years earlier.[4] And a medieval Jewish midrash, as usual almost impossible to date, reports that Abd

al-Malik "shall build the house of the God of Israel," certainly a reflection of the presence of the
Dome of the Rock on the site associated for centuries with the destroyed temple.[5] I shall suggest
later an explanation for how all these texts may be
understood, but the point is clear, even from these
partial and fragmentary sources, that Christianity
and Judaism were somehow involved in shaping the
original perception of the Dome of the Rock.

All these examples, even Muqaddasi's text, are
short references or inferences from the evidence of
outsiders, to the construction or utilization of the
building. The building itself, however, contains four
documents that are, by physical necessity or because of the existence of a date, more or less contemporary with the time of its completion. In the
order in which we perceive them today, these documents comprise its location, its architectural
forms, its mosaic decoration (as well as a few other
decorative fragments that belong to the original

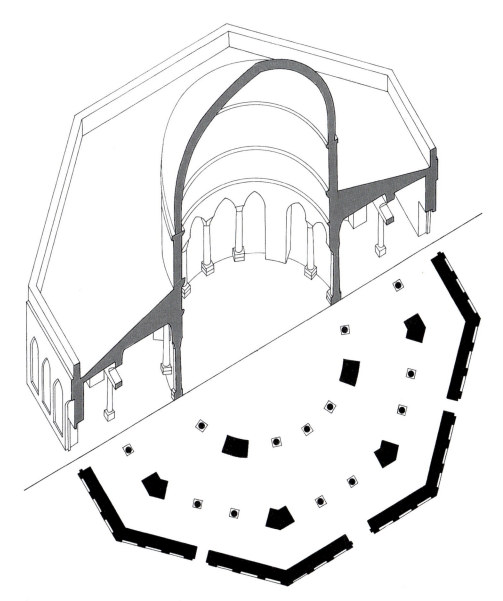

*Figure 20. Dome of the Rock: plan, section, and elevation. The porches have been eliminated since their exact shape is not
certain.*

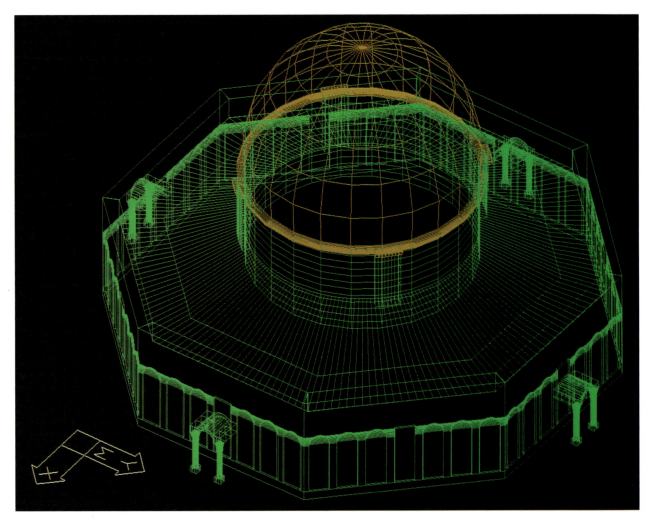

Figure 21. Dome of the Rock, as reconstructed by the computer, with porches added.

building), and the inscriptions from two of its entrances and in the frieze on the octagonal arcade. By dealing with the inscriptions first and then, in sequence, with the mosaics and other forms of surface decoration, the shape, and the location, I shall present the documents in their order of informational specificity, the precision and accuracy with which they can be defined, described, and explained. It is what Max van Berchem called the "archaeological index" of a document, the range of its value in elucidating a monument. As we shall see, even the inscriptions, the clearest document involved, lead to questions without immediate answers.

A small technical note is needed before proceed-

ing. Figure 22 provides the codes based on cardinal points for piers or segments of the octagon and on the measurement of angles from a 0° in the middle of the Southern segment. These are a mix of arbitrary or self-evident numbers and letters used in labeling photographs and consequently in identifying them.

The Inscriptions

The most important and most spectacular inscription is located inside the building, as a continuous mosaic frieze of some 240 meters just below a cornice that supports the ceiling on either side of the octagonal arcade. It was thought by some that the inscription originally continued on the outer side of the circular arcade. This is not very likely, because the text as it stands delivers a rhetorically completed argument and does not seem to require a continuation. Still, the possibility cannot be excluded that some additional statement on either or both sides of the arcade disappeared when the Crusaders refurbished the building for their own purposes, or during the numerous repairs of Mamluk and Ottoman times.[6]

The inscription was read, for the most part, by Melchior de Vogüé, the first scholar and explorer allowed to work inside the building. It was then carefully reviewed and published by Max van Berchem and is included in the *Répertoire Chronologique d'Epigraphie Arabe*.[7] Considering the conditions under which he worked, with a ladder and candles, Max van Berchem's readings are remarkably accurate and

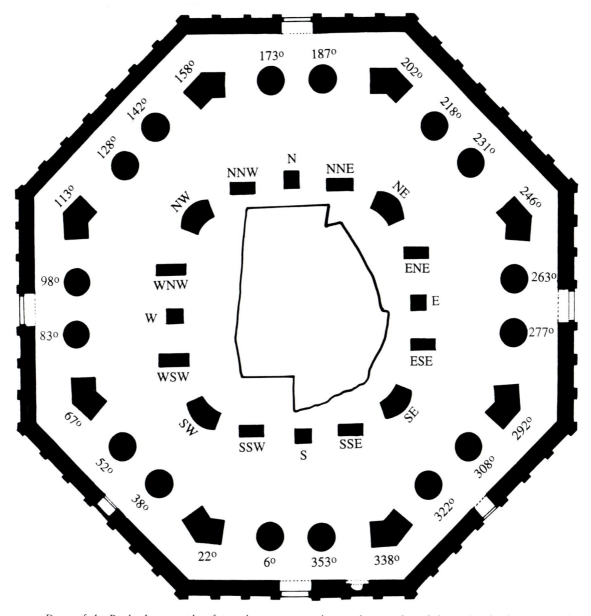

Figure 22. Dome of the Rock, diagram identifying the mosaics on the circular arcade and drums (cardinal points) and on the octagon (angles on a north-south axis).

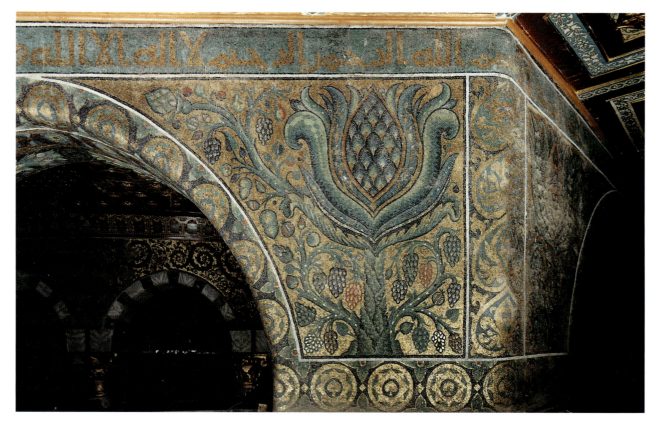

Figure 23. Dome of the Rock, mosaic on the outer face of the octagon with the beginning of the first section of the inscription (338°).

only a few of his guesses turned out to be wrong. During the restorations carried out in the 1960s, Dr. Christel Kessler was able to study the inscription at close quarters. She corrected some of van Berchem's readings and pointed out the unexpectedly large number of diacritical marks found in the text on the inner face of the octagon. She published some of her findings and included in particular a very useful drawing of the inscription which gives a sense of its actual appearance and its idiosyncracies.[8]

Over twenty years later, Sheila Blair published a full translation of the inscription in the context of her interpretation of when the construction of the building was begun,[9] and Heribert Busse included complete German translations in several of his numerous studies on early Islamic Jerusalem. Because of the importance of the inscription as a source for understanding the monument, an appendix to this book contains the Arabic text with a few technical

observations. I am also providing a translation immediately below, with the passages that are also found in the Koran capitalized. Koranic quotations are identified according to the standard "Egyptian" version and the numbering of verses is, therefore, different from the ones in the *Répertoire*. I have not tried to give a literary flavor to the translation, and have made it as literal as possible. The illustrations (figs. 42–49) present most of the inscription on the inner face of the octagon.

The inscription begins on the outer side of the octagon (fig. 23), just at the corner between the southeastern and southern sides (338°), where the rosette ending the outer sequence of the inscription is visible around the corner. There are only two words with some diacritical marking on the outer side: *tattakhidu* on the northwestern face (113°) and *taqabilu* on the southeastern one (308°). Rosettes serve to separate segments of the inscription from each other; there does not seem to have been any

Figure 24. Dome of the Rock, outer octagon, section where al-Ma'mun replaced Abd al-Malik's name with his own (292°).

attempt to make them fit with architectural parts, except the south face of the octagon which includes one whole section of the inscription. The inner face of the octagon contains a single, continuous statement without rosette or other means to divide it into parts, and some fifty letters are provided with diacritical marks. It begins on the upper right corner of pier 22.

The Outer Face

"In the name of God, the Compassionate, the Merciful, there is no god but God, One, without associate. SAY HE IS GOD, ALONE,[10] GOD THE ETERNAL, HE DOES NOT BEGET NOR IS HE BEGOTTEN AND THERE IS NO ONE LIKE HIM [K 112]. Muhammad is the envoy of God, may God bless him. [ROSETTE] In the name of God, the Compassionate, the Merciful, there is no God but God, One, without associate. Muhammad is the envoy of God. INDEED

GOD AND HIS ANGELS BLESS THE PROPHET; O YOU WHO BELIEVE SEND BLESSINGS ON HIM AND SALUTE HIM WITH FULL SALUTATION [K 33:56]. [ROSETTE] In the name of God, the Compassionate, the Merciful, there is no god but God, One. PRAISE TO GOD WHO BEGETS NO SON AND WHO HAS NO ASSOCIATE IN POWER AND WHO HAS NO SURROGATE FOR (PROTECTION FROM) HUMILIATION AND MAGNIFY HIS GREATNESS [K 17:111]. Muhammad is the envoy of God, may God bless him and His angels and His envoys and peace unto him and the mercy of God. [ROSETTE] In the name of God the Compassionate, the Merciful, there is no god but God, One and without associate. TO HIM IS DOMINION AND TO HIM IS PRAISE; HE GIVES LIFE OR DEATH AND HE HAS POWER OVER ALL THINGS [combination of K 64:1 and K 57:2]. Muhammad is the envoy of God, may God bless him and grant his intercession on the day of resurrection for his community. [ROSETTE] In the name of God, the

Compassionate, the Merciful, there is no god but God, One, without associate. Muhammad is the envoy of God, God bless him. [ROSETTE] Has built this domed structure the servant of God, Abdallah, the imam al-Ma'mun, Commander of the Faithful, in the year seventy-two. May God accept it from him and be satisfied with him. Amen. Lord of the worlds, to God is praise. [ROSETTE]." (It is obvious from logic and from the evidence of mosaic cubes (fig. 24) that the name of the caliph Abd al-Malik had been replaced, while the date has remained the same.)

The Inner Face

"In the name of God, the Compassionate, the Merciful, there is no god but God, One, without associate. TO HIM IS DOMINION AND TO HIM IS PRAISE, HE GIVES LIFE OR DEATH AND HE HAS POWER OVER ALL THINGS [combination of K 64:1 and K 57:2]. Muhammad is the servant of God and His envoy. Verily God and His angels send blessings to the Prophet. O YOU WHO BELIEVE SEND BLESSING ON HIM AND SALUTE HIM WITH FULL SALUTATION [K 33:54]. May God bless him and peace upon him and the mercy of God. O PEOPLE OF THE BOOK, DO NOT GO BEYOND THE BOUNDS OF YOUR RELIGION AND DO NOT SAY ABOUT GOD EXCEPT THE TRUTH. INDEED THE MESSIAH JESUS SON OF MARY WAS AN ENVOY OF GOD AND HIS WORD HE BESTOWED ON HER AS WELL AS A SPIRIT FROM HIM. SO BELIEVE IN GOD AND IN HIS ENVOYS AND DO NOT SAY 'THREE'; 'DESIST, IT IS BETTER FOR YOU. FOR INDEED GOD IS ONE GOD, GLORY BE TO HIM THAT HE SHOULD HAVE A SON. TO HIM BELONG WHAT IS IN HEAVEN AND WHAT IS ON EARTH AND IT IS SUFFICIENT FOR HIM TO BE A GUARDIAN.[11] THE MESSIAH DOES NOT DISDAIN TO BE A SERVANT OF GOD, NOR DO THE ANGELS NEAREST (TO HIM). THOSE WHO DISDAIN SERVING HIM AND WHO ARE ARROGANT, HE WILL GATHER ALL TO HIMSELF [K 4:171–172]. Bless your envoy and your servant Jesus son of Mary AND PEACE UPON HIM ON THE DAY OF BIRTH AND ON THE DAY OF DEATH AND ON THE DAY HE IS RAISED UP AGAIN. THIS IS JESUS SON OF MARY. IT IS A WORD OF TRUTH IN WHICH THEY DOUBT. IT IS NOT FOR GOD TO TAKE A SON. GLORY BE TO HIM WHEN HE DECREES A THING HE ONLY SAYS 'BE' AND IT IS. INDEED GOD IS MY LORD AND YOUR LORD, THEREFORE SERVE HIM; THIS IS THE STRAIGHT PATH [K 19:33–36].[12] GOD BEARS WITNESS THAT THERE IS NO GOD BUT HE, (AS DO) THE ANGELS AND THOSE WISE IN JUSTICE. THERE IS NO GOD BUT HE, THE ALL-MIGHTY, THE ALL-WISE. INDEED THE RELIGION OF GOD IS ISLAM. THOSE WHO WERE GIVEN THE BOOK DID NOT DISSENT EXCEPT AFTER KNOWLEDGE CAME TO THEM (AND THEY BECAME) ENVIOUS OF EACH OTHER. WHOSOEVER DISBELIEVES IN THE SIGNS OF GOD, INDEED GOD IS SWIFT IN RECKONING [K 3:18–19]."

In addition to the long mosaic inscription, there were plaques with writing nailed on the wooden beam above the doors of the Dome of the Rock, two of which, on the eastern and northern doorways, have been preserved. The text was painted in gold over a blue background. Whether already done at the time of Abd al-Malik in the late seventh century, the effect of gold over blue may have represented or imitated the mosaics inside the building, although the notion of writing the text of the Revelation in gold met with opposition in the earliest *Books on Koranic Leaves* (*Kitab al-Masahif*) from the tenth century. Such opposition usually indicates common practice and there may not be any need to connect the execution of these door inscriptions with the mosaics inside.[13] The inscriptions were still *in situ* at the turn of the century, one over the eastern doorway, the other one, only partially preserved, over the northern one. Today both are kept in one of the small Mamluk sanctuaries in the Haram. Max van Berchem, who published the inscriptions, argued that the eastern one had seven lines from the Umayyad period, most likely the time of Abd al-Malik, while the last two lines, which contain the historical information about the sponsorship of the work, were replacements from the time of al Ma'mun at the beginning of the ninth century. For reasons that are not at all clear, these historical lines are repeated and appear as two sets of two lines set next to each other. The northern plaque is incomplete, and it is some twenty centimeters shorter than the eastern one; it also repeats the historical statement and its pious first part is close to the eastern one, but not identical. It is likely that each of the building's four doors was provided with such inscriptions containing the same historical information, but with variations in their religious content. The texts of these inscriptions as read by van Berchem are also found in the Appendix.

The East Door

"In the name of God, the Compassionate, the Merciful, PRAISE BE TO GOD EXCEPT WHOM THERE IS NO GOD, THE LIVING, THE EVERLASTING, THE CREATOR OF HEAVEN AND OF EARTH, AND THE LIGHT OF HEAVEN AND OF EARTH [K 2:255, partly, or 3:1; 2:112 or 6:101, both in part], the Upholder of Heaven and earth, ONE, UNIQUE, HE DOES NOT BEGET NOR IS HE BEGOTTEN AND THERE IS NONE LIKE HIM [K 112, minus one word], One, LORD OF POWER, YOU GIVE POWER TO WHOM YOU PLEASE AND YOU TAKE AWAY POWER FROM WHOMEVER YOU PLEASE [K 3:26]. All power is to You and comes from You, our Master, and it returns to You, Master of power, Merciful, Compassionate. HE HAS WRITTEN MERCY FOR HIMSELF, HIS MERCY EXTENDS TO ALL THINGS (K 6:12 and K 7:156).[14] Glory to Him and may He be exalted over what polytheists associate [to Him]. We ask you, our God, by Your mercy, by Your beautiful names, by Your noble face, by Your immense power, by Your perfect word by which heaven and earth stand together and by which, and with Your mercy, we are preserved from the devil and we are all saved from Your punishment on the day of resurrection, by Your abundant grace, by Your great nobility, by Your clemency, Your power, Your forgiveness, and Your kindness, that You bless Muhammad, Your servant and Your Prophet, and that You accept his intercession for his community. May God bless him and give him peace and the mercy of God. And this is what was ordered by the servant of God Abdallah, the imam al-Ma'mun, Commander of the Faithful, may God prolong his life, under the rule of the brother of the Commander of the Faithful Abu Ishaq, son of the Commander of the Faithful

al-Rashid, may God prolong him. By the hand of Salih ibn Yahya, client of the Commander of the Faithful, in *rabi' II* 216 [May-June 831]."

The North Door

"In the name of God, the Compassionate, the Merciful, PRAISE BE TO GOD EXCEPT WHOM THERE IS NO GOD, THE LIVING, THE EVERLASTING [K 2:255, in part, or 3:1]. There is no partner to Him, One, UNIQUE, HE DOES NOT BEGET NOR IS HE BEGOTTEN AND THERE IS NONE LIKE HIM [K 112, except for first words). Muhammad is the servant of God and His envoy, WHOM HE SENT WITH GUIDANCE AND THE RELIGION OF TRUTH TO PROCLAIM IT OVER ALL RELIGIONS, EVEN THOUGH THE POLYTHEISTS HATE IT [K 9:33 or 61:9]. Let us believe in God and what was revealed to Muhammad and IN WHAT WAS GIVEN TO THE PROPHETS FROM THEIR LORD; WE MADE NO DIFFERENCE BETWEEN ONE AND THE OTHER AND WE ARE MUSLIMS TO HIM [K 2:139 or 3:78, slightly modified]. God bless Muhammad, His servant and His prophet, and peace upon him and the mercy of God, His grace, His forgiveness, and His pleasure." This is followed by a statement with the name of the caliph al-Ma'mun and the date of 831, as on the eastern door.

Commentary

The significance of these inscriptions is enormous at several different levels and I shall divide my comments into three categories. The first is essentially technical and specific; it includes precise information about the building as well as such matters as the history of the Arabic script and the chronology of the Koranic text, which lie outside of the concerns of this book and which are, for the most part, beyond my competence. The second one seeks to interpret a text incorporated into a building: what does it mean? To whom is it addressed? By whom was it composed? The third one is speculative and derives from the second: are the inscriptions limited to explaining something about this building only? Or do they have wider implications for Jerusalem and for its period? The inscriptions lend themselves to many interpretations. In retrospect, it is amazing that they have been ignored for so long.

Most of the scholarly concern with these inscriptions has been relatively technical and detailed. It has involved the paleography of the script, the nature of Koranic quotations, and the date. The difficulty with any paleographic analysis of the inscriptions is that there is nothing comparable to them in length or conception from early Islamic times. The strictly contemporary milestones erected by Abd al-Malik along some of the major roads of his empire have letters of strikingly similar shapes and a limited use of diacritical marks as well. The reasons why some words and letters but not others are provided with ways to improve or to secure their reading, hardly leap forward, either for the milestones or in the Dome of the Rock, which is the more remarkable because of the length of the texts. The last two decades of the seventh century and the first two of the following one are identified by later writers as the time when diacritical marks appear in Koranic texts in order to facilitate reading of Arabic by foreigners (missionary purpose) and to classify textual problems (exegetical purpose). Nonreligious texts known in papyri were rarely provided with systematic signs of any sort.[15]

Perhaps, as has been suggested for some early manuscripts, a general aesthetic aim predominated over a referential or informational one, as Koranic quotations are not singled out for diacritical marks, and as it is the spelled-out number "eight," hardly a particularly significant word in the inscription but nicely located in the last line, that is provided with one on a milestone.[16] The possibility of an even more focused aesthetic purpose is, on the other hand, strengthened by two features. First, the diacritical marks occur only twice on the outer, darker side of the octagon in the Dome and nearly fifty times on the inner and more visible side, whose decorative designs were also highlighted. Second, the shape, size, and location of these marks does not seem to have been standardized as it would be in later times. It can be argued that, just as in several pages from early manuscripts, the use of diacritics lacks consistency if it is understood in terms of differentiating letters, but makes sense as a means to attract a reader's attention.[17] Thus can be explained the unusual three vertical dots (fig. 48) that precede the verb *shahada,* "witness," in the middle of the western side of the octagon, which refers to God's own statement about Himself. With this striking and unique composition of dots begins the final proclamatory statement of the inscription, and while the marks may indeed identify the letter *shin* rather than *sin,* they are primarily a visual signal of the importance of the text that follows them.

I leave to specialized scholarship the task of placing the style of writing found in the Dome of the Rock within the evolution of the Arabic script during the first centuries of Muslim rule. When compared with the thousands of pages of the so-called "Kufic" *masahif* or parchment pages with the text of the Koran, the Dome of the Rock inscriptions are striking by the clarity and directness of their script.[18] But, since they are almost alone in having both date and locale, it is difficult to relate them meaningfully to texts copied in books or even to the epitaphs that begin to appear from the early ninth century onward. Furthermore, it is still open to question whether the mosaicists of the Dome of the Rock knew Arabic and designed the inscription directly on the wall or copied a prepared model, probably painted or inked on some construction material like wood.[19] In short, it is simplest to conclude at this stage that, whatever place the inscriptions of the Dome of the Rock assume in the history of Arabic writing, the visual expression of that writing was as clear as was possible at the time, and that diacritical marks were used to emphasize the appearance of the writing and to increase one's awareness of it as a continuously flowing belt holding together the whole decoration of the building.

Relatively little attention has been given to the rather extraordinary fact that the Koranic passages from these inscriptions, if this is indeed what they are, precede by over two centuries any other dated or datable quotation of any length from the Holy Book including pages from manuscripts.[20] There are, of course, presumed or acknowledged Koranic excerpts among the small number of inscriptions from the first two centuries of Islam, some still preserved, others known from medieval sources or from a few modern or pre-modern descriptions of monuments that have disappeared.[21] And the official coinage developed by Abd al-Malik utilizes, as does the eastern door inscription of the Dome of the Rock, the so-called "mission" verse (9:33 or 61:9) as the enabling statement for its message. The proclamation of faith on the obverse of most gold and silver coins is identical to that of *surah* 112 found several times on the Dome of the Rock. These examples and especially the lengthy version in the Dome of the Rock make it all the more curious that their evidence is rarely discussed in the considerable western scholarship dealing with the formation of the Koranic text and is simply ignored by a Muslim scholarship upholding the tradition of a text fixed by a commission appointed for these purposes by the caliph Uthman (644–656), with minor later, primarily orthographic, changes.[22]

Succinctly put, the issue is whether the passages in bold characters that have equivalents in the accepted Koranic text should be considered as actual excerpts from an existing written or oral recension, which would have been by then more or less definitively closed. Such is the conclusion reached (in a footnote) by A. Brockett, the only scholar to have considered the Dome of the Rock in his studies of the transmission of the Holy Text.[23] If so, two corollaries emerge. One is that an oral tradition is more likely to have affected the text on the Dome of the Rock than a written one. This could explain the changes from the first to the third person in quoting divine pronouncements about Jesus, and to the collages of different passages that occur there and elsewhere in early inscriptions. It is easier and more natural to manipulate one's recollection of texts (or images, for that matter) than it is to recompose and modify chosen fragments from a written manuscript. The other conclusion is that there must have been a social, political, or intellectual mechanism for the composition of the inscription and, therefore, for the conceptualization of the building's purpose. If one agrees that the passages involved are Koranic "quotations," then at least one

dimension of that mechanism is clear. A learned and thoughtful individual or group chose to excerpt parts of a written or, more likely, remembered Holy Text in order to formulate an iconophoric or aesthetic message about a building.

But is it necessary to assume that these were all Koranic "quotations"? An extreme alternative is to consider *all* the so-called quotations as parts of a text composed for the Dome of the Rock and including statements and expressions that are also found in the Holy Writ, but that were not necessarily excerpted from it.[24] If this is so, the two instances of change in person would have reflected a version of the same account other than the traditional Koranic one, not a change in the Koranic text, but an alternate reading of the same model.[25] As we shall see shortly, it may well be appropriate to consider the inscriptions, especially the mosaic one, as a single text without a clear separation between contemporary statements and quotations from the Holy Book. In much later times, the latter were often introduced with the formula *qala Allah tala'* ("said God Most High") in order to separate Koranic excerpts from other types of statements. Here, it can be argued, it is only the previous knowledge of the whole Koran by the viewer which permits him to identify quotations, as nothing sets them off in the writing itself.

It is possible to consider intermediary solutions. The two passages dealing with Jesus (4:171–72 and 19:33–36) and the final proclamation (3:18–19), which together occupy most of the inner side of the octagon may indeed be quotations, while the other apparent quotations are simply parallel statements of a religious nature that would have been part and parcel of a collective expression of beliefs without necessary ties to the Revelation itself. Further work on this subject is complicated by the paucity of information from the early centuries, as it would be necessary to investigate the vocabulary of religious and pious behavior toward the end of the first century of Islam. It is probable that a relationship could be established between formulas used in social, personal, and religious behavior and their presence in a holy text, without assuming that the former are citations of the latter.[26]

Thus we must, I believe, leave unanswered in part the question of the specificity of Koranic quotations in these inscriptions. On balance, I suspect that it is probably reasonable to assume that this is indeed what they were and, therefore, to interpret variations in terms of oral versus written tradition or some other similar procedure. But other interpretations cannot be excluded.

One detail of these inscriptions has received more attention than the rest. It concerns the dedication at the end of the last segment on the outer wall of the octagon. Since it was first published by Melchior de Vogüé and then republished and analyzed by Max van Berchem, the name of al-Ma'mun, who ruled from 813 to 833, as the monument's patron had to be reconciled with the date of the building which is clearly 72 A.H./691–692 C.E. There is by now general agreement with van Berchem's explanation of a *prise de possession* through changes in an inscription of the Umayyad building by a later, Abbasid, caliph. It was important for the latter to preserve the original date, since the whole point was the imposition of a new legitimacy on an older monument.[27] For an understanding of the monument and, in fact, the whole city of Jerusalem, al-Ma'mun's action is interesting in two ways. One is that this particular Abbasid caliph also restored sanctuaries in Mekkah and Madinah. In the former he left two long inscriptions describing the trophies he sent there and the events whose memory he sought to perpetuate.[28] The pattern of involving the three holy cities—Mekkah, Medinah, and Jerusalem—in a demonstration of Muslim legitimacy to rule continued under the Fatimids, as we shall see below, and found its best known expression under the Ottoman Suleyman the Magnificent in the sixteenth century, when all three cities became more or less what they remained until the twentieth century. In other words, what appears as a childish and incompletely executed act of vanity, is in fact a very deliberate claim to the ownership of a place whose holiness, of whatever sort, has already been established. Al-Ma'mun's action is also interesting from the point of view of his particular policies, and to these we shall return as well.

Some concern has also been expressed as to whether the date 691–692 (72 A.H.) corresponds to the beginning of the building's construction or to its completion. Usually such inscriptions, which could not have been mounted much before the completion of the building, determine the end of a job. But there are strong reasons to believe that in this case at least, it was important to commemorate the beginning of a long and complex operation.[29] I shall return to this question after a discussion of all the data available for the building.

It is understandable why the date and the name of the founder have been so frequently discussed by scholars. Dates and names are the backbone of historical knowledge. But there is one detail in this segment of the inscription that may not have received the attention it merits. It is the use of the Arabic word *qubbah* to describe the building. In classical and modern Arabic, the word means "cupola" and, by common extension, a "domed building," frequently a mausoleum. In this sense, it is perfectly reasonable to interpret the word as an appellation for the hemispheric dome and the double octagon surrounding it, in short, to see it as the verbal equivalent of the standing building. The problem is that all the uses of the word *qubbah* in the first century of Islam appear to refer to temporary coverings, most often to tents. Just as with the Koranic "quotations," we could then consider the inscription in the Dome of the Rock as containing the first example of a new usage for a traditional Arabic word. But it is also possible that the usage had already been established in Jerusalem. In a Greek poem composed shortly before the Muslim conquest, probably ca. 631–635, the patriarch Sophronius describes, in the complex of the Holy Sepulchre, a "holy cube" (*hieros kubos*) with its "heavenlike" (*ouranosteros*) combination of four items whose names have not been preserved in the corrupt manuscript. One of the peculiarities of this passage, which has troubled its editor and translator, is that it does not make clear what the word *kubos* meant. It could have its usual Greek meaning of "cube" and refer to some small construction or even object in the Holy Sepulchre. Or it could refer to the dome over the tomb of Christ, in which case it would be a local Palestinian, perhaps even Jerusalemite, variant. Sophronius, accustomed to local speech, might have adopted the spoken Arabic or Aramaic word for a temporary cover and used it to define the constructed dome in the Holy Sepulchre.[30] Such a direct passage from spoken Arabic to written Greek, if justified, would have the curious implication of bypassing a Syriac intermediary, which had already appeared in a sixth-century hymn to a church in Edessa.[31] As for so many features of the Dome of the Rock, there are two explanatory paths, one that leads to local issues of the Late Antique world in western Asia, and the other to the uniqueness of Jerusalem.

→ ◆ ←

WHAT SORT OF TEXT is formed by these inscriptions? And to whom was it addressed? The mosaic inscription should, I believe, be considered a single text that begins on the outer face of the octagon at the east end of the southern arcade, just after one of the rosettes, and ends on the inner face at the south end of the southwest arcade; further, each of the four doors provides an additional, probably (but not necessarily) related, statement, of which only two have been preserved.

The inscription at the east entrance is a perfectly clear statement. It begins by praising God, His uniqueness, and His power which is indivisible. Then His universal mercy is proclaimed in two short clauses that make sense, on their own, as one continuous phrase or statement ("He has written mercy for Himself, His mercy extends to all things"). The second clause is a fragment from Koran 7:156, modified from the first to the third person, but it can simply be considered a logical rather than a scriptural extension of a theologically more profound statement (possibly a fragment from K 6:12) that establishes mercy as a prerogative of God. Then, after a brief repetition of the Muslim doxology, there is a prayer for the Prophet with two significant characteristics. One is the evocation of God's many facets, the earliest example of the listing of the sacred names and functions of God that will become a major fixture of traditional Islamic theology and a major expression of individual

or group piety.[32] The second characteristic of note is the importance given to the resurrection and judgment, to the dangers coming from the devil, and to the Prophet Muhammad as an intercessor between the community of believers and the Divine, in short to the theme of eschatology so prominent in Jerusalem. The end of the inscription is a reference to its patron, in this case the caliph al-Ma'mun, but, as this historical part of the inscription is written with letters of smaller size than the ones used in the religious part, and as a break line clearly exists above the beginning of the historical section, Max van Berchem's conclusion that al-Ma'mun's two lines replace some comparable statement from the time of Abd al-Malik should be accepted.[33] The historical section in the Abbasid version is unusual for the mention of other members of the caliph's family and the official in charge of the work.

I shall return below to the events surrounding al-Ma'mun's patronage in Jerusalem. The main point of this summary of the inscription is to propose that it bears a striking resemblance to the Christian liturgy, as it was practiced at the time, and of course, to some aspects of Jewish liturgical practices as well. Praises in part from the Holy Text (as the Psalms or certain passages from Isaiah are used in the Jewish and Christian liturgies) are followed by requests for God's infinite mercy in granting salvation at the time of judgment by an invocation to an intercessor. And, as in Christian and occasionally in Jewish liturgies, litanies also evoke the ruling prince.[34]

The inscription on the north door has been preserved only in part. It too begins with a doxology, followed by the proclamation of the Prophet's mission with special emphasis on the universality of his message within the prophetic tradition given to Christians and Jews.[35] And, before the reference to the Abbasid caliph, the blessing of God is called upon the Prophet. Four possible Koranic quotations are used, but all four examples are incomplete (two words missing in K 112), modified (modification of 3:84 if it was indeed the model used),[36] or uncertain in the sense that two Koranic passages could have been combined in order to create a statement for the Dome of the Rock. These peculiarities are dispelled or become unimportant if, once again, the text of the inscription is considered as a doxology *cum* litany directed this time to the missionary message of the Prophet and to its unique quality.

Nothing in these inscriptions says that they were made expressly for the eastern and northern doors of the Dome of the Rock. Some uncertainty exists, for instance, as to whether they were really preserved *in situ* during the time of the Crusades. Perhaps they were covered with Christian images or Latin inscriptions. In any event, their location, at least as it appeared in 1900, was probably not an accident. The east gate facing the Mount of Olives, just beyond the valley of cemeteries leading to the entrance to Hell, invokes the Last Judgment and the astounding power of God, while the north gate is today the Gate of the Prophet and of the mission he transmitted to all Muslims. We shall see later that the "gate of the Prophet," the *bab al-nabi*, was a concept as well as a place in the development of Muslim Jerusalem and that its location was to the south of the esplanade. At this stage and with a slight reservation as to whether these plaques are necessarily in the locations for which they were originally made, the meaning that can be assigned to two of the entrances into the Dome of the Rock makes it all the more regrettable that nothing has remained from the other two doorways. The preserved inscriptions evoke two themes for the building: mission and eschatology. It is reasonable to argue further that eschatology predominates and is deeply bound to mission, since dozens of early epitaphs which are known from the ninth century on in Egypt use the "mission" verse 9:33 as the means of entry for the deceased into eternal protection and life.[37] The relatively short inscriptions on the doorways can thus be seen as independent texts containing doxologies and prayers comparable in genre and structure to parts of the Christian and (possibly) Jewish liturgies, emphasizing the agency of the Prophet within the world of God in converting others and in preparing the way to the judgment which follows the resurrection.

The same structure can be proposed for the inscription inside the building, but its interpretation is more complicated. Structurally, it is a single text divided into seven unequal sections. Six of these sections are on the outer side of the octagon. The first five are praises to God and the Prophet that begin with and include elsewhere what became more or less standard formulas of the Muslim profession of faith ("In the name of God, the Compassionate, the Merciful"; "There is no God but God, One, without associate"; "Muhammad is the Envoy of God"). It is nearly impossible to know how common, consistent, and canonical, so to speak, these formulas were by the last decade of the seventh century, but the appearance of most of them on the new coins of Abd al-Malik, more or less contemporary with the Dome of the Rock, indicates that they were accepted as common statements, almost as proclamations, of the new faith and of the sociopolitical order that came with it. Four of the five sections contain passages from the Koran or parallels to the Holy Scripture. Three of these passages proclaim the oneness and greatness of God, and one asserts the blessing of God and His angels on the Prophet. The fifth section is limited to the official proclamation of faith; the sixth contains historical information about the building, its founder, and its date. It ends with a formulaic response typical of liturgical practice, at least in Christianity: "Amen, Lord of the worlds, praise to God."

The entire inscription on the inner side of the octagon is organized as a single section within the text. It begins by recalling God's name and the blessings of God and His angels on the Prophet. These statements are combined with two possibly Koranic passages with appropriate references to God and His Oneness. Both of these passages are also found on the outer side and their reappearance here is suggestive of automatic liturgical repetition. Then, three large excerpts from the Scripture are set in logical sequence and broken only once by a non-Koranic call for God to bless Jesus, son of Mary, God's envoy and servant, just as He blessed His envoy and servant Muhammad. The logic of the sequence is quite clear: Jesus is acknowledged as a Prophet, not as Son of God, since the power of God is beyond the need for progeny, and the true faith requires submission to God who is swift in punishing those who do not accept his message. This last statement is solemnly introduced by the verb *shahada*, "to witness," which is so essential to self-assertion in Islam.

The progression of the text is strikingly comparable to the liturgy of the catechumens in the Christian mass.[38] A series of litanies and what liturgical books call "exclamations" (the proclamation of "honor, glory, and worship to the Father, the Son, and the Holy Spirit, now and ever and unto ages of ages") precede and follow formal readings from the Scriptures. I am not, at this stage, proposing a Christian model for the inscription inside the Dome of the Rock, but I am suggesting that the rhetorical, psychological, and emotional pattern of prayers, praises, and blessings leading to a long combination of divinely revealed passages is a model probably used in many faiths with a revealed text and a transcendental God. It was certainly present in the Christian liturgy when St. Basil the Great and St. John Chrysostom standardized it in the fourth century. The comparison must remain a structural one, as I am not aware of an incident or a story that could explain how Christian practices, even those open to non-baptized applicants seeking instruction, could have affected the carefully chosen officials in charge of a building ordered by a Muslim ruler. But neither in Judaism nor in the little we know of early Muslim practices can I find anything suggesting the rhetorical structure found in the Dome of the Rock inscriptions.

If my interpretation of its structure is accepted, the operative part of the inscription which gives it its particular meaning lies in the "readings" from the inner face of the octagon, which, as have seen, contains the largest number of visual signs in the shape of diacritical marks calling attention to it and which is, in fact, the easiest part of the inscription to see.

As was pointed out many years ago,[39] these readings, set in the context of repeated proclamations of God's Oneness, iterate the position of Jesus in Islam as a prophet and envoy and claim that this explanation of Jesus is proper and true, that it does not imply any malice toward Jesus, that Islam is the appropriate faith for those who received the Reve-

lation, and that God will (or at least can) castigate those who do not believe in His revelation. Two aspects of this text composed of three Koranic passages run together require particular attention. One is that a conscious parallel is drawn between the Prophet Muhammad, blessed by God and angels at the beginning of the text, and Jesus for whom divine blessing is asked in the only addition to a Koranic passage ("Bless Your envoy and Your servant Jesus") following a quotation mentioning the angels that accompany Jesus (K 4:172).[40] The "People of the Book" (at that time, primarily Christians and Jews who share in the divine Revelation with Muslims) are mentioned at the beginning of the long quotation, but there is no reference anywhere in the Dome of the Rock to Jews or to any Old Testament figures and events. This absence is striking when contrasted with nearly all written accounts of contemporary events, or with the later histories of the Haram.[41] Written accounts, like the early *fada'il*, constantly comment on Jews and Jewish religious behavior and beliefs, and mention Christians and especially Christianity only incidentally.

The second curious aspect of this text lies in its choice of quotations. Out of the ninety-three verses in the Koran dealing with Jesus, the five that were chosen avoid the problematic issues like the virgin birth and especially the death and resurrection of Christ, where the fundamental divergences between Islam and orthodox Christian dogma are most obvious.[42] The most notable choice is of 4:157, which implies that the crucifixion was but a semblance and about whose exact interpretation much discussion occurred quite early.[43] Absent are references to the miracles performed by Jesus like the celebrated story of Jesus breathing life into the clay sculpture of a bird (3:49). It is, of course, dangerous to draw conclusions from the absence of statements, but it seems reasonable to argue that the "reading" offered in the Dome of the Rock is what would be called today an "ecumenical" one, stressing an image of Jesus that is fairly neutral except on two points, that he cannot be the Son of God because of the nature of God, and that he is in no way diminished in being the "servant" (*'abd*) of God. Some aspects or implications of these propositions were fully accepted by several Christian movements of the time, especially the various Monophysite groups with considerable following in Palestine.

The mode of expression throughout the Dome of the Rock is praise, the praising of God in Whose name all things exist and Whose blessing and that of His angels is called upon His envoys and on mankind; then the praising of the Prophet Muhammad who is the servant and envoy of God, but also an intercessor for men; finally, and only inside the building, the praising of Jesus, servant and envoy as well but not an intercessor. The readings exhibit three moods: eschatological (almost exclusively on the two gates and especially on the eastern one); missionary and exhortative (on the north entrance and inside the building); liturgical and expository (a carefully chosen part of the Muslim way of understanding Jesus presented inside the building, within the rhythmic framework of repeated pious formulas and proclamations).

For whom were these messages meant, and who was responsible for them? The second part of the question is easier to answer. Because of the mention of the caliph's name and the replacement of Abd al-Malik's with al-Ma'mun's, there is no doubt that the statements on the Dome of the Rock were chosen by the highest authorities in the Muslim realm, whoever they were and wherever they lived, probably in Damascus in 692 and Baghdad later on. The coincidence between the statements, Koranic or not, on coins and those on the building confirms that the ruling authority framed the inscriptions. A second component is an awareness by Christians and Muslims that Jerusalem in the seventh century was a Christian city. Christians dominated the city and, while they may have been divided among themselves, they were aware of being different from and superior to the upstart Muslims and to the Jews who were beginning to return to the city. The third component was Islamic learning. By that, I mean the ability to manipulate the interest in pious statements or holy verses in order to meet social, political, religious, and other challenges.[44]

It is more difficult to understand for whom the inscriptions were made. It could have been for the Muslims of Jerusalem, as the inscriptions identify for them traditional, pre-Islamic, Jerusalem associations like the end of time and the resurrection, now fitted into new Islamic dress. The inscriptions would have provided them with new obligations toward the dominant Christian population around them and would emphasize specifically Muslim obligations like conversion. A faithful Muslim, entering the Dome of the Rock and circumambulating it, could read the whole inscription on the octagon in a systematic way by walking once clockwise and once counterclockwise around the octagon. Alternately, he could pick out segments of the inscription and read the carefully composed text in sections sufficient unto themselves. In a sense, perhaps, the reading of the inscription is not, for the Muslim visitor, in the past or today, a goal to reach, rather the inscription exists as an aid in experiencing the building, the space, which has a special meaning for Muslims.

The inscriptions could also have been chosen for Christians, as so much in them focuses on the new truth about their religious beliefs. The eschatological themes are also valid for Christians. The idea of making a religious building, especially a visually impressive one, available to those outside the faith was not new: it was certainly part of Byzantine practice in Constantinople and intended to impress and convert barbarians and nonbelievers. Still, while theoretically not impossible, the idea that an inscription inside a Muslim building was meant for Christian eyes is not very likely.

It is also possible that the inscriptions were viewed as an intrinsic and essential part of the building. Writing, because of its denotative qualities, identifies purposes and expectations for the building so that future generations unaware of the circumstances that created the edifice might learn something of the ambitions and beliefs of its founders. Writing, at this level, has the practical potential to label an accomplishment like a title on a frame. Ultimately, the receiver of the written message is God, who is commemorated in the building.

SOME ADDITIONAL, if speculative, aspects of the inscription may be elucidated by comparing it to other inscriptions on buildings and objects in earlier times. The traditional explanation for the presence and use in the Dome of the Rock of a long inscription with a specific message is quite simple. Writing had, already by the late seventh century, formally or subconsciously, replaced images as the Muslim way of imbuing objects and buildings with meaning or simply of communicating pious thoughts or sanctioned ideas to the faithful.[45] The fact that, in these very years and by order of the same caliph, Abd al-Malik, most gold and silver coins replaced images with writing confirms the notion of a momentous shift in visual expression. To be understood or interpreted, letters and words require different competencies from images[46] and thus the presence of a long inscription with a narrative content implies a major change in those who were expected to absorb its message. Such a change, conjectured by many scholars without real demonstration,[47] may well have taken place by the time of the building of the Dome of the Rock, at least among the ruling circles responsible for it. But it is impossible, as far as I know, to show with a single example that the reading or writing of inscriptions on buildings or objects were the processes by which meanings were established and understood.

A rapid survey of the inscriptions whose texts have been preserved by early chroniclers and geographers, sets the Jerusalem inscription within its context of comparable documents and allows for a few speculations about responses to its existence. I have limited my discussion to the first two and a half centuries of Muslim rule, before the lengthy inscriptions in the mosque of Ibn Tulun in Cairo and, a bit later, in the mosque of Cordova. The latter usher in a different and fairly consistent procedure whereby the variations in set formulas, in invocation and in quotations from the Koran are carefully elaborated statements about the buildings involved.[48] This classical type of procedure with a clear pattern of standards and variations is easy to correlate with the Abbasid cultural and political equilibrium more or less in place by the ninth century, an equilibrium that involved the coherent acceptance of linguistic, political, cultural and ideological methods for argument and decisions.[49] The language was Arabic; the political stance was hierarchical from the caliph to the local tax collector; the cultural component was the Muslim structure for law and thought; and the ideology was Sunni. Such was not the case during the first two centuries of Muslim rule, and especially not during the Umayyad period, when experimentation of all sorts and coexisting languages created a far more colorful social setting.

The easiest inscriptions to understand are those of the eighth century—one Umayyad and all the others Abbassid—in the pan-Islamic sanctuaries of Mekkah and Madinah.[50] Their main purpose is to identify and laud the work done by the caliph in building or restoring various parts of buildings. They all contain what in the Dome of the Rock I called the doxology, then praises addressed to God and to the Prophet, the latter being frequently followed by the Koranic statement of the prophetic mission (9:33). In Madinah the interesting emphasis on the social responsibilities of the caliph probably corresponds to some concrete objective of al-Mahdi's policies around 778 to 782; at the very least the inscriptions have an unusual way of defining his image, something which, many centuries later, will be accomplished through a set number of attributes for princely patrons such as "the learned," "the just," and so forth.[51] The short inscriptions in Mekkah are merely indicative of the religious or pious functions of a place. They serve as practical labels for pilgrims and only occasionally commemorate the patronage of a caliph.

The founding inscription from the mosque of Damascus exists in two versions, a short one from the tenth century reproduced by the historian Mas'udi and a later one from a local Damascene source.[52] The two texts share some of the same pious formulas and ways of witnessing the faith, and both mention not only the building of the mosque but also the destruction of the church that had been there previously. Their dates differ by one year, and only the later one contains the Throne Verse (K 2:258). It is possible but unlikely that there were two foundation inscriptions in the mosque and, as a preliminary hypothesis, I prefer to think that the second version includes later additions or some later rewrite of the original, shorter inscription. The important point, however, is that both versions include the most significant aspect of the Damascus mosque, the one which remained as a key part of the memories associated with it, namely the destruction of the church on the site. That socio-political statement suggesting a confrontation between Christianity and Islam, together with a fairly routine statement of faith, was meant from the very beginning to be the principal message of the inscription and, by extension, of the mosque.

A most unusual example of inscriptions known from written sources consists of the two extensive statements added to the original decoration of two unique objects, or perhaps inscribed on them like museum labels with an explanatory text. One was on a side (the word used is *safihah*) of the crown (*tåj*) of the Kabul-Shah, a prince from the area of modern Afghanistan. He gave the crown in submission to the army of Harun al-Rashid in 815, as an emblem of his conversion to Islam. The other one, dated a year later in 816, was a plaque (*lawh*) attached to the throne of the same Kabul-Shah.[53] Both items were put inside the Ka'bah in Mekkah and, as reported by the chronicler of the holy city, the crown was actually hung inside the sanctuary. The inscriptions relate how the objects were returned to Harun al-Rashid, to whom they had belonged before, and why they were placed as trophies in the holiest Muslim sanctuary. The aim was to commemorate ephemeral, even if dramatic, occurrences by making them permanent reminders of the caliph's victory over unbelievers.

One other long inscription is found in written sources. Allegedly Umayyad from the time of al-Walid and known through an eighteenth-century French transcription, it is said to have been found in the mosque of Amr in Fustat in Cairo.[54] It consists for the most part of a set of prayers for the prophet Muhammad and for the caliph who enlarged the mosque. Its Koranic citations are very similar to the ones in the Dome of the Rock.

When we turn to preserved examples, there are, first of all, epitaphs, found for the most part in Egypt in a continuous series that begins around 790.[55] Epitaphs became quite lengthy, using phrases or quotations from Scripture that are remarkable for their repetition with variants expressing different social, cultural, and religious attitudes. They are also remarkable for the clarity of their main themes: belief in God and in the Prophet's mission, the forthcoming resurrection and judgment, forgiveness and intercession on the Last Day. These are also some of the themes in the inscriptions on the doors of the Dome of the Rock and the praises and prayers found throughout the building. In fact the Mission verse (9:33) and *surah* 112 are found in nearly all early epitaphs, and many of the other Koranic passages from the Dome of the Rock match those in funerary inscriptions. This parallel confirms eschatology as a major component of much of early Muslim pious expression and provides a psychological context for the Dome of the Rock. And, in a more interesting way, it argues for the existence in early Islamic times of a pious language in which excerpts from or parallels to the scriptures, formulas for the proclamation of the faith, and ways to pray or praise could be combined with each other according to the individual needs of a person or place.[56] This pious language is important, because, initially uttered and written in Arabic, it remained in Arabic even in areas where other languages predominated. It became an essential ingredient in what may be called an "Islamic language" different from dozens of local spoken and written forms of Arabic.[57]

A rather peculiar preserved inscription in Madinah is really a painted graffiti dated 735 in a private house. It contains two long Koranic citations dealing with faith as well as the signature of its maker.[58] Another one, equally puzzling, is the fragment found on a mosaic floor in Ramlah in Palestine. The floor seems to have come from a private house, and the inscription, located inside an archway similar to a mihrab, seems to be a citation from the Koran (7:205), although the caution I have urged earlier about identifying Koranic sources should possibly apply here, too.[59] In both these instances, the context of the inscription is insufficiently clear to allow significant conclusions.

It is then altogether possible to fit the Dome of the Rock inscriptions within an evolving language associated with a Muslim way of expressing thoughts, fears and hopes that are themselves fairly universal. We can conclude that a set of formulas had emerged in early Islamic times to express the specifically Muslim vision of the unity of God and of the functions of the Prophet. It is strange, however, that the earliest statement of this vision, in the Dome of the Rock, is the most complete and the longest, as if a complete written theme had been created first, which would then have been repeated with variations or used in summary form elsewhere. Furthermore, the fact of the existence of a set of socially accepted formulas does not explain *why* such a long inscription should have been put inside that particular building. Nothing in the inscription itself nor in the later ones from the early centuries of Muslim culture explains the decision to use this particular mode of visual expression on a building. Even the indicative purposes of a label ("this *qubbah*"), or the date and name of a patron-donor (including, in this particular case, the change from one caliph to another), are found in the least visible parts of the building. In short, while the inscription demonstrates the existence of a type of pious text, the type itself is not requisite for a building.

Arab Muslim power and its art did not spring out of nothing. Since time immemorial inscriptions have been used to proclaim the divine and the power or piety of men, especially kings, while graffiti recorded more mundane pains and hopes of men and, occasionally, women. More specifically and closer to the late seventh century and the Umayyads, the writing of long inscriptions had become particularly common in Late Antiquity and early Byzantine times. Greek epigrams in a grand classical tradition were composed in honor of important or holy people, and even Sophronius, the patriarch of Jerusalem at the time of the Muslim conquest, authored some. Furthermore, between the third century and the end of the sixth, such epigrams were often associated with statues of consuls or magistrates. In the celebrated case of the Church of St. Polyeuktes in Constantinople, a long poem praising the founder and describing the church was inscribed inside the building as a frieze above a cornice with vegetal motifs.[60] Founders were also praised in the sixth-century Church of Sts. Sergius and Bacchus in the Byzantine capital. Such inscriptions, with or without literary flavor but always prominently displayed on a building or object, seem to disappear—or become much more rare—by the end of the sixth century. A later example, from around 843, is part of the decoration in the entrance complex of the imperial palace after the end of the Iconoclastic controversy,[61] and emphasizes an ideological rather than a literary or simply a laudatory content.

In spirit and content these Late Antique inscriptions are quite different from those in the Dome of the Rock or most early Islamic monuments, but the idea of incorporating writing within the ornamental scheme of a monument can be seen, especially with respect to mosaic inscriptions, as the continuation of Late Antique practices, a visual integration of writing into the building that is quite different from the plaque with information or a label identifying an object. In this respect, the Dome of the Rock is more readily connected with Late Antiquity than with the new Muslim world.

The Mosaics

Like its inscriptions, the mosaics of the Dome of the Rock have been known since de Vogüé's publication of over a century ago. Their splendor has been recognized by many visitors to Jerusalem while statistically inclined recorders of the past have calculated that the 1280 square meters (or 12,800 square feet) of mosaics in the Dome of the Rock make it the largest repository of medieval wall mosaics before the Norman church in Monreale. Black and white illustrations of the mosaics have been available in an almost complete photographic survey published in Creswell's monumental volumes on early Islamic architecture.[62] It is, however, only with the publication in 1962 of Richard

Ettinghausen's *Arab Painting* with three good color reproductions that the brilliance of the mosaics was shown. These plates were technically revolutionary for their time, but the manner of presenting them in the book limited the selected details to two dimensions, and did not show their architectural setting.[63] The major overhaul of the Dome of the Rock in 1959–1962 included the restoration of its mosaics as well as a complete photographic survey of every part of the building before and after restorations, but, to my knowledge, examples from this survey were never published.[64] A new photographic survey of the mosaics, for the first time complete and in color, was accomplished by Mr. Said Nuseibeh in 1992–93 and a selection of his work is included in this book (figs. 23–55).[65] It is easy to be carried away by the technical and expressive qualities of the mosaics, but the recognition and description of these qualities in the late twentieth century have a subjective side that is not necessarily valid for the time of their creation. Since this chapter deals with the late seventh century and the building of the Dome of the Rock, I shall concentrate on those features or attributes of the mosaics that illustrate or reflect decisions made in the seventh century and expectations or perceptions reasonable to assume for that time. Two such categories are the sources for the forms and subjects in the mosaics and the meanings, if any, to be attributed to these forms. In fact sources and meanings are precisely the two subjects which have exercised scholarship since the first publication of de Vogüé's book on Jerusalem and especially after the appearance of Creswell's volume in 1932.[66]

There is a more or less general scholarly agreement on the main source for the motifs used in the Dome of the Rock and for the style or styles in which they were executed. That source was the rich visual repertory of Late Antiquity in the Mediterranean and Iran; samples from this repertory appeared in nearly every available medium and with several stylistic variants.[67] Put in such general terms, the statement is no doubt true; but it is also self-evident and redundant, as nothing *a priori* required the Dome of the Rock to be decorated in a particular way. The Muslim world had not yet acquired an artistic personality of its own, nor am I aware of a religious, political, or legal directive about representations or about any sort of decoration that would have directed the Muslim patrons of the building either to choose available forms or to create new ones. It is also more than likely, although unprovable, that the mosaicists and probably the designers of the decoration came from Constantinople, since only the capital of the Byzantine empire was able to maintain at that time a corps of craftsmen capable of the high technical competence found in the Dome of the Rock.[68] In short, it is difficult to seek origins other than Late Antique ones (always recalling that the Iranian world should be included)[69] for the vocabulary of the mosaics and a place of original employment other than Constantinople for the craftsmen who made them. On the other hand, it is possible to understand some of the choices made by patrons and designers of the Dome of the Rock by simply looking at what remains, and detailed photographs of high quality permit the analysis of every segment of the mosaics, showing how craftsmen worked and how successful or unsuccessful restorations have been during centuries of preserving the decoration. Parallels with other monuments can be suggested, but they are fraught with methodological problems. A formal parallel between, let us say, sixth-century Ravenna in Italy and late seventh-century Jerusalem requires, for historical validity, many intermediary documents or assumptions; and the documented presence of Egyptian Christian workers in Palestine does not demonstrate a Coptic origin for artistic motifs. In fact, the uniqueness of the Dome of the Rock undermines even the best instances of logical reasoning or artistic history, for the process of selection and creation that led to an idiosyncratic program of mosaic decoration in that seventh-century building was necessarily an unusual one.

As to interpretations of meaning, if we exclude some complicated ones that existed in the late Middle Ages and that are occasionally revived today,[70] two approaches have predominated. One, exemplified by the work of Marguerite van Berchem, argues in fact (although not in words, since theories are abhorrent to this particular approach) that the absence of well-known carriers of meaning like representations of people, buildings, or landscapes defines the mosaics of the Dome of the Rock as ornamental, that is to say, as serving exclusively to beautify a building.[71] A second approach proposes meanings based on the iconographic or evocative explanation of selected motifs. Crowns and jewels, so prominent on the inner face of the octagon (figs. 42–49) and on the two drums of the dome (fig. 27), have been identified as the trophies of the rulers defeated and conquered by the early Muslims and represent an offering to the sanctuary in Jerusalem. The Ka'bah in Mekkah was used for such offerings until the early tenth century, and there are many representational models in Late Antique art for crowns and jewels hanging over or around a sacred place.[72] Other scholars take their cue from the vegetal motifs that dominate the program of decoration, especially the large trees, realistic or imaginary, often covered with precious stones, which are so prominent on nearly all rectangular vertical spaces and most obvious on all the piers of the building. Simple or complex arguments and easily acceptable or more convoluted parallels have led to explanations of the mosaics as evocations or even representations of Solomon's Temple and Palace, part of Jerusalem's mythical lore, or else of Paradise, access to which was believed to be available in Jerusalem at the end of time. In fact, traces of the original Paradise were seen in Jerusalem itself, through a tree standing on the platform of the Haram and associated at times with God's original creation.[73]

Individually or in some combination, these explanations may well be the right ones, but they do not necessarily impress themselves on the pious or the sightseeing visitor to the building. The texture and composition of the decoration do not highlight clearly and systematically contrasts in motifs. Such motifs as are highlighted—trees and jewels for instance[74]—have no evident and generally accepted external referents for the visitor today or, I dare say, in the past. Their forms and the manner of their execution may well belong to the ways of Late Antiquity, but there are no representational or

symbolic meanings obviously associated with them, such as exist for Christian or imperial subjects.[75]

Before proposing my own explanation of the iconography of the mosaics and making suggestions about the process by which their message was formalized, it is essential to understand how these mosaics are perceived. I am proposing three different ways of seeing them, two of which have been available to all visitors to the Dome of the Rock throughout time, while the third one is peculiar to our own time as it involves seeing the mosaics in photographs. I shall then turn to the more traditional question of the meaning of this unique decorative system.

First of all, there are several of what I would like to call "fixed" places from which to see the mosaics, places in which the visitor—by choice or necessity because of the building itself—pauses and remains more or less motionless. Such are the four entrances which provide an immediate and particularly powerful access to the mosaics within the whole monument (figs. 25–26). Because of the symmetry of the building more or less the same effect is repeated four times, the external source of light being the only variable. Other fixed points—where one prays, for instance, or simply sits to meditate and to rest—provide alternate and more varied views of the mosaics, slightly different angles, more or less wide fields of vision. But nearly all the fixed points normally available have two characteristics pertinent to the perception of the mosaics and their understanding: they all cut through the whole building and thus acknowledge the mosaics as a succession of planes set transversely and, usually, perpendicularly to the path of vision. Wherever and however one looks into the interior of the building, the same sequence of planes—formed by the octagon, circular arcade, drum, circular arcade, octagon, outer walls and windows—appears. It is always clear that whatever can be seen of the inscription in mosaic on the octagon or the rest of the decoration signals continuity of design through either exact or approximate repetition without apparent beginnings or endings.[76]

One scholar dealing with the Dome of the Rock

Figure 25. Dome of the Rock, interior from the south door. The picture attempts to illustrate in one image the totality of what is visible as one enters the building. The lights have been equalized to highlight as much as possible of the interior. Note the lit center without the rock being clearly visible, the rings of ornament, especially mosaics, and, in particular, the artful way in which every plane of the building is visible.

has apparently realized that the mosaic decoration consists of a set of five ring-like surfaces (both sides of the octagon, circular arcade, two drums) set at different distances and angles from the same central point, which are only perceived, at any one time, in sections.[77] Both the designs and the technique of embedding mosaic cubes highlight some aspects of the compositions over others. Thus, the inward face of the octagon is much more colorful and much more comprehensible than the outward face. This is so primarily because the design expresses the "ring" function of a collection of items

set around a sacred spot, and in this scheme, the outer face of the octagon is more difficult to see in general and impossible to see across the building. The view of the inner face is also enhanced by the brilliance of its mother of pearl inlays and the variations in the angle of setting that make the mosaic cubes stand out from the darker surroundings. The major exception to a sense of continuity in the mosaics occurs in the decoration of the soffits of the octagon's arches. These long ribbons contain cubes with many more color variations than elsewhere in the building. Each soffit is unpredictably different

Figure 26. Dome of the Rock, interior from the north door. There is almost no difference from what would be seen on the south door (fig. 25).

from every other one and the composition of each so artfully arranged that the eye is drawn from the outside inward (figs. 25–27). They are like punctuation marks within a continuous discourse whose exact objective is not, at first glance, very clear.

A second way of viewing the mosaic decoration of the Dome of the Rock is that of a person moving in a circular path around the rock; reading the inscription on the sides of the octagon, which begins on the southern side, requires two successive walks around the inside the building, one clockwise and the other in reverse. The visitor moves along

(or between, if he is between the octagon and the circular arcade) a succession of decorated panels that do not progress (or at least do not appear to do so) toward a specific place or image that would seem to be the point of the whole exercise. It is as though the viewer were walking in an unending alley framed by two rows of hedges. The repetitive trees, bushes, and jewels set in vegetal rinceaux provide the reassuring presence of a surrounding space without surprises, and as one walks along the differences between individual panels of decoration are minimized. The colorful soffits are visible, but rarely in their entirety, and it is rather the large tie-beams covered with gilded bronze plaques and the lightly carved marble friezes that convey the viewer around a hallowed enclosure (fig. 27). The richly colored soffits of the arches catch the light coming from the outside and, like the landing lights of an airstrip, serve as beacons to lead the visitor around the building.

A third way of viewing the mosaics, the one most commonly used by art historians, extracts them from their architectural context and treats them as two-dimensional panels adapted to architectural spaces, defined by the constructed shapes they cover. But, in fact, the mosaics are designed, most of the time, to escape from the constrictions of these shapes rather than to emphasize the forms of their construction. This escape is accomplished in two ways: by dissolving the built forms in a festival of color not directly connected to the building's construction; and, as appears most clearly on the soffits of the octagon, by arranging the decoration in an asymmetric way, so as to emphasize passage from one zone of the building to the next one, rather than to privilege the specific structural shape of the soffit as an independent unit. The lower drum is a single band organized around sixteen closely packed vases each topped by a pair of wings and spouting a more or less symmetrical pair of spiral rinceaux (fig. 31). The upper drum is divided by windows into sixteen independent units (figs. 28–30). Elsewhere, large triangular areas with two curved sides—long rectangular ones, squat squarish ones, and long bands on the inner curves of the intrados—act as independent panels with different types of designs based on vegetal motifs occasionally associated with jewelry or insignias of some type.

It is in terms of the requirements of such flat areas that Marguerite van Berchem organized the only coherent presentation of the mosaics, a perfectly sensible one for the art historian who deals primarily with the relationship between forms and designs set in comparable spaces. But before assessing that particular relationship, which leads necessarily to the question how these mosaics were most

likely designed, we must, even if only hypothetically, define and explain the mosaics as part of a patron's commission.

These mosaics are found throughout the Dome of the Rock. They decorate the uppermost part of all vertical surfaces except for the cupola and the inner face of the outer walls. They were even included in the decoration of the outside of the building, but little is known about this rare example of exterior decoration.[78] Inside, they are part of a decorative program that began with some kind of floor covering. The rugs of today with their predominantly red colors were probably preceded by mats of some sort, which would have been restful to bare feet and easy to clean.[79] Colorful marble columns coiffed by richly ornamented capitals and piers and walls covered with marble plaques run from floor to ceiling. Whether the present combinations of marble plaques are the original ones is unclear, and it is difficult to define and explain the patterns created by these panels.[80] At times they form closed symmetrical compositions, at other times certain panels are orphaned in incongruous ensembles. Regardless of the patterns (or lack thereof), these pieces of cut marble transform flat surfaces into ordered spaces separated from each other by moldings and introduce subdued color tonalities as a key component of the building's interior. Creamy white dominates on flat surfaces and luscious green or gray on the columns, but the main feature of the marble zone in the elevation of the Dome of the Rock is the contrast between rigid frames and richly fluid surfaces. The contrast is strengthened by the ring of gilt marble[81] that follows the capitals along the circular arcade, and by the entablature of wooden beams covered with gilt plaques above the capitals of the octagon.

The mosaics occupy nearly all the vertical faces above the marble, and seen as a block, they provide consistency to the monument; motifs not easily identifiable in their detail appear like rich silk draping the upper part of the interior. This textile effect is strengthened by the shining brilliance of the mosaic surfaces and the glitter of the moving light from the windows, which competes with the

Figure 27. Dome of the Rock, interior, the eastern side of the building. The angle of the photograph is artificial, but it permits one to see the rich decoration in the mosaics and the contrast in width between the two octagonal areas. The rugs and ceiling are contemporary, for the most part.

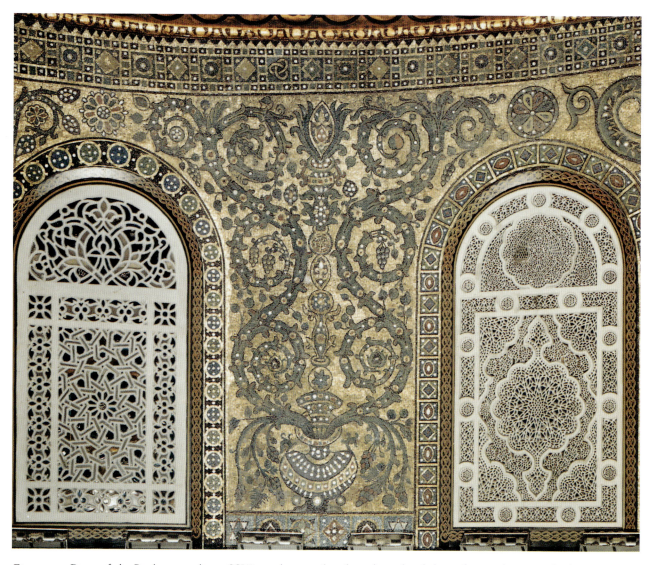

Figure 28. Dome of the Rock, upper drum, SSW panel, restored and partly replaced, but reflecting the original schema.

flickering light of hundreds of hanging lamps. The mosaics in the drums can be broadly distinguished from those in the ambulatories in color and in plan. In the drums, the gold background dominates and provides a forceful luminosity to the center of the building. In the ambulatories, the darker blue-greens of the vegetal motifs create a mysterious, shadowy ring around the light in the middle. One of the unique features of the Dome of the Rock is that the central focus of its plan is visible from all parts of the building and, as a result, the darker mosaics of the ambulatory continue beyond the

brightly colored central beam. It is as though the glow of light in the middle were something to contemplate, not something toward which one strives, since the "reality" in which the viewer stands reappears on the other side of the luminous center. There is, thus, a statement made by the mosaics within a broadly conceived decorative program, in part an iconographic statement, which emphasizes the center by manipulating frame and boundaries. But it is also, as is appropriate in architectural decoration, a functional statement directing the ways in which the visitor to the building is expected to

Figure 29. Dome of the Rock, upper drum, SW panel, restored but reflecting original design.

behave. On a more prosaic operational level, the mosaics of the Dome of the Rock act simultaneously as colorful forces manipulating spaces into light or dark areas, and defining the relationship between these zones, and as the continuous surfaces that hold the interior spaces together.

Nothing remains of the original ceiling of the Dome of the Rock. The coffered wooden panels, covered with decorated leather, are twentieth-century restorations of presumably Mamluk creation, and the dome itself is a contemporary recasting of an Ottoman dome. We can only speculate

about the Umayyad ceilings and perhaps propose that carved woodwork, akin to what remains in the Aqsa Mosque, was used in the Dome of the Rock as well.[82]

INSTEAD OF PROVIDING a new or modified list of motifs found in the mosaic decoration, I shall present the decoration as a series of panels or units of design, at times repeated. All the designs were chosen from pre-existing patterns and adapted to the requirements and opportunities of the building. By looking at the mosaic decoration in terms of identifiable units of composed surfaces rather than as "phonetic" motifs arranged in sets, one can propose a process that leads to the choices and, possibly, to the motivations behind the process.[83]

I will describe the units as they appear in the five main zones of decoration—the two drums, the circular arcade, and the two sides of the octagonal arcade—and will deal separately with the soffits of the arches of the octagon which pose a special problem. Finally, I will discuss whether it is reason-able to seek an iconographic meaning for the themes of these mosaics or whether to explain them as the articulation of some ideological, pious, imperial, or other idea. For the location of the mosaics in the building, see the diagram in figure 22.

The Upper Drum

Sixteen mosaic panels cover the upper drum, separated from each other by windows. A band of squares topped by a "crenulation" of gold cubes creates a border at the base of the dome proper

Figure 30. Dome of the Rock, upper drum, NNW panel, probably much redone.

(figs. 28–30). The squares are separated from each other by many squares with a single white mother-of-pearl dot. Every larger square contains one of two alternating motifs: a shining ring of gold around a red and green cube, or a diamond shaped gold border around a red or green fill. Originally, there may well have been a single and consistent rhythm in the sequence of these small motifs and the filling color, but too many thoughtless repairs have introduced inexplicable variants. Two curious details may, however, be noted. On the S and SSW (fig. 28) panels a knot is found close to the vertical axis of the design, and on the NNW (fig. 30) and NW there are several representations of tulip-like floral cups. It is difficult to argue for any deep significance associated with these details, but they may reflect some esoteric meaning, or they may be signatures of artisans or of teams of artisans. Most of this border has been much repaired, as can be illustrated by comparing it to the few instances (for instance S and SW, fig. 29) where a probably original Umayyad lower border has been preserved. The dully repetitive squares around the windows clearly belong to a very late "restoration."

Of the major designs in the drum, one (SSE) has been redone in a way that can bear no relationship to whatever was there originally, and seven (WSW, W, WNW, NNW, NW, SE, S) have been repaired or redone so clumsily that they reflect only the general shape of the initial design. The other eight panels are sufficiently close to each other in manner of execution and design to imply that they are all more or less successful modifications of original patterns and that some details in all of them are from Umayyad times. The SW and SSW panels (figs. 28–29) have retained more of the original design than the other panels: a heavily bejewelled vase (possibly framed by small trees) from which two vegetal variants emerge. One consists of two rinceaux, one on either side of a thin rod of bejewelled ornaments, culminating in a motif frequently seen in the Dome of the Rock: a sort of vegetal chalice harboring a crown or a bejewelled almond-shaped ornament; the rinceaux extend above the windows until they meet a rosette set on the vertical axis of each window. The

second variant is concentrated on the central rod and projects half palmettes covered with florets in mother-of-pearl on either side of the rod; the upper part of the design consists of large half palmettes turning back toward the center where bejewelled wings frame leaf patterns or costume jewelry.

These designs are executed on a gold background and the shining gold-plated glass cubes and mother-of-pearl fragments found in every lavish detail give this drum a rich splendor that almost compensates for the technical and compositional detraction of so many poorly restored panels. There is no internal evidence for dating these mosaics to establish an acceptable chronology for the restoration and repair of the panels, but all of them except one (SSE) probably reflect a design composed of the two variants. Whether the original design was in fact Umayyad cannot be demonstrated without technical and comparative analyses, but it is reasonable to argue that it provided a comparable effect.

The Lower Drum

Between two thick borders of diamonds with lines and dots of gold and mother-of-pearl set on green backgrounds, sixteen symmetrical compositions with the same dimensions share the same basic pattern. On the central axis, a jewelled vase holds various ill-defined items such as bejewelled pillows, decorative arches, or roundels, usually topped by a pair of wings framing a crown (figs. 31–32). The compositions vary considerably in the proportions of these respective parts and the exuberance of the various items piled up on the vases, and there seems to be no compositional, iconographic, or formal logic in the variations that occur, such as the sequence of thinner units found in the SSE, S, and SSW; differences in the shapes of the crowns and the presence of little arcades rather than pillows, as on the SE and W (fig. 32). The same difficulty in explaining variations affects the rinceaux, with their considerable differences in the fruits or leaves ending each volute or in the density of mother-of-pearl studs.

To these observations there are two exceptions.

Figure 31. Dome of the Rock, lower drum, S panel, reflects original design, but probably entirely redone in later times.

One is the NE unit (fig. 31), which contains no wings in the upper part of the composition and has extra crowns in the axial construction and unequal proportions between volutes in the scrolls. The central axis of this unit resembles patterns in the inner octagon, and I propose to attribute most of it to a restoration from a time when the original motifs were no longer understood but when there was still considerable competence in the laying of mosaics. The second exception, only partial, is found in the W unit, where the crown in the middle has been replaced by a floral design, while the rest of

the composition seems consistent with those elsewhere in the drum except for occasional repaired patches. The W panel is also remarkable in that it contains in its upper border the Fatimid inscription dating a repair (*murammah*) of the glass mosaics (*ballur*) in 418/1027–1028 (fig. 32). Some scholars have concluded that all the mosaics from the drum should be dated to the early Fatimid period,[84] which is possible, although I prefer an alternative explanation that restorations of high technical quality were accomplished in Fatimid times and included misunderstandings of original patterns. But,

Figure 32. Dome of the Rock, lower drum, W panel, partly restored. The inscription refers to glass mosaics and gives the date 418H/1027–1028 C.E.

Figure 33. Dome of the Rock, circular arcade, NE panel. The lower section is completely redone.

whoever made the repairs and whenever, the basic scheme remained that of the original Umayyad decoration of the *qubbah* in the foundation inscription and in early medieval texts.

The visual message of this initial program is quite clear: to create on a gold background a seemingly continuous band of brilliantly lit green scrolls out of which sixteen colorful constructions culminate in the wings associated with royalty in the Iranian tradition surrounding a beautiful tiara, without apparent cultural identification, and a variant of a lotus shape.[85] The requirement that the mosaics in the lower drum be perceived as an unbroken entity is further demonstrated by the care taken to hide or, at the very least, to downplay the separation between individual units of composition. Visible

from everywhere, but never seen all at once, the mosaics of the lower drum were intended to look the same from any vantage point, without a dominating moment or place, or a single focus.

The Circular Arcade

The mosaics of the circular arcade, at least in their present shape, are the most difficult to perceive in any consistent way, and because of their spatial awkwardness, restorations, and modifications of all sorts, the least rewarding to study. They are located directly above the marble facing of the arches and piers below, and end with a long wooden border set at an angle to the vertical face of the wall and painted, quite recently, in rather

Figure 34. Dome of the Rock, circular arcade, SW panel, repaired.

garish colors. The large squarish spaces of the corner piers project from the rest of the decoration, separated from it by a border of gold roundels with rosettes inside and gold florets between the roundels. In the one instance of the SW pier, this border decoration is continued into the lower part of the main design (fig. 34). All piers certainly had similar borders, and the green and gold cubes found there now are later additions. It is possible, although less clear, that such a border extended above and possibly framed all the mosaics of the arcade.

Four continuous compositions begin (or end) with narrow vertical rectangles on the sides of the piers and then continue through three units of symmetrical design whose compositional axis corresponds to the top of a column. The circular arcade, in contrast to the drums, has no single continuing design, but a series of eight discrete compositions (four projecting piers and four triple arcades) on two different planes. Even a rapid glance at the mosaics of this arcade reveals so many oddities in composition or details of execution that there is little doubt of many repairs and restorations. It is possible that a microanalysis of sizes and qualities of cubes could suggest a chronology of these repairs, but except for the history of mosaic technique, such a chronology would be of little value because the basic structure of the original design is fairly clear, even though most of the significant later changes like the "lettuce heads" on the NE pier or over the ENE column are simply awful (fig.

Figure 35. Dome of the Rock, circular arcade, NE panel, left side.

Figure 36. Dome of the Rock, circular arcade, NE panel, right side.

33). The original design consisted of scrolls of two slightly different leafy types issuing either from vases or from a thick arrangement of acanthus leaves and then unrolling in harmoniously composed volutes (figs. 35, 36). There probably were jewel-like effects of colored mosaics or mother-of-pearl on some of the tendrils, as on the SW pier (fig. 37), and on some of the terminal flowers and leaves. But I am rather doubtful about the presence of structured compositions of ornament such as appear now on the right side of the NE pier, and I prefer to argue that only the left side of that pier has preserved its original design, including even spaces for a border now gone. The mosaics of the circular arcade are not good examples of the origi-

nal Umayyad decoration. But to the extent they do represent it, they suggest a rather subdued decoration of lightly lit green leaves on a gold background without any emphasis on a particular motif, form, or effect.

The Outer Face of the Octagon

The mosaics of the octagon have been much better preserved than those of the drums and circular arcade, largely because they were protected from the most vulnerable part of the building, its dome. They were probably also less affected by such changes as may have occurred in the use of the building—for instance, under the rule of the Crusaders. Only the southeastern section (292° left, 308°, 322°, 338° right) underwent considerable changes, including the addition of jewels, apparently at a time when the objects and motifs represented had lost their original meaning, but when competent mosaicists were still available. There are numerous traces of repairs, and in a few places more significant changes may have been made, but, on the whole, the basic design of the original decoration remains. The thirty-two decorated panels are carefully framed by the inscription above and by a broad band of roundels below, which, when appropriate, merges into the design of the soffits. Gold, light green, and very dark green areas dominate in the border and create patterns which can be read as gold on two kinds of green or in other combinations of these colors.

The decoration of all the panels is constructed around a composite tree, best preserved in its original shape in the northern arcade (158°–202°; figs. 38–39). The trunk may be read as a leafy vertical composition or a succession of heart-shaped elements imbricated into each other; many variations occur on both of these motifs, as, for instance, a trunk that appears to have been split open and stuffed with vegetal and other forms (292° right).[86] The most unusual compositions occur above the trunks of trees. Thick tendrils bearing fruits and long leaves often designed in chevrons or other non-natural patterns broaden out symmetrically to enclose an ovoid, highly decorated shape. The latter may have been related to representations of pomegranates, but they have undergone many modifications and whatever vegetal origin they may have had is often obscured. Bunches of grapes or dates hang down or project into corners. The de-

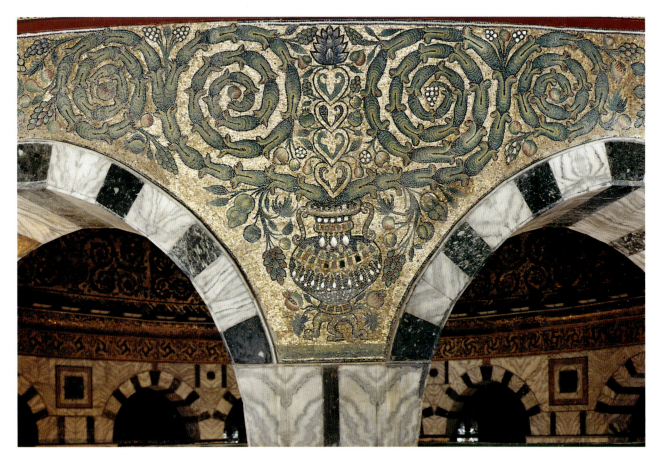

Figure 37. Dome of the Rock, circular arcade, N panel with second type of base in the design.

Figure 38. Dome of the Rock, outer octagon (158°), restored.

sign is highly symmetrical, except when the panels are over a pier and extend over a spandrel. The extension of the floral designs into these triangular corners is often rather awkward and, in one striking example (22°; fig. 40), the restorer simply left the area blank. One tree (0°; fig. 41) contains two words whose date and purpose remain a mystery (see n. 83).

It is true, as earlier writers have already pointed out, that the construction of such artificial tree-like units is unknown in the vocabulary of Mediterranean mosaic or painted designs, but occurs in late Sasanian secular buildings and objects, silver or textiles, from Iran.[87] While perhaps presenting an interesting puzzle for a study of the transmission of sources for these motifs, Iranian origins do not explain what these motifs are doing in this building. I propose to interpret them, located as they are, just under the litanies invoking the powers and qualities of God and the position of His Prophet, as a ring

of non-terrestrial trees surrounding a sanctuary, a shrine. That they are artificial constructions of the imagination of artists and patrons with a wide artistic vocabulary at their disposal is clear enough, but beyond their possible function of representing a world other than that of the senses, they also evoke something else. They are full of life, their tendrils and branches bursting with life-creating force and heavy with fruits: the "other" world of the trees is shown as a living world.

This set of mosaics is also instructive about a creative process that is probably applicable to other sectors of the mosaic decoration. It suggests that a single type of tree design was provided to the artisans who were then fairly free to develop their own variants. It is logical enough to assume this way of organizing whatever work force was available, but such a method is reaffirmed by the mosaics themselves. As one looks at the sequence of these richly laden tree forms, one can imagine that artisans competed to create the most effective, most luxuriant tree.

The Inner Face of the Octagon

The inner face of the octagon has a more complicated structure than the outer one because of the piers projecting inward from the arcade. But, in addition, its general composition was more carefully thought out, no doubt because it is the most consistently visible part of the mosaic decoration. Narrow borders with several different repeated motifs, all from traditional Mediterranean patterns for borders,[88] outline broad areas of decoration without intruding into those areas, in contrast to what happens on the outer side of the octagon (figs. 42–49). On top of every arch a dark blue circular shape with a five, six, or eight point star in gold separates one section from the next. Just as everywhere else in the mosaic decoration, there are

many areas of minor repairs and several major transformations, but the basic organization of the decoration is the original one, even when, as in the cases of 67° to 22° (fig. 43), the execution is awkward.

The rectangular segments of eight piers contain variations on the same theme: a bed of acanthus leaves from which emerge two symmetrically arranged rinceaux with two volutes each, the rinceaux always different from each other in details (fig. 42 or 43). The sixteen long and narrow spaces on the side of the projecting piers are at present divided into two groups. Eight of them contain trees the trunks of which are covered at times with jewels, but which in several instances (338° right or 292°) appear to be almost illusionistic representations of palm trees with heavy bunches of dates (fig. 44); a few others (202°, left and right) are depicted according to the conventions of Late Antique art for the representation of trees, but their

Figure 39. Dome of the Rock, outer octagon (277°), repaired.

exact botanical identification is not clear.[89] The other eight are curious composite constructions of vases, plants, and other ornaments (fig. 46), topped off with some sort of fruit or a colorful, flower-like creation. There does not seem to be an order or a rhythm in the choice of one or the other motif, nor is it possible to argue that one is later than the other, although the second type has been affected by many more alterations than the first one.[90]

The most striking feature of the inner face of the octagon is the way the sixteen panels appear to spread from the capitals of the columns to the top of the arches on either side. From a vase or comparable vessel, or in a few cases from a tree trunk, a symmetrically constructed arrangement of branches extends toward the top of the spandrels and encloses a central bud in the manner of the compositions on the outer face. Most of the branches end with a rich array of fruits, among which pomegranates, dates, and grapes are recognizable, or with

flowers (fig. 42). Some branches are covered with jewels, while others are also encrusted with sets of small floral scrolls. The most stunning feature of these panels is that they all display crowns, pectorals, brooches, tiaras, bracelets, and other jewelry (figs. 42–49) and the bright colors transform the panel into a brilliant display of overwhelming wealth, a fantasy of riches or possibly the iconographic expression of some now unintelligible message. Even obviously redone panels (like 38° or 52°) shine like originals. Furthermore, the fascination with jewels has extended to many other parts of the decoration of the inner face of the octagon, so that motifs on piers and fill-ins on the spandrels between arches and piers occasionally contain sequences of jewels, specific pieces of jewelry, or precious stones set in the most incongruous ways. In a few possibly restored areas, the festival of jewels—brooches, bracelets, nacklaces, pectorals, earrings—is almost overwhelming (fig. 49).

The effect of this inner face as a brilliant ring of

Figure 40. Dome of the Rock, outer octagon (22°), restored.

Figure 41. *Dome of the Rock, outer octagon (128°), later (?) inclusion of a small inscription,* lilah al-hamd *("praise to God").*

jewels and color is not only powerfully visual, it is also unique and no other monument with comparable decoration exists or has been recorded. Also unique is the combination of natural vegetal and manufactured elements in a continuous sequence in which no two panels are alike and yet appear the same.[91] This diversity within sameness provides yet another clue to explain the decoration of the Dome of the Rock.

The task of identifying and cataloguing the jewelry systematically is still to be done, but many scholars have already noted that the vast majority of the items represented, when they can be identified, are the official insignia or decorative apparel of Byzantine emperors and, most particularly, empresses, or of high dignitaries of the Byzantine court, as they appear in the mosaics of Ravenna, ivory diptychs, and elsewhere.[92] In one instance only (231°) have I detected the wings of an Iranian crown. The more insidious problem is whether

these features should be explained, as I did over thirty-five years ago, as culturally specific elements recognized as such and represented in order to specify Byzantine or Iranian, male or female, associations; or whether they must be interpreted as expensive offerings in a shrine, or as evocations of something else: a building, a memory, or an expectation.

This problem cannot be resolved yet, but nearly every area of the mosaics in the Dome of the Rock contrasts an initial impression of sameness with endlessly inventive variations which seem to frustrate the likelihood of a single purpose.

The Soffits of the Arches

It has already been pointed out that the mosaics on the twenty-four soffits of the octagon's arches play an unusual, but very sophisticated, part in the overall effect created by the decoration of the Dome of

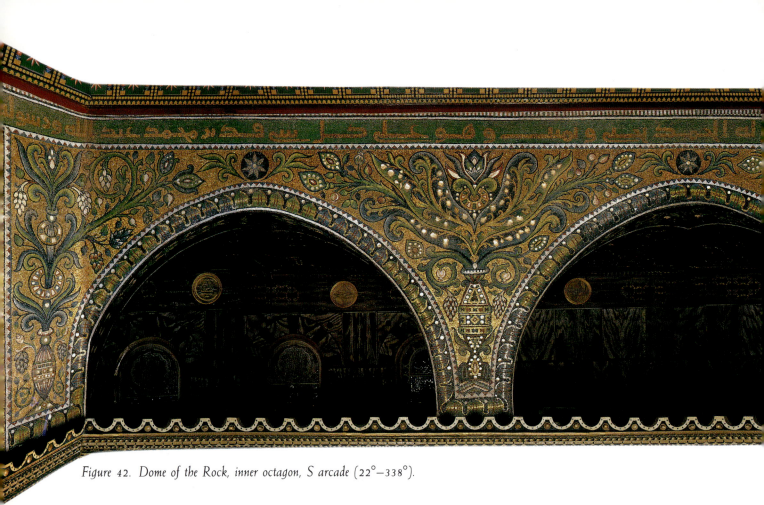

Figure 42. *Dome of the Rock, inner octagon, S arcade (22°–338°).*

Figure 43. *Dome of the Rock, inner octagon, SE arcade (338°–292°).*

Figure 44. Dome of the Rock, inner octagon, E arcade (292°–246°).

Figure 45. Dome of the Rock, inner octagon, NE arcade (246°–202°).

Figure 46. *Dome of the Rock, inner octagon, N arcade (202°–158°).*

Figure 47. *Dome of the Rock, inner octagon, NW arcade (158°–113°).*

Figure 48. Dome of the Rock, inner octagon, W arcade (113°–67°).

Figure 49. Dome of the Rock, inner octagon, SW arcade (67°–22°).

the Rock, a series of diacritical or punctuation marks that interrupt the flow of the dark green ornamental rings. These soffits are unusual is several other ways. Even though they are all composed and executed in the same manner, they are all different from each other. One-fourth of their surface is taken by the border from the outer face of the octagon which serves as a transition from one space to the other; the roundels involved in this border are the same throughout. Each soffit also has a long narrow band with three variant designs: an elegant vegetal scroll (fig. 50), a succession of multi-petaled, multicolored rosettes, sometimes with intermediary heart-shaped florets (figs. 51, 52), or a succession of alternating rosettes and half-rosettes (fig. 53). The last of these motifs is found on only three consecutive arches (22°, 38°, 52°) in the southwestern quadrant and, since this particular quadrant's mosaics above the soffits have been much repaired, it is possible that the mosaics on these soffits belong to a late but highly competent restoration. It is tempting to imagine that scrolls and single rosettes originally alternated, but the evidence is not conclusive.

With two exceptions (338° and 277°), to which I shall return, a single motif occupies one half of each soffit. No two motifs are alike, but there are obvious groupings among them with internal variations: guilloches (83°, 113°); vegetal scroll (128°, 202°, 246°, 263°, 308°); vegetal rings with realistic fruits like grapes or pomegranates, appearing at times with baskets and other implements (142°, 218°, 353°, 22°, 526°) (fig. 53); cornucopias and vases mixed with vegetation (173°, 187°, 231°); more or less geometricized units (242°, 322°, 6°); two very remarkable series (38°, 67°) of large leaves carrying identifiable fruits and sheafs of grass (figs. 54–55).[93] Of the two exceptional soffits, one (277°) has an allover pattern of medallions and the other (338°) a similar pattern of leaves. The former shows an unusually awkward execution that must be attributed to a later repair.

In all the soffits, even the last two, the central and highest point on the arch is always clearly indicated as the axis of composition, even though the ways of marking that axis vary considerably. Fur-

thermore, one half is always better executed than the other, even in instances like 277° which were clearly restored. The explanation is almost certainly that a master craftsman executed one half of the design and an apprentice finished it up with considerable leeway. Beyond this I am not able to propose any reasonable explanation for the sequence or location of any one particular decorative pattern[94] and no clear iconographic purpose seems sufficient to explain the realism of some of the fruits or the presence of any of the items shown on the soffits. It is, however, possible that different motifs were associated with different teams of artisans and that the thematic variety exhibited by the soffits illustrates a degree of freedom for these teams to show their competence and the range of their abilities. Yet it could also be argued that the soffits were an exhibition of a single team's breadth of possibilities. Whatever the correct interpretation, the soffits remain a stunning array of decorative elements, whose quality and imagination far surpass all the examples I have been able to gather in the mostly Mediterranean sources for these motifs. But, even though their execution is of superior quality, these panels find close parallels elsewhere, especially the floor mosaics so common all over the Mediterranean. In this, they are strikingly different from the rest of the building's mosaics.

Wherever one looks at these mosaics, even in the most damaged upper drum of the dome, there is an unusual equilibrium between a small number of basic patterns of composition and subjects—vegetal scrolls, trees, body or costume jewelry, composite constructions of objects like vases of vegetal ornament, and so on—and the considerable variations in their actual execution. Two explanations can be proposed for this contrast. One explanation alluded to above is that there were several teams of mosaicists at work in the decoration of the building, each group with its own formal and technical procedures. Probably called or hired from elsewhere, most likely Constantinople but perhaps Saloniki or even Italy, these teams were given broad mandates or briefs based either on oral descriptions of what was wanted or on choices made through some sampling system in current operation.[95] Then each team covered the space assigned to it and perhaps (as could be suggested by the soffits of the arches) divided the work among the team. This explanation could apply to the time of Abd al-Malik's construction, but it also might be relevant to repairs and restorations before those carried out during the 1960s, when once again mosaicists were brought from elsewhere (Italy). In all instances, however, the models used were of the late seventh century and the Umayyad period.[96] Eventually, the microanalysis of the technique of mosaics in the manner accomplished in San Marco in Venice and in Torcello could provide precise groupings of teams, or of original creators and later restorers operating according to their own tradition. Then a true chronology of repairs will indeed be possible. But it is worth noting that high levels of technical competence appear in several restorations, thus suggesting the availability of qualified craftsmen over many centuries.

The second explanation for the contrast between a coherent vision and a great variance in execution lies in the apparent uniqueness of the Dome of the Rock decoration. It is possible to argue that a tradition existed for the transformation of the interior of buildings, usually churches or other ecclesiastical structures like baptisteries, through mosaics. Santa Constanza as the earliest of a Roman series, a celebrated group of fifth- and sixth-century churches and baptisteries in Ravenna, and St. George in Saloniki are all examples of buildings in which mosaics were used to create a powerful impact. The Church of the Holy Sepulchre in Jerusalem, the Church of St. John in Ephesus, religious and secular buildings in Gaza known from texts, and the still standing Church of St. Catherine on Mt. Sinai, all somewhat closer to the Dome of the Rock, also contained important mosaic panels.[97] But the only buildings earlier than the Dome of the Rock where interiors were truly dominated, in fact transfigured, by mosaics are the small baptisteries and mausoleums of Ravenna, the very special Church of St. George in Saloniki installed in a Roman mausoleum, and possibly the Gaza buildings. Except perhaps for the last, it is difficult to postulate a relationship to Jerusalem and its Umayyad patrons. In other words, there was no immediate model for the mosaics in the Dome of the Rock and the decoration is the result of many different responses to imposed themes. What were those themes and directives?[98]

What is most evidently absent from this decoration is a clear hierarchy in the importance and significance to be given to individual forms. What is present is the rich texture of an exuberant, often bejewelled and luxuriant foliage around an architectural space. It is partly a vegetation derived from the surrounding world of nature, and partly an imaginary vegetation, full of fantasy, embellished with hanging crowns and jewels directed toward the center of the building. Just as the inscriptions were, in the final analysis, prayers and readings for a place rather than for men to peruse, so it is that this luxuriant fantasy of variations on the theme of nature directs its display of wealth to the consecrated space rather than to the pleasure or instruction of the pious. The idea of an art not to be seen, of a message not to be received, was a new one, or almost. While in the Christian and pagan spheres, liturgies, a priesthood, and several levels of narrative and ritual behavior almost always organized holy spaces toward a goal—the altar, the tabernacle, the relic of a saint, a consecrated image, the place of sacrifice—only in the Ka'bah in Mekkah was there a shared knowledge that expensive offerings from many lands had been donated to a sanctuary but these donations were not seen by the faithful except on a few, very rare, ritual occasions. In the Dome of the Rock, a rich and imaginary landscape was depicted on which wondrous gifts were exhibited.[99] It was a landscape to be seen and felt, not one in which specific ritual actions were required.[100]

Whether access to these mosaics was restricted as in Mekkah, or as it would become later on in Jerusalem, cannot be demonstrated for the Umayyad period. But it is likely that their brilliance was heralded by yet another unique aspect of the Dome of the Rock, the fact that the exterior of the building was also decorated in color. Hardly anything is known about these exterior mosaics, of which a few fragments were seen late in the nineteenth

Figure 50. Dome of the Rock, soffit of octagon (308°).

Figure 51. Dome of the Rock, soffit of octagon (292°).

Figure 52. Dome of the Rock, soffit of octagon (60°).

Figure 53. Dome of the Rock, soffit of octagon (22°).

Figure 54. Dome of the Rock, soffit of octagon (38°).

Figure 55. Dome of the Rock, soffit of octagon (67°).

century, but it is tempting to assume that the colorful sixteenth-century tiles that now cover the building replaced an equally colorful mosaic decoration. Such external decoration in color is virtually unknown before Umayyad times,[101] but it is once again the memory of Mekkah and a series of other pious associations affecting the Dome of the Rock that may explain the decoration of the building.[102]

The Shape of the Building

The first of two related issues that have dominated the rather considerable literature on the shape of the Dome of the Rock considers the sources for its plan and for some of its construction features like tie-beams and stained glass windows.[103] None of the numerous studies dealing with minute details of construction or decoration discusses the elevation of the building as a whole nor, in more general ways, the manner in which its structure affects and controls the visitor's vision and behavior. The elevation, however, plays a significant part in the second issue of scholarly concern with the Dome of the Rock: the modular base and the system of proportions that govern its geometry and the magnetic and harmonious effect of that geometry.[104]

The Dome of the Rock is a building of extreme simplicity (figs. 19–21). Its skeleton is clearly visible under mosaic or other decoration, inside or outside: an octagonal ring of two ambulatories around a high cylinder, the whole fitted over an enormous but uneven asymmetrical outcropping of black rock. Its four entrances were originally alike, with small vaulted porches covered by mosaic ceilings projecting from the doors. There was no single or multiple entrance or facade and nothing seems to indicate which, if any, of the existing four entrances would have been the preferred one. The outer walls are like a thin membrane, hardly needed for the construction, a temporary veil like a theatrical flat or a Japanese screen. Initially some scholars had even wondered whether the original *qubbah* was not an open building, a possibility denied by the physical evidence but suggested by the visual one.

The Dome of the Rock appears as a monument constructed in order to make a statement for the whole city of Jerusalem and for its surroundings (figs. 56–57). In a most dramatic way, it is the first landmark in the city seen by anyone coming from the East, turning the corner of the Jericho road at Bethany or climbing to top of the Mount of Olives where the high tower of the Church of the Ascension stood. It is a constant magnet as one moves up from the South, although the steepness of the hill and the height of the walls make it disappear from view before it emerges again, slowly and almost theatrically, as one enters the area of the platform through the underground passages of the Triple and especially the Double Gates (fig. 57). It is less striking from the North, where the terrain of the city climbs steeply up and soon hides it from view, but it is very effective seen from the West, from the older Christian city. It became the visual rival of the Holy Sepulchre and the Nea church. It is seen immediately as one leaves the Holy Sepulchre (fig. 58), signaling the rebirth, under a new Muslim guise, of the old Jewish Temple area, and it is taller than the Christian sanctuary, even though the hill on which it is located is slightly lower than Golgotha.[105] It competes also with the Nea by occupying another visible outcrop in the complex topography of Jerusalem. Even though the exact condition of the Nea at the end of the seventh century is uncertain, it must at least have been an impressive ruin on a rocky edge.[106] The deliberate attempt to be visually arresting at a distance explains the unusual height of the central cylinder of the Dome of the Rock, a feature recognized in all of its later representations, for example, the Crusader sculpture of it now embedded on the portal of the Sultan Hassan madrasah in Cairo,[107] made popular by Bernhard von Breydenbach in the late fifteenth century.

But the Dome of the Rock was not only a remote visual sign, a magnetic invitation to visit, or the mark of a Muslim presence. Its effectiveness is not the same in all parts of the city, nor is its presence heralded through other monumental signs, like, for instance, minarets in Cairo, or obelisks and cupolas in later Rome. Just as is true for important

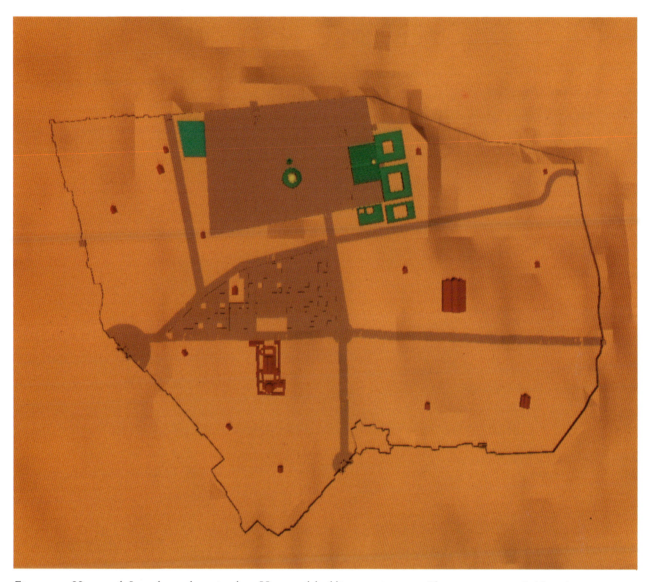

Figure 56. Umayyad Jerusalem, schematic plan. Umayyad buildings are in green, Christian ones in red. Note the concentration of Umayyad constructions around the platform of Mt. Moriah on the upper right.

buildings in Isfahan and probably in many other Near Eastern cities, the magnetic force is transmitted to the streets leading to it, for a view of the Dome disappears as one comes close to it.[108] It cannot be seen from the street along the Herodian western wall of the Haram and only reappears once the platform is reached. For the late seventh century only southern accesses to the platform are documented (fig. 59), but there may have been a southwestern entry through an underground passageway and some sort of access from the north and the northwest may have existed, although the

life and layout of that quarter of town under the Umayyads remains very unclear.

The first point, then, about the architecture of the Dome of the Rock is its forceful message to the whole city. This message was self-contained in the sense that the shape of the colorful, shining building with its small, almost invisible, entrances, did not *a priori* require a visit inside to understand it, in contrast to the Holy Sepulchre, and to most Christian martyria and churches, whose clearly marked facades convey a hierarchy of form and function for the exterior of the building and an urgency to

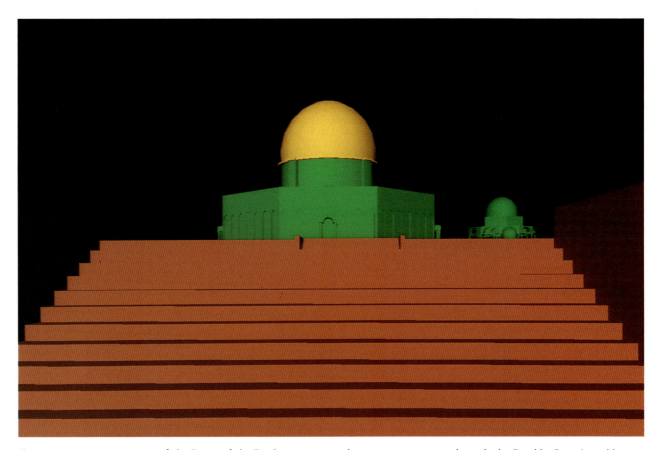

Figure 57. A reconstruction of the Dome of the Rock as it appeared to someone entering through the Double Gate (possibly already already known as the Gate of the Prophet) under the Aqsa Mosque. The Dome of the Chain is to the right.

participate in whatever takes place inside. It belongs to a relatively rare category of shrines, architectural compositions that seem more important by what they are than by what happens in them. The most obvious comparable shrine is one of particular significance for our purposes, the Ka'bah in Mekkah, which has been mentioned more than once as a parallel to the Dome of the Rock.

The attributes of a shrine are still evident once one has reached the platform of the Haram itself and especially the second platform, whose justification in Umayyad times, although difficult to determine, appears to be primarily to make the Dome of the Rock higher. After the dramatic view of the Dome of the Rock from wherever one enters the lower platform, the power of the whole building diminishes, as the visitor, advancing, sees only a succession of identical wall segments with four small porches, without the funneling effect of an

elaborate facade. We know nothing about who was permitted or who was required to enter the shrine, or whether rules existed to determine access, although the relatively insignificant doorways suggest that entry must have been limited to those who already knew what the building it was.[109]

Two particularly important architectural characteristics, already alluded to in the discussion of the decoration, are expressed through the sophisticated manipulation of very simple architectural elements. One is what Creswell called the "annular" character of the building, its ring-like sense of circular movement with no indication—through decoration or planning or elevation—of a hierarchy of parts, of an obvious beginning and end. The only sense of a direction lies in the inscriptions that begin on the southern side of the octagon and are read clockwise and counterclockwise in succession. Is it possible to deduce from this that, in the late seventh century, the normal entrance into the building was from the south and that two consecutive walks in opposite directions were expected (or required) of those who entered? Most early Islamic settlements were to the south of the platform and one of the underground passages from there to the platform opened directly on to the Dome of the Rock. But from the point of view of the building, south was the *qiblah*, the direction of prayer, and one may question whether a Muslim building with pious functions would have had its major entrance to the south. In short, such internal hierarchies in the annular space of the building as may emerge remain quite uncertain in the absence of a known or likely context of pious behavior. This difficulty will weigh heavily in the explanation I shall ultimately propose for the Dome of the Rock.

One point about the ring-like arrangement already noted by several observers is that the apparent geometric purity of the layout of the two arcades has, in fact, been slightly altered in one place.[110] The location of the supports of the central circular arcade and the columns of the octagon have been shifted by about 3° which insures that the visitor is able to see clearly the supporting arcades across the whole building. It appears that one is expected to see through the building, from darkness to the light in the middle and to darkness again before reaching the outer wall and the door leading outside. The horizontal gaze of the visitor crosses the building and does not end in an apse or on the statue of a god inside the monument (figs. 25–26). This relatively small detail is indicative, I feel, of the very thoughtful way in which the designers of the Dome of the Rock used the models and principles at their disposal. The absence of other hierarchies in the organization of the annular space may therefore be seen as the result of a fully thought-out architectural decision.

The second essential feature of the Dome of the Rock is the domination of the central cylindrical space set over the rock by a shaft of brilliant light at the core of the building. There is nothing unusual or unexpected about the focus on the main dome in a centrally planned building. The peculiarity of the Dome of the Rock is that neither the cupola nor even the rock can be perceived from most places inside the building, only the light from the drums under the dome as it beams down. For the dome the matter is clear, as the height of the cylinder (over three times that of the ring) makes it nearly impossible to see the crowning achievement of the building unless one stands directly under it, which is difficult to do since the circular arcade circumscribes the rock quite closely. The dome was primarily for external display, to be seen throughout the city and its surroundings, not as a phenomenon inside the building, as in the Pantheon, the Rotunda of the Holy Sepulchre, and the Church of the Ascension atop the Mount of Olives. It is more difficult to ascertain whether the rock itself was visible inside the building. In later years and until quite recently, all sorts of screens or balustrades shielded it from view and, even today, when only a very low balustrade surrounds it, the rock cannot be easily seen (fig. 25). This may mean that the building was planned in such a way that the specificity of the holy object—a rock to be touched or perhaps only seen—was replaced by the general evocation of something holy but almost invisible, a secret shared by the faithful, an invisible presence consciously designed into the building.[111]

Let us turn now to a reconstruction of the process by which the Dome of the Rock was created with a clearer sense of what it is that we are trying to understand. It is not the plan or a set of dimensions that requires explanation, rather it is a completed, still standing, object with its own unique set of formal and visual peculiarities. As to the basic shape, a circle surrounded by a double octagonal ambulatory, there is little doubt that the model for the Dome of the Rock was a fairly common type in Late Antique and Early Christian or early Byzantine architecture. Originating in the mostly funerary architecture of the late Roman empire (the tomb of Diocletian in Spalato, of Santa Costanza in Rome), it became a common form for baptisteries all over the Christian world and included the two monumental ones built in Ravenna for the Orthodox and for the Arians, with mosaic decoration, as we have mentioned, comparable in its effectiveness to that of the Dome of the Rock. The shape was found occasionally in commemorative churches, most strikingly in Jerusalem in the rotunda around the Holy Sepulchre, the octagonal Church of the Ascension on the Mount of Olives, and the so-called Tomb of the Virgin in the Kedron valley.[112] It appears even in secular buildings, or for buildings intermediary between secular and religious such as the Great Palace in Constantinople.[113] It appears in a small group of congregational churches, usually connected with some formal or official setting, such as the archbishop's palace at Bosra in southern Syria, San Vitale in Ravenna, or the somewhat later Carolingian Palace church in Aachen. Two Palestinian examples are the Church of the Virgin on Mount Gerizim and the mysterious octagonal church (if this is what it is) recently discovered in Caesarea.[114] As Ecochard and others have demonstrated, all of these buildings were planned according to standard ratios between the circumference of the circle circumscribing the whole building and the one around its focal center. And Doron Chen may well be right in arguing that all these ratios approximate the Golden Mean and were current in Palestinian building practices.

But the plan of the Dome of the Rock is distinguishable from the plans of most comparable buildings by its inordinate size and by the perfection of

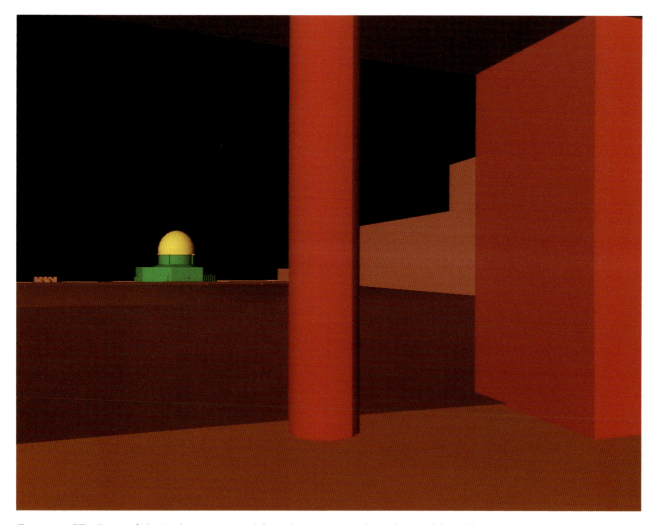

Figure 58. The Dome of the Rock as it appeared from the entrance to the Holy Sepulchre. The column belongs to the cardo *or main street from which the church was reached.*

Figure 59. Umayyad Jerusalem, bird's-eye view from the southeast: from left to right, the new "settlements," the Aqsa Mosque, the Triple Gate, the Dome of the Rock, the Dome of the Chain.

its symmetries around multiple axes without visible focus or direction. In terms of size, the churches of San Vitale and Aachen , the possible *martyrium* in Caesarea, and the two sanctuaries of Jerusalem are the only ones that are close to the Dome of the Rock, and in both the Church of the Ascension and San Vitale, the circle circumscribing the building has the same diameter as the Dome of the Rock. In terms of axes, only the Church of the Ascension and the church at Caesarea are symmetrical on several axes and appear to lack an apse for an altar or a monumental entrance, but both are only known from miserable archaeological remains.

Since so few of the comparable examples have been preserved, it is difficult to demonstrate the originality, or lack thereof, of the elevation of the Dome of the Rock. But the still standing examples of Aachen, Ravenna, and, immensely redone though it is, of the Holy Sepulchre, as well as liturgical or symbolic information derived from written sources, separate the Dome of the Rock quite radically from its parallels. Alone among them, it has a dome that is more important as a sign to be seen from afar than as a visible focus of an interior architectural composition. And alone among them, it has no focus toward which one is directed to go, only one around which one may process. The whole geometry of the building's construction creates a visually magnetic shell for something sacred or holy, but does not make the liturgical usage clear and, in this respect, it separates itself from the whole liturgical tradition of Christian churches and baptisteries.

Altogether then, the conclusions to be drawn from an analysis of the architectural forms of the Dome of the Rock are remarkably similar to the ones derived from the consideration of its decoration. All the forms belong to the language of Late Antique art in the Mediterranean area. In all aspects of planning, design, and even construction (ashlar masonry, piers, columns), the Dome of the Rock could have been a work of seventh-century Byzantine, Italian, possibly even western European architecture, for the remarkable feature of all the arts issuing from the Roman empire was their technical potential to provide for new needs and new functions. They had accommodated Christian art and contributed to Jewish and Buddhist arts.[115] These imperial arts and workmanship are the source in the new Muslim culture for an architecture for the mosque and a new type of palace, in addition to providing a template for urban order.

How did they affect the Dome of the Rock, a monument enclosing a mystery and proclaiming its presence in a city, a monument whose fact of existence was more significant than whatever other function it may have had? Because of the quality of its harmonious proportions (and its decoration), it transcends its meanings and its functions and exercises a continual visual magnetism. Some unusual manipulations of the geometry—the inordinate height of the cupola, the slight shift in positions of some of the columns, the power of light in the center of the building—have led to a work of architectural art that demands rationalization in each period of its history, because no one can remain indifferent to its aesthetic merit and at the same time no one has adequately explained its intended purpose.

On a more prosaic and technical level, the intriguing question is how the design of the Dome of the Rock came about. Did an idea, a wish, come from a single person or from a group of people? Was it then translated into building by an architectural team? Were specific proposals made from an existing vocabulary? Should we, then, conclude that there existed closer models to the shape of the building than we know? However one answers these questions, if indeed they can be answered at all, the sophistication of thought and imagination in the shaping of the building remains astounding.

The Location of the Building

The last original document I present about the Dome of the Rock is its location. It is indeed difficult to imagine the incorporation of this specific and idiosyncratic spot—an enormous rocky and shapeless outcrop with an underground cavern—into the building's design, unless there were a deep meaning associated with that spot. But, in reality, as we have seen in connection with the story of the caliph Umar's trip to accept Jerusalem for Islam, there was no clear and unequivocal single meaning attached to the Rock at the time of the conquest. It probably served as a reminder of the Temple for Jews, but no one knew then (or, for that matter, knows now) how this huge promontory would have accommodated the Temple.[116] It was hidden from view by Christians, who covered the area with refuse; for them it was probably an unidentified part of the justly destroyed Temple. It is particularly difficult to understand what the rock meant to Muslims at the time of the conquest, because later associations were easily projected backwards into the seventh century. In trying to stay as close as possible to the sources of the time and to a certain conception of historical logic in that area, I proposed that in 637–640, Muslim Arabs and the first Jewish and Christian converts to Islam associated several allusions in the Koran or from the early Traditions with the ruins on Mount Moriah. There was the first qiblah, the mihrab Dawud, perhaps already some general and vague associations with the isra', the Night-Journey of the Prophet to the masjid al-Aqsa (K 17:1), and possibly also with the spaces of Solomon's Temple and palace.[117] But I argued that in 637–640 these associations were very general and involved in fact the whole city of Jerusalem, with the ruined southeastern corner simply as the convenient locus for associations that required topical specificity.

Four major changes took place during the half-century that separates the conquest from the building of the Dome of the Rock. First, a quasi-imperial state was created under the leadership of the patrician Arab family of the Umayyads, an empire in size (in 690 it extended roughly from present day Algeria to the Oxus in Central Asia) and wealth, perhaps also in the ambitions of leaders like Mu'awiyah or Abd al-Malik and some of their brilliant local governors. But its political and administrative organization and its ethos were still very much those of what has been called an "Arabian kingdom."[118] A number of stories from Christian and Muslim sources associate Jerusalem with Umayyad imperial ambitions or, at the very least, with expressions of authority and power. The Muslim chronicler Tabari is very brief and simply says that in 661–662 Jerusalem was the place where allegiance was sworn to Mu'awiyah.[119] Christian sources are more extensive, but also more bizarre and less credible, exhibiting the kind of inventiveness that assumes an audience without direct knowledge of the events described. A chronicle of 664 relates that Mu'awiyah was made king in Jerusalem, where he walked from Golgotha to Gethsemane, and eventually to the Tomb of the Virgin in the valley to the east of the Haram. The total bypass of the Haram itself is peculiar and the whole event is interpreted as a wicked one, since a destructive earthquake occurs as a result. The chronicler adds that the amirs proffered their right hands to Mu'awiyah, that an order went out announcing his kingship in all the villages and cities of his realm, and that people were instructed to issue "proclamations and invocations" in his honor.[120] The text adds that Mu'awiyah, unlike other kings, never wore his crown, but I am not clear about the point of this particular remark. An account of various disasters, dated to 716, alleges that the caliph Sulayman, a contemporary of the chronicler, had gathered all the treasures of the

"Saracens" (i.e., the Umayyad rulers) and put them in a single treasury in Jerusalem.[121] Later sources make similar assertions about Abd al-Malik and al-Walid.

It is difficult to know what conclusions to draw from these accounts except that, in ways and for reasons which cannot be entirely understood in our own time, Christian traditions about this area associated the proclamation of rule by early Umayyad caliphs with Jerusalem, where the only space available to Muslims for such an event was the former Temple area or the Haram al-Sharif to be. Thus, largely later sources describe the caliphs Sulayman and Umar ibn Abd al-Aziz as holding court under many domes on the platform of the rock.[122] The *Kitab al-Aghani* reports that Khalid al-Qasri, one of the more brutal and successful Umayyad governors, is said to have claimed that he would, if so ordered, move the Ka'bah to Jerusalem, as evidence of the preeminence of the Palestinian city.[123]

This assertion must be related to the most celebrated, if much debated, explanation of the Dome of the Rock by its relationship with Umayyad imperial power and imperial ambitions. This explanation holds that the building was erected to serve as the place of pilgrimage, the *hajj*, for Muslims denied access to Mekkah by the revolt of Ibn al-Zubayr, the leader of an old Mekkan family representing a religious and political party deeply antagonistic to the Umayyads. Ultimately, the building would have been an assertion of Umayyad *mulk* or imperial right, since Abd al-Malik expected Jerusalem to replace Mekkah as the focal point of the Muslim pilgrimage. There are objections to this explanation, but, as an interpretation, it fits well with the development and expression of an Umayyad sense of their own strength.[124]

In the earliest forms in which they are known, however, all the early texts that can be connected to the Dome of the Rock are characterized by their terseness and their brevity, as though the events they describe were either commonly known or of little importance. They are sometimes like fantasies, especially the Christian accounts, as though the author had not observed whatever happened, and the impression they leave is that no one really knew much about Jerusalem. Curiously, the administrative function of Jerusalem was never clear. After its foundation in 715, Ramlah became the capital of Palestine province, and Jerusalem was just a settlement in Palestine administratively subject to a governor residing in Ramlah.[125] Thus, with the possible exception of the time of Mu'awiyah (661–680), Jerusalem does not seem to have played a significant role in the administrative structure of the Umayyad empire, yet it was a city where Muslims and Christians competed in daily life, in death, and especially in proclaiming their religious memories, vying with a newly returned Jewish community. Therefore, the Umayyads as Muslims and Arabs sought control of the urban landscape, especially obvious in a small city with many monuments, and it is not accidental that two historians who did not take the visual component unto account called the Dome of the Rock "an architecturally metropolitan building."[126]

A second change, more difficult to evaluate with respect of the Dome of the Rock, involves the reappearance of a Jewish community in Jerusalem. The sources, Muslim or Jewish, are not very enlightening because they are all late and affected by constant reinterpretations of early Islamic history.[127] It seems reasonable to propose that early Muslim rule allowed a number of Jewish families to establish residence in Jerusalem. They settled, if not immediately then very soon, near the northern edges of the former Jewish Temple area where some of them were apparently involved in the transformation of that area, certainly the biggest source of employment for the city. From the evidence of later accounts, the work associated with Jews was primarily menial and comprised what would be called today custodial and maintenance work, mostly keeping the place clean. For instance, the regular cleansing of the Rock was for a while in Jewish hands.[128] At this level of involvement, it is hardly likely that the new Jewish immigrants could have made a significant contribution to a Muslim interpretation of the Dome of the Rock.

A more promising source regarding a Jewish impact might have been Jewish converts to Islam, who were usually more educated than the simple sweepers and often occupied significant positions in the new Muslim establishment. The presence of at least one of them, Ka'b al-Ahbar, at Umar's side at the time of the conquest was mentioned earlier. Over the following two generations, the impact of these converts was certainly reflected in the Muslim legends about pre-Islamic, largely Hebrew, prophets,[129] but it is nearly impossible to figure out whether any of the associations between the Haram in general and the Rock in particular that can be traced to transferals from Judaism had been made by 690 or thereabouts. The figure of Abraham, for instance, which was to loom so large in the holiness of medieval Palestine *and* of Mekkah, may have already been connected with the Rock by then.[130]

In other words, while the return of significant numbers of Jews to Jerusalem is clear and their role in the economic and practical life of the city and most particularly of the Haram likely, no document can provide, to my knowledge, an explanation for the holiness of the Rock for Muslims that derives from the new Jewish presence in Jerusalem. At the same time, I know of no evidence that would indicate, in early medieval times, a specific Jewish attitude toward the Rock in the destroyed Temple, as has been attested while the whole Haram was deserted. But the existence of major new buildings in Jerusalem was interpreted in some Jewish messianic circles as the revival of the Temple without any identification of specific places.[131]

There is, however, one concrete instance in which a Jewish transferal may indeed be proposed for this period, even though it does not immediately affect the Rock, its overall impact was considerable—that is, the use of the words *Bayt al-Maqdis*, "The Holy House," to refer to the Haram area, while *Iliya* (from the Latin name of the city, *Aelia Capitolina*) remained the name of the city. At some point *Bayt al-Maqdis* become the name of the city and *al-Haram al-Sharif* the name of the sanctuary, but the change was not completed until much later, and for several centuries there was considerable confusion about the matter.[132]

Within the Muslim community, the fifty years

between the beginning of its rule in Jerusalem and the building of the Dome of the Rock exhibit or suggest momentous changes, which appear in the *hadith* literature and separately in more popular pious practice. The distinction between *hadith* and popular piety is partly an artificial one, as the Traditions of the Prophet often justified, even if *post facto*, religious behavior. But it is one of the contentions of this book that the history of holy places consists of a constant, friendly or antagonistic, dialogue between popular practice and the formal acceptance or rejection of that practice by the religious establishment, which in the case of Islam is the consensus of learned men.

The identification of the first *qiblah* and the location of the *mihrab Dawud*, which were known to the first Muslims to enter Jerusalem, continued to be important in Muslim views of the city, but they do not seem to have affected the interpretation of the Rock during the period under consideration. Quite recently Joseph van Ess has reviewed the *hadith* literature and pointed out that there exists a significant body of Traditions dealing with the Rock under the Dome that were eventually rejected by the official establishment of Muslim religious learning. They acquire a particular significance for our purposes because they parallel the anomalies of the building itself and its decoration within the artistic traditions from which the building's design originated. And, even if the stories involved were thought to be forgeries by ninth-century critics, the fact that they existed is important in its own right, inasmuch as the reasons for the rejection were theological and did not include alternate explanations of the Dome of the Rock.

Here are some of the instances brought out by van Ess. When carried away to Jerusalem at night (K 17:1), Gabriel told the Prophet, as they approached the Rock: "Here your Lord [i.e., God] ascended into Heaven." Muhammad ibn al-Hanafiyah, one of the more interesting early shi'ite leaders, is supposed to have said that the Syrians "pretend that God put His foot on the Rock in Jerusalem, although only one person ever put his foot on the rock, namely Abraham when he made it the *qibla* for all mankind." And, then, a certain

Hisham b. Umar reported from his father that Abd al-Malik had said about the Rock that "this is the rock of the Compassionate One on which He had set his foot."[133] These stories and Traditions were associated with an intellectual movement claiming the possibility of imagining God's body. This doctrine of corporeal (*mujassimah*) existence existed as early as the beginning of the eighth century and argued for an anthropomorphic God.[134] Classical Islam, especially after the debates of the ninth century, rejected this idea and proclaimed the *hadiths* that reflected it as forgeries, but the point remains that the idea existed toward the end of the first century of the *hijrah*, that it made a direct and specific association between the Rock and the footstep of God leaving the earth He had created, and that the name of Abd al-Malik is involved, at least indirectly, in its transmission. The parallel is clear with the event commemorated in the Church of the Ascension, also, it will be recalled, a tall building, on top of the Mount of Olives. And, as was the case with the Christian tradition, the place from which God ascends into the heavens is also the one to which He will return to judge men,[135] as the end of time was a central concern of all believers at the end of the seventh century. The very fact that Christian and Jewish sources mention the Dome of the Rock can be explained by the collective anticipation of all Abrahamic faiths in the end of time in Jerusalem.

As a commemoration of the place of God's Ascension—and thus of His return—this particular explanation of the Rock satisfies more of the objective features of the Dome of the Rock as it was built than any other and it also provides some clues for its later fate in the memory of Muslim culture. But it is only proper to mention another association with the Rock, which may have existed as early as the time of the conquest, but which acquired particularly striking features by the end of the century: the *isra'* or Night-Journey, that mystical trip alluded to in the first verse of the 17th surah—"Glory to [God] Who took His servant for a Night-Journey from the *masjid al-Haram* [the sacred space of Mekkah] to the *masjid al-Aqsa* [the Farthest Mosque] whose precincts We did bless, in order that We may show him [the Prophet] of Our signs; for He is the One who hears and sees [all things]." Regardless of the historical context of this revelation, which has been the subject of considerable debate in medieval commentaries and in contemporary scholarship,[136] it is clear that, at a reasonably early date, the association was made between the Journey of the Prophet and Jerusalem, perhaps even the platform of the Haram, as is indicated, for instance, in Ibn Ishaq's *Life of the Prophet* written a century later, in which the *masjid al-aqsa* of the Koranic text is identified as *bayt al-maqdis* at Iliya (*wa huwa bayt al-maqdis min Iliya*).[137] By the end of the seventh century, as I now believe, the *isra'* was already connected with the even more extraordinary vision of the Prophet's journey into Heaven, his own ascension known as the *mi'raj*, which was destined to have a tremendous development in later Muslim thought.[138] That association between the ascension of the Prophet and his Night-Journey would have still been, at that time, a general one affecting the whole of the platform of the Haram or even the entire city, with the Rock itself playing no part in it, at least formally. It was an idea that was most effective at the level of popular piety, rather than the level of official expression. The official authorities required several centuries to take hold of the spaces available to them and to recognize them through architecture and decoration.

→ ◆ ←

IT IS PROPER NOW to sum up the evidence from the four different kinds of documents—inscriptions, decoration, shape, location—that clearly pertain to the last decade of the seventh century and to propose an explanation of the building erected over the Rock by order of the Umayyad caliph Abd al-Malik. Between 640 and 690 the main "events" involving the Muslim community were the expansion to the east and to the west, a polymorphous contest with the Byzantine empire and its Christian allies within areas controlled by Muslim rule, the formation of a state, and the often bloody conflicts within the fledgling community. All of these events took place outside

of Jerusalem and for the most part outside of Palestine. But slowly and in ways that can no longer be reconstructed, two religious themes were taking root in Jerusalem, even while a more secular one was pervasive. The first religious theme, the Night-Journey, was specifically Muslim in most of its features, even if it is typologically related to many such flights by divinities or holy figures, and a number of narrative accretions were transforming it into a story. The *isra'* was, at that time, associated in a very general way with the large space of the Herodian Temple transformed into the *Masjid al-Aqsa* of the Revelation, while more popular practices were elaborating the additional theme of the *mi'raj*. The second major theme was much more specifically associated with the Rock and involved one segment of a myth long associated with Jerusalem, the city's place in God's creation and, most particularly, its role at the end of time as the place of God's return for the Last Judgment. The Islamization of this theme was occurring at several levels, at times concrete and popular and at other times abstract and intellectual. And within it, a bare Rock, with surface traces that could be interpreted as footprints, was dramatically imagined as the spot from which God left the earth and to which He will return. The more secular aspect of this theme was that the past of the city created by David and Solomon and transformed by Constantine and Justinian could be used to legitimize a new authority. This was especially so, as the predominantly Christian population of the city, the fledgling Jewish community, and the probably small number of Muslims who had come to live there all shared the memory of a "royal city," and all maintained a network of information that extended wherever in the world Christians, Muslims, or Jews lived.

As a result of these factors, in the area associated with the Prophet's Night-Journey a shrine was built on the past and future spot of God's presence on earth, and it was built so as to be visible throughout the city and its surroundings. The building follows a *martyrium* type developed in Late Antiquity, but, since it was not associated with any liturgical practice or pious behavior, it modified the geometric purity of a designer's dream exclusively for visual effects, some inside the building (the spacing of supports) and others outside (the unusual height of the dome and the colorful decoration). The decorative scheme using variations on a relatively small number of patterns from Late Antiquity is remarkable for its sensory qualities and low iconophoric charge. The inscription incorporated into the building's decoration is a litany of proclamations of the oneness of God and of praises to the Prophet followed by an acceptance of Christ as a prophet and a servant of God in the city of His Passion and in full view of the place of His Ascension. While pious reasons and local conflicts and memories explain why the Dome of the Rock is where it is and, to a degree, why it is shaped and decorated the way it is, these reasons do not yet explain the time of its construction.

One possibility, hinted at by Goitein, is that, whatever religious associations were eventually involved, it was the political sense and acumen of Mu'awiyah, the founder of the Umayyad dynasty (661–680), that required an expression of dynastic presence in the Christian city of Solomon and Constantine, and that Abd al-Malik, in 692, simply completed the physical manifestation of Mu'awiah's vision, after dealing successfully with a host of internal and external problems. It is even possible that in such details as the choice of inscriptions or the decoration, he introduced some emphases of his own.[139]

A second possibility, argued recently by Sheila Blair mostly on the basis of a careful reading and interpretation of the inscription and the decoration within the architectural context, is that the Dome of the Rock is Abd al-Malik's attempt to create, in the sacred city of Jerusalem, a shrine for a pilgrimage whose exact nature, however, was not fully spelled out.[140] An essential point, and a very cogent one within the context of the author's arguments, is that the character of the building belongs, together with the changes in coinage and administrative practices, to a set of decisions that followed Abd al-Malik's full assumption of control over Muslim possessions.

The third possibility is the classical, later, Muslim one adopted by Creswell and many other

scholars. It specifically argues that, because control of Mekkah was in the hands of Ibn al-Zubayr who represented a very special pious local, Hijazi tradition and whose family was deeply opposed to the Umayyads, Abd al-Malik tried to replace Mekkah with Jerusalem, and the Dome of the Rock was meant to be an equivalent of the Ka'bah. It is an explanation that more or less requires that the building be planned before 692, when Mekkah was "liberated" from Ibn al-Zubayr's rule.[141]

These sundry explanations may not be as contradictory to each other as they have been made out to be. There were reasons for the building of a Muslim shrine almost from the moment of the conquest, and subsequent events, whether they affected the Muslim community or the Umayyad empire, always found a resonance in Jerusalem. These explanations were accepted by one cultural group or another, and the search for a single interpretation is a misguided effort for a community without ecclesiastical authority during its own formative decades. Finally, the only decision that could not have been reached in a consensual way was the decision actually to order the construction and to provide funds for it. Adjusting somewhat the arguments developed by Sheila Blair, I prefer to see the date of 692 as the beginning of the implementation of an idea and the fulfillment of needs that were earlier and not necessarily entirely the same as those that inspired Abd al-Malik. Furthermore, a very coherent explanation of the building is in fact provided by the oldest local source on Jerusalem's past, al-Wasiti's *Fada'il*. According to it, two individuals, Raja' ibn Hayweh and Yazid ibn Salam, were appointed by Abd al-Malik to organize the construction of a building over the rock to shelter Muslims from heat and cold. Craftsmen were gathered from everywhere and, when the construction was completed, the managers said that "there is nothing in the building that leaves room for criticism." This account, from which all pious sentiments are absent, is clearly a later reaction to an existing building, remarkable for its sense of the monument's esthetic qualities and uniqueness of purpose.[142]

A definitive answer to the question why the

monument was built may well depend on our response to a query brought up with particular acuity in a recent work by Myriam Rosen-Ayalon[143]: was the Dome of the Rock an end in itself or part of a wider "master plan" to transform Herod's platform into a *masjid?* The query is not as anachronistic as it seems, for, in dealing with every aspect of the making of the Dome of the Rock, the conclusion seems inescapable that there were teams of people releasing funds, approving designs, guiding mosaicists, supervising building and decoration, choosing texts for inscriptions, and so forth. Who were these people? Where and how did they come together?

I shall return to this question, but it would not be right to leave these considerations of the Dome of the Rock without reflecting on the undeniable presence of a building whose features are so clearly delineated, so powerfully visible, and aesthetically so rewarding. Looking at it no longer with the eyes of a historian trying to understand a moment in the past or even of a believer receiving some spiritual nourishment from praying in it, one might argue that much of its power as a work of art derives from the almost embarrassing beauty of its features and the absence of any immediately identifiable message. In this sense, it is a remarkably contemporary work of art, which imposes itself by its forms more than by its meanings.

CHAPTER THREE

The Haram and Its Buildings

The Aqsa Mosque

The largest building on the Haram is the mosque abutting the enclosure's southern edge, commonly known as the "Aqsa Mosque" (figs. 60–61). It is, in its contemporary shape, unusual in composition and structure. Its function as the covered congregational hall typical of hypostyle mosques is obvious and still operational; it is clearly oriented toward the *qiblah* through seven north-south arcades, and it is now provided with all the appropriate fixtures of a mosque: an elaborate mihrab in the center, a minbar or chair for the preacher, platforms for the reading and recitation of holy texts, rugs on the floor, even a handsome dome on the axis and in front of the mihrab. Yet it stands in an anomalous relationship to the surrounding space. Unlike all mosques of its kind, it does not have a clearly delineated courtyard of its own, unless one considers the whole Haram as the *sahn* or court of this prayer hall. It does not seem to be aligned with anything else, nor is it in the center of the southern wall of the Haram. The wisdom of contemporary scholarship sees the Aqsa Mosque as lying on the axis of the Dome of the Rock and much has been made

out of that relationship. That a relationship exists cannot be doubted, but it is a broad relationship, not set in terms of formal planning, as none of the key elements involved—the south wall of the Dome of the Rock, the steps in the center of the south side of the upper platform, the axial nave and main entrance to the Aqsa Mosque—are on the same axis. Mechanical precision need not be expected in the late seventh century, but awareness of an awkward absence of axial sequence is unavoidable whenever one leaves the mosque or stands at the southern doorway of the Dome. In the language of architectural criticism, the boundaries of the building on all but its southern side are either indeterminate or do not follow the norms associated with a mosque.[1]

In addition to compositional peculiarities, the Aqsa Mosque exhibits a large number of structural ones, in spite of the fact that it is so obviously a hypostyle hall on columns (fig. 60). Its external eastern face is a composite of different styles of construction; it has several small or large halls to the east and west of its southern part which seem to fulfill some now vanished purpose; its supports under the contemporary whitewash can be seen to

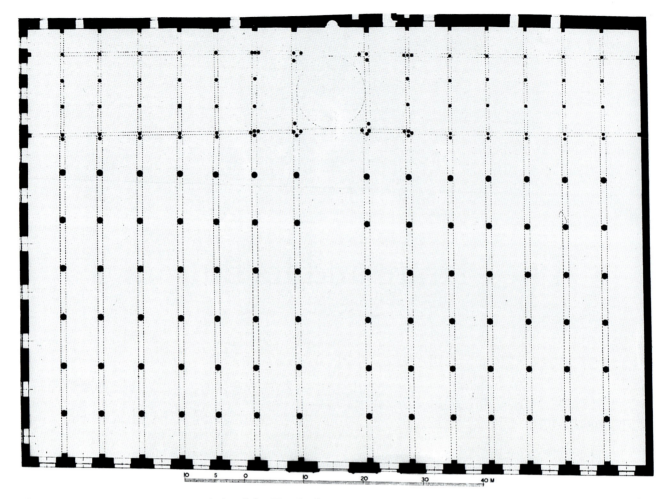

Figure 60. Aqsa Mosque, reconstructed plan (after Hamilton).

be quite different from each other and appear to have been distributed randomly. It is altogether clear that the building visible today is the result of many restorations, repairs, and other interventions, and the problem lies in reconstructing the history of the building and in figuring out what, if anything, can be attributed to the Umayyad period, perhaps even to the time of Abd al-Malik.

We know, from the testimony of the Gallic bishop Arculf, that by 670–680 there was a sizeable mosque, constructed of wood for the most part and of mediocre quality, somewhere on the Haram, and it is reasonable to argue that it was located between the platform of the Dome of the Rock and the southern end of the enclosure. The only other written evidence about the mosque that comes from Umayyad times consists of several pas-

sages from papyri datable between 709 and 714, the archives of Qurra ibn Sharik, then governor of Egypt.[2] On several occasions, it is asserted, laborers were sent from Egypt for work on "the mosque in Jerusalem" and they were paid and fed through taxes from Egypt. I have pointed out earlier that, shortly after the taking of Jerusalem by the Muslims, the city acquired a permanent labor force employed or available for public works. Just as in the second half of the twentieth century all over the developed world, additional labor was provided from countries with excess population whenever some major enterprise was undertaken in centers of power, and it is reasonable to conclude that sufficiently major work was being done in the mosque of Jerusalem during the caliphate of al-Walid (705–715) that local labor could not deal with it or lacked some competencies required for the project. But it is not possible to conclude from these fragments of evidence that al-Walid was responsible for building an Umayyad mosque in Jerusalem. All that *is* certain is that labor was required to work on the mosque there, just as it was required in other major cities under Umayyad control, Damascus, Medinah, and Mekkah, where al-Walid is credited by later chroniclers or by inscriptions with the sponsorship of mosques.[3]

In short, the present building is confusing, and the more or less contemporaneous sources are tantalizing but limited. The earliest written source describing the mosque as it was at the time is the account by Muqaddasi composed in 985, three centuries after it was built.[4] Although often quoted and discussed, its salient features bear repeating for their relevance here. After praising the mosque's qualities in general terms, Muqaddasi mentions one or more earthquakes that damaged it in the middle of the eighth century, especially the one in 747 or 748, which must have been quite destructive, as it is recalled by many chroniclers. The mosque was then restored by order of the caliph al-Mahdi (775–785), and it is clear that what Muqaddasi describes is, with two exceptions, attributed by him to the time of that caliph. This "Abbasid" mosque had twenty-six doors, of which eleven were on the eastern side and undecorated. It is thus possible to reconstruct a mosque of fifteen north-south arcades

Figure 61. Aqsa Mosque, schematic interior, looking toward northeast.

of eleven columns each (fig. 60). The central entry was provided with a heavy brass door and one of the doors on each side of the axis was gilt. The central arcade is described as higher than the rest and as having a "magnificent dome"; its ceiling was covered with sheaths of lead except in the back where there were mosaics.[5]

The two exceptions in Muqaddasi's account are a porch erected between 828 and 844 by Abdallah b. Tahir, and some "ancient" (i.e., pre-Abbasid) portion that remained "like a beauty-spot" and is described as "near the mihrab." However one interprets details, Muqaddasi's mosque is simple to imagine: fifteen arcades perpendicular to the qiblah, a cupola in front of the mihrab, elaborate doors on the northern side, simple doors on the eastern side. The existence of so many doors on the eastern side can easily be explained by the fact that one of the two major entrances into the Haram was a wide underground passageway beginning at the so-called Triple Gate on the outside and emerging a few meters to the east of the mosque (fig. 62).

From written sources, then, we can propose five possible, but not necessary, Aqsa mosques: the one seen by Arculf, the one built by Abd al-Malik as a companion to the Dome of the Rock, the one built or redone by al-Walid that required outside labor, an early Abbasid one associated with al-Mahdi, rebuilt after an earthquake and more or less identical to the one described by Muqaddasi, and then a very different one described by Nasir-i Khosraw in 1045.[6]

The question is whether anything in the mosque restored or rebuilt by al-Mahdi can be assumed to be still Umayyad. The answer depends on the interpretation of the archaeological evidence admirably presented by R. W. Hamilton as a formal report on the repairs carried out in the mosque between 1938 and 1942.[7] Without entering into a detailed analysis of the often very complicated technical arguments of the book, its archaeological conclusion of a sequence of buildings has generally been accepted, even if controversies continue about the dating of the building sequences that were revealed. According to the archaeological evidence, there were three successive major constructions be-

fore the transformations effected by the Crusaders after 1110: Aqsa I, which extended from the south wall of the mosque some 50.80 meters northward (19 meters shorter than the present building) with archaeologically unconfirmed eastern and western limits and no certainty about the central nave; Aqsa II, which extended to the northern end of the present mosque and included a wider central nave as well as a dome in front of the mihrab (figs. 60, 62); its beams were decorated with striking carved wooden panels and some of its columns were provided with beautiful new capitals; Aqsa III, in which the central nave and sections of side naves were redone and whose total number of naves was reduced to seven.[8]

With minor variations, three collations between archaeological and written sources have been proposed. It is unlikely that any of them can be demonstrated to be the correct one, because the written sources are too few and too remote and the archaeological evidence too confused by centuries of unrecorded repairs or intrusions. Yet a rapid summary of the three available interpretations helps in providing a context for the variation I propose. One suggests that Aqsa I is the work of al-Walid because of the papyri from his time; Aqsa II, the Abbasid reconstruction of ca. 771–780, and Aqsa III, a Fatimid reconstruction of the eleventh century.[9] A second collation proposes that Aqsa I is the very first mosque, the one seen by Arculfus; that Aqsa II is an Umayyad creation because of its impressive visual quality, attributed variously to Abd al-Malik or to al-Walid; and that Aqsa III is either an Abbasid mosque or a Fatimid one—the difference between the two is considered, in this hypothesis, unimportant since it assumes, wrongly as it turns out, that only restorations and decoration differentiate Abbasid from Fatimid work.[10] The third collation attributes Aqsa I and Aqsa II to Abd al-Malik and al-Walid, respectively, and Aqsa III to the Abbasids. It introduces an argument true for any early Islamic city, that the Muslim population of Jerusalem increased rapidly, especially after the building of the Dome of the Rock.[11]

The difficulty has been, it seems to me, that far too often incompatible data have been paired in

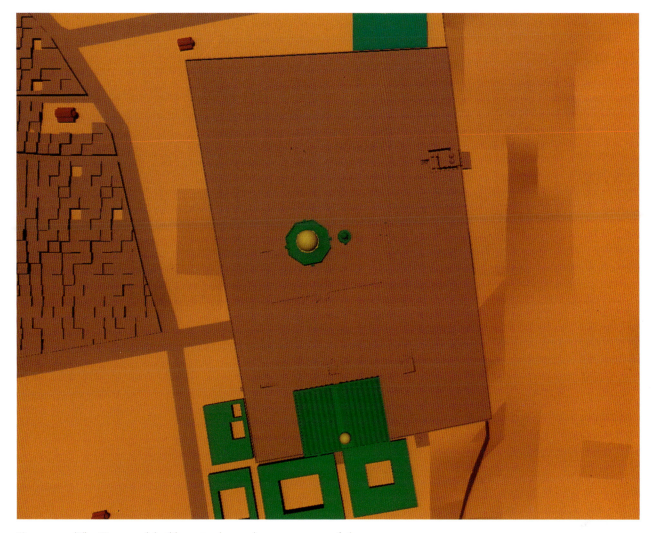

Figure 62. The Umayyad buildings in the southeastern section of the city.

these collations. The written observation of a visitor like Arculf or of a native like Muqaddasi cannot really be combined with an archaeologically defined, physically demonstrable change or even with simple assessments of structural and decorative properties. Some other way is required for an eventual reconstruction of the building's history. Before proposing my own attempt at a reconstruction, I would like to add three documents that, I believe, have not been properly utilized in the various collations and that clearly belong, at least in archaeological terms, to Aqsa II: the Greek (not Arabic) graffiti found on the tie-beams of the mosque, which are not later than the eighth century according to paleographers and which refer in rather ob-

scure ways to the materials used in construction and decoration[12]; the tie-beams themselves which have often been repainted but on which some traces of old decoration have been preserved; and especially the carved wooden panels that were fixed like consoles on those parts of the beams that extended beyond the wall sections they crossed.[13]

The absence of Arabic graffiti suggests that the leaves were put on during the earlier Umayyad period rather than later, when the speaking and writing of Arabic replaced Greek and Syriac. None of the motifs in the vegetal ornament, at times mixed with geometric themes or embedded in decorative niches and conches, shows the influence of the decorative designs and approaches developed in the ninth century in Iraq and rapidly adopted all over the Islamic world.[14] They do, however, exhibit both the floral exuberance and, more rarely, the geometric rigidity often found in stucco ornament from Qasr al-Hayr West and Khirbat al-Mafjar, both princely residences of the second quarter of the eighth century.[15] As with the mosaics of the Dome of the Rock, a relatively small number of basic designs—a vase with vegetal growth, two rows of circular floral or leafy motifs, compositions with multiple leaves, geometric interlaced diamonds, niches with vegetation—appear in different variations, as though several artisans or crews worked simultaneously. At least two unfinished panels have been preserved that argue for a workshop with intermittent employment opportunities. It is difficult to imagine the effect of these deeply carved plants and geometric designs in the center of the original building. There certainly were mosaics in the drum of the dome, as there are now, and possibly elsewhere, as many fragments of mosaic panels, probably from floors, were found during the excavations.[16] One fragment consisted of a mosaic incrusted crenellation panel in the shape of a trefoil which must have been located on the roof, and it appears from what remains that, in contrast to the decoration of the Dome of the Rock, that of the Aqsa Mosque served primarily to highlight the architecture. Stylistically, the ornament of the richly decorated Aqsa II could be Umayyad or early Abbasid; the graffiti favor the former.

The simplest way of integrating these various pieces of the Aqsa puzzle in a coherent solution may be the following: Abd al-Malik wished to transform the simple mosque built several decades earlier, because it was too small, because it no longer carried the new message his Jerusalem was meant to convey, perhaps because, as so many scholars have suggested, the shrine-congregation combination was part of the city's expected formal arrangements,[17] and perhaps even because he needed to employ the labor force assembled in the city. The work dragged on for a decade or more and al-Walid brought in additional labor and resources to finish it.[18] The size of the mosque was increased at some point in the process of construc-

tion. Aqsa I and Aqsa II, as archaeologically identified, are most likely artificially separated moments of a building period that may well have lasted a generation or more. The mosque was to serve as an effective congregational space for the growing Muslim community, but it was also to secure a place in the city of Jerusalem. At the southern boundary of the sacred space of the city, dominating the new Muslim settlements and easily connected to them (figs. 63–65), with its naves and dome it faced Justinian's Nea across the ravine of the Tyropaeon valley, just as the Holy Sepulchre and the Dome of the Rock faced each other farther north. Its interior was brilliantly decorated with carved wood and mosaics because the Aqsa Mosque, much more than the Dome of the Rock, was the space in which the community of Muslims met regularly and recognized as exclusively its own.

With this perspective, attempts to separate neatly the work of one prince from that of another and to relate any one of them to this or that version of the building are likely to fail as long as there are no pious, ideological, political, or aesthetic records to distinguish the works of different patrons. The Abbasids confirmed what the Umayyads had done and appropriated it as their own creation, as witnessed by the celebrated inscription of the Dome of the Rock. They repaired a building after it had been damaged by one or more earthquakes, but they probably reused capitals made for the Umayyad construction because, in spite of considerable political and ideological divergences, the Muslim social and pious ethos did not change with the new dynasty. The Fatimids did indeed create something new in the eleventh century and their Aqsa III was meant to carry a different message.

The Haram

The existence by 700 or 725 of the Dome of the Rock and the Aqsa Mosque implies that there was already a high platform for the former and that, at the very least, the southern half of the Haram esplanade had been cleared of debris and flattened out. There is no documentary evidence to confirm when these spaces were prepared for building. Only careful large-scale excavations and perhaps the establishment of a chronological dictionary of construction techniques could explain how and when the platform of the Dome of the Rock materialized as well as a reasonable history of the outer walls.[19] We are therefore left with conjectures, or else we can assume, as have most scholars, that the earliest descriptions we have, those of the tenth century, are valid for still earlier times unless proved otherwise. Yet one of my methodological arguments has been that the testimony of Muqaddasi or Ibn al-Faqih should be viewed primarily as statements of late Abbasid or early Fatimid times, only applicable to the seventh century if other information justifies it. Therefore, instead of resorting to the evidence of these later texts, we can try to deduce what may have been done in Umayyad times from the two major buildings and from the more hypothetical conclusion, that a permanent work force of masons, carpenters, and other laborers existed in the city of Jerusalem. Furthermore, as has already been suggested by several scholars, agreement on the date and function of some parts of the Haram affects our reading of many other parts on technical and stylistic grounds.[20] Finally, the most important achievement of the late seventh century was the reintroduction of the former Temple area as an active element in the city. It was no longer a static image of destruction and desolation but a dynamic symbol and a lively place of urban life so that whatever happened in the city affected it, just as its presence affected the city. This point was forcefully demonstrated by the excavations carried out to the south and southeast of the Haram, which brought to light considerable new and largely unexpected data about early Islamic and Umayyad times.

The Dome of the Rock and the Aqsa Mosque, obviously visible as they were ca. 700, required a specific spatial context in the Haram that can be deduced through logical and comparative analyses, while a more general urban context is provided by new archaeological data. Finally, there is the enigmatic Dome of the Chain, standing to the east of

the Dome of the Rock, with which I will deal separately.

Let me recall, first of all, that the area of the Herodian Temple and the second-century Hadrianic monuments had been left unbuilt during Christian rule and that it was filled with all sorts of architectural (and other) debris, including the numerous large columns from Herod's celebrated *stoa* raising the Temple enclosure at its southern end as well as a gate at the location of the present Golden Gate on the east side of the enclosure (figs. 16–17). As argued earlier, from the very beginning of their rule, the Muslims organized a labor force to clear the area, and it is possible to reconstruct the results of their work, at least hypothetically.

At the southern end of the Temple area, the terrain was smoothed and old remains covered up for the erection of the first mosque before 670. At least one entryway up to the level of the esplanade was used or had been cleared to become usable, either the Double Gate, now located under the Aqsa Mosque, or the Triple Gate farther to the east (fig. 63). The former is probably more likely, as it remained the most significant entrance in the Muslim memory of the Haram, acquiring eventually the name of *bab al-Nabi*, "Gate of the Prophet," in memory of Muhammad's arrival during his *isra'* or Night-Journey. Although this identification poses a practical problem in interpreting the buildings excavated to the south of the Haram, it still seems to be the most reasonable one. Then, under Abd al-Malik or al-Walid, when Aqsa II was being built on a much grander scale, the Double Gate would have been totally redone and redecorated to befit its position as the main entrance into a sacred precinct.

This conclusion incorporates the results of studies and observations made over the past decades which have not yet been included in broader surveys of Islamic architecture. It shows that the Umayyad patrons had accomplished two things. The first one, very much in line with our own twentieth century attitudes toward restoration, was to clear and repair the older Herodian foundations at the southern end of the esplanade and as much of the superstructure as remained standing, for instance the Double and Triple gates. It would be idle to speculate as to how much had really been left of Herod's work or of Hadrian's, and how much of what now can be seen—usually very little since the interior of the Double Gate is rarely accessible and quite dark—is Umayyad. This is clearly an area where studies in comparative construction techniques would be essential. The second Umayyad accomplishment consisted of decorating the Double Gate with a lintel on the outside and of covering the surface of the first two cupolas inside the gate with an unusual mixture of geometric and vegetal designs. The lintel may or may not have been carved in Umayyad times,[21] and, if it looks awkward in the present configuration of the Double Gate, it is mostly because the walls around and above it have been redone so frequently. In Umayyad times it is most likely that the *stoa* of Herod was still largely standing and, therefore, that the middle part of the southern wall of the Haram, at the approximate level of the Double and Triple gates, was an open gallery.[22] Such a gallery would explain the peculiarity of two decorated domes in front of the Double Gate (fig. 66), which are almost invisible in the darkness now but would have been quite effective with light from the front and sides.

A more secure conclusion, also reached by many others, is that the Golden Gate on the eastern side of the Haram (fig. 17) is related to the Double Gate by its shape, its construction, and its decoration. The two gates share the same plan—a sequence of square spaces arranged in pairs, with the pair closest to the outside wall surmounted by two domes on pendentives—and each gate is embellished with an elaborately carved vegetal frieze on the outside framing low doorway. Like the Double Gate, the Golden Gate in its present form is a rearrangement of structural and decorative elements from several periods. However impressive it looks from afar and however effective is its interior of low slung cupolas on high drums, it is a composite work of architecture whose awkwardness and lack

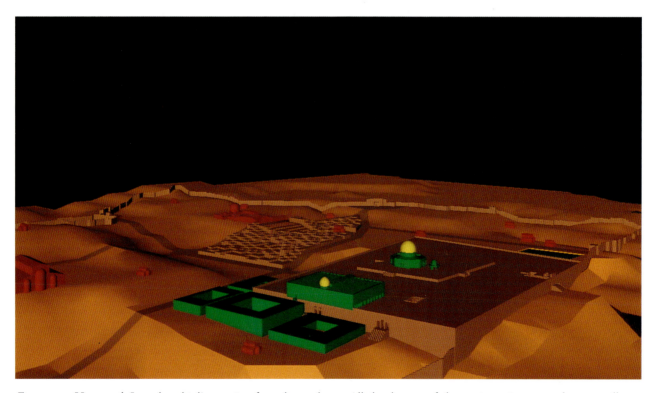

Figure 63. Umayyad Jerusalem, bird's-eye view from the southeast. All the elements of the previous picture are there as well as the two southern gates, the Golden Gate, and the remaining Christian churches. The settlement between the Holy Sepulchre and the Haram is set there as an example only.

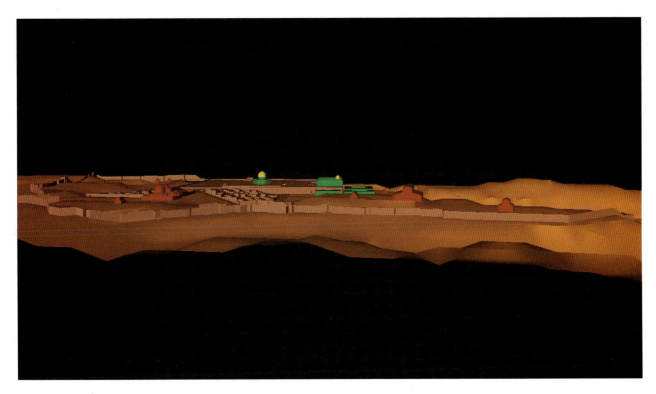

Figure 64. Umayyad Jerusalem from the west with Christian buildings in the foreground.

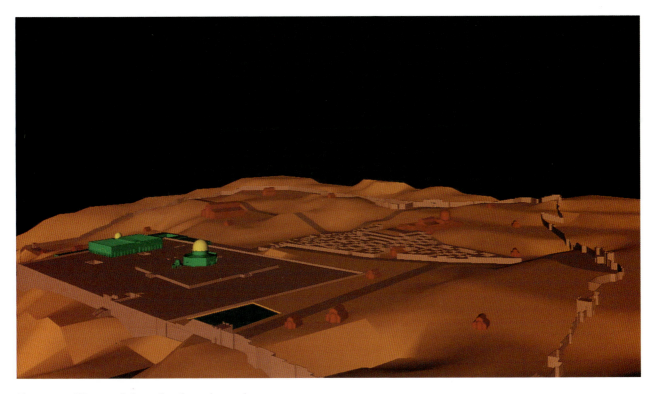

Figure 65. Umayyad Jerusalem from the northeast.

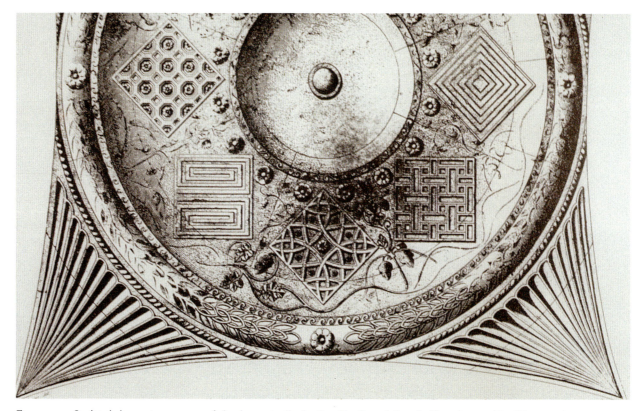

Figure 66. Sculpted decoration on one of the domes inside the Double Gate (after de Vogüé), possibly Umayyad.

of proper proportions in the relationship between parts reflect rapid construction.[23] The more intriguing question about the Golden Gate is why it was redone and decorated with such care. It was hardly an important point of entry into the city or the Haram, as the terrain in front of it is particularly steep, and its meaning for Christians as a place to celebrate the Entry into Jerusalem was hardly of significance to Muslims. Even in Herod's Temple it was primarily a ceremonial gate.

One explanation for the development of the Golden Gate is the eschatological meaning that it would have acquired already in Umayyad times as the gate to the place where the Last Judgment would occur. Or, it may have been simply a signal that the area behind it was once again religiously active. An elegant frieze outlining the entryway, like that of the Double Gate, is also found in the Holy Sepulchre, in the present twelfth-century facade.[24] The meaning of all three gates was conveyed in decorative pan-Mediterranean rather than distinctive Christian or Islamic terms, as writing or images would have been, since their message as entryways was intended to a large extent for others than the faithful who already had access to what lay behind them.

Thus, two gates to the south and one, probably never used, to the east are certain. A fourth public gate led from the city to the southwestern section of the Haram. The old Herodian bridge held by Robinson's Arch (fig. 67) was probably still in use, with a small underground passage leading to what is known today as Barclay's Gate, a single entrance with a simple lintel over the doorway, into a tunnel-like approach to a set of steps.[25] Although usually inaccessible, the passage and the gate are still there. There may possibly have been another gate farther north on the western side, perhaps in the area of today's Gate of the Chain, which is also a double gate with Herodian and Roman

Figure 67. "Robinson's Arch," the remains from Herodian times of a bridge or a grand stairway leading to the Temple area. The photograph was taken around 1960, before the transformation of the whole area to the southwest of the Haram. Note the very different masonries which form a history of the building.

antecedents,[26] but this is speculative. The Double and Triple gates on the northern edge of the Haram had not been developed in any significant way in Umayyad times, but may well have already been cleared of debris.[27]

We can only speculate about the original size, shape, and function of the platform on which the Dome of the Rock was built, and whether it even existed at all before the Muslim appropriation of the Haram. It is not in the center of anything, it is an irregular polygon, and its main constructions are not on any of its more obvious axes. There is, therefore, no doubt that its existence and dimensions were dictated by reasons that have little to do with the development of the Haram. At the least, it was a way to conceal remains that would have been difficult to remove and ideologically dangerous to preserve. What these remains were is, of course, impossible to say. It is also impossible to know how the platform was reached in Umayyad times and our reconstruction (fig. 63) of four sets of stairs is based exclusively on a taste for symmetry. Only the southern one is probably accurate, as it is on the axis of the Dome of the Rock and not of the Aqsa Mosque. Although it faces the mosque, it is really an access to the shrine of the Dome of the Rock. If the present location of the steps is identical with the original one, they were directed toward the north. The point, to be elaborated more fully below, is that from the very beginning, these sets of stairs exerted a direction, a vector, in the organization of space on the Haram.

Thus, the vast esplanade of the Herodian Temple was shaped into a surface able to support buildings, with new or restored entries, and the slow work was begun of fixing up outside walls which had fallen into disrepair. We shall probably never know how much was actually accomplished during the ninety odd years of Umayyad rule, but much was achieved in the making of a Muslim sanctuary.

The Muslim "Quarter"

Who were the Muslims of Jerusalem? Where did they live? And since they ruled the city, where was their administrative center? Written sources, almost entirely of the remote variety for the first century of Muslim occupation, suggest a pattern that, on the whole, conforms to the logic of the time and the peculiarities of the Holy City.[28] Based on texts gathered by others, I propose the following way of addressing the questions. Some thirty Arab Muslim[29] tribes or tribal groups settled in Palestine, mostly Yemenis, some of whom established themselves in Jerusalem. Individual tribal leaders were even exiled to Jerusalem in Umayyad times,[30] as would happen so frequently later in Mamluk times and as had already happened under Byzantine rule. There are also instances of individuals who chose to settle there, as did one Muhammad b. al-Rabi' of the Khazraj tribe, who died in Jerusalem in 718 at the ripe old age of ninety-three.[31] But I have not encountered a single example of a person who settled in Jerusalem during the seventh century for pious reasons, as happened fairly frequently from the ninth century onward.

It is difficult to define the administrative position of Jerusalem within the new empire, at least during the first eighty years or so of Muslim rule. Things became much clearer after the foundation of Ramlah by Sulayman b. Abd al-Malik, some time around 715. Located in the coastal plain at the edge of the Judean hills, Ramlah rapidly became a significant producing and trading center and the official capital of the province of Palestine. Jerusalem was turned into a sort of *sous-préfecture* with religious and touristic importance, although that may not have been the original intention of the early Umayyads. Among the milestones of Abd al-Malik, two proudly proclaim distances from Jerusalem in beautiful lapidary script, and one of several early bronze coins minted in *Ilya Filastin* even shows on the obverse the representation of a standing caliph. The investiture of Mu'awiyah and the visits and other activities sponsored by Abd al-Malik and his sons certainly indicate that a special political as well as religious significance was assigned to the city at the outset.

The most curious case is that of the caliph Sulayman, one of al-Walid's sons. He is known primarily for the creation and development of Ramlah, but his name clearly relates him to the first great builder in Jerusalem, and his flamboyant personality as well his attempt to take Constantinople, the last such attempt in early Islamic times, suggests grander ambitions than those of a local ruler. He received the allegiance of Arab leaders in Jerusalem, and a later account relates that a governor of his was forced by Umar II, Sulayman's successor, to swear an oath on the Rock. His caliphate was very short (715–717), and it is only minute bits of ill-digested later stories that suggest he may have wanted to transform Jerusalem, or at least the Haram, into a royal and holy city and to separate that special, symbolic city from the political and economic activities concentrated in Ramlah.[32] Unfortunately, however tempting the argument may be, it is, given the available information, nothing but an interesting speculation.

There is something odd about being able to see and reconstruct the magnificent architectural creations of the first Muslims of Jerusalem without being able to sense who they were, what they did, and where they lived. A few segments of tribes with families and attendants, a few individuals coming on their own, possibly a judge or a tax collector representing the caliph or his governor in Ramlah, some staff for occasional ceremonial visits by caliphs—these are minimal data for a reconstruction, even in one's imagination, of Muslim participation in the life of the city. The problem is compounded by the rather extraordinary and certainly quite unexpected results of excavations carried out to the south and southwest of the Haram,[33] but as these excavations have not been published in full, one must rely on somewhat romanticized descriptions and reconstructions and on references to documents, both published and unpublished, that are not always properly interpreted.[34]

It seems clearly established that over foundations dug across layers of Byzantine occupation, several large buildings were erected, partly on the spectacular steps leading to the Herodian Temple. They form a sort of L around the southwestern corner of the Haram, and since Fatimid tombs and other debris were found in the excavated fill, it is reasonable indeed to conclude that these buildings were early Islamic or Umayyad. One of the buildings was a bath, and the others, of which only foundations remain, are massive rectangular constructions with multiple gates (usually on opposite sides), interior courtyards with porticoes, and two floors of long dark rooms, apparently arranged in rows. Nothing can really be deduced about these interiors except that they are typologically related to a well-known form of military and civilian architecture used for everything from barracks for soldiers to warehouses. What is missing for a reconstruction of the interiors is any sense of the openings there might have been for light, of the modulations that may have existed in the spatial arrangements, and of the ornamental surface of the walls. It is true, as several commentators have noted, that the basic model for these constructions was also used for the Umayyad princely villas, but I have strong reservations about interpreting any of these buildings as palaces, *a fortiori* as residences for caliphs. One of them might have been a *dar al-'imarah* in the broadest sense of the word, an administrative building in which records are kept, taxes collected, and other mundane activities are handled, such as the management of the labor force on the Haram. The other buildings would have been places for the settlement of immigrating Muslims from Arabia, hostels for traveling pilgrims, possibly caravanserais for the keeping and safeguarding of merchandise.

In general, very little tangible evidence exists for the enormous population changes which affected all newly Muslim cities, both old cities with new immigrants and newly created ones.[35] In Jerusalem, the limitations imposed on preempting living spaces belonging to Christians or used by them made it necessary to develop a new architecture that includes both official buildings of state and living quarters. Both had a particularly original development in later Islamic urban architecture. But I must confess that, after studying the published evidence and trying to imagine how those large structures functioned, I keep feeling that the pieces provided by the standing remains do not quite fit with each other. If a Double Gate was so important as an entrance, why was it partly blocked from view by one of the buildings? Something is still out of focus in the evidence we have and what we see.

If most of the preceding is still speculative, we are on somewhat surer ground in relating these buildings to the city. They are today separated from each other and from the Haram by well paved streets. These streets are probably, but not necessarily, restored from earlier times, and it is their earlier existence that may be responsible for the unusually large (84 by 96 meters) rectangular shapes of the buildings. The streets also connected the Muslim area to the rest of the city and to three formal entrances to the Haram, the Double and Triple gates to the south, and the smaller "Barclay" gate to the southwest. Furthermore, a most unusual small gate led directly into the Aqsa Mosque from the roof of the main building to the south of the mosque. The existence of this fourth entry has been ingeniously proposed by Ben-Dov on the basis of a curious break in the masonry of the Haram. The gate has been compared to the princely doors from palace to mosque known to have existed in Damascus, Kufah, and Cordova and assumed to be a standard Umayyad element in royal structures in cities. Its probable existence has in fact been one of the arguments for interpreting the building as a palace. But a passageway does not a palace make, and inasmuch as the doorway leads to the extreme southwest corner of the mosque and not, like everywhere else, to a space near the mihrab, it could be just as easily argued that it was a gate for women. Once again a tantalizing concrete bit of archaeological evidence must remain unexplained because too much of its physical and social context is missing.

The excavated buildings can be imagined most securely by considering their impact on the city (fig. 63). Their location on the rapidly descending slopes of Mount Moriah, just below the enormous, newly refurbished platform of the sanctuary, gave them a prominent immediacy. To anyone coming from the south or from the east, they announced the presence of the living next to the monumental exaltation of the holy. From the west they rose in competition with a whole range of Christian institutional buildings on Mount Zion and on the slopes leading up to it, highlighted by Justinian's Nea church. In a way it almost does not matter what happened or was meant to happen in these buildings. Their primary role was to show that a new group dominated the city and its holiness.

The Dome of the Chain

The *qubbah al-Silsilah*, or Dome of the Chain (fig. 68), is a most unusual building, recently visible again after many a decade of repairs and consolidation. Located immediately to the east of the Dome of the Rock, it consists of a hexagon covered by a cupola, surrounded by an eleven-sided polygon on eleven columns; a mihrab was added later on the qiblah side. The interior surfaces of the dome were covered with mosaics. Its overall diameter of some fourteen meters makes it the third largest building on the Haram.[36] The earliest remote sources mention its existence, and contemporary scholarship has generally accepted the statement in one of them that it was built by order of Abd al-Malik. Since it is known to have existed by ca. 850, and since all the earlier major buildings on the Haram are Umayyad, it is reasonable to assume that one of the Umayyad rulers sponsored the building. But which one? Mu'awiyah, who is said to have brought a dome all the way from Baalbek and who became caliph in a ceremony probably somewhere on the Haram? Abd al-Malik, who sponsored the Dome of the Rock nearby, but whose needs for a smaller building are not evident? Al-Walid, who built a lot of buildings everywhere? Sulayman, who may have thought that it was a wonderful place to meet the Queen of Sheba? All are possible and none is even remotely demonstrable. Only Abd al-Malik is mentioned by later sources, but this attribution may have been an automatic later reaction and in fact nothing in the shape or decoration of the building argues for an Umayyad sponsor.

In reality the important question is not so much who built the Dome of the Chain as *why* it was built. At some point in the history of the Haram, the interest in eschatology became pervasive and the Dome of the Chain became the place of Judg-

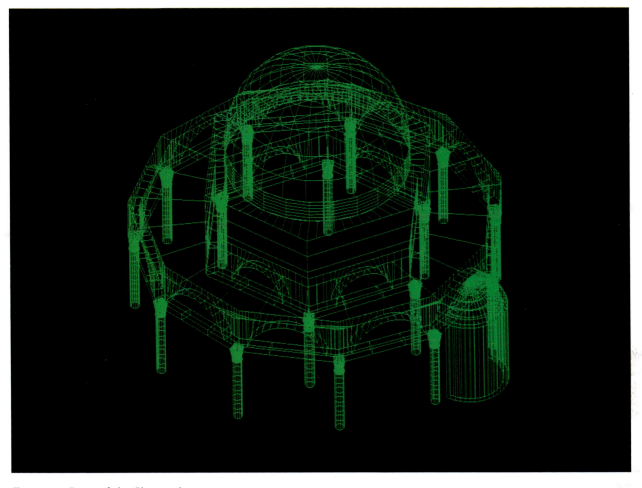

Figure 68. Dome of the Chain, schematic reconstruction.

ment, with themes associated with a chain that would stop the wicked and let the just pass through. Then it was related to the *mihrab Da'ud* of the Koran, which was a place of judgment. Such an association is clearly later than the original building, inasmuch as the mihrab in it is a later addition. Some medieval sources, and a few modern scholars, identify it as a *bayt al-mal*, a treasury of the local Muslim community that existed in some early mosques. But, aside from the fact that the existence of these establishments as separate buildings is doubtful, the construction of the Dome of the Chain, open to all comers and without a protected vault, does not lend itself to the keeping of bullion. Rosen-Ayalon quite recently made an observation that may be more fruitful than all the earlier ones. She noted that the Dome of the Chain is located

in the exact center of the Haram, at the meeting point of its two axes, the only building on the whole Haram, in fact, that is in the middle of anything. Furthermore, it is on the same axis as a secondary mihrab in the present Aqsa Mosque, in an area later associated with the visit to Jerusalem of the caliph Umar. In other words, the Dome of the Chain is somehow related to the whole platform and marks a place on it that is independent of other buildings and that was, for a while at least, an important sign or signal. Rosen-Ayalon's suggestion is that it was meant to indicate the *omphalos*, that navel of the universe otherwise assigned to the Church of the Holy Sepulchre.[37] It is indeed possible to accept such an explanation as one of many Umayyad attempts to reflect or to adapt motifs from the earlier practices of the city. If so, it would have been a borrowing that did not take root in Islamic culture, and eventually gave way to the more vivid theme of the Last Judgment. Finally, an originally secular function cannot be excluded for a building that seems to forecast the pavilions and kiosks of later times used for secular activities and ceremonies.

The form of the Dome of the Chain is quite extraordinary, and no other example is known to me of a hexagon enclosed by an eleven-sided polygon or even a decagon. It is apparently impossible to design an eleven-sided building on geometric principles alone, which makes it even more difficult to explain the Dome of the Chain, although an unusual form could have been conceived and designed for an unusual purpose, or perhaps there were seventeen columns available and this puzzling building is nothing but an unplanned afterthought in the endless activity of building up the Haram.

→ ✦ ←

Before summarizing what we can conclude about the new Jerusalem completed and functioning by about 730–750, it is well to recall that the Umayyads as patrons and the Muslims who swore allegiance to them were but one segment, the wealthiest and most powerful one no doubt but certainly not the most numerous, of the population of Jerusalem. Most of what is known about the non-Muslim population of the city comes from written sources and from inferences implicit in later developments. It should also be added that there are archaeological documents for the Umayyad period other than those of the Haram and its immediately adjacent area, but these documents are bits and pieces from which few useful conclusion can be drawn at this stage of our knowledge.[38]

From written sources we know that Christians remained the largest group in the city. Many among them were priests, monks, and nuns attached to the large and still functioning ecclesiastical establishment. A survey made many years ago, based on a Georgian liturgical calendar of the tenth century, identified some eighty-one Christian sanctuaries in the area of Jerusalem that were operating in early Islamic times, eighteen of them in the walled city. Not only were religious services and other activities carried out in the Nea, the Holy Sepulchre with its many chapels, and the church on Mt. Zion, but new sanctuaries were erected, such as a church at Gethsemani built around 675 under the sponsorship of an abbot formerly associated with the Holy Sepulchre.[39]

The greater visibility of non-Greek monks and priests as well as worshippers is explained by the exodus of the Greek Byzantine leadership from the Holy City, a phenomenon that affected much more than Jerusalem; evidence suggests that monophysite allegiances were maintained all over Syria and Palestine in the absence of the coercive power of Byzantium. It also seems that pilgrimages to the Holy City, so frequent before the Persian invasion of the early seventh century, now involved primarily Georgian, Armenian, probably Coptic, Jacobite, and Nestorian faithful, while western pilgrims were still relatively rare. In a sense, then, under Umayyad rule Jerusalem began to reflect more than before a variety of Christian traditions and pilgrims from many Christian lands. Yet it still remained a city with a universal Christian meaning, as is illustrated by a story told by the Byzantine historian Theophanes. According to him, in 737 one Tiberios, alleged to be the son of Justinian II, was taken prisoner by the Arabs somewhere in Anatolia. Great honors were bestowed on him, and his captor, one Sulayman b. Issam, gave him imperial honors and brought him into Jerusalem surrounded by flags and carrying a scepter.[40] The story is certainly apocryphal, if for no other reason than the fact that the real son of Justinian II was killed in 710 or 711, but it illustrates simultaneously the prestige of Jerusalem among Christians and its somewhat mythical status under alien rule.

There is very little documented evidence about when and where Jews reestablished their presence in Jerusalem, about how numerous they were, and about where they came from. I have alluded to possible Jewish activities as attendants and workers on the Haram, as intermediaries in the elaboration of Muslim knowledge and doctrine on the pre-

Islamic past, as occasional converts to Islam, in short as active participants in the momentous events of the seventh century in Jerusalem. But it is very difficult—in fact, nearly impossible—to extrapolate these activities into spaces where Jews might have lived and where their synagogues or other communal institutions might have been. From later times it is reasonable to argue that the rising terrain to the north of the Haram became a Jewish quarter, but there is also evidence for Jewish presence in the valley near the western wall of the Muslim sanctuary and near the Damascus Gate. It is possible that the division of cities into fairly strict ethnic or confessional quarters is a later phenomenon and that families with different religious allegiances lived near each other. Also from later evidence, one might suggest that, already under the Umayyads and their relatively lax control over their empire, Jews from Iraq and Iran settled again in Jerusalem. The Karaite movement with strong roots in Iran began to appear in Jerusalem late in the eighth century, and the Samaritans of Palestine were no longer persecuted. Thus, even if concrete evidence is lacking for the Umayyad period itself, it is indeed plausible to imagine that the Jews of Jerusalem, like its Christians, reflected a broader sample of regional and doctrinal differences than had been true before.

In spite of the uncertainties surrounding the actual mix and distribution of people in Jerusalem, a fairly coherent picture of the city in late Umayyad times does indeed emerge. Jerusalem became visually organized around two competing poles. One is the older, western one with the Christian sanctuaries of the Holy Sepulchre and the Nea, facing opposite directions and proclaiming *their* truth as they pointed to the destroyed Jewish Temple and its pagan imperial successors. The other pole comprises the newly created complex on Mount Moriah, with the Dome of the Rock and the Aqsa Mosque transforming the ruins of Herodian and Roman monuments into a striking statement of the new faith (figs. 63–65). It is difficult to doubt that this proclamation was deliberately planned as a formal statement of Muslim presence intelligible to any Christian walking away from the Holy Sep-

ulchre (fig. 58) or climbing toward Mount Zion. It is, on the other hand, more difficult to define the psychological context of that statement. During the decades of the Cold War, I had argued, from the more limited story of the Dome of the Rock alone, that it was a confrontational statement, a proclamation of dominating presence and absolute truth. In the relatively more irenic times of today, it is easier to posit competition without necessary conquest or even assumption of superiority as a more accurate interpretation. The very nature of the Dome of the Rock and of the Aqsa Mosque— abstract geometric forms of shining brilliance without representational signs or identified symbols— can readily be adapted to changing emotional and religious climates but, regardless of the meanings given to these forms at different times, it was the Umayyad vision for and of Jerusalem that transformed the small walled city into a dynamic composition of spiritually and culturally charged monuments whose interplay was designed to be part of the city's attributes.

The monumental display of Jerusalem overwhelmed in large measure the daily lives of people, and the linkage between human activity and the monuments was through the commemoration of death in its peculiarly Jerusalem-centered form of eschatological expectation. The *Apocalypse* of Pseudo-Methodius of Patara, a Christian vision, reflected the monumental and political transformation of Umayyad Jerusalem.[41] Jewish apocalyptic writing explicitly referred to the revival of the Temple under Muslim rule. And, at least in the interpretation I propose, the Dome of the Rock was, among many other things, a monument to Muslim eschatological thought through the remembrance of God's creation, while Traditions of the Prophet's sayings and commentaries on the Koran began, slowly and at times hesitantly, to connect Jerusalem with the end of time and the divine Judgment.[42]

The complexity and the fascination of Umayyad Jerusalem lies, then, first of all in its blend of religious emotion, commemorative function, ultimate expectation, imperial ambition, *and* an irretrievable daily life. All of these elements helped to shape the built spaces, individually used by a few but visible to all. This achievement is remarkable enough in itself, for it illustrates two broader conclusions: the technical and conceptual potential of the visual language of Late Antique art whose forms allowed so many possible meanings to so many different people; and the ways in which the new Islamic order was being created. A recent book argues that the making of an Islamic cultural identity went through four phases successive in logic but possibly contemporary with each other: a "polemic" one to establish itself in relationship to other communities, a "liturgical" one to organize its own rites, a "didactic" one to formulate its traditions, and a "juridical" one to codify these traditions.[43] Umayyad Jerusalem does not reflect the time of codification, but it does illustrate nearly all other aspects of cultural self-identity as defined in this scheme. The polemic phase is demonstrated in its assumption of beliefs and associations made for earlier religious systems and in its reviving as its own a sacred space that had lost some of its former intensity. The liturgical aspect is displayed in the building of a mosque which acknowledged its own rituals. The didactic function is found not only in the formulation of traditions, but also in the effort to make them visible to others, perhaps even to proselytize them. Together with the urban upheaval it effected and the visual power of its main monument, the Dome of the Rock, the Umayyad patronage of Jerusalem must indeed be considered one of the most original and most effective agents of urban change known anywhere.

CHAPTER FOUR

The Fatimid City

THE MAIN DECADES OF imperial Umayyad investment in the city of Jerusalem (roughly 690–720 C.E.) had two lasting results for the city's fabric. One is obvious, still discernible today—that is, the monumental transformation of the ruined area of the Jewish Temple of Herod into a Muslim sanctuary facing the Christian monuments on the city's western hills. That sanctuary did not as yet have a single identifying name in the middle of the eighth century but it was endowed with many pious associations. A corollary of this transformation was probably a redistribution of people in the city, but information on this matter is too scarce to allow reliable conclusions. The second result, even less secure, is the establishment, possibly derived from older Christian and Roman imperial practices, of what we would call today a buildings and grounds department, a group charged with maintaining the religious and ceremonial buildings, with some sort of official budget and a labor force of masons, stone-cutters, carpenters, perhaps mosaicists and painters, whose size depended on available state funds augmented by private donations, which could be adapted to current needs. Like so many comparable institutions today, this labor force kept itself

busy clearing debris from destroyed or damaged buildings—the ruins of the Herodian Temple and its Roman imperial successors, or Christian churches abandoned for lack of attendants—or repairing a wall, a roof, or a floor. Several remaining inscriptions or fragments of inscriptions attest to continuous work on the Haram. Around 910 C.E., a woman, probably the mother of the caliph al-Muqtadir, had some part of the terrace repaired. A more formal statement commemorating the actual construction (*binā'*), rather than mere repairs, of the walls of the Haram is recorded for 961–962 under the sponsorship of the Ikhshidid ruler of Egypt, and more complex works, to which I shall return, are recorded for the eleventh century.[1] Whether these repairs and constructions reflect the existence of a "master-plan" or, at least, of a coherent "master" vision of the shape of the Haram, if not of the whole of Jerusalem, or whether they were all *ad hoc* decisions without overall conception is difficult to determine, but my sense is that the latter is more likely and that the relatively haphazard organization of Umayyad constructions continued for a while.[2] The assumption of a more or less permanent work force has an important implication for the architecture of Jerusalem: traditional and local ways tended to persist in spite of outside influences so that, when there is innovation, as happened under the Crusaders or in Mamluk times, the impact is all the more striking.

Many other events and interventions affected Jerusalem during the three and a half centuries that followed Umayyad constructions. There were earthquakes in 747 or 748 (a major one), 856–857, 859–860, 1016 (another major one), and 1034 or 1035. Archaeologists and historians have cited them to explain visible or putative reconstructions of buildings as well as events in the life of individuals,[3] but their actual value as documentary evidence is very arbitrary and they can rarely be used credibly without corroboration. Next to these natural disasters there were major or minor expressions of concern from the Abbasid capital, Baghdad, as specially earmarked funds were sent for specific repairs to the major monuments above and beyond continuous aid for maintenance. On three occasions, the caliphs themselves visited Jerusalem, making time-consuming detours from their pilgrimages to Mekkah or using the occasion of trips to Syria and the Byzantine frontier for visits to the city. Al-Mansur came in 758 and in 771, al-Mahdi in 780. Curiously, no record exists of a visit by al-Ma'mun, the caliph who had substituted his name for that of Abd al-Malik on the Dome of the Rock, and who was in Damascus in 830–831. From the second half of the ninth century onward, the official presence of Baghdad in Jerusalem somewhat declined, but this political passivity coincides with the growth of historical and geographical compendia, sponsored from the cultural capital of the Muslim world, that provide important resources for the knowledge of Jerusalem. Effective political power was now located in Egypt, in Fustat, and, after 969, in Cairo. The successive dynasties of the Tulunids, Ikhshidids, and Fatimids were all active in Palestine, each one with its own style and its own agenda. No official visit to Jerusalem by a ruler from Egypt seems to have occurred, but Khumarawayh, the eccentric son of Ahmad ibn Tulun, went in 888 to Ramlah, the provincial capital in the coastal plain, and there was in the Holy City some sort of ad-

ministrative structure to collect taxes and to keep order, although, as we shall see, it is difficult to know when this structure was established or whether it continued an old, perhaps even pre-Islamic, institution. The endemic tribal struggles in the countryside, which affected much of Palestine, especially during the tenth century, must have had an effect on the city of Jerusalem, particularly by making access to it more difficult and more dangerous. And there were riots and other kinds of disturbances within the city. Yet these were also the times when the remote Carolingians invested in churches and hostels in or around Jerusalem and, out of probably very simple and prosaic activities by the Latin church, the myth of Charlemagne as the first crusader began to grow. Finally, the Geniza documents from Cairo began to shed light, especially in the eleventh century, on hundreds of individual lives and events involving the Jews in Jerusalem, catching the historian between fascinating, if trivial, detailed accounts and the difficulty of finding in them patterns useful for the visual reconstruction of the city.

Initially I thought that a strict chronology of events affecting the city's physical shape could be established, but, as Moshe Gil's valiant attempt has shown,[4] masses of trees and bushes totally obscure the forest or compel one to see it only in terms of a single community or a single issue. A somewhat blurred picture does emerge of a Jewish city in the eleventh century, but it is presented through a large number of individual stories, without acknowledging the Christians and Muslims who were there as well, without a visual account of a space with hills, walls, and gates, and without any sense of how far back the life of this particular time could be projected. And for the specific concern of this book with the physical shape of the city, there is only a spotty sequence of very heterogeneous bits of information, many of which are problematic. For these reasons, I decided to give up a systematic chronology of what happened to the Umayyad city of ca. 745 and to begin with the city as it must have existed around 1050. My reasons for choosing the latter date and then looking back lie in a major eyewitness description from 1047, several earlier datable structural changes to the city and to some of its major monuments, the rich Geniza material from the eleventh century, and the fact that the first Muslim *fada'il* or "praises" of Jerusalem are datable to around 1019. However incomplete and at times incompatible these documents are, their concentration makes it reasonable to attempt a reconstruction. In a retrospective view I shall pick up three features of the city of 1050, which clearly distinguish it from the Umayyad city, and suggest that they are the result of a process over several centuries that can be imagined in its general lines, if not in every detail. The themes I shall highlight are the evolution of beliefs and of piety, the impact of external political power, and the uniqueness of the population mix within the city.

Jerusalem in 1050: Nasir-i Khosraw's Account

On 5 March 1047, Nasir-i Khosraw, a forty-two-year-old Persian from Marv in Khorasan (today's Republic of Turkmenistan), arrived in Jerusalem accompanied by his brother and a Hindu manservant. They stayed until May, when they departed for Mekkah, a journey of some fifteen days from Jerusalem. They returned on 2 July and left for Egypt shortly thereafter.

Nasir-i Khosraw was no ordinary traveler, nor was he on an official mission, even though he had served as a bureaucrat of some sort in his native land. He was a middle-aged man who had studied philosophy and theology, had written some poetry, and who decided, suddenly, to seek his personal salvation from a somewhat dissipated private life by accomplishing the pilgrimage to Mekkah, in principle an obligation for all Muslims. As he relates himself, he paid off his debts, "renounced everything worldly, except for a few necessities," and began a journey that was to last five and half years. He returned home on 23 October 1052 and moved to a small valley in Badakhshan, in contemporary Tajikistan just north of the Afghan frontier, where he became a major figure in Isma'ili thought and, more generally, in the explosion of eleventh-century thinking about faith and reason, nature and divine Revelation, personal righteousness and duty to established authority, ultimate salvation and immanent life. Buddhism and Christianity also spawned similar seekers of truth during this century, and Nasir-i Khosraw was not the only Muslim of his time to have sought the path of salvation, in part at least, through extensive travel. Scholars have debated whether the journey of 1047–1052 followed or preceded Nasir-i Khosraw's adoption of Isma'ilism as his interpretation of Islam and his activities as a teacher and missionary of that branch of shi'ite Islam. This particular question is not overly important for our purposes of understanding the city of Jerusalem, but it may have some bearing on the overall interpretation to be given to his *Sefernameh* or *Travel Book*, a rather peculiar book about a rather peculiar trip.[5]

There were long stretches of road carefully measured, so that, in the manner of a contemporary frequent flyer, Nasir-i Khosraw can proclaim at the end that he covered 2200 *parasangs* (somewhere around 6600 miles). In many places, especially crossing the Arabian peninsula, he describes the peculiarities of medieval travel in the Near East: waiting for weeks until a caravan could be formed, fighting for bed and board, complex financial arrangements, boredom barely alleviated by visits to depressing settlements. But he does not really write to help later pilgrims, but to record his own experience away from his homeland. The personal nature of the trip is further emphasized by the idiosyncratic route which led him to avoid Baghdad and the central world of Islam, and to cross northern Iran, Azerbayjan, and eastern Anatolia as fast as possible.[6] There are three longer descriptions of cities visited more than once, usually with the different visits telescoped into a single account: Mekkah, the alleged goal of the whole trip; Cairo, the Fatimid and Isma'ili capital which he describes in glowing terms; and Jerusalem. Other places are barely mentioned, at best cursorily identified by a few characteristics, with the curious exception of Tinnis in the Egyptian delta, whose textile manufacturing plants clearly fascinated Nasir-i Khosraw.

The long description of Jerusalem is no doubt

because of the special role the city was expected to play within the Fatimid order at its apogee in the middle of the eleventh century. The author states that he made sketches (*taswîr*) of what he saw and that he took notes in a diary (*rûznâme*). The acknowledgment of such procedures is rare enough among medieval travelers from any land, but, when it occurs, it usually involves major sanctuaries—as, for example, those of Jerusalem drawn by Arculf in the seventh century, or those of Mekkah found in Azraqi's ninth-century survey of the Arabian sanctuary—rather than strictly local ones.[7] Since his account of Jerusalem, like the one dealing with Mekkah, was meant to provide an impression of Jerusalem for people who had never been there, he guaranteed the accuracy of what he wrote by volunteering that he was not writing from memory but from notes taken on the spot. And, probably with the same objective of making a space understandable to those who would never go there, his account of the Haram is like a recorded walk through the sanctuary. One can follow his footsteps and reconstruct what he saw. The rest of the city is summarized in less specific terms.

The City and Its Gates

Bayt al-Maqdis or "Quds" ("Holiness" or "the Holy one"), as Nasir-i Khosraw tells us it is called colloquially, was at this time a pilgrimage city for all Muslims, who went there if they could not make the pilgrimage to Mekkah, and more especially for Syrians and Palestinians when they celebrated the circumcision of their male children (up to 20,000 were said to gather there for such occasions). It was probably because of the pilgrimage that Jerusalem was provided with an endowed hospital, well stocked in drugs and potions and with several salaried physicians, located somewhere in the western part of the city, probably north of the Haram. Christians and Jews came, he says, from the Byzantine world or elsewhere to local churches (*kilisia*) or synagogues (*kunisht*). This is the only mention of Jews in Nasir-i Khosraw's text, a curious omission if we recall the significant Jewish presence in the city at that time. The Church of the Holy Sepulchre is

mentioned at the end of his account as an edifice of considerable size rebuilt by the Byzantines after its destruction by order of the caliph al-Hakim, and filled with painted and mosaic images, and usually many priests and monks.[8]

The Persian traveler notes that Jerusalem is located on a rocky terrain, without water and trees, but with well irrigated rich villages around it, supposedly with twenty thousand, presumably male, inhabitants.[9] Its walls are of stone and mortar and its iron gates protect access to stone-paved streets which can easily channel rain water; there are tall buildings, nice bazaars, and artisans grouped according to their specialities or to some other ordering system.[10] This idyllic picture of a nearly perfect city provided by Nasir-i Khosraw is, without doubt, the idealized one he wanted to leave with people who would never set foot in Jerusalem.

The most original feature of the city lay to the east of the walls and the mosque: the deep valley of Gehenna with ancient mausoleums followed by the huge expanse of the *Sâhirah*, apparently a reference to the slope of the Mount of Olives, with more tombs. The *Sâhirah*, says our traveler, is the place where the resurrection will take place, and many people from all over the world take up residence there in order to be present when the end of time comes. Throughout the area, he says, are places for prayer and for special requests to God and to the various intermediaries leading to Him. The traditional entrance of hell was, it will be recalled, in the valley of Gehenna and legend had it, in Nasir-i Khosraw's time, that one could hear the voices of people in hell. Our systematic traveler went to the designated place but, he says, heard nothing, yet, while describing the setting of Jerusalem, he calls twice on God's mercy, thereby demonstrating his own personal piety and recalling, albeit indirectly, the ultimate role of Jerusalem formulated many centuries before him.

Nasir-i Khosraw's city can easily be set in space (figs. 69–72), and sources other than his account allow us to fill in a number of features that he mentions in very general terms. Two of them, the shape of the city and the new state of the Holy Sepulchre, plus some information about population which is not in Nasir-i Khosraw's text, are integral to my reconstruction of the Fatimid city.

While Nasir-i Khosraw simply acknowledges the powerful impression of the city with its walls and gates, contemporaneous geographers, like Muqaddasi half a century earlier, provide the names of the gates and other important details about the city, and a passage in a historical text, however controversial, offers some information about the actual dimensions of the city in the middle of the eleventh century.

Eight gates are mentioned by Muqaddasi, of which seven pose no particular problem: the Gate of the Mihrab of David certainly corresponds to today's Hebron or Jaffa Gate on the western side, since by the tenth century the place mentioned in the Koran to which David had retreated was often localized on the top of the citadel, adjacent to this major gate; the Zion Gate, on the western end of the south wall, is known today as the Gate of the Prophet David because it leads to the holy complex of Zion with an alleged tomb of David, a complex whose inclusion or exclusion from the walled city before the Crusades is a matter of controversy (see below, p. 167); the Jericho Gate, called today the Gate of St. Stephen, is on the east side of the city; the Damascus Gate or the Gate of the Column ("Bab al-Amud"), is more or less in the center of the northern wall; the Gate of Jeremiah's Grotto ("Bab jubb Armiyah"), possibly the gate known today as Herod's Gate (or "Bab Sahirah"), also on the northern wall, but farther east[11]; and the Gate of Siloam is somewhere in the eastern part of a south wall that no longer exists[12]; the Gate of the Nea[13] must also have been on the southern half, probably not very far from the Sion Gate. Several possibilities exist for the eighth gate, the Gate of the Palace or of the Court ("Bab al-Balat"), none of which is really convincing. The interesting point about Muqaddasi's list is that all the gates except one, the Jericho Gate, refer to other features of the city or its immediate neighborhood. Two refer also to personages from religious lore, but one of them, Jeremiah, is a secondary figures in the history of Muslim prophets. In contrast to the Haram entrances, the gates to the city were mostly of practical and local interest, without the other meanings and names that appear much later.

For our purpose of imagining the city, two further observations missing from Nasir-i Khosraw or underplayed by him need mention. First, there was a citadel, qal'ah, in Jerusalem, which was the traditional seat of power on the western wall that had been either restored or rehabilitated for the use of Fatimid (and perhaps earlier) officials whose existence is implied in several sources.[14] Second, according to all Muslim accounts, Jerusalem was a city well provided with food and other merchandise, but there is no mention of the bazaars. That there were more than one is perhaps implied by some of the Jewish sources, which do not include references to non-Jewish commercial life.[15] And it is easy to conclude, simply because of its location, that a bazaar north of the Holy Sepulchre was restricted primarily to Christians.

Some doubts have been thrown recently on one fact about the city which had been generally accepted. Around 1033, the caliph al-Zahir brought to an end the extended Jerusalem created by Eudocia in the fifth century by shortening the southern wall to approximately its present extent. A text by a Christian chronicler of the following century, Yahya ibn Sa'id al-Antaki, asserts that in 424/1032–1033 the walls of the city were built (the verb used is bana) by order of the caliph al-Zahir and that many churches were destroyed, including the church on top of Mount Sion, which by implication would have been outside of the city's walls.[16] It has recently been pointed out that Yahya's text contains confusions about the sequence of earthquakes that would have led to these restorations or to new monuments, and that nothing in the text refers to "new" walls.[17] Since the shortened walls essentially returned to the layout of the old Roman walls, they were not, stricto sensu, new. Furthermore, enough hard and circumstantial evidence exists about a shift of direction for the main entrances to the Haram to justify the conclusion that al-Zahir shortened the south walls of the city to approximately their present alignment, but this does not mean that no one lived in the area south (and especially southeast) of the city, simply that those

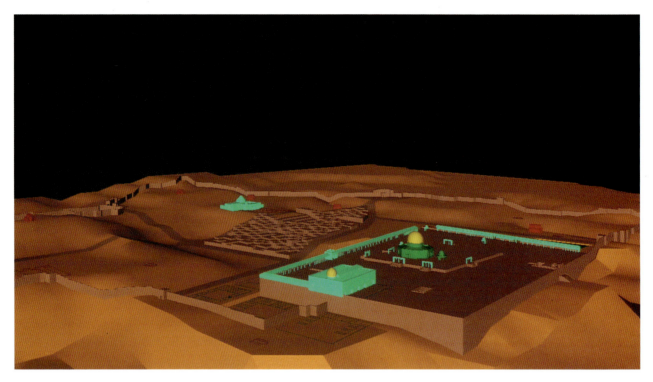

Figure 69. Jerusalem in the eleventh century, schematic view from the southeast. Note the shortened wall on the south side corresponding to the present one. The ensemble of the Holy Sepulchre is in the middle left; the arcade on the west and north sides of the Haram, the large Western Gate, the arcades over the steps leading to the platform of the Dome of the Rock are new Fatimid creations. Some of the domes may be earlier.

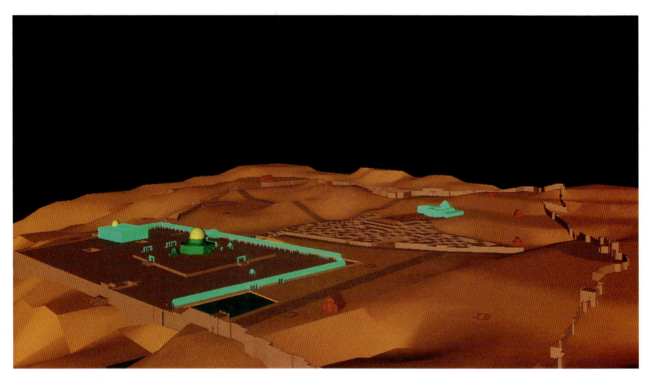

Figure 70. Jerusalem in the eleventh century, schematic view from the northeast.

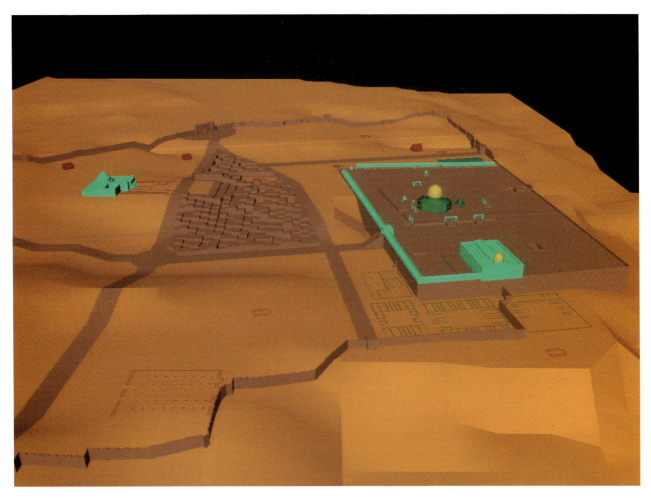

Figure 71. Jerusalem in the eleventh century, schematic view from the south.

Figure 72. Jerusalem in the eleventh century, schematic view from the east.

who lived there were no longer protected by the wall.

The Holy Sepulchre

There is no doubt that in September of 1009, an order of the Fatimid caliph al-Hakim, the so-called "mad" caliph, was carried out and the Holy Sepulchre was looted and then destroyed.[18] Many reasons are given as to why al-Hakim issued this order, but none is really satisfactory. It may have been just one episode in a continuous series of destructive actions against Christian and Jewish buildings—a constant theme in Christian and Jewish writing—which were a form of retaliation for alleged Byzantine attacks on Muslim buildings in Constantinople; or an expression of the caliph's own newly formulated religious beliefs; or a puritanical assault on a celebrated monument reputed to contain expensive treasures and to have witnessed miraculous events viewed by Muslims as fraudulent if fascinating.[19] The patriarch, according to some sources, had been warned of the coming assault and managed to hide many of the treasures in safe places. Every stone is reported to have been violently separated from every other stone, but much of the earlier church is still there. Furthermore, relations between Byzantines and Fatimids were not particularly bad during these years and, in fact, western European Christians seem to have been more seriously affected by the story of the destruction of the sanctuary than the Byzantines.

We are obviously dealing with another one of these transformations which centered on Jerusalem during these centuries, the manipulation of an actual event, however minor, into a series of mythical accounts, each satisfying an emotional or ideological purpose. Whatever happened, a sufficiently major transformation of the Holy Sepulchre took place in the early decades of the century that it is reasonable to connect it to a destruction caused by the religiously obsessed al-Hakim rather than by an earthquake. Furthermore, the connection of this transformation with the exercise of power by Fatimid caliphs is supported by the fragment of an inscription found in the Holy Sepulchre and now somewhere in Istanbul, which goes as follows: "In the name of God, the Compassionate, the Merciful, the august order has come from the high authority [al-amr al-'âli, a very rare formula] to protect (say-ânah) this mosque and to restore ('imârah) it and that no protected people (dhimmi) enter it in order to [lacuna] or for any other purpose. Let no one challenge this order and let it be executed in full, with the will of God."[20] Van Berchem has connected this inscription with a small mosque erected, against all alleged earlier agreements, inside the complex of the Holy Sepulchre some time before 940 or even 930, after the Christians of Jerusalem had sided with the rebel Muslim movement of the Qarmatians. Like its counterparts built on either side of the Holy Sepulchre after the Crusades,[21] this mosque served less a practical purpose for Muslims than the ideological one of asserting Muslim power over Christians. The inscription, however, is datable to the eleventh century on paleographic grounds and would be a renewed assertion of Muslim rule that would make sense around the time of al-Hakim's persecutions or else when the reconstruction began after 1033, during the reign of al-Mustansir, and which was completed before the visit of Nasir-i Khosraw in 1047.[22]

The reconstruction was a major event recorded by Greek, Arab Christian, and Arab Muslim sources, and the expensive liturgical objects brought to it from Constantinople were duly recorded by Fatimid customs officials.[23] Although specific details are bound to remain in dispute, the main points of the reconstruction (fig. 73) are two: the entrance facing the Dome of the Rock was abandoned and a new entrance created that faced northward, more or less corresponding to the contemporary entrance; and the new building closed into itself with its constructions and open spaces invisible from the outside, except for the dome or dome-like structure over the Anastasis. The visual presence of the holiest Christian sanctuary was diminished and processional access to it was restricted. A large Muslim sanctuary, jealously protected, reinforced Muslim presence, and the Umayyad order with equal visual sectarian expression in the city of Jerusalem had been broken. It is

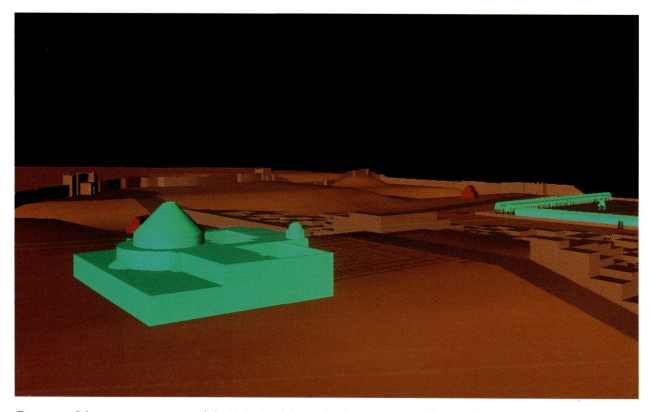

Figure 73. Schematic reconstruction of the Holy Sepulchre in the eleventh century. The ensemble is seen from the northwest as a closed space with a high conical dome over the Anastasis. The older building is outlined on the ground.

odd that this change occurred during the relatively benign and open rule of the Fatimids, but, as I shall show below, al-Hakim and his successors only confirmed the deterioration of the older equilibrium. It should be noted, however, that the reconstructed church could hold eight thousand people, according to Nasir-i Khosraw, and that it contained many gold and silver crosses, elaborate vestments, expensive textiles, paintings or mosaics, icons or, at least, images, of Abraham, Isma'il, Isaac, of Jacob with his sons, precisely and probably not fortuitously the prophets also honored in the Haram. There were also narrative paintings of *Christ's Entry into Jerusalem* and of a *Last Judgment* with representations of heaven and hell, including the denizens of the latter. It is clear that, just as in the seventh century, the Christians were more than happy to show off to a Muslim visitor the technical qualities of their art. But it is also interesting that Nasir-i Khosraw does not mention (or was not shown) representa-

tions of the Crucifixion or the Resurrection, which must have been there, events in the life of Jesus that were interpreted quite differently by Christians and Muslims. The *Entry into Jerusalem*, by contrast, has ecumenical appeal, while eternal reward and punishment are essential aspects of both Christian and Muslim messages. In other words, at least some of the images in the Holy Sepulchre may well have been meant for non-Christians as well. Nothing has, apparently, been preserved of these eleventh-century paintings and mosaics, but something of their technique and quality may be imagined from small ornamental fragments discovered two decades ago and attributed to the very beginning of the Crusades, when local craftsmen still predominated.[24]

On the whole, Nasir-i Khosraw's account does not do justice to the extent and variety of non-Muslim presence in the city. The Holy Sepulchre, the most hallowed place of Christian belief, was the responsibility of a patriarch, one of five at that time. The names and dates of most of these patriarchs have been preserved. Their political and religious orders as well as their revenues came mostly from Constantinople and their status was negotiated between Fatimid and Byzantine rulers. Many other Christian establishments existed in and especially around the walled city. Among eastern churches, there were Jacobites, Armenians, and particularly Georgians who built the monastery of the Holy Cross to the west of the city.[25] It is even possible, although the evidence is circumstantial, that by 1063 or so, a true Christian quarter had been established, funded by the taxes levied on the island of Cyprus,[26] probably in the area between the Holy Sepulchre and the citadel, where it is now located.

While the Byzantine political predominance and the existence of oriental schismatic or heretic establishments are not surprising, the resurgence of the Latin presence is more unexpected. Already by the early ninth century, almost a third of the Christian clergy in Jerusalem appear to have been Latin.[27] The merchants of Amalfi were allowed by the Fatimid caliph al-Mustansir to build or sponsor a monastery, a church, a hospital, and two hostels, one for men and the other for women, somewhere near the Holy Sepulchre.[28] The most remarkable Latin activity was pilgrimage. It is well documented for the eleventh century through groups of religious and feudal leaders, men and women, for whom the trip seems to have been a sort of psychological release as well as an expression of conspicuous consumption comparable to the grand tours of northern aristocrats in the eighteenth and nineteenth centuries or the exotic cruises of today. In 1065, seven thousand men from south Germany are said to have participated in such a pilgrimage; two thousand of them returned, after fascinating and often tragic adventures.[29] Whatever these journeys did for the souls of the pilgrims, they certainly led to an increase of both the factual and the legendary information about the Holy City.

But their impressions were not written down as fully as were those of early Christian pilgrims, who were emotionally involved in the discovery of hallowed spaces and who shared a common culture with most of the city's leadership. Like modern tourists, these later Latin visitors were foreigners to all the local inhabitants, even fellow Christians. The terseness of most of the texts reporting these Latin pilgrimages of the tenth and eleventh centuries do not add enough to the other sparse information we have to help us very much in placing these Christian visitors within the spaces of the city.

The Jewish Population

Matters become even more difficult to visualize when Jews are added to Muslim and Christian crowds. Jews are mostly absent from the large books on medieval Jerusalem published in the early part of this century or in the nineteenth century because so little was known about them. But since World War II the Geniza fragments have added so substantially to the available documentation that the names and actions of thousands of Jews can be recovered, at least in part. Much has been written on this population, on its makeup and on precisely what it did at the time of Nasir-i Khosraw, and many controversies have already arisen on how to interpret the data.[30] For the purpose of reconstructing or imagining the physical city, I will limit myself to a few observations only.

First of all, the Jews were divided into three main groups: the Rabbinites, probably the majority, who came from everywhere, even though the core was probably Palestinian; the Karaites, from Iraq and Iran, who were very active both intellectually and socially and maintained close connections with Karaites elsewhere; and the Samaritans, also Palestinian, who were probably not very numerous in Jerusalem. The relations between these groups were far from harmonious, and conflicts arose over trivial as well as significant matters. As a result, the *gaonate*, the highest Jewish authority in the city, was much occupied in the administration of justice. The Jewish community was made up of separate groups and a hierarchy of restricted functions, each with some sort of spatial requirement, not necessarily with an architectural identification.

Second, far more consistently than Christians and Muslims, Jews were in constant epistolary communication with other Jews everywhere and, although the sources are not very clear on this point, a considerable movement in and out of Jerusalem, by individuals and by whole families, seems likely. Already in the eleventh century there are instances of pious Jews who, when old or suffering reverses in fortune, came to Jerusalem to die and be buried there. Contemporary Jerusalem was far more important in the lives and emotions of Jews everywhere than to Christians or Muslims. For Christians the physical Jerusalem was, with significant exceptions like the Crusades, less important than its symbolic transfers into the liturgy and the hope of salvation, and for Muslims, the awareness of Jerusalem was only beginning to take shape. Jews needed space to meet co-religionists from far away, and their formal and informal institutions existed primarily as places for contacts.

Third, it is very difficult to identify and locate Jewish spaces in the Jerusalem of the eleventh century. Official institutions met on the Mount of Olives, where certificates of learning, for instance, were awarded, and there was a "community house" (dâr al-jamâ'ah) inside the city, but there are few clear references to synagogues, except for a rather complicated story dealing with a cave used as a place of prayer.[31] Whether a Jewish quarter existed is controversial.[32] In fact, an event took place in 1011 that illustrates the difficulty of seeking, in genuine and authentic sources, answers to questions that were not asked at the time. The funeral cortege of one Paltiel was attacked by Muslim ruffians; the incident led to the establishment of new rules about Jewish funeral processions. One could imagine a procession going from the south of the city, where the deceased lived, through quarters that housed both Muslims and Christians, and leaving through the eastern Jericho gate.[33] The remarkable feature of this story is not the funeral procession, inasmuch as we have no other account of another funeral procession to verify that the new rules were followed, but the proximity of dwellings used by people with different religious allegiances. As we do not have any real evidence about the existence of a Christian quarter until later in the century, I prefer to hypothesize that, in the middle of the century, there was a great deal of haphazard informality about where people lived. Although the case of Jerusalem may be an exceptional one, this hypothesis may call into question, at least before the major upheavals of the twelfth century, the rigidity of the separation into ethnic or religious quarters that has been seen as characteristic of traditional Islamic urban order from the very beginning.

Around 985, Muqaddasi wrote, in an oft-quoted sentence, that the Muslims of Jerusalem were ignorant and weak in religious learning and that Jews and Christians had the upper hand in running the city. Half a century later Nasir-i Khosraw hardly mentions Christians and Jews, and his description of Muslim piety, if not learning, is quite favorable. Yet all evidence points to a remarkable increase in the number of non-Muslims in the early part of the eleventh century. Obviously, Nasir-i Khosraw was only interested in *his* people, just as western pilgrims or Jewish letter-writers only mentioned members of other religious groups when they were hurt or annoyed by them. Reflecting the way the Holy Sepulchre had turned inward to its own spaces, allowing a few non-Christian visitors occasionally, the city became a construct of separate groups aloof in their own religious agendas, intermingling but hardly speaking to each other.

The Muslim Sanctuary

The major part of Nasir-i Khosraw's story deals with the huge Muslim sanctuary of Jerusalem. He calls it the *masjid*, at times modifying the generic term with *adîneh*, "Friday," or *jâmi'*, "congregational," thus seemingly reflecting even in the eleventh century some continuing uncertainty about the precise name used for the grandiose creation of the Umayyads. The uniqueness of the place is recognized by the Persian traveler because of its overall dimensions and character and because of the fundamental reasons for its creation. Nasir-i Khosraw, who spent a long time looking at the sanctuary from different angles, describes first its height, which exceeded everything around it, then its dimensions, which were recorded on the building itself, an inscription that may well be on the fragments preserved at the northern edge of the sanctuary,[34] and, finally, the sheer quality of its rich masonry and its carefully paved ground. Then he explains that it is what it is because of the rock "which God commanded Moses to make the direction of prayer." Solomon built a *masjid* around the rock which served as the "*mihrab* for all creation,"[35] and so it remained until the Prophet Muhammad transferred the *qiblah* to Mekkah. The essential points here for understanding the city in the eleventh century are the formal statement of the sanctuary's relationship to the pre-Islamic revelation to Jewish prophets, in this case

Moses, and the acknowledgment of the rock as the reason for the existence of the sanctuary. The intermediate history of the city between Solomon and the eleventh century is not mentioned, although what Nasir-i Khosraw saw took physical shape during that period.

Having introduced the sanctuary as a whole, Nasir-i Khosraw proceeded with his visit, starting from within the city and the main (presumably) bazaar, located somewhere north or northwest of the Holy Sepulchre, and moving westward to a splendid gateway (*dargâh*), which corresponds to the present principal entrance of the Haram known as *Bab al-Silsilah*, the Gate of the Chain. That gateway

Figure 74. The Fatimid western gateway to the Haram al-Sharif, a reconstruction. The steps are not mentioned in Nasir-i Khosraw's text, but are required by the terrain and its likely debris, although the exact height of the stairs is conjectural.

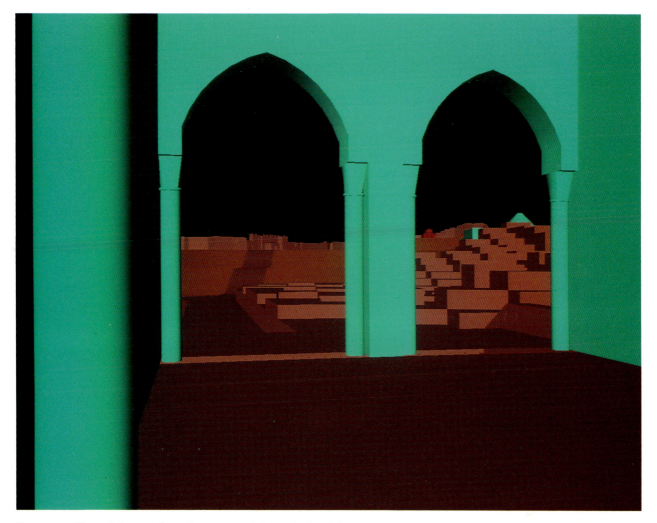

Figure 75. View of the city from the new gate. The Holy Sepulchre appears above the conjectural houses.

consisted of several elements according to Nasir-i Khosraw, which are not all fully understandable, as, for example, the two "wings" (janab) on either side of the domes. The reconstruction we are proposing (fig. 74) is based on the Jerusalem pattern of double dome entrances established in the Herodian Temple and restored by the Umayyads, but other possibilities may exist as well. The majestic staircase we have placed in front of the gate, is not mentioned by Nasir-i Khosraw, but it seems required by the terrain.[36] After the partial closing of the southern gates to the Haram, this gateway was meant to be the main link between the city and its sanctuary. As one stood on its threshold, one could contemplate the whole city to the west, including the Holy Sepulchre (fig. 75), and as one climbed

toward the Haram, one would be dazzled by its doors decorated with gilt brass, its colorful mosaics that shone whenever the sun's rays fell on them, and a formal inscription, also in mosaic, with the name and title of the Fatimid caliph.[37]

Once on the esplanade of the Haram, Nasir-i Khosraw was aware of a portico leading southward and then eastward toward the covered part of the mosque (what is known today as the Masjid al-Aqsa), for which he uses—at the beginning of his account, and not later when he visits it—the unusual term of maqsurah, usually meaning the place inside a mosque reserved for the ruler and frequently marked by some sort of architectural or decorative element. Having glimpsed the mosque to his right, Nasis-i Khosraw turned northward to his left along a portico of sixty-four arches which followed the western side of the sanctuary. He passed by another gate, the Gate of Hell (*Bab al-Saqar*), then turned eastward, probably still following a colonnade, and encountered two more gateways, *Bab al-Asbât*, Gate of the Tribes, and *Bab al-Abwâb*, Gate of Gates, with three passageways. To the right, on the surface of the esplanade but close to the portico, a dome on tall columns decorated with lamps (*qanâdil*) and known as the *Qubbat Ya'qûb*, commemorated the place where Jacob, usually associated in the Muslim tradition with Abraham and Isaac or Isma'il, prayed.

By the northeastern corner was a portico and a large dome with an inscription identifying it as the *mihrab* of Zakariyah, who was one of the traditional figures honored under Christian rule and in Umayyad times, even though it was not necessarily the same personage. Outside the Haram space, but presumably quite close to it, although Nasir-i Khosraw does not say so directly, there was an area with two sufi establishments,[38] containing many fine *mihrabs*. It was only on Fridays that the members of the mystical order went to pray in the mosque proper.

Then Nasir-i Khosraw proceeded southward along the eastern wall which seems to have remained without a portico. He described the Golden Gate as a handsome monument of stone, "so finely hewn that one would say it has been made of a single block" (fig. 76). He acknowledged its elaborate designs and mentioned two impressive iron doors alleged to have been made for Solomon. Once inside the building, he could see two additional doors, probably closed in Nasir-i Khosraw's time as they are now: the *Bab al-Rahmah*, Gate of Mercy, and the *Bab al-Tawbah*, Gate of Repentance. The hall (*dihliz*) in front of them was a mosque decorated with beautiful carpets. The whole ensemble was associated by Nasir-i Khosraw with the place where God accepted David's repentence and it apparently retained its redemptive quality as he prays there for cleansing the sin of disobedience and for divine grace to be distributed to all the Prophet's servants through the holiness (*harmah*) of the Prophet. The oratory was serviced by a differ-

ent group of people than those who dealt with the rest of the sanctuary, although Nasir-i Khosraw gives no information about the nature of the difference. Many people, he writes, come to pray and meditate, as they face the eastern wall separating them from the place of judgment and resurrection.

Proceeding southward along the eastern wall, the pilgrim descended into a mosque, some ten by twenty meters in size, with a stone roof supported by marble columns. The mosque contained as its main *mihrab* the Cradle of Jesus, and additional *mihrabs* on either side were attributed to Mary and Zakariyah. Appropriate Koranic passages dealing with both of them are inscribed in the *mihrabs* and one of the columns has traces of Mary's fingers as she grasped it while in labor. The space described here is part of the rather poorly maintained halls that lead today to the vast underground area now known as the Stables of Solomon, which include the small Single Gate, probably a later creation, and the Triple Gate used in Umayyad times as one of the main entries to the Haram. In Nasir-i Khosraw's time there does not seem to have been a connection between the underground mosque and the halls below, whose subsequent use as stables by the Crusaders certainly transformed their appearance. Since the Crusaders did not associate Jerusalem with the birth of Christ, they probably limited the use of this area to purely military purposes. In Ayyubid and Mamluk times, the place of Christ's birth became again the main commemorative function of this area, but on the whole it remained a secondary space in the whole sanctuary.

Then, Nasir-i Khosraw moves to the building he clearly calls the *masjid al-Aqsa*, although from afar it had been just a *maqsurah*.[39] His description of the building contains measurements taken from many places, a numbered list of columns, and many details about the techniques used in construction and decoration. Scholars have compared his description with the equally precise but shorter passage by Muqaddasi describing the building around 985. The major intervening events were the two earthquakes of 1016 and 1034, which probably damaged the building seen by Muqaddasi, and the shortening of the city walls completed in 1033, which made much

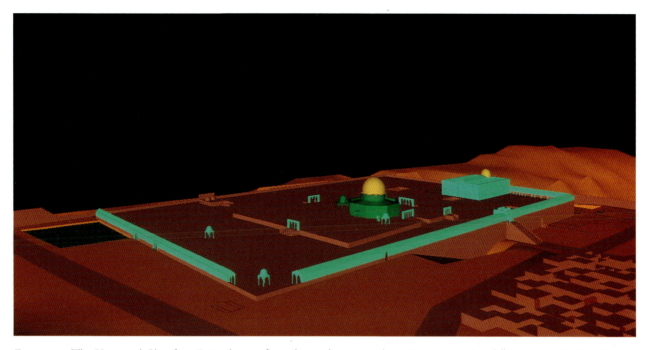

Figure 76. The Haram al-Sharif in Fatimid times from the northwest, a schematic reconstruction. There was probably also a balustrade around the central platform. The exact location of the small homes is not certain.

of the southern wall of the Haram into a city wall. It is therefore legitimate to explain the discrepancies between the descriptions of Nasir-i Khosraw and Muqaddasi as the results of reconstructions and to reconcile these discrepancies with the archaeological record of the building and with its present shape, the result of many changes by the Crusaders, the Ayyubids, the Mamluks, and, to a smaller degree, the Ottomans.[40] But so far, these fragments of information have not been brought together in a systematic manner. It is, in fact, probably impossible to accomplish with certainty, because, as has been amply demonstrated more than once, written, visual, and archaeological documents are never constructing the same building, but different versions of the same building. The observations that follow deal primarily with the impression likely to have been given by the building and limit themselves to features about which little doubt can be had.

The mosque seen by Nasir-i Khosraw (fig. 77) had seven gates to the north and ten to the east, indicating a considerable shrinking in size compared with the Umayyad mosque following consolidation after either destruction or a more realistic

assessment of the population of the city. The abandoned naves were on the western side, where a newly completed arcade abutted the mosque, in all likelihood, an assymetrical building with parallels in several reconstructions of early Islamic mosques.[41] We know that much of the present axial nave of the mosque was redone in Fatimid times. This is particularly true of the dome area in front of the *mihrab*, a particularly striking architectural ensemble that has never been studied as a whole. It begins with a triumphal arch (fig. 78) decorated with mosaics: on a golden background two grandiose vegetal assemblages—genetically related to the artificial trees of the Umayyad vocabulary of the Dome of the Rock, but somewhat constrained in design and without the exuberance of the model—above a thick ornamental band of frets on either side of a curious floral composition (fig. 79) whose location gives it an emblematic importance impossible to find in other sources. Above the floral assemblages a long inscription, which has never received the attention it deserves,[42] reads as follows: "In the name of God, the Compassionate, the Merciful, GLORY TO THE ONE WHO TOOK HIS SERVANT FOR A JOURNEY

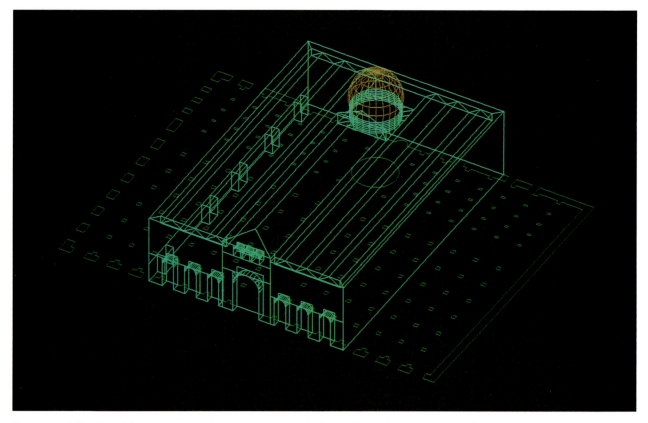

Figure 77. The Aqsa Mosque in Fatimid times, reconstructed plan and wire-frame elevation. The plan of the older mosque appears on the ground.

Figure 78. The Aqsa Mosque in Fatimid times, reconstruction.

BY NIGHT FROM THE MASJID AL-HARAM TO THE MASJID AL-AQSA WHOSE PRECINCTS WE HAVE BLESSED (K 17:1, in part). Has renovated (*jaddada*) its [presumably the mosque's] construction (*'imârab*)[43] our lord Ali Abu al-Hasan, the *imam* al-Zahir li-A'zaz din Allah, Commander of the Faithful, son of al-Hakim bi-amr Allah, Commander of the Faithful, may the blessing of God be on him, on his pure ancestors, and on his noble descendants. By the hand of Ali ibn Abd al-Rahman, may God reward him. The (job) was supervised by Abu al-Qasim *al-sharif*[44] al-Hasan al-Husaini [small lacuna] may God help him."[45]

This inscription is important in several ways. It is the earliest citation remaining in Jerusalem of the key Koranic revelation dealing with the *masjid al-Aqsa* and proclaiming what Nasir-i Khosraw repeats in his account: that "this," meaning the mosque, "is where God transported Muhammad from Mekkah on the night of his ascension (*mi'raj*)." The inscription identifies the mosque as the place where the miraculous event occurred and proclaims that fact with a dramatic and most unusual (at least in mosques) formal arch.[46] For, as made clear in the inscription noted by Nasir-i Khosraw at the entrance to the Haram, holiness is closely associated with the genealogy of the Fatimids and with the source of their power.

Furthermore, the inscription provides the name of the caliph al-Zahir, who ruled between 1021 and 1036. The same caliph is mentioned in another inscription, no longer extant, which was recorded by the pious traveler Ali al-Harawi, who visited Jerusalem in 1173 during the rule of the Crusaders.[47] There the precise date of October 1035 is given for the completion and decoration of the cupola and one Abdallah ibn Hasan al-Misri is identified as the mosaicist. The person in charge of the work was Abu al-Qasim Ali, an important Fatimid vizier, who died in March 1045. He is probably the very person named in the inscription on the triumphal arch, where his correct name was not remembered by some later restorer.[48] Whatever the details, it is reasonable to point to the year 1035 as the time of completion for what the Fatimids rebuilt and Naser-i Khosraw saw.

Once the pilgrim had passed under the triumphal arch with its proclamation of faith under the benevolent rule of the Fatimid dynasty, he entered into the domed space in front of the *mihrab*. Such a space is not at all unusual as the place reserved for the prince or the governor representing him but serving also to mark the focal center of a sanctuary. The remarkable feature of the Aqsa mosque is the extensive mosaic decoration of that space. The ornamental pendentives (fig. 80) are covered with gold, except in the center where a huge dish-like shape with wreaths of vegetal motifs and peacock eyes is embedded in the architectural form.[49] The effect of these pendentives is quite striking and, especially when the sun shines on one of them, something like the awe reported by Nasir-i Khosraw at the sight of the mosaics of the domes at the entrance to the Haram can still be felt. Between the square and the dome proper there is a drum with sixteen panels of mosaics alternating with sixteen windows (figs. 81, 82). These mosaics have been studied in some detail by Henri Stern, whose conclusions can be adopted in the following way. The vases carrying floral crowns or small water basins and surrounded by thick bushes or trees can be related to the Umayyad decorative vocabulary of the late seventh and early eighth centuries. And, although somewhat repetitious, the sixteen panels are richer in texture than the floral compositions of the triumphal arch. Such stylistic distinctions need not reflect different periods. Actually, the designs appear in the drums at the scale on which they were made, while on the triumphal arch they are magnified to a rigidity absent from the original models. This point argues for the novelty of the triumphal arch in the architectural vocabulary of the eastern Mediterranean at that time.

In summarizing his comments on the Aqsa Mosque, Nasir-i Khosraw, like the sophisticated architectural critic that he was, reflects that it was a building making two different impressions, depending on whether the doors were open or closed. When open, external light came more or less at ground level from the north and the east. When they were closed, light came from the clerestory of

Figure 79. The Aqsa Mosque, interior, mosaic on "triumphal arch." The inscription is found on the upper part of a much restored wall.

the central nave and from side windows and therefore from above. In both instances, the building manipulated natural light to create different effects, and Nasir-i Khosraw, like most visitors today, was deeply affected by the esthetic power of the Aqsa Mosque.

In his description of the Aqsa Mosque, Nasir-i Khosraw mentions the impressive bronze doors added to the northern entrances into the mosque by the Abbasid caliph al-Ma'mun. These gates were probably damaged when Nasir-i Khosraw saw them, because, as we know from an inscription, in 1065 the whole northern facade (*wajh*) of the mosque was redone by order of the caliph al-Mustansir.[50] A more interesting, although also minor, observation is that, according to Nasir-i Khosraw, there were large chests in the mosque which, as in Mekkah, were associated with the

principal cities of Syria and Iraq and probably were used for liturgical or social practices about which little else is known.

Nasir-i Khosraw's more important observation begins with his mention of the various cisterns, channels, and pools that are found all over the area in front of the Aqsa Mosque. Their existence is fairly easy to explain by the fact that the surface of the esplanade sloops down toward the mosque where water would tend to collect. But he continues by calling attention to four gates to the outside in the south part of the Haram. His account poses some problems of identification and placement to which I shall return later in this chapter, but his mention of the gates in relation to the mosque is important for the overall interpretation of the sanctuary in Fatimid times. The gates are: *Bab al-Nabi*, under the Aqsa Mosque, Gate of the

Prophet, through which the Prophet is believed to have come to the Haram, where there is a trace of the shield of Hamza ibn Abd al-Muttalib, a relative and companion of the Prophet—its beautiful masonry is attributed to Solomon; *Bab al'Ayn*, Gate of the Spring, facing toward the spring of Silwan, possibly the so-called Single Gate on the eastern end of the South wall; *Bab al-Khittah*, Gate of Forgiveness, referring to an enigmatic allusion in Koran 2:58 to the need for forgiveness as one enters a city; and *Bab al-Sakînah*, a reference to an old Semitic term for the holy contents of the Ark of the Covenant (K 2:248). According to Nasir-i Khosraw the Ark had once been at the site of the gate, but was taken away by angels as the Koranic reference mentions that angels will bring it back to Jerusalem; the entry itself was used as a mosque and contained many *mihrabs*, which suggests that it

was no longer open to the outside. It can be concluded from these statements that the south and southeastern areas were still common ways of access to the Haram, even after the shortening of the southern wall. But they also show the coexistence in the names of gates, as in so many other features of Jerusalem, of topocentric indications and, especially, holy connotations.

Having skirted it from all sides, Nasir-i Khosraw turned toward the central platform, called *dukkân* in the text.[51] He explains its existence by the height of the rock that had been a (or the) pre-Islamic *qiblah* or direction of prayer—in a more general sense a religious requirement comparable to the Muslim one but not identified with any special religion, another instance of the Persian traveler's curious reluctance to mention Jews and Judaism. The platform and its supporting walls are enclosed by

Figure 80. Mosaic on "triumphal arch"; detail of ornament on apex.

Figure 81. The Aqsa Mosque, eleventh-century pendentive in dome.

Figure 82. The Aqsa Mosque, mosaic on the drum below the dome.

marble plaques and form what Nasir-i Khosraw calls a *hazîrah*. The term, an interesting one for the definition of religious spaces in Islamic culture, means "enclosure" and has been used most consistently for the area around mausoleums, particularly the tomb of the Prophet in Madinah. Its broader connotation is that of a *hortus conclusus*, a "closed garden" with commemorative associations[52] that has a pronounced development in later Persian poetry and architectural programs. How much of these later considerations are appropriate for the eleventh-century Haram is uncertain, and it may be prudent to argue simply that Nasir-i Khosraw considered this platform a special and restricted area with collectively accepted meanings and with many opportunities for individual religious practices. A balance between collective and private behavior was developing in many urban cemeteries during this period.

There are four domes on this platform. The main one, the Dome of the Rock, was described by Nasir-i Khosraw as being in the middle of the platform, which was itself in the middle of the whole sanctuary, although neither description is architecturally accurate. Nasir-i Khosraw's description of the structure of the Dome of the Rock is, on the other hand, precise. The measurements he provides are so numerous that one can almost imagine him walking around, measuring and counting everything he can, writing it all down, and then adding whatever he was told about heights he could not measure himself. But he writes nothing about the mosaic decoration of the building, even though we know from an inscription that the mosaics of the drum were repaired, if not redone, in 1027–1028.[53] The capitals are extolled as particularly beautiful, as are also the many wonderful silver lamps with inscriptions and an enormous candle, nearly four meters high, sent by the Fatimid ruler in Egypt. The importance of the Fatimid caliphs in the organization and maintenance of the building is also expressed in three inscriptions (probably out of four original ones) that were not seen by our traveler because they were set inside a narrow gallery at the base of the dome.[54] They begin with Koran 9:18: "INDEED THE MOSQUES OF GOD WILL BE MAIN-TAINED (*'amara*) by those who believe in god."[55] Then a proclamation of al-Zahir's titles and of his order to repair (*'imârah*) the dome is followed by the name of the person in charge of the restoration, Sadid al-Dawlah Ali ibn Ahmad, otherwise unidentified; by the date (1022–1023); and, in the eastern inscription, by an extraordinary and very "secular" prayer: "May God give durable glory and power to our lord the Commander of the Faithful, may He give him possession of the East and of the West, and may He find him deserving of praise at the beginning and at the end of his actions."

Like the Umayyad inscription of the Dome of the Rock and its modification by al-Ma'mun, these texts are much more than records of the technical task of repairing or rebuilding the dome. They constitute a takeover of a holy place by a dynasty, what van Berchem called a *prise de possession*, shown not to men, but to God alone; and the inscription, facing the space of the Resurrection, offers to God the glory and success He has bestowed on the ruler. Thus the unique atmosphere of the Dome of the Rock with its mixture of legitimating authority and meditation on ultimate things was preserved by the Fatimids, but its formal expression was not visible and accessible to all visitors. The spirit or mood of the building seems to have sufficed to endow it with emotional and pious power, although it is possible that other visible written expressions had been removed before Nasir-i Khosraw saw it, either by the Crusaders or by the sunni leaders of Ayyubid or Mamluk times. The Persian traveler notes that there are always people in the Dome of the Rock, many pious individuals (*'abidān*) as well as attendants who keep it clean, and he adds that this is the third holiest place of God (*khāneh-i Khoda*), where prayers are particularly valuable. Yet the only explanations he gives for the holiness of the rock itself are two relatively minor and partially contradictory ones: that Abraham had been there with Isaac as a child, who left his footprints on it; and, mentioned at the end of his description of the platform and somewhat out of the logical sequence of his account, that the Prophet prayed there during his *mi'raj*, that the rock rose to honor the Prophet, and that the Prophet put his hand on the rock and froze it in mid-air, thus explaining the cave underneath. Both stories are imaginative interpretations of existing physical features, but hardly profound religious events. The Dome of the Rock thus appears under the Fatimids as a magnificent aberration, carefully maintained as a sanctuary for individual piety.[56] Princes patronized it and left in it statements of their power and their humility, but no true explanation for its construction, only a few popular stories about the rock that derive from local folk lore in response to the queries of pious tourists. A memory has been lost, purposefully or not, but a space exists, which, because its physical presence, its esthetic quality, and its location, demands an explanation, if no longer a justification.

The later, post-Crusader, meaning of the Dome of the Rock as the place of the Prophet's ascension began slowly to emerge. The official acknowledgment of the Prophet's Night-Journey was made in the Aqsa Mosque, but it was on the platform of the Dome of the Rock that his ascension was celebrated. The other domes on the platform are Gabriel's Dome, where, writes Nasir-i Khosraw, the Prophet's mount came to carry him through the heavens, and the Dome of the Prophet, where he actually mounted Buraq, his heavenly steed, both small, undecorated commemorative domes on four

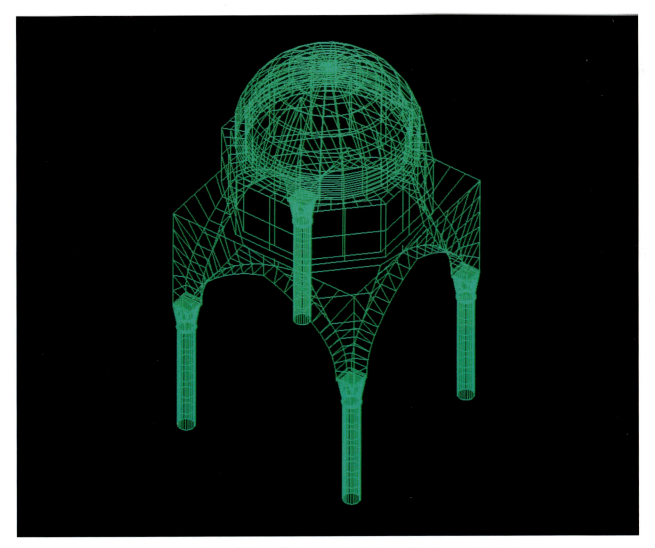

Figure 83. *Schematic reconstruction of one of the small domes on the platform of the Dome of the Rock.*

columns (fig. 83); and, finally, the Dome of the Chain, formally connected to David who allegedly hung there a chain that could only be reached by the innocent. Nasir-i Khosraw thus maintained an eschatological meaning to the Dome of the Chain, made visually specific by the presence of a beautiful *mihrab*, probably a reference to David's *mihrab* (K 38:21).

The last feature of the platform mentioned by Nasir-i Khosraw was the set of six stairways leading up to it, all of them with a different number of steps and an arcade where the steps reach the surface of the platform. A stairway was located on the eastern and the northern side, bearing the unenlightening names of "eastern" and "Syrian" (or "northern"), respectively. Two on the western side were more elaborate. One, more or less on the axis of the Dome of the Rock, had an inscription on one of its columns referring to a construction (*'amal*) dated in 951–952 and attributed to a master builder (*bannâ'*), Ahmad ibn Abi Bakr, a very rare official identification of a builder in early Islamic times.[57] The other stairway on the western side is almost certainly the present southwestern stairway, which is closest to the main entrance to the Haram. Nasir-i Khosraw does not describe it, but he is quite precise on the two southern ones, and writes that the one on the axis is called *maqâm* ("station") of the Prophet because it is the one the Prophet ascended to climb on the platform, while the southeastern one is called *maqâm Ghûri*, the "Ghurid station," in honor of the Fatimid prince who decorated it with an inscription bearing his name (now gone).[58] Whatever the reasons may have been—need for repairs, changes in piety, or dynastic glory—there is little doubt that the Fatimids were responsible for the complete renovation of the southern accesses to the upper platform of the Haram.

A few additional observations about the stairways are worth making. Their technical name varies from one source to another, perhaps from one period to the other: sometimes simply "stairs" (*marqat*, pl. *marâqi*); *maqâmât*, "stations," where one stops for some commemorative purpose; *qanâtîr*, "arcades," a purely technical appellation; or *mawâzîn*, "scales," as they are called now, presumably to weigh the deeds of those who pass through them. Nasir-i Khosraw used the word *maqâm* and Max van Berchem, noting that the original inscriptions, when known, were always located on the inside of the arcade, has cogently argued that these passageways were in fact thought of as the boundaries of the platform, not as means of access to it. To the south, the top of the stairway was like a mihrab indicating the *qiblah*, but it was also the place through which the Prophet had passed. It illustrates the deeper meaning of the mihrab as a direction but also as a means of access for divine grace, thus providing an Islamic parallel to the apse of the Eastern Church which was also both a boundary and a passageway.[59] That deeper meaning would have extended to all the stairways, whose arcades served as a sign separating areas of varying emotional and pious intensity.

The second observation deals with the form of the arcade, a rather original architectural morpheme in the sense that no ensemble of the first millennium of our era, to my knowledge, exhibits a few arches as a unit of design independent of a building (fig. 84). Its appearance in Jerusalem can be explained as the revival of the old, allegedly Semitic, practice of endowing single columns or groups of columns with holiness or with some symbolic value.[60] The conscious use of this form appears to have begun under the Abbasids, since tenth-century writers already mention the existence of such arcades, and, as in several other instances, the Fatimids assumed and completed tasks begun earlier. The other explanation would be that columns were available from the rich debris of Jerusalem and the compositional units made from the "spolia" acquired their connotative meaning from some quality intrinsic to them. The second explanation seems preferable to me, because I am not convinced that symbolic association is fixed and permanent, but the question should remain open.[61]

It is also worth pointing out that the eccentric location of the two stairways that are not on the axes of the platform or of the Dome of the Rock—the eastern one on the south side and the southern one on the west side—probably met the practical needs of a Muslim population that lived, for the

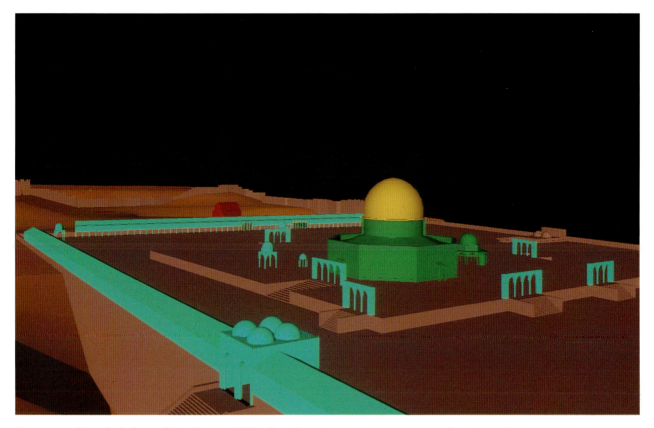

Figure 84. Central platform of the Haram al-Sharif in Fatimid times, a reconstruction, from the southwest.

most part, to the south and to the west of the sanctuary. It is curious that Nasir-i Khosraw's careful account ends with two seemingly random observations: that on the northern section of the esplanade there was a small mosque with low walls called *mihrab Da'ud*, but what it really was, says our traveler, was Solomon's footstool from which he watched the Temple being built; and, the last and strangest point he makes, is that the most peculiar thing he saw in the Haram was a walnut tree.

The Muslim sanctuary of Jerusalem, according to Nasir-i Khosraw, was a fascinating mix of associations with religious memories and of practices that issued from beliefs. The associations were, first of all, with the two prophet-kings: David and Solomon, and then a series of non-royal prophets who, in the Muslim tradition crystallized a century or so earlier, were the forerunners of Muhammad, each one bringing some particle of the divine revelation. David, the ruler who asked God's pardon after committing an otherwise ill-defined sin, at least in

the Koran, is the prototypical man of faith, imperfect but seeking forgiveness; and Solomon is the mythical builder, to whom all grand architectural projects are attributed, especially the ones requiring unusual effort or having striking visual effects. In Jerusalem, the series of prophets included Abraham, Moses, Jacob, Isaac, Zakariyah, and Jesus, all of whom were commemorated with new constructions or in existing spaces—spaces natural or man-made, Muslim or earlier, whose original function was often forgotten. These traditional prophetic associations were being replaced, or at least surpassed, by the Prophet Muhammad, his Night-Journey and, more and more, his ascension. The Night-Journey had been commemorated since the beginning of Islam through the Prophet's arrival at the Aqsa Mosque and his presence by the rock, even though the exact reason for his being there was always unclear. His ascension was now the main event commemorated on the upper platform, although it did not yet involve the Dome of the Rock. The first steps in the endowment of the land with Muslim holiness were taken during the centuries preceding the Fatimids, part of a complex cultural and religious transformation which, during the eleventh and twelfth centuries under the broad impact of shi'ism as well as the Christian successes in Syria and Palestine, modified the visual landscape of the Muslim world through the building of commemorative structures. Before then, and always with the exception of Mekkah and Madinah, the informal memories of popular traditions and folk practices predominated over the authorized ones and did not lead to significant architectural undertakings.[62]

Turning to practices and beliefs, Nasir-i Khosraw leaves us with an impression of a variety of activities taking place on the Haram, among which prayer, the fundamental Muslim act of piety, predominates. He describes a large number of places reserved for private prayer on the Haram, many identified by mihrabs, probably but not necessarily flat niches which might have been decorated with vegetal or geometric ornament or else provided with inscriptions. Such panels, often done in ceramic and usually with a funerary or commemorative purpose, are well known in later Islamic art.[63] A second practice, described but less clearly defined by the Persian traveler, was meditation, an exercise particularly favored by mystics who gathered just outside the northeastern corner of the Haram; even the great Ghazali is said to have spent some time there a few years before the arrival of the Franks. Meditation is normally private, but there were two very special themes for collective inspiration in Jerusalem: eschatology, raising concerns about divine mercy and the need for atonement; and the Journey of the Prophet, which was only beginning to acquire significance and layers of meanings. A third practice was pilgrimage, which Nasir-i Khosraw recognizes for all the faiths in Jerusalem, and for which he identifies a special regional Muslim character, in addition to its occasional role as a substitute for Mekkah. The last pious practice is commemoration, which, at least from the account of Nasir-i Khosraw, was the spiritual acknowledgement of a memory and did not require any specific behavior. There is no evidence,

for instance, for the kind of offerings that are so typical of later shi'ite sanctuaries and of so many tombs of saints everywhere. But it is also possible that folk behavior was not recorded by our sophisticated traveler, especially if he preferred to show all Fatimid places as consistent with authorized Islamic behavior.

Prayer, meditation, pilgrimage, and commemoration, all centered on pious memories and on the end of time, were the Muslim ways of the Haram. In its memories and practices Jerusalem did not have the specificity of Madinah, where the life and death of the Prophet was the exclusive focus, or of Mekkah with its Abrahamic memory and the pilgrimage, or even of some shi'ite sanctuaries in Iran and Iraq. But, at the same time, nearly all parts of the Haram had some holy significance, which illustrates a key feature of the Islamization of Jerusalem, the formal association of existing spaces with piously meaningful purposes and events. This process, much advanced under the Fatimids, was to be arrested during the Frankish occupation and only completed at the end of the thirteeenth century.

The most interesting Fatimid achievement, however, was symbolic. Formally, the Christian and Muslim hills no longer confronted or even faced each other, but remained enclosed within their respective spaces. The entrance to the Holy Sepulchre was now from the north rather than the east, and a small mosque was built near it as a sign of the ruling power. The Haram was provided with a majestic gateway so that the whole living city to the west could be contemplated from a Muslim sanctuary. Inside the Haram, a portico framed the holy space and acted as its boundary to the outside world; the central platform had become a *hazîrah*, an inner sanctified area with its own very special signs embodied in the small arcades at the top of the stairs; and the Dome of the Rock rose from a yet higher level of holiness within the *hazîrah*, an architectural masterpiece whose initial purposes were no longer quite clear and whose new meanings were not yet quite formed, but whose visual power was made holy by its setting. Fascinated as they were with ceremonial processions,[64] the Fatimids organized the spaces of the Haram into an orderly sequence, carefully described by Nasir-i Khosraw, whereby the visitor first experienced the whole area as he walked around it, then entered the mosque with its dramatic celebration of the Prophet's journey and the Fatimid ruler, and finally ascended the highest place of commemoration, the Dome of the Rock. Technically and morphologically, the Fatimids used the materials and techniques—stones, columns, arcades, mosaics, domes—that were part of the local environment, and in this sense they completed the space in the Late Antique fashion of the Umayyads.[65]

The Formation of Fatimid Jerusalem

Many factors affected the city of Jerusalem between the time of the Umayyads in the middle of the eighth century and the dawn of the eleventh. Too little is known or has been made available about the development of the arts and of culture in the core lands of Islam and in Jerusalem, in particular, to explain simply and neatly how the rich texture of the Muslim city seen by Nasir-i Khosraw came about. My purpose here is not to outline the broad cultural history within which the city of Jerusalem existed, but rather to argue that the Fatimid city is the culmination of several processes in which Islam-wide developments were mixed with purely local ones. It is reasonable to call the eleventh-century city Fatimid because, at least in my judgment, the character and policies of the Fatimid state were largely responsible for it, just as the Umayyads were responsible for its quality and shape in the eighth century. It is less appropriate to call it Abbasid in the two centuries between Umayyads and Fatimids, because the caliphs in Baghdad played a relatively small part in the transformation of the city, and these intermediate centuries were less affected by a state agenda than by the growth of Islamic culture. That early medieval Islamic order managed ultimately to resist and repel Christian, Byzantine and Western, incursions, at least in the Levant, and to incorporate within its fold "fringe barbarians" like Kurds, Berbers, and Turks. Particularly active in the visual transforma-

tion of Jerusalem as well as contributing to its character in the eleventh century were the political patronage, the evolution of piety, and the ethnic and religious equilibrium that were characteristic of the new Islamic culture.

Political Patronage

The direct involvement of Abbasid caliphs in the buildings of Jerusalem is limited to a short period of time during the reigns of al-Mansur (754–775) and al-Mahdi (775–785), both of whom visited the city on the occasion of their pilgrimage to Mekkah or, in the case of al-Mansur's second trip, of a military expedition farther west. These visits play a minimal role in the great remote chronicles written in Baghdad later in the ninth century, but they were reported by local sources, both Muslim and Christian, and by the *fada'il*. Various repairs or reconstructions to the Aqsa Mosque and to the Dome of the Rock were attributed to visits by caliphs, which at times included very detailed accounts of the ways funds for repairs were found. Modern scholars have similarly sought to connect sequences of archaeologically retrieved constructions and reconstructions with these imperial visits.[66]

I propose to handle these events in a different manner. Nothing argues for or against al-Mansur's or al-Mahdi's contribution of additional funds to the Jerusalem offices in charge of building and civil engineering, just as nothing compels or makes impossible the dating of any repair to the second half of the eighth century. Such repairs as well as the long range and slow refurbishing of the Haram are fully documented by inscriptions dated or datable to 901–904, 913–914, 951–952, 961–962.[67] At times it is possible to identify a member of the Abbasid family, usually a woman, as the sponsor. But in all likelihood there were other sponsors, as is suggested by a group of very badly preserved inscriptions with private property titles and endowments near the Haram and elsewhere in the city.[68] In short, these centuries of primarily Abbasid rule should be interpreted, I believe, as centuries during which the Muslim presence was establishing itself in Jerusalem, the enormous sanctuary was being cleared of debris and made to appear a formal space, and Abbasid power was exercised through tax collecting and the efficient handling of occasional urban troubles.[69] Except for extreme cases, like the Crusades, this local history was uninterrupted by political difficulties and persecutions.[70] Even though the exact administrative structure of Jerusalem remains ill-defined and the existence of a permanent police force or the location of governmental offices (probably in what is now the citadel or the Tower of David) are still uncertain,[71] it is clear that a routine Muslim life was taking root and a reasonable mix of people[72] settled in Jerusalem and became part of its physical growth and development without significant involvement of the Abbasid dynasty in Baghdad.

In this general and not particularly original conclusion it is necessary to make an exception of the activities sponsored by al-Ma'mun (813–33), a caliph who never set foot in the city, but who replaced Abd al-Malik's name with his own in the Dome of the Rock and added long statements to the inscriptions on the doors, and whose name still remained in the eleventh century on the principal gate of the Aqsa Mosque, probably part of a row of arches erected there by Abdallah b. al-Tahir, al-Ma'mun's trusted viceroy.[73] The main explanation for al-Ma'mun's visibility in Jerusalem lies in the importance of his reign and his policies in formalizing the standard Muslim intellectual, philosophical, and religious positions that were to dominate mainstream Islam for centuries to come.[74]

Comparable to Al-Ma'mun's intervention in the city are three takeovers of built spaces by means of additional constructions and the near magical effect of inscriptions: the Fatimid inscriptions on the Haram and in the Aqsa Mosque; the takeover by Saladin and the Ayyubids, less clearly visible in architecture and epigraphy but quite evident from written accounts[75]; and the intervention of Suleyman the Magnificent, who rebuilt the walls of the city and redecorated the outside of the Dome of the Rock. In all these instances and with varying degrees of intensity and success, specific rulers or dynasties reasserted their control, their protection,

and their rights in the city and especially in its holy places. All of this was done in expectation of divine succour for the ruler and of the eternal awards associated with Jerusalem. These were the very rulers who also asserted their power—or, in the case of the Fatimids, tried to do so—through sponsoring construction and inscriptions in Mekkah. As the Fatimids ultimately failed to control the city of the hajj, it is reasonable to assume that the favors they showered on Jerusalem resulted from their inability to control Arabia.[76] What was accomplished by Suleyman, al-Zahir, or al-Ma'mun was a Muslim parallel for what Abd al-Malik had done to Christian Jerusalem, Justinian to Constantinian Jerusalem, and Constantine to the Jewish and Roman imperial city: making visible the association between the realm and the legitimizing power of God. They were intercessors between man and God through the spaces they created, and at the same time, like the David of the Koran and, in a way, the Old Testament, they also sought salvation and received divine pardon through their works.

One other example of Abbasid intervention, less dramatic that the one cited above but more suggestive for understanding the atmosphere of Muslim Jerusalem at that time, was the increasing use of the city as a place for the burial of celebrated persons from elsewhere. One of the Ikhshidid rulers of Egypt was buried there in 933 and so was Ibn Karram, the religious firebrand, in 869. The geographer Muqaddasi also mentions religious and tribal personalities whose tombs were near the city.[77] It is not clear how frequently this occurred, but it certainly was related to the reputation of Jerusalem as the place of the Resurrection. These are probably the centuries during which the eastern slope of Mt. Moriah, facing the Mount of Olives, became one of the two main Muslim cemeteries of the city, the other one being on the western side of the city, although there is some uncertainty about the confessional division of cemeteries, just as there is some doubt about the division of the city into ethnic and religious quarters.

In short, Muslim political patronage in Jerusalem, as opposed to social intervention, was sporadic during the centuries after the Umayyads, but it culminated in a major and probably successfully completed Fatimid effort to transform the Haram al-Sharif into a powerful visual statement emphasized by their inscriptions. That achievement is difficult to capture now, as later rulers, Christian or sunni Muslim, wanted to disassociate themselves from what was to them an alien power, and a heretical one at that.

In the last decades of the eleventh century, Arab and Turcoman tribesmen fought over the countryside and made access to the city difficult and dangerous, according to many written sources. It is almost impossible to assess the degree of insecurity that may have actually existed, since Chrtistian pilgrims, Muslim mystics, and Jewish travelers still came in and out of the city during the last decade of the century. In 1092 or thereabouts, Ghuzz tribesmen even appointed a member of the minority Jacobite sect by the name of Mansur al-Balbayi as administrator of the city.[78] It may reflect total chaos in the administration of the city that only a representative from a minority within a minority could be found to run it, or, on the contrary, great openness that Jerusalem was free of religious prejudice. Whatever the explanation, this particular administrator, if he really existed, did not last, and just before the arrival of the Crusaders, Fatimid power was restored, however shakily.

The Evolution of Piety

There is no way of tracing the evolution of Muslim pious behavior as it would have affected the physical shape of Jerusalem or the ways the city was understood by its inhabitants or by the faithful who were far away. We are only beginning to know how the truly pan-Islamic sanctuary of Mekkah evolved before the destructions of the tenth century by extremist Qarmatian movements, but for most other places, including most particularly Jerusalem, such evidence as exists in the great compendia by LeStrange, Mednikoff, and Marmarji has not been analyzed in anything approaching the systematic manner employed for written passages and archaeological finds dealing with Jewish or Christian monuments and activities. Much can be done, as I

will try to show in dealing with three sources: the two geographical sources of Ibn al-Faqih and Muqaddasi, the names of the gates to the Haram, and the newly written fada'il.

Ibn al-Faqih, a native of western Iran, completed his work of geographic mirabilia and memorabilia around 905, but all we have left is a series of excerpts from the original.[79] His account of Jerusalem, a relatively long one, consists of two unequal parts. The first and longest is a collection of pious stories relating the city to the divine revelation in the Koran, to nearly every Jewish prophet, to Zakariyah, John, Mary, and Jesus, but not to the Prophet Muhammad, who appears only insofar as he proclaims God's revelation on earth. The references to these prophets are rarely connected with places and are mostly reactions to the first Temple or the resurrection and Last Judgment. The spaces are imaginary in this part of the account; only the rock on which God rested at the time of creation and to which He will return is actually identified and located. The shorter part of Ibn al-Faqih's text reads like a list of measurements, building materials, and people: a thousand lamps in the Haram use annually a hundred jars of oil each; there are eight hundred thousand mats and forty-five thousand lead joints; sixty-five people can fit in the cave under the rock; there are twenty columns in the Dome of the Chain (actually there are seventeen). These lists, however, which are sometimes accurate, although usually impossible to verify, give no intimation of the reasons for major buildings like the Dome of the Rock. Smaller buildings, probably because their commemoration of the Prophet's Journey was of relatively recent association, are more precisely identified. Eight gates are listed for the Haram, a minaret is mentioned, and the mihrab of David is located in the western part of the city, presumably in the present citadel. The overall impression is that numbers are given because they make a description credible, a conclusion supported by a slightly later adab source, the al-'Iqd al-Farîd written in remote Spain, which relates that the Muslim sanctuary of Jerusalem was provided with ten mihrabs and fifteen domes,[80] both numbers quite unlikely.

At the end of his account Ibn al-Faqih writes that Jesus ascended into heaven from the Mount of Olives, and it is over the *Sirât* bridge, spanning the valley of Gehenna between the Mount of Olives and the city's mosque, that the just will go to their reward. This work for the education and delight of Baghdadi elites associates with the land of Jerusalem, but not with its specific spaces, a rich trove of stories and aphorisms from Adam to Jesus and eventually to the end of time. Fleeting mentions of the prophet Muhammad, the caliphs Umar, Abd al-Malik, and al-Walid are buried in accounts of buildings more notable for their statistics than for their purposes.

A very different impression is provided by Muqaddasi, a native of Jerusalem, in his great geography datable to around 985. He too is fascinated by statistics and gives the number of columns and other information about construction that has much exercised modern scholars. On the city as a whole, he presents two opposing views. On the one hand, it is well provided with water and food from surrounding villages, and its streets reverberate the call to prayer. But on the other, the baths are dirty, Muslim learning is almost non-existent, Jews and Christians in the city are brutal and domineering, and merchandise is overtaxed. I do not quite know how to interpret this inconsistency except as one between the typical statements by bureaucrats that "everything is wonderful" and the author's irritation with actual conditions.

Muqaddasi's main emphasis is on the sanctuary, but his description is neither systematic like Nasir-i Khosraw's nor clearly selective like Ibn al-Faqih's. It ranges from mention of specific buildings to broad statements about the whole Haram. Like Nasir-i Khosraw, Muqaddasi provides an interesting vocabulary for architectural analyses that begs for lexicographic investigation.[81] Even though his comments about decoration and other forms of embellishment are confusing, they convey something of the brilliance of the Dome of the Rock and the Aqsa Mosque, and Muqaddasi concludes that nothing similar exists in the world of Islam or that of the Infidels. Like most early medieval writers, he does not express esthetic reactions, possibly because there was no commonly accepted vocabulary for this sort of discussion, perhaps because the monuments of Jerusalem, and especially the Dome of the Rock, were unusual precisely because their esthetic appeal overshadowed religious meanings.

Equally unsettling is Muqaddasi's description of pious purposes and religious functions. He mentions the two small cupolas of the Prophet and the Ascension on the upper platform and simply lists *mihrabs* or *maqams* ("locations") for Mary, Zakariyah, Jacob, Muhammad, and Gabriel. To these names he adds the fascinating prophet al-Khidr, who belongs to Jerusalem's holy personages but is not frequently mentioned in early periods. But Muqaddasi's most original contribution is a series of references to *maqams* that are unique to his book: the "place" of the Ants who spoke to Solomon (K 27:18–19), the place of Light, of the Ka'bah (presumably identifying the place where the Makkan sanctuary will come on the day of judgment), and of *Sirât* (the bridge of K 1:5). These themes either deal with Solomon, hardly an unusual feature in Jerusalem, or the equally common Last Day. The presence in this one source of all these features requires explanation. An answer may lie in a curious comment by Muqaddasi, just after he has given his list of sacred spots on the Haram, that on the east side of the sanctuary,[82] nothing is built and there is no colonnade, and he gives two reasons for this. One is that the caliph Umar said: "Reserve in the western part of this *masjid* a place of prayer for Muslims" and, as a result, the eastern part was left untouched so as to show respect for the words of the caliph. The second reason is that, had the covered area (that is, the Aqsa Mosque) been extended to the southeastern corner, the Rock would not have been on the axis of the mihrab. The center of the mosque would have been much farther east than in the mosque as it was at the time of Muqaddasi, when the mihrab was not on the axis anyway.

The two reasons provided by this late tenth century author illustrate superbly the two processes of understanding that dominated Muslim piety in Jerusalem at this time: justification through recourse to a precedent at the time of the Prophet or the caliph Umar, a process that is central to the establishment of values in the Islamic ethos, even if precedents had to be invented; and the evaluation of architectural and urban spaces in terms of the formal identification of symmetries, axes, and the relationship between built forms. This particular process is relatively new in early Islamic descriptions of cities[83] and it would be interesting to trace its evolution. Both of Muqaddasi's reasons for the lack of building on the east side of the Haram, especially the first one, can be further explained in characteristic medieval fashion as answers to questions by his unknown readers: where will the Ka'bah come on the Last Day? why is there nothing on the eastern side of the Haram? since the chair on which Solomon sat is there, where are the ants who were afraid that Solomon would crush them under his feet? and so on. The point is that Muqaddasi, perhaps more openly and more visibly than most other writers on Jerusalem, was himself affected by the Umayyad buildings in a city so full of invisible memories and expectations. But he did not choose or wish to understand the historical contexts of the city that inspired Abd al-Malik or al-Ma'mun. He had to find an explanation within a Muslim epistemological system which developed after these main buildings had been built.

The reality of Jerusalem was precisely in the constantly changing relationship between space and memory, and the explanations of one by the other. A striking example is given by the names of the gates to the Haram as given by Muqaddasi and Ibn al-Faqih.[84] Ibn al-Faqih mentions eight gates (David, *Hittah*, Prophet, Pardon, *wadi*, Mercy, Tribes, House of Umm Khalid). All of them except the *wadi* gate are listed in Muqaddasi who has additional names, some of which may apply to two doorways in a single portal: *mihrab* of Mary, pool of the sons of Israel,[85] al-Hashimiyah, al-Walid, Abraham, *Sakinah* (Ark), and *Saqar* (Hell). Part of the problem with these lists is localizing them on a plan of the Haram,[86] probably a hopeless task without much more evidence than we are likely to muster. The principal problem is that certain religious and abstract Muslim names like *Nabi* (Prophet), *hittah* (Pardon), *rahmah* (Mercy), *tawbah* (Forgiveness), *sakinah* (Ark of the Covenant), remain asso-

ciated with the sanctuary regardless of the modifications introduced to it. Several of them were interchanged in the tenth or eleventh centuries when the southern entries lost some of their importance or were simply blocked off. The *Hittah* gate, for instance, was moved to the north of the Haram and the Gate of the Prophet to the west. In addition to pious names, the gates to the Haram were also given local topical names (pool of the Children of Israel to the northeast) or names of people, possibly identifying clans or families settled nearby (Umm Khalid, al-Walid). These names sometimes replaced names of figures like Abraham and David and often were themselves replaced in later times.

These geographical and primarily descriptive sources demonstrate a certain amount of confusion in nomenclature and probably in the actual meanings of specific places, but not in the constellation of possible meanings. It is in part to formalize a Muslim orthodox position on Jerusalem, possibly as a reaction to shi'ite successes in the tenth century, that the *fada'il* or "praises" of the city appear early in the eleventh century.[87] Much in them simply codifies and elaborates on the answers to be given to the pious about what Jerusalem in general and the Haram in particular were supposed to signify, commemorate, and evoke for the faithful. For these reasons I am more sceptical than some recent writers have been about the value of the *fada'il* for the reconstruction of history, especially of the early Islamic and Umayyad history of the city. For the Umayyad period, archaeological, epigraphic, and visual information is far more authentic than written sources with an ahistorical bias, but these texts are of enormous importance in understanding the eleventh century.

Only one *fada'il* text has been published and very little has been written about problems posed by many of the stories contained in them.[88] Their most striking feature is the importance, wealth, and precision of stories related to the ancient Jewish past of Jerusalem, with David and Solomon as the fascinating principal heroes. Then, especially as the story of the Prophet Muhammad's Night-Journey is being developed, his miraculous journey becomes an encounter with what one of the "praises" calls the "massed prophets of the pilgrimage"[89] and each episode in the journey acquires elaborate narratives. In many of these stories, occasional Koranic references are overwhelmed by an immense, learned or popular, literature of Jewish origin.[90] There is, of course, nothing surprising about Jewish heroes in the landscape of Jerusalem, as a traditional Jewish imagination became fully enmeshed with a new Muslim one, both having been elaborated, for the most part, outside of Jerusalem itself. One can speculate that the conditions of the city after the Umayyads—the Jewish population was growing while political and ideological confrontation was primarily between Muslims and Christians—created a climate in which the monuments and spaces required a past that downplayed the politicized dynasties of the Umayyads and Abbasids, that developed the account of Umar's participation in the taking of Jerusalem by the Muslims, and, most particularly, that incorporated the memory of those who first built the city.[91] The Christian past of the city, however important it was in determining the city's shape, hardly remains in the Muslim memory of the city.

To extend a point made earlier, the *fada'il* are relatively consistent in identifying sacred spaces, often but not always in explaining their sacredness and relating what action should be carried out in any one of them—usually a set of prayers, the normal prostrations of Muslim worship, or special prayers dealing with the hope of forgiveness and the search for light and guidance.[92] As in all such texts from any religion, repetition is frequent in the narrative sequence but, curiously, a sort of sacred cosmology begins to emerge, of Muslim holy cities existing even before creation.[93] The focus of this Islamization of an eternal sacred history is necessarily the Prophet Muhammad and it is his miraculous journey that becomes the link between belief and Jerusalem.

The early *fada'il* are remarkable precisely because they reflect so strikingly the coexistence of these two currents, the lives of Old Testament figures and the Prophet's mission. Christianity and the events of Islamic history are, if not absent, quite secondary in this pious account fashioned in the

eleventh century. Whether this manner of understanding Jerusalem was the result of a conscious and official Fatimid ideological position or of more localized pious tendencies remains an open question.

A New Equilibrium

It is possible to imagine Jerusalem around 600 as a city focused almost entirely on its Christian sanctuaries, concentrated on either side of the empty area of the Jewish Temple with its Herodian and pagan ruins, and on a host of pious and liturgical Christian activities. The official language was Greek, but Latin, Syriac, and a number of Near Eastern languages were spoken as well both by visitors and more permanent residents, all of whom shared the broad culture of Mediterranean Late Antiquity. By 725, a Christian population probably still dominated in terms of numbers and was still concentrated in the same areas of the city and its immediate surroundings, but its makeup had changed, with a greater proportion than before of faithful from western Asia and the Caucasus. The main change, however, lay in the return to Jerusalem of a Jewish population and in the unexpected appearance of Arab Muslims who transformed the old consecrated area of Mt. Moriah into a stunning display of architectural monuments. Although difficult to confirm, it is reasonable to assume that Jews and Muslims settled in the eastern part of the city and more specifically, at least when they arrived, in the lower southeastern area, and that Arabic began to replace Greek as the language common to all inhabitants of the city.

By the middle of the eleventh century, all these communities were present and active in Jerusalem and a new equilibrium can be suggested for the city. The considerable changes brought to the structure of the city, most particularly the Haram and the Holy Sepulchre, affected the life and the behavior of Muslims and the traditional Christian communities in the city. Not much more than has already been argued can be said about the early Muslims of Jerusalem, since a few inscriptions are our sole actual documents for their economic, social, and cultural life outside of the Haram.[94] One can only infer the restoration, at some unknown moment, of the citadel on the western wall of the city as an administrative and military center. The traditional Christian community is better known through ecclesiastical chronicles, the lives of saints, and literature in Arabic.[95]

The story of these Christians *in partibus infidelium* is a curious one. For a while they partook of the grand history of Christianity in and around the Byzantine empire, as when John of Damascus thundered against iconoclasts from the safety of a Palestinian monastery. They were also missionaries of sorts, as they made translations of the Gospels into Arabic some time after 750.[96] Around the same time that Theodore Abu Qurra was engaged in written and oral debates with Muslims, Christians were emigrating to the safety of the Byzantine empire, "fleeing the boundless evil of the Arabs," according to the somewhat opinionated chronicler Theophanes.[97] But still in 724, a group of rich landlords from Iconium (today's Konya in central Anatolia) came as pilgrims to Jerusalem,[98] and, as we saw earlier, the Byzantine emperor was much involved in the rebuilding and refurbishing of the Holy Sepulchre in the first decades of the eleventh century. During this same period, Georgian and Armenian monks were setting down roots in the Holy City.

The fragmentary evidence allows us to emphasize two main aspects of the old Christian population in Jerusalem. They remained the custodians of the holy places, most particularly the Holy Sepulchre, and it was their responsibility to maintain them in proper order, whatever this meant at any one time, and to accept and treasure the gifts brought to the holy sites from everywhere in the Christian world, gifts that spawned stories about the principal churches of Jerusalem as repositories of immense wealth and, therefore, as magnets for looting. The other significant aspect of that Christianity is its linguistic arabization, so that, by the time of the Fatimids, the majority of the Christians in Jerusalem had acquired an Arabic culture comparable to the Greek culture of their predecessors, one which brought them closer to the dominant

Muslim culture and separated them to some degree from the main streams of Christian orthodoxy.

This point becomes particularly striking when one considers another Christian presence in Jerusalem, that of the Latins. This is not the place to review the mixture of fact and fancy that surrounds the appearance in Jerusalem of a clergy from western Europe, the growth of Latin pilgrimage which by the eleventh century had become an industry, or the celebrated, if not necessarily authentic, treaties alleged to have been signed by Charlemagne and Harun al-Rashid.[99] Much in the story of these relations, even during their own time, reflects the political competition between eastern and western emperors, as the patriarchs of Jerusalem seem at certain times eager to seek alternate patrons in ways repeated in the nineteenth century and even in our own times.

It is clear from the *Commemoratio de Casis Dei*, written in the first half of the ninth century, that a significant proportion of some two hundred and fifty-seven Christian religious found in Jerusalem were Latins,[100] including the hermits celebrating services in the Church of St. Mary (possibly the *Nea* inside of the city, or the Tomb of the Virgin in the valley of Jehosaphat, which is closer to the area where hermits had their cells) in Greek (eleven of them), Syriac (six), Latin (five), Georgian (four), Armenian (two), and Arabic, still known as the *saracenic* tongue (one). It is probably reasonable to assume that, like the confessionals today in the basilica of St. Peter in Rome, these services corresponded to the real or presumed needs of the population. It is also probable that the proportion of Latins increased in the tenth and, especially, the eleventh centuries, as pilgrims became more and more numerous and included even Swedes and Norwegians.[101] Many of the sanctuaries visited by these pilgrims were in the valley of Jehosaphat and on the Mount of Olives, where a German was, for a while, abbot of a monastery.[102] Finally, it is probable that the overall number of continuously used churches gradually declined in the centuries between the Umayyads and the end of Fatimid rule, or disappeared altogether, like the church of Sion, which was *in medio Jerusalem* in the eighth century and apparently in ruins after the shortening of the walls that did not include it within the city.[103]

Except for the Holy Sepulchre, Christian monuments in the city were few but Christians must have been quite visible, often in clerical garb, going from one place to the other, feeling and touching all the places consecrated by Christ and His apostles, moving beyond the walled city to the Mount of Olives, to Bethany, to the monasteries of the Judean desert and, in fact, all over Palestine.

Liturgical and ritual obligations did not require as much ostentatious movement from the third confessional component of Jerusalem, the Jews. Our knowledge of them has a degree of precision and of detail unknown for the other communities, thanks to the Geniza documents from the Cairo synagogue.[104] Three points are pertinent to the argument of this book. First, while it is almost impossible to reconstruct or even to imagine the actual character of the private or collective spaces occupied by Jews, there was a synagogue somewhere near the western wall of the Haram, perhaps because Jews lived nearby or because they gathered at times near the gates to what was to them the Temple area. There are, furthermore, intriguing references to a cavern used as a meeting place, perhaps as a synagogue.[105] The second point is that, like some of the Christians, some Jews, probably the Karaites, lived outside the walled city, and some formal meetings of the *gaonate* and the yeshiva took place on the Mount of Olives. Pilgrims went there as well and in some Talmudic sources, Divine Presence (the *shekhina*, the Jewish precedent to the Muslim *sakinah* mentioned earlier) had moved from the Temple Mount to the Mount of Olives.[106] A letter written in 1057 relates that, against the payment of a tax, Jews were allowed to pray out loud on top of the Mount of Olives.[107] The third point is that, especially under the Fatimids, Jerusalem became a major intellectual, educational, and religious center and a magnet for the Mediterranean Jewish community; it was considered the center of Jewish leadership by Muslim authorities.[108] At the same time, it was a community divided into major factions, some doctrinal like the Karaites and the Samaritans, others social, economic, or cultural (local versus visitors, the learned versus the ignorant).

Such divisions can probably be postulated for Christians or Muslims as well, but, for the historian of the city, the difficulty lies in translating this information into spatial terms, into a reconstruction, even a sketchy one, of the city's fabric at a certain point of time. The monumental foci—the Haram al-Sharif and the somewhat diminished complex of the Holy Sepulchre—were either Muslim or modified Early Christian, in both cases the result of external imperial interventions. It may be appropriate to add the Mount of Olives, which dominates the walled city without a major monument in the eleventh century, but clearly the site of continuing Christian and Jewish activities since the Umayyad period and occasionally appearing in Muslim sources as the holy place of the Resurrection. The daily and common life of the city took place between these major nodes, mostly within the walls, but probably also in the formerly enclosed areas to the south of the city, where ruins and debris from former buildings could easily have accommodated various types of settlements. As I have already suggested, there may be some doubt about the actual segregation of the religious communities into quarters. It is more likely, especially if we consider the small overall area of the protected city, that families of different religious allegiances shared living spaces and only segregated their places of pious and ritual behavior. This would mean that, in line with a practice already established when Jerusalem was exclusively Christian, distinctions among people were determined less by where they lived than by where they worshipped. Formal Christian processions through the city may have been abandoned or forbidden under Muslim rule, but there remained, as today, the movement of people at specific times or days. It was in the streets of Jerusalem that the communities encountered each other. Occasional conflicts occurred between them, although the eighth to eleventh centuries seem to have been relatively free of major confrontations rising from the city itself rather than from external interference. Yet the most striking implicit feature of most written sources is how much the communities ignored each other's presence.

On a purely political level, this situation began to change during the second half of the eleventh century, as Turkish and Turcoman soldiers as well as marauding Arab tribesmen seem to have altered the mood of the city and increased the arbitrary powers of ever-changing Muslim governors.[109] The Crusaders arrived at a city much more militarized than it had been for centuries; this may explain the difficulties they encountered in taking the city, which had not been besieged since the Persians came in 614, almost four hundred years earlier.

The city also included extensive cemeteries between the city itself and the Mount of Olives and probably also to the north and west of the city, embodying myths and expectations. Too many men and women have come to die or be buried in Jerusalem since the eleventh century to permit a valid topography of the dead, surrounding the living, protecting them, and ultimately joining them on that last day awaited by all.[110] A few remaining epitaphs from the tenth century introduce a curious twist to these conclusions. On the tomb of a Muslim from Damascus who died in 937, the standard inscription contains the following unique addition:"O you who sit on my tomb, try not to be proud; I used to be like you and you shall be like me in your coffin. Curses on whoever jumps over [the tomb] or opens it." Three other Muslim epitaphs contain comparable statements, and one example of a similar malediction occurs on the undated tomb of a Christian who died in 979, where the tomb is proclaimed sacred (*maḥrûmah*) by virtue of the "word of God" inscribed on it, and it is forbidden to buy or to sell it.[111] Max van Berchem suggested, with some reservations, that these statements reflected old and generic Semitic attitudes and concepts about the sanctity of tombs and the bodies they contain. But no other instances exist of such statements in the enormous corpus of medieval epitaphs in Arabic. It seems more fruitful to me to imagine that, in the city of Jerusalem with its many communities and subdivisions within communities, cemeteries were the only places where one could indulge one's animus against the others with relative impunity.

The Shape of the Holy

AT THE PENTECOST, according to the *Acts of the Apostles* (2:1-12), "devout Jews drawn from every nation under heaven" were present in Jerusalem and were amazed to hear simple Galilean fishermen suddenly speak the languages of "Parthians, Medes, Elamites, inhabitants of Judaea and Cappadocia, Pontus and Asia, Phrygia and Pamphylia, Egypt and the district of Libya around Cyrene, visitors from Rome, both Jews and proselytes, Cretans and Arabs." The apostles were thus able to tell in everyone's tongue "the great things God had done." The vision of the New Testament is that of devout Jews (or simply men in some versions of the text) from most known nations still lingering in Jerusalem many weeks after Passover, or perhaps living there more or less permanently. The universality of the new divine message was miraculously brought to them in their own tongues and not in the Hebrew or Aramaic in which they presumably communicated with each other, but it is equally remarkable that there were so many "foreigners" in the city of the Temple during difficult times in the struggle between imperial Rome and various Jewish factions.

The Pentecost is a great feast of the Christian church celebrated in moving liturgies and through countless representations from early Christian times onward. It was acclaimed and proclaimed as, among other things, the moment that redeemed mankind from the linguistic incomprehension created by the fateful episode of the Tower of Babel. But, like so many of the texts and monuments discussed in this book, the particular passage on which all liturgies are based is far from clear. Its interpretation, in fact its very words, has been the subject of much discussion, so that the traditional account may well be the transformation, if not even an invention for the purest of purposes, of an event whose implications developed much later.[1]

Such a transformation need not be seen as an obfuscation, or a denial of an original truth, or even the deliberate creation of a falsehood, but rather a moment in the natural growth of a living entity, the city of Jerusalem, sanctified many centuries earlier as the site of the Jewish Temple and the capital of the Jewish kingdom. By the time we picked up the story, in the late sixth century of our era, there were no Jews in Jerusalem, which had become a Christian city on a Roman imperial canvas. In the seventh century it entered into the orbit of a new Muslim community and state, while retaining the presence of Christians and gaining the return of Jews. When we leave the story, in the second half of the eleventh century, these three religious communities with a vast array of internal distinctions and divisions were leading parallel and apparently reasonably peaceful lives within the boundaries of the modified Roman city and awaiting separately, in a commonly held belief, the end of time.

Two paradoxes—or, at the very least, unexpected results—accompany this development of four centuries. One is the coexistence of different, in many ways even antagonistic, religious communities in a small urban space without political or economic functions that would have justified the presence of "people from many nations." For, beyond intraconfessional linguistic differences certainly also characteristic of other holy cities like Rome or Mekkah, Judaism, Islam, and Christianity each asserted formally and unequivocally the divinely ordained uniqueness of its own system of belief and the falsehood of the other two, a falsehood made all the more damnable since the same God revealed Himself to all three faiths. Two reasons why this coexistence was possible have deeply permeated the preceding pages: the shared sacred history of prophets and kings as common resources for feeding imagination and creating myths; and the consistency of Jerusalem-centered piety and pious behavior, regardless of confessional allegiance. Along with common assumptions about eternal life or the proximity of hell and paradise, the three communities had common immediate requirements like the identification of holy places, hostels to accommodate short-term visitors, ways to collect funds and to communicate with co-religionists elsewhere. With variations of emphasis, pilgrimage, commemoration, instruction, meditation, death, preservation of one's own holy spaces, and some level of belief in the Ascension and Resurrection are integral to all three religions. These themes, present in the Jerusalem of the seventh century as they are today, became permanently attached to the city, forming what may be thought of the continuous component of its holiness and the enactment of that holiness by the faithful. The four

centuries we have considered are the ones during which Islam, the last of the monotheistic revealed religions, creates its own manner of acknowledging its relationship to the city. From complex and ill-defined beginnings in which many memories as well as royal power were involved, Islam moved to a forceful assertion of the Prophet's presence through the Night-Journey (isra'), the Ascension (mi'raj), and a host of associated motifs like the meeting with the prophets of old. It is always essential to recall that the profound originality of Jerusalem, at this level of analysis, is not that specific sacred and ritual themes remained as constant fixtures of its history—most holy cities are like that—but that several systems of faith played out *simultaneously* their ways of commemorating these themes. As the passage from the *Book of Acts* illustrates so well, even though rational explanations why so many different people from so many different lands were in Jerusalem are difficult to find and the reasons may never be clearly understood, they nevertheless *were* there, and they bore witness to a mysterious and paradoxical phenomenon demonstrating God's omnipotence. Even in today's world of sanitized sameness, the Old City, in particular, still hosts dozens of groups exercising their own expression of belief, with parallel rituals that, most of the time, do not clash with each other, although, now as before, secular power maintains civil peace.

Although Jerusalem is unique in its catholicity, it is particularly original in the forms that catholicity took, the visual expression of the city's piety, the shape it gave to what is holy in it. The monuments commemorating some holy event or ritual, almost overwhelmed the city. Even though King David and King Solomon cannot be given credit for thinking of the topography of Jerusalem like Frank Lloyd Wright or William Randolph Hearst, it is nonetheless true that the west to east sequence of rises and gulches, the towering Mount of Olives on the side of the rising sun, the convergence of all land features from the north and south toward the spur of Mount Moriah, are all forceful natural features that can easily shape human belief and fantasy. Without in any way espousing a determinism of natural geographical shapes, I am arguing that the sharply defined valleys and rocky outcrops of the area where Jerusalem grew became places for the collection of memories. Wittingly or not, Mount Moriah, the hillock in the physical center of the area, was highlighted first by the Jewish Temple in several massive forms, then by a Roman imperial ensemble, and, after some four or five hundred years of abandonment, by the spectacular ensemble of the *masjid al-Aqsa*, eventually to become the Haram al-Sharif, the Noble Sanctuary, and its centerpiece, the Dome of the Rock. The Islamic city developed around 700 C.E. by the Umayyads included, on the level of formal arrangement, the full exploitation of the city's topography, manipulating the perception of monumental foci through height (a dome on a high drum) and location (entries from the south, control of spaces between the Holy Sepulchre and the Mount of Olives). In the eleventh century, under the Fatimids, closed compositions restricted entry but favored visual nodes like a monumental gateway and shining inscriptions where the techniques and materials used to achieve visual objectives—domical structures, stairways and arcades, columns, mosaics, marble, and interior proportions—derive directly from the urban art of the Roman empire. To the extent that this reliance on the classical heritage is part of any definition of medieval art, early Islamic Jerusalem is a fully medieval achievement, including both the reuse of classical spaces and the expression of new ideas and purposes in the terms of classical art. The question can even be raised, although probably to be answered in the negative, whether a sort of master vision for the space of the Haram existed from the very beginning of the Muslim takeover when it would have been inspired by dozens of Roman imperial cities, whether in ruins or in use.

Another paradox of Jerusalem is that a small number of buildings and of spaces served a large number of hallowed functions—commemoration, pilgrimage, prayer for forgiveness and eternal life. These functions had common themes that differed in their specific associations, as, for instance, the prophet's Muhammad's mystical presence came to dominate the places where early kings and prophets were occasionally still remembered. The hallowed history of Islamic Jerusalem, like the Christian and probably like the Jewish one as well, incorporated broad religious themes and specific connections that changed in intensity over time and were even exchanged for one another. We saw this most clearly in the Dome of the Rock, whose early royal and eschatological meanings turned into associations with Moses and Abraham, and eventually with the prophet Muhammad. Comparable, if less striking, modifications can be demonstrated for the Double Gate, the Golden Gate, the Dome of the Chain, the side areas of the Holy Sepulchre, the spaces of the Ascension on top of the Mount of Olives, and so on.

There are several explanations for the phenomenon of architectural power in this small city. One is the hypothesis developed in this book of a continuous work force being maintained by whatever authority controls the city. Such a work force, which may well have continued through the Ottoman period, ensured the minimal preservation of monuments and allowed for the continuous reuse of built spaces for new purposes, a point more easily demonstrable for the Mamluk and Ottoman periods, but, in my argument, also possible because of a building tradition that could well go back to the Roman empire, if not earlier, and that preserved traditional forms and techniques. Another reason is the sheer quality of the major monuments of the city, and especially of the Dome of the Rock, poised as the visual magnet of shining gold and brilliant color, in the midst of greenery, as it is now, or contrasting vigorously with the stark barrenness of stone pavements as was the case only a few decades ago, and always emerging above the beautiful stones of the city whenever and wherever one climbs up from the streets.[2] Its colors, its height, its location, and the harmonious geometry of its shape are all abstract values, because the care with which they are ordered removes or at least reduces whatever specificity of meaning they may have. It is a victory of esthetic achievement over parochial piety and its bravado may reflect something of the arrogance of the princes who sponsored it, but it is piety that made it possible in the first place. In this respect, it is an illustration, with few parallels—the Taj Mahal is one—of the transformation of a hallowed place into a work of art that may end by limiting its holiness. Perhaps this explains in part why so many religious authorities have feared works of art.

Other cities, of course, also have monuments of striking architectural quality. The peculiarity of Jerusalem is that the area of the walled city and its immediate surroundings is so small that its hallowed spaces occupy an inordinate proportion of the city. The monuments, in fact, energize the whole city, and any analysis of the built space of medieval Jerusalem is a synechdoche-like discussion of faith and rituals organizing daily life throughout the city. There is a sense in which the early medieval city of Jerusalem and even the Mamluk one were meant to proclaim the opportunity for salvation and eternal life. Its architecture is poised to greet the end of time and the liberation of all.

At the beginning of this book, I imagined that Jerusalem should and could be compared to other holy cities for pilgrims, from Compostella to Benares, Zagorsk to Mekkah, and that it should and could serve as an example for some sort of paradigmatic "holy city," an urban space in which believers of different faiths participate in comparable activities. And it is, in many ways, true that the religious associations of Jerusalem, its physical layout, and the activities in it have parallels elsewhere. Yet, on balance, one key difference exists between medieval Islamic Jerusalem and all other religious centers, including Muslim ones. It is that three religions were able to share in the holiness of the city and use it for their separate purposes. The reason does not lie in an early medieval display of ethnic pluralism and ecumenical acceptance; it is rather that the self-assured sense of legitimate power by the ruling elites of the Umayyad, Abbasid, and Fatimid dynasties led to an ethos that minimized the need for coercion or the arbitrary exercise of force to effect control. In spite of notorious cases like the persecutions and destructions ordered by the Fatimid caliph al-Hakim, differences were not seen as being important and there was tolerance for parallel expressions of the same pious thoughts and the celebration of the same, if transfigured, holy figures. This fragile harmony between faiths, probably frequently broken in daily life, distinguishes early Islamic Jerusalem from all other holy cities. The plurality of Jerusalem's holy existence was maintained under Mamluk and Ottoman rule, even if the conditions for its maintainance were sometimes coercive, corrupt, and mean-spirited. Perhaps the vision of four harmonious centuries before the Crusades is an idyllic view simply derived from the absence of truly contradictory evidence. But it may also have been, like the passage on the Pentecost in the Book of *Acts* and like so many of the accounts that remain part of the city's lore, an uncertain moment more significant for the image it projects through its monuments than for the reality it conceals.

Appendix A

Using Computer-Aided Design Programs for
Urban and Architectural Reconstructions:
The Case of Early Islamic Jerusalem

Mohammad al-Asad

THIS APPENDIX addresses the subject of architectural representation. More specifically, it deals with the use of computer-aided design (CAD) programs for representing historical works of architecture and urbanism, taking early Islamic Jerusalem and a number of its important buildings as examples.[1]

Authors on architecture, whether writing as historians, critics, or theoreticians of architecture, usually need to supplement their writings with images. These images consist of two-dimensional drawings like plans, longitudinal sections, and elevations or three-dimensional drawings such as perspectives and axonometrics. Other media which represent a work of architecture include photographs and three-dimensional models. Through these various media one can represent works of architecture that exist in their entirety or survive only partially as well as buildings which were completely destroyed or were never executed, but for which information exists to allow for reconstructions.

These methods of representation make reference to external physical realities, but differ in the degree to which they interpret these realities. They can attempt to mimic an external physical reality, as with a photograph, or to abstract it, as with a plan drawing. A photograph of a completely or partially surviving work of architecture provides a record of how that work appeared at a certain point in time defined by various elements such as specific lighting conditions. A 50 mm lens approximates the angle of vision of the human eye; a wide angle or zoom lens registers different angles of vision. Regardless of how faithfully a photograph may attempt to mimic the manner in which the human eye perceives an object, photography not only involves an interpretation, but also a degree of abstraction of that object since it transforms three-dimensional information by transferring it to a two-dimensional plane.

A variation on the photograph for representing a work of architecture is the motion picture, which adds the element of movement. It has not, however, achieved the ubiquity of the photograph for the purpose of architectural representation, in part because it is more expensive to produce and more cumbersome to exhibit.

Paintings and drawings, whether free-hand or drafted, provide versatile methods for representing works of architecture. Certain drafted two- and three-dimensional drawings, such as plans, sections, elevations, and axonometrics, do not aim at reproducing an external physical reality as much as providing information about it. Such information can include the dimensions of a work of architecture, the relationship between its different components, and between the work and its surroundings. Although these methods do not always attempt to register the manner in which the object appears to the human eye, they at least maintain the integrity of its dimensions, a characteristic which the effects of perspective sacrifice.

Since a perspective drawing relies on the diminution in size of objects at a distance, it does not preserve the actual dimensions of a work of architecture. However, it approximates the manner in which a work of architecture appears to the human eye. Perspective drawings can vary in the degree to which they imitate an external physical reality. They therefore differ in their representation of features such as texture, light, shade, and intricate details. They can include the sketchy and schematic, which rely on evocation rather than mimesis, and the highly detailed which aim at producing high levels of realism. Like photography, perspective drawings inherently include a degree of abstraction since they transfer three-dimensional information to a two-dimensional plane, but because of the arbitrary quality of the drawing medium, the abstraction is twice removed from the original object.

Three-dimensional physical models are only occasionally used for the purposes of architectural representation. Often, they are used by architects to explain unbuilt designs to clients. Models can provide highly realistic representations of a work of architecture. In contrast to drawings and photographs, they maintain its three-dimensional character. They usually differ from the original object in scale and in the materials used for construction. Like perspective drawings, they can range from the schematic—such as the massing model—to the highly detailed that attempts faithfully to emulate textures, colors, and intricate architectural details.

Since models are not always easy to move, they are directly accessible only to a small number of viewers. In contrast, the reproduction of drawings and photographs is relatively easy. If a model is to reach a wider audience, it usually needs to be photographed. In such a case, the three-dimensional character of the model is lost and the result is a representation of a representation, or two levels of abstraction from the original object.

CAD (computer-aided design) programs provide the latest addition to the available methods for architectural representation. These programs have the potential to influence significantly the manner in which architectural historians deal with past works of architecture. CAD programs are computer software that can be used to create digital objects in two and three dimensions. The results can be presented as wireframes (using separate lines resembling strands of wire, see fig. 3), as shaded surfaces, or as solid objects (fig. 4).[2]

This method of representation combines the qualities of the traditional methods discussed above and, in some cases, offers advantages over them. It is a very powerful tool for creating two- and three-dimensional drawings such as plans, longitudinal sections, elevations, axonometrics, and perspectives. A major strength of these programs lies in their versatility. With traditional drafting methods, obtaining a new view of an object requires the construction of a new drawing. With CAD programs, one can create a single comprehensive three-dimensional geometric model of an object, and subsequently obtain an infinite number of two- and three-dimensional views of the object from that single model.

Consequently, a CAD three-dimensional geometric modeling system can provide highly comprehensive documentation of an architectural object. Since a comprehensive three-dimensional CAD geometric model should enable the computer user to view an object from an infinite number of points, the construction of an object using CAD programs requires the input of a relatively complete set of geometric information about the object. In contrast, no reasonable set of traditionally drafted two- and three-dimensional drawings can provide an equivalent number of views of an object. Traditionally drafted drawings will, at best, only illustrate parts of the object.

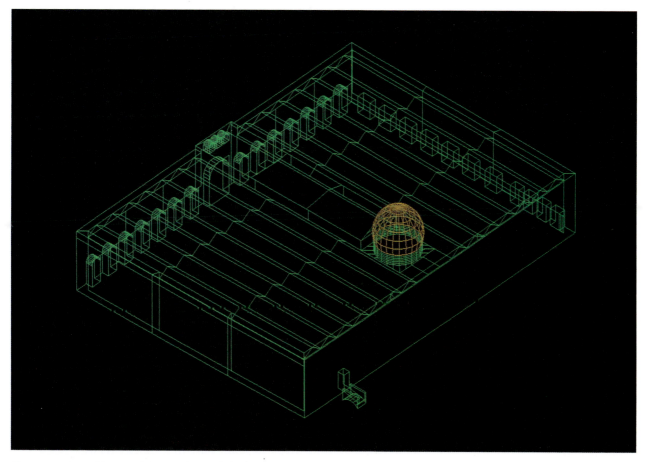

Figure 3. Aqsa Mosque, Umayyad period, bird's-eye view from the southwest, wire frame version.

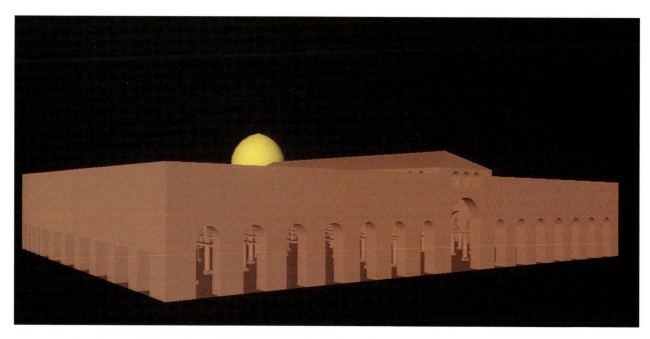

Figure 4. Aqsa Mosque, Umayyad period, bird's-eye view from the northeast, shaded version of the same drawing as in figure 3.

Although the computer screen is a two-dimensional surface, CAD programs have the ability to preserve the three-dimensional character of a given object. In order to construct a three-dimensional CAD geometric model of the object, one needs to input information defining the x, y, and z coordinates of its various entities. This allows CAD programs to combine the qualities of two-and three-dimensional drawings with those of a physical three-dimensional model.

CAD programs allow for high levels of accuracy in the representation of a work of architecture or urbanism in comparison to drafted drawings or physical three-dimensional models. Dimensions and coordinates can be specified with extreme precision. Also, since information is fed into the computer through the intermediacy of devices such as the keyboard and mouse, the relation between the human hand and the resulting computer-generated model is indirect. Consequently, human errors resulting from factors such as a trembling hand—which are not uncommon in hand-drafted drawings or hand-made physical models—are eliminated. In addition, since all views of an object constructed using a CAD program belong to a single geometric model, accidental discrepancies between the dimensions of similar elements in different views are avoided.

Changes are easy to make with CAD-generated models. Similarly, CAD programs allow for ease of replication and for the three-dimensional projection of objects. They also allow for distributing the elements of the model among layers each of which can be viewed or worked on separately. In addition to enabling the computer user to view a model through a variety of two-and three-dimensional representational drawings such as plans, sections, elevations, axonometrics, and perspectives, CAD programs allow for the simultaneous display of different views. Moreover, changes made to one view are automatically updated in the database to affect all others.

Numerous CAD programs have shading and rendering capabilities which transform line drawings into highly realistic images containing features such as textures and shadows. Photographs can also be incorporated into a CAD-generated model to create highly realistic effects. A number of CAD programs have animation capabilities which approximate the experience of walking—or flying—through or around an object.

All in all, CAD programs are flexible systems for the visual documentation of architectural objects and provide high levels of interaction between the object and the viewer. They allow the user to create comprehensive two- and three-dimensional objects in relatively little time. This last remark needs further elaboration since constructing a complete CAD model of a complex architectural object can be time consuming, and if one is only interested in a single view of that object, the construction of a complete model may be inefficient. Under such circumstances, a CAD program can use a two-dimensional Cartesian coordinate system in which only x and y (but not z) values are represented in a single two-dimensional plan. If more than one view is required, the construction of a complete three-dimensional digital model may be well worth the time.

CAD programs are more than merely advanced drafting tools. They have the potential of transforming the manner in which architectural historians address historical works of architecture and urbanism, especially for the purpose of reconstruction. On a basic level, these transformations show similarities to the changes which word processing programs have had on the act of writing. Before the advent of word processing, typing the final draft of a manuscript was separate from the act of writing it. Now, boundaries between creating and typing the final statement of a written work have become amorphous.

In a similar manner, the advent of CAD programs has meant that one can integrate the research needed for reconstructing a work of architecture with the process of representing the final results. Because of this integration, finished drawings can easily be made available at various stages of the research process. As research progresses, the model from which drawings are created can be easily modified and updated. When using traditional methods of architectural representation, initiation of the presentation phase needs to wait until the research is completed.

The changes introduced by CAD programs can function as a double edged sword. On the one hand, these programs provide the historian with additional time to carry out research since the presentation phase is no longer a separate phase which cannot be initiated until the research phase is completed. The negative consequence is an example of the rule of diminishing returns. Since changes can be made up to the last moment, one can spend far too much time making what only amount to minor changes.

CAD programs can also function as valuable tools for teaching architectural history. The interactive nature of these programs allows the user to explore thoroughly a past work of architecture or urbanism through still and moving images. These programs can be customized to allow the user who has little or no training in the use of CAD programs to view an object with relative ease. Through these programs, the student can explore a past work of architecture or urbanism with a degree of thoroughness not possible through the images of traditionally printed texts. Because of their ability to simulate internal and external views from above ground level, these programs allow the user to experience a work of architecture or urbanism in a way not readily available even to visitors to that work.

An integral part of this study of early Islamic Jerusalem has been to create a series of two- and three-dimensional drawings which explain the evolution of the city during the period under consideration. The drawings illustrate the city and a number of its major buildings at three moments in time. The first is during the second quarter of the seventh century, just before 637, when control of the city transferred from Christian to Muslim hands (fig. 11); the second belongs to the second quarter of the eighth century, during the Umayyad period (fig. 63); and the third belongs to the middle of the eleventh century, during the Fatimid period (fig. 69).

The drawings include site plans showing the city at the three points in time, plans of the city's im-

portant buildings, and axonometric and perspective views of the city and its buildings. A number of the perspective views are taken at ground level, and are intended to explore the evolving relationships between the city's major monuments, primarily the Dome of the Rock and the Church of the Holy Sepulchre (fig. 58).

Computer-aided design technology has proven to be ideal for this project. We used this technology to construct a digitized three-dimensional model representing the city of Jerusalem as it may have existed during the late Byzantine period (fig. 12), and modified the model through additions and deletions to represent the city at the two other points in time under consideration. From the final model we were able to obtain easily a large variety of two- and three-dimensional views (figs. 56-59). Constructing this variety of views using traditional methods would have been unrealistically time consuming. Additionally, since CAD programs allow the user to make changes and additions with little difficulty, we were able to begin constructing the model of the city as soon as the research project was initiated, and to incorporate new results as they became available.

The digitized model of the city contains a number of architectural and urban elements most of which underwent changes during the period under consideration. These include the topography of the city, its urban components (city walls and gates, streets, residential neighborhoods, and the Haram platform) and individual monuments, the most important of which are the Church of the Holy Sepulchre, the Dome of the Rock, and the Aqsa Mosque.

We began inputting data for the digitized model of the city using AutoCad release 11, and converted to release 12 after it became available. We primarily used an IBM Personal System/2 model 80 386 which processes data at 20 Mhz for this task. The machine was initially equipped with 8 MB of Random Access Memory (RAM) and later expanded to 14 MB. Its hard-disk drive has a capacity of 320 MB. In order to run AutoCad, the machine had to be equipped with an 80387 math co-processor chip. For the purposes of presentations and animations, we relied on the much faster UNIX-based Silicon Graphics, Inc. IRIS workstations operated by Princeton University's Interactive Computer Graphics Laboratory. Large AutoCad drawings which take over three minutes of regeneration time on the IBM 80 386 only need about thirty seconds on the Silicon Graphics workstations.

We were able to create high quality line drawings of the AutoCad drawing files using a 600 dots per inch (dpi) laser printer. For the purposes of rendering the AutoCad line drawings, we relied on the Silicon Graphics, Inc. Inventor program. Most of the computer images used in this book are reproductions of these rendered images.

The Inventor program also has animation capabilities. Consequently, we created a series of animations which simulate the experiences of flying around and walking through the city and a number of its structures during the various periods under consideration. These animation sequences were converted into a short documentary video (about ten minutes) dealing with this project.[3]

Abeer Audeh and I worked on inputting information for this project over a period of about two years, both of us working on the project on a half-time basis. Both of us were trained as architects and I had previous training in the use of the CAD programs. However, neither of us was trained as a computer programmer; we worked on AutoCad in the capacity of software users. When transferring the information to the Silicon Graphics, Inc. Inventor program, which was still in its earlier versions, we worked in collaboration with Princeton University's Interactive Computer Graphics Laboratory personnel who had specialized technical knowledge in computer graphics programs.

The digitized model of the city consists of over 25 separate drawing files connected to a master file using external file referencing. (External referencing permits files to be combined for viewing or plotting, but also to retain their specific identities for individual editing, viewing or plotting.) Each of the files contains one of the city's buildings or part of its urban composition such as the topography, walls, or streets. The largest of these drawing files

occupies about 0.8 MB of memory. When combined, the files take up over 7.0 MB of memory, which is an extremely large amount of memory for AutoCad to process. Limiting the size of the drawing files using CAD technologies presented a major challenge for this project.

As the size of a file grows, CAD programs function at a slower speed. The maximum CAD file size which can be processed at an acceptable speed (or even processed at all) depends on the computer hardware and CAD software used. Still, the data contained in this project proved to be very large for the software and hardware technologies currently available to most users. In order to control the size of these CAD files we had to keep representations of architectural details such as surface decorative features to a minimum since such details occupy large amounts of memory. For example, a digitized three-dimensional CAD model of an Ionic capital can take up more memory than a simple building.

As a result of this restriction, we had to concentrate more on forms and spaces than on surface decorative elements or the "skin" of buildings. This approach has provided our CAD-generated objects with a degree of minimalism and abstraction. Since surface decoration plays an integral and very important role in most pre-modern architectural traditions, a study of such traditions usually needs to include representations of their decorative characteristics. When dealing with large CAD files, one way of representing decorative details is to supplement these files, which need to concentrate on forms and spaces, with traditionally produced drawings and with photographs of architectural details. These drawings and photographs can even be copied into the computer through scanner or ray tracing and incorporated into the CAD model. One can also create additional separate CAD files concentrating on drawings of architectural details. For example, we produced two versions of the Aqsa mosque (figs. 3-4) for this project. The first version is connected to the master file linking the various files of the whole city through external referencing and represents the exterior of the structure. This version occupies about 0.3 MB of memory. The other version is more detailed and consists of two files which are independent of the master file but are connected to each other through external referencing. One of these two files represents the exterior of the Aqsa mosque, the other its interior. Together, the two files occupy about 1.9 MB of memory.

Of course, one should keep in mind that new generations of more powerful computers that can process large amounts of information at higher speed are continuously becoming available. This means that the difficulties presented by large CAD file sizes will diminish in the future, and a single file or a group of connected files will be able to include considerably more architectural details.

This resulting simplification and abstraction of the CAD models of the city raises another issue related to the use of CAD technologies for the purposes of architectural and urban reconstructions. CAD programs have the capability of creating highly realistic images. In the case of architectural reconstructions such realism can be misleading since computer generated images can be sufficiently effective to convince the viewer that what is presented is a faithful representation of a preexisting physical reality, even though the reconstruction may be of a conjectural nature. In the case of the Jerusalem project, we primarily present possibilities about what might have existed, and do not claim to replicate a preexisting reality. Consequently, a degree of simplification and abstraction of the CAD-generated images is desirable since it serves to remind the viewer that these images are an approximation of what might have existed and not realistic representations of preexisting urban and architectural compositions.

As mentioned earlier, in order to construct a three-dimensional CAD geometric model of an object, one needs to provide a set of comprehensive and precise geometric information about it. We therefore had to input specific data about the city's architectural, urban, and topographic elements, even when accurate data was not available. This necessity of inputting a comprehensive and precise set of geometric information can be avoided when using traditional drafting methods. With traditional

drafting methods, one can deal with the unavailability of geometric information for a part of an object by simply not representing that part. Therefore, if the information available for the facade of a building is insufficient, one would not draw that facade.

As a result of the precision which CAD programs require for generating geometric models, these programs do not allow for some of the "fudging" that can take place using traditional drafting methods. For example, with a traditionally-produced perspective drawing, the draftsperson can easily modify dimensions or manipulate relationships between components of the object, but a three-dimensional CAD-generated geometric model uses one set of dimensions for all views, and calculates perspective drawings using specific mathematical formulas that maintain a consistent relationship between the various components of the object.

Because we had to provide a complete and precise set of geometric information for the geographic, urban, and architectural elements of the city—even when sufficient information did not exist—we needed to differentiate these elements according to the degree of certainty of our reconstruction. We considered relying on a visual system of differentiation, but since we had already used color in the CAD geometric model of the city for the purposes of chronological differentiation, we decided that adding another visual system of differentiation would only result in confusion. Consequently, we decided that the differentiation of elements according to the degree of certainty of their reconstruction would be done through the text rather than the images.

The representations of the city's topography provide an example of the challenges faced in using CAD programs for a project of this nature (fig. 5). The city is located on a hilly, and extremely uneven terrain. Constructing a three-dimensional model of its contours and connecting the contours to the city's architectural and urban components is in itself a challenging task. An additional challenge arises from the fluidity and continuously changing character of the topography of an urban setting which result from changes in factors such as

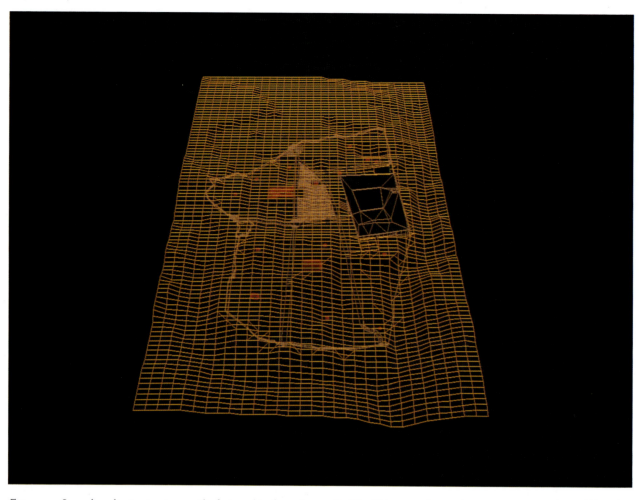

Figure 5. Jerusalem, basic structure grid of city plan from the south. The Haram is the partly empty space in the middle right, while the better lit section is the "living" area, reconstructed as a model.

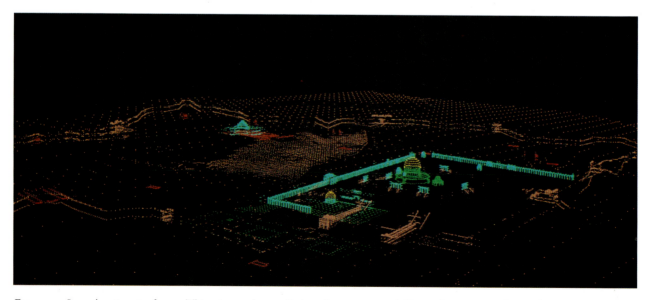

Figure 6. Jerusalem in wire frame. This picture shows all the information available in the computer, from whatever period. The city is seen from the southeast with the Haram in front and the Holy Sepulchre in the back.

habitation patterns and geological conditions. Our knowledge of the city's topography during the period under consideration is scarce. We decided to deal with this lack of adequate information by beginning with what is known. We therefore used the topography of the bedrock underneath the city as the point of departure since the bedrock reflects the overall characteristics of the contour above it. Taking the topography of the bedrock as a guide, we represented the city's topography by constructing a three-dimensional mesh on a 50 by 50 meter grid and fitted the mesh with the city's urban and architectural features which we reconstructed for the late Byzantine period. We modified the topography to accommodate the architectural and urban developments which took place in the city during the two later periods under consideration (figs. 5-6).

Had our goal been to provide an archaeological reconstruction of the city, and to register only that of which we are certain, this approach would not have been acceptable because it involves an approximation of the city's topography. However, since our aim is to present visual impressions of how the city might have existed during the periods under consideration, this approach towards representing the topography of the city proves quite suitable.

Finally, had this study of Jerusalem's urban and architectural development extended into the present, we would have followed a reverse chronological order for its reconstruction. This means that we would have begun by constructing a three-dimensional geometric model of the city as it exists today, and from there, we would have moved back chronologically. In other words, we would start with the known and move towards the lesser known.

These remarks have dealt only with the *production* of images. A final word on the *display* of these images. One can, of course, display CAD-produced images using a computer screen. CAD images can also be transformed into more traditional formats, such as slides and photographs, which can be viewed directly or reproduced in printed works like books, journals, or brochures. It is also becoming increasingly possible to combine digital and traditional display methods. Both still and moving images can be projected directly from a computer to a large screen, and currently available printing technologies can now directly convert electronically stored images into high quality printed ones which can be viewed separately or as part of a printed work.

This is not to say that computers should displace traditionally printed works for the display of images, but that they should be used in conjunction with them. Under present circumstances, the book or journal remains the indispensable physical object for the display of images. In most cases, print media are cheaper to obtain and easier to handle and transport than a computer. If nothing else, looking at a printed page remains more comfortable than staring at a computer screen.

Appendix B

The Inscriptions of the Dome of the Rock:
Arabic Text

Outer Face of the Octagon

بسم الله الرحمن الرحيم لا اله الا الله وحده لا شريك له قل هو الله احد
الله الصمد لم يلد ولم يولد ولم يكن له كفو احد محمد رسول الله صلى
الله عليه ٭

بسم الله الرحمن الرحيم لا اله الا الله وحده لا شريك له محمد رسول الله
ان الله وملئكته يصلون على النبي يا ايها الذين امنوا صلوا عليه وسلموا
تسليما ٭

بسم الله الرحمن الرحيم لا اله الا الله وحده الحمد لله لم يتخذ(٥) ولدا
ولم يكن له شريك فى الملك ولم يكن له ولي من الذل وكبره تكبيرا محمد
رسول الله صلى الله عليه وملئكته ورسله والسلم عليه ورحمت الله ٭

بسم الله الرحمن الرحيم لا اله الا الله وحده ولا شريك له له الملك وله
الحمد يحيى ويميت وهو على كل شئ قدير محمد رسول الله صلى الله عليه
وتقبل شفعته يوم القيامة في امته ٭

بسم الله الرحمن الرحيم لا اله الا الله وحده لا شريك له محمد رسول الله
عليه ٭

بنى هذه القبة عبد {الله الامام المامون امير} المؤمنين في سنة اثنين
وسبعين تقبل (٥) الله منه ورضي عنه امين رب العالمين لله الحمد

{ ٥ } *indicates the location of possibly diacritical marks on the mosaics*

Inner Face of the Octagon

بسم الله الرحمن الرحيم لا اله الا الله وحده لا شريك له له الملك وله الحمد يحيى ويميت وهو على كل شئ قدير محمد عبد الله ورسوله ان الله وملئكته(٥) يصلون على النبي يا ايها الذين امنوا(٥) صلوا عليـه و... اء وا تسليما (٥)صلى الله عليه و السلم عليه و ر حمت (٥)الله يـا اهل الكتاب(٥) لا تغلوا في دينكم (٥)ولا تقولوا(٥) على الله الا الحق انما(٥) المسيح عيسى ابن (٥) مريم رسول الله وكلمتـه (٥) القيها الى مـريم وروح منه(٥) فامنوا(٥) بالله ورسله ولا تقولوا(٥) ثلثله(٥) انتهوا(٥) خيـرا(٥) لكم انما(٥) الله اله واحده سبـحنه ان يكون له ولد له مـا في السموت وما في الارض(٥) وكفى بالله(٥) وكيلا (٥) لن

يستنكف(٥) المسيح ان يكون(٥) عبدا(٥) الله ولا الملئكه(٥) المقربون(٥) ومن يستنكف(٥) عن عبدته(٥) ويستكبر(٥) فسيحشرهم(٥) اليه(٥) جمـيعـا(٥) اللهم صلي على رسـولك وعـبدك(٥) عـيـسى ابن(٥) مـريم والسلم عليه يوم ولد ويوم يموت ويوم يبعث(٥) حيا(٥) ذلك عيسى ابن مـريم قول الحق الذي فيه(٥) تمترون(٥) مـا كان لله تتخذ(٥) من ولد سبحنه اذا(٥) قضى(٥) امرا قائما(٥) يقول(٥) له كن فيكون ان الله ربي وربكم(٥) فاعبدوه هذا صرط مستقيم(٥) شهد الله انه(٥) لا اله الا هو والملئكة واولوا العلم فيما(٥) بالقسط لا اله الا هو العزيز الحكيم ان الذين عند الله الا سلم وما اختلف(٥) الذين اوتوا الكتب(٥) الا من بعد ما جاهم(٥) العلم بغيا(٥) بينهم(٥) ومن يكفر(٥) بايـيت(٥) الله فان الله سريع الحساب

East Doorway (After Max van Berchem)

(1) بسمله ... الحمد لله الذي لا اله الا هو الحي القيوم بديع السموت والارض ونور
السموات(2) و الارض وقيم السموت والارض آلاحد الصمد لم يلد ولم يولد ولم يكن له كفؤا
أحد ملك آ (3)الملك تؤتي الملك من تشاء وتنزع الملك ممن تشاء كل ملك لك ومنك ربنا واليك
مصيره رب العزة (4)آلرحمن الرحيم كتب على نفسه الرحمة وسعت رحمتـه كل شئ
سبحانه وتعالى عما يشركون نس(أ)لك اللهم بر (5) حمتك واسمائك الحسنى وبوجهك الكريم
وسلطنك العظيم وبكلمتك التامةالتي بها تقوم السموت والارض (6) وبها نعصم برحمتك
من الشيطن وننجي بها من عذابك يوم القيمة وبنعمتك السب وفضلك العظيم وبحمدك
وقدر(7)تك وعفوك وبجودك ان تصلي على محمد عبدك ونبيك وتتقبل شفعته في امته
صلى الله عليـه والسلم عليـه ورحمت و(8a)الله مما امرب عبد الله عبد الله الامام المأمون
أميـر المؤمنين أطال الله بقاءه في ولاية أخي أميـر المؤمنين أبي إسـحـاق بن أميـر
(9a)المؤمنين الرشيد أبقاه الله وجرأ على يدي صلح بن يحيى مولى أمير المؤمنين في شهر
ربيع الآخر سنة ست عشرة وما[ئتين]

North Door (After Max van Berchem)

(1)بسمله ... الحمد لله الذي لا إله إلا هو الحي القيوم لا شريك له الاحد الصمد لم يلد ولم (2)
يولد ولم يكن له كفؤا احد محمد عبد الله ورسوله أرسله بالهدى ودين الحق ليظهره على
الدين كله(3) ولو كره المشركون آمنابالله وبما انزل على محمد وبما أوتي النبيون من ربهم
لا نفرق بين احد منهم ونحن (4) له مسلمون صلى الله على محمد عبده ونبيه والسلم عليه
ورحمت الله وبركته ومغفرته ورضوانه

ABBREVIATIONS

ArtB   Art Bulletin

BEFAR   Bibliothèque des Ecoles Françaises d'Athènes et de Rome

BGA   Michael Jan de Goeje, ed., Bibliotheca Geographorum Arabicarum, 8 vols. (Leiden,
            1870–1894)

BSOAS   Bulletin of the School of Oriental and African Studies

DOP   Dumbarton Oaks Papers

DOS   Dumbarton Oaks Studies

EI²   Encyclopaedia of Islam, 2d. ed. (Leiden, 1954–)

IEJ   Israel Exploration Journal

IJMES   International Journal of Middle Eastern Studies

INJ   Israel Numismatic Journal

IOS   Israel Oriental Studies

JA   Journal Asiatique

JRAS   Journal of the Royal Asiatic Society

JSAH   Journal of the Society of Architectural Historians

JSAI   Jerusalem Studies in Arabic and Islam

MIFAO   Mémoirs publiés par les membres de l'Institut Français d'Archéologie Orientale du Caire

PEQ   Palestine Exploration Quarterly

PO   Patrologia Orientalis

QDAP   Quarterly of the Department of Antiquities in Palestine

RBi   Revue Biblique

RKB   Realexikon der byzantinischer Kunst (Stuttgart, 1975–)

RCEA   Etienne Combe, Jean Sauvaget, Gaston Wiet, eds., Répertoire chronologique d'Épigraphie
            arabe (Cairo, 1931–present)

RMM   Revue du Monde Musulman et de la Méditerranée

RSO   Rivista di Studi Orientali

TM   Travaux et Mémoires

ZDMG   Zeitschrift der Deutschen Morgenländischen Gesellschaft

ZDPV   Zeitschrift der Deutschen Palastinavereins

Bayt al-Maqdis I	Julian Raby and Jeremy Johns, ed., *Bayt al-Maqdis, Abd al-Malik's Jerusalem I* (Oxford, 1992)–Oxford Studies in Islamic Art 9
Bieberstein-Bloedhorn	Klaus Bieberstein and Hanswulf Bloedhorn, *Jerusalem, Grundzüge der Baugeschichte*, 3 vols. (Wiesbaden, 1994)
Creswell, *EMA*²	Keppel Archibald Cameron Creswell, *Early Muslim Architecture*, Vol. 1 (Oxford, 1969, 2d ed.); Vol. 2 (Oxford, 1940, 1st ed. only)
Gil, *Palestine*	Moshe Gil, *A History of Palestine 634–1099* (Cambridge, 1992; from Hebrew edition of 1983)
Hamilton, *Aqsa*	Robert W. Hamilton, *The Structural History of the Aqsa Mosque* (Jerusalem, 1949)
LeStrange, *Palestine*	Guy LeStrange, *Palestine under the Moslems: A Description of Syria and the Holy Land from A.D. 650 to 1500* (Beirut, 1965; rpr. from 1890 original edition)
Mednikoff, *Palestina*	Nikolai A. Mednikoff, *Palestina ot Zavoevaniya ea Arabami do Krestovykh Pohodah*, 2 vols. (St. Petersburg, 1902)
Rosen-Ayalon, *EIM*	Myriam Rosen-Ayalon, *The Early Islamic Monuments of al-Haram al-Sharif. An Iconographic Study* (Jerusalem, 1989)–Qedem 28
van Berchem, *Matériaux: Haram*	Max van Berchem, *Matériaux pour un Corpus Inscriptionum Arabicum*, Pt. 2: *Syrie du Sud*, Vol. 2: Jérusalem, "Haram," MIFAO 44 (1927)
van Berchem, *Matériaux: Ville*	Max van Berchem, *Matériaux pour un Corpus Inscriptionum Arabicum*, Pt. 2: *Syrie du Sud*, Vol. 1: Jérusalem, "Ville," MIFAO 43 (1922)
Vincent-Abel	Louis Hugues Vincent and F. M. Abel, *Jérusalem II: Jérusalem Nouvelle* (Paris, 1922–1926)

NOTES

Introduction

1. The story of the conquest of Jerusalem by the Crusaders has often been told. Particularly well informed and well written accounts are those of Steven Runciman, *A History of the Crusades*, vol. I (Cambridge, 1953), pp. 279–88, and in Kenneth M. Setton, ed., *A History of the Crusades*, vol. I (Philadelphia, 1958), pp. 333–37.

2. Max van Berchem, *Matériaux: Haram*, pp. 31–36, for a specific example, and pp. 23–107, for the mood of the Ayyubid period and its reconstruction of the past.

3. This is a simplified statement about a complicated development first identified by Ira M. Lapidus, *Muslim Cities in the Later Middle Ages* (Cambridge, 1967), a book which spawned many further investigations. The phenomenon it describes began as early as the twelfth century in Syria, but it is after the defeat of the Crusaders that it became more prevalent, at least in the lands west of Iran.

4. The whole theme of the Holy Land has been wonderfully elucidated in the recent book by Robert L. Wilken, *The Land Called Holy* (New Haven, 1992).

5. Michael H. Burgoyne and others, *Mamluk Jerusalem* (Buckhurst Hill, 1987). By-products of this project are Archibald G. Walls, *Geometry and Architecture in Islamic Jerusalem, A Study of the Ashrafiyya* (Buckhurst Hill, 1990), and numerous articles and brochures published in the periodical *Levant* or under the sponsorship of the Festival of Islam Trust. The publication of this survey is a landmark in the study of the city; even if the interpretative chapters are less successful than the descriptive ones and lack considerable elaboration and discussion, any scholar can easily find in this publication nearly all the available documentation. Short emendations and debates on specific points of fact or of interpretation are, at this stage, more important for an understanding of Mamluk Jerusalem than a rehash of available data. I am not aware of any subsequent discussions, commentaries, or interpretations of the city based on these wonderful documents, a sad reflection of the state of the field.

6. Michael Meinecke's huge opus, *Die Mamlukische Architektur in Ägypten und Syrien*, 2 vols. (Berlin, 1992), is a superb, if difficult, entry into the subject and contains a very extensive bibliography.

7. For examples of smaller cities see Hayat Salem-Liebich, *The Architecture of the Mamluk City of Tripoli* (Aga Khan Program, Cambridge, 1983); and Mohammed-Moin Sadek, *Die Mamlukische Architektur der Stadt Gaza* (Berlin, 1991).

8. See Richard Krautheimer, *Rome, Profile of a City 312–1308* (Princeton, 1982); and Gilbert Dagron, *Naissance d'une Capitale, Constantinople et ses institutions de 330 à 452*, 2d ed. (Paris, 1984).

9. The two most recent reconstructions with full references to older studies are the article "Baghdad" by Abd al-'Aziz Duri in *EIM²*; and Jacob Lassner, *The Shaping of Abbasid Rule* (Princeton, 1980), especially the second part from p. 139 onward.

10. Al-Azraqi, *Akhbar Mekkah*, ed. F. Wüstenfeld (Leipzig, 1858; rpr. Beirut, 1964); Oleg Grabar,

"Upon Reading al-Azraqi," *Muqarnas* 3 (1985). Although much has been written about the present spiritual and physical setting of the pilgrimage, relatively little research has been done on the topographic and visual history of Mekkah. For an important study of Jerusalem and Mekkah together, see Francis E. Peters, *Jerusalem and Mecca, The Typology of the Holy City in the Near East* (New York, 1986). See also now his most recent study, *The Hajj* (Princeton, 1994).

11. Mujir al-Din, *Al-'uns al-Jalil fi ta'rikh al-Quds wal al-Khalil* (Cairo, undated original edition in two volumes, subsequent editions in 1968, 1973, and 1992); partial translation by Henri Sauvaire, *Histoire de Jérusalem et d'Hébron* (Paris, 1876). Max van Berchem called Mujir al-Din "le chroniqueur" because of the systematic precision of his information, but this title is inappropriate as he does not provide the formal history of a space. Something like "l'antiquaire" would have been better.

12. The most accessible introductions to these sources are R. Stephen Humphreys, *Islamic History, A Framework for Inquiry* (Princeton, 1991); Bernard Lewis and Peter M. Holt, eds., *Historians of the Middle East* (London, 1962); Abd al-Aziz Duri, *The Rise of Historical Writing among the Arabs*, ed. and trans. Lawrence Conrad (Princeton, 1983). An example of more specific analysis is Tarif Khalidi, *Islamic Historiography: The Histories of Mas'udi* (Albany Press, 1975).

13. Albrecht Noth and Lawrence Conrad, *The Early Arabic Historical Tradition* (Princeton, 1994).

14. See below, chapter 4. For an introduction to the Abbasid geographers, the best is André Miquel, *La géographie humaine du monde musulman jusqu'au milieu du 11e siècle*, 4 vols. (Paris 1967–1988). Thoughtful remarks on Jerusalem appear throughout as well as wonderful appreciations of individual writers (see vol. 4, pp. 134–36, as an example).

15. See below, pp. 52–55, for the meaning of the Dome of the Rock.

16. The most impressive statement on these topics is found in the recent volumes of Josef van Ess, *Thelogie und Gesellschaft im 2. und 3. Jahrhundert Hidschra: Eine Geschichte des religiosen Denkens im frühen Islam* (Berlin/New York, 1991). For a simpler introduction, see R. Stephen Humphreys, *Islamic History*, pp. 20–23.

17. Over the years I have used two editions of *Al-'Iqd al-Farid*, one by M. al-Ariyani (Cairo, 1940), the other one by Khalil Sharaf al-Din (Beirut, 1986). In the former, the relevant passages are in vol. 7, pp. 297ff., and in the latter, in vol. 6, pp. 204–6; see also Le Strange, *Palestine*, p. 4; Mednikoff, *Palestina*, vol. I, pp. 157ff., for a lengthy study; and Walker Werkmeister, *Quellenuntersuchungen zum Kitab al-'Iqd al Farid* (Berlin, 1983).

18. Greek and Latin sources are difficult to find, except for travelers' accounts about which, see below, pp. 137–38; for Western Asian Christian sources, see Andrew Palmer, *The Seventh Century in the West-Syrian Chronicles* (Liverpool, 1993) which has a good bibliography. For Jewish sources, a most convenient introduction is Joshua Prawer, ed., *The History of Jerusalem: The Early Islamic Period* (Jerusalem, 1987), also with many further references; the articles are all in Hebrew.

19. There is an extensive literature on messianic thought; see, for instance, William Alexander McClung, *The Architecture of Paradise: Survivals of Eden and Jerusalem* (Berkeley, 1983); or the classic by Norman Cohn, *The Pursuit of the Millennium* (London, 1957). More directly involved with the early Middle Ages is Paul J. Alexander, "Medieval Apocalypses as Historical Sources," *American Historical Review* 73 (1968); and *The Byzantine Apocalyptic Tradition* (Berkeley, 1985). For Jerusalem see Raphael Patai, *The Messiah Texts* (Detroit, 1979); and then specific texts like those discussed by Bernard Lewis, "An Apocalyptic Vision of Islamic History," *BSOAS* 13 (1950), and "On that day. A Jewish apocalyptic poem on the Arab conquests," in *Mélanges d'Islamologie: Volume dédié à la memoire de Armand Abel*, ed. Pierre Salmon (Leiden, 1974).

20. Gilbert Dagron and Vincent Déroche, "Juifs et Chrétiens dans l'Orient du VIIe siècle," *TM*, 19 (1991).

21. See, for example, Bianca Kühnel, *From the Earthly to the Heavenly Jerusalem: Representations of the Holy City in Christian Art of the First Millennium* (Rome, 1987), and Marie-Thèrèse Gousset, *Iconographie de la Jérusalem Céleste* (Thèse Univ. de Paris IV, 1978).

22. Nearly every year a new floor mosaic is discovered. For a recent survey with excellent illustrations, see Michele Piccirillo, *The Mosaics of Jordan* (Amman, 1993).

23. Ibid., pp. 81–95; the best description after repairs to the panel is in Herbert Donner and Heinz Cüp-

pers, *Die Mosaikkarte von Madeba I* (Wiesbaden, 1977; English version, Kampen, 1992); for interpretations one must still go back to M. Avi-Yonah, *The Madaba Mosaic Map* (Jerusalem, 1954), R. T. O'Callaghan, "Madaba, Carte de," in *Dictionnaire de la Bible, Suppl. V* (Paris, 1951), and B. Kühnel, *From the Earthly to the Heavenly Jerusalem*, pp. 89ff.

24. John Wilkinson, trans., *Jerusalem Pilgrims before the Crusades* (Warminster, 1977). The texts themselves are found in many other places as well. The most studied of the pilgrims is Arculf, a bishop from Gaul, who also provided drawings that are often used; see, for example, Walter Horn and Ernest Born, *The Plan of St. Gall*, 2 vols. (Berkeley, 1974); and Richard Krautheimer "Introduction to an 'Iconography of Medieval Architecture,'" *Journal of the Warburg and Courtauld Institutes* 5 (1942).

25. Al-Muqaddasi, *Ahsan al-Taqasim fi Ma'rifat ul-Aqalim*, ed. Michael Jan de Goeje, *BGA*, vol. 3 (Leiden, 1906); the parts on Syria and Palestine translated by André Miquel (Damascus, 1963); discussion of authors in Miquel, *Géographie humaine*, vol. 1, pp. 313ff. Le Strange, *Palestine*, pp. 5–6. Mednikoff's book appeared before the publication of the text.

26. Nasiri Khosran, *Sefer Nameh*, ed. and trans. Charles H. A. Schefer (Paris, 1881; rpr. Amsterdam, 1970), pp. 19–26 of Persian text; English trans., Wheeler M. Thackston Jr., *Book of Travels* (Albany Press, 1985), pp. 21–38.

27. Emmanuel Sivan, "The Beginnings of the Fada'il al-Quds Literature," *Der Islam* 94 (1971); Ernst A. Gruber, *Verdienst und Rang; die Fada'il als literarisches und gesellschafisches Problem im Islam* (Freiburg, 1975). An earlier but still very impressive elucidation of Muslim traditions in Jerusalem is J. W. Hirschberg, "The Sources of Muslim Traditions concerning Jerusalem," *Rocznik Orientalistyny* 17 (1951–1952).

28. Al-Wasiti, *Fada'il al-Bayt al-Muqaddas*, ed. Isaac Hassoun (Jerusalem, 1979). New comments by Nasser Rabbat in "The Dome of the Rock Revisited," *Muqarnas* 10 (1993), and by Moshe Sharon in "The Praise of Jerusalem," *Bibliotheca Orientalis* 49 (1992).

29. Tübingen Ms. 27; see Sivan, "The Beginnings of the Fada'il al-Quds Literature," p. 264.

30. Salah al-Din al-Munajjad, "Qit'ah min kitab. . . .al-Muhallabi," *Majallat Ma'ahad al-Makhtutat al-Arabiyah*, 4 (1958); Miquel, *Géographie humaine*, I,

pp. 309–12; Georges Vajda, "La Description du Temple de Jérusalem," *JA* (1959).

31. See Georges Vajda, "Isra'iliyyat," *EI²*.

32. Donald P. Little, "The Significance of the Haram Documents," *Der Islam* 57 (1980), serves as an introduction to articles published later by Little in *Arabica* 29 and *ZDMG* 131 (1981); Huda Lufti, *Al-Quds al-Mamlukiyya: A History of Mamluk Jerusalem based on the Haram documents* (Berlin, 1985).

33. Monik Kervran, Solange Ory, and Madeleine Schneider, *Index Géographique du Répertoire Chronologique d'Epigraphie Arabe*, vols. 1–16 (Cairo, 1975), which is a useful, if only partial, guide to the *Répertoire*.

34. Archibald G. Walls and Amal Abul-Hajj, *Arabic Inscriptions in Jerusalem: A Handlist and Maps* (London, 1980), lists ten new ones, five of which are epitaphs. Moshe Sharon has announced the publication of all Jerusalem inscriptions.

35. M. van Berchem, *Matérieux: Ville*, pp. 32ff.

36. Henry I. Bell, ed., *Greek Papyri in the British Museum*, vol. IV (London, 1910), pp. 75, 135, 139, 142, 285, and 296. The appropriate Greek texts were translated into English by Bell, "Translations of the Greek Papyri," *Der Islam*, vols. 2 (1912), 3 (1913), 4 (1914), and 17 (1927). As we shall see later, the exact interpretation of these fragments is not as simple as it seems.

37. The most complete study based on the Geniza fragments and on many other sources as well is that of Shelomo Dov Goitein, *A Mediterranean Society*, 5 vols. (Berkeley, 1967–1988), and *Cumulative Indices*, vol. 6, by Paula Sanders and S. D. Goitein (Berkeley, 1994). Two earlier studies have not lost their value: Jacob Mann, *The Jews in Egypt and in Palestine under the Fatimid Caliphs* (New York, 1920; rpr. 1970); and M. Gil, *Documents of the Jewish Pious Foundations* (Leiden, 1976). M. Gil is one of many scholars who keep on publishing fragments in Hebrew that are of interest regarding Jerusalem.

38. A summary is found in Yacov Meshorer, "Coins of Jerusalem under the Umayyads and Abbasids" (in Hebrew), Joshua Prawer, ed., *The History of Jerusalem: The Early Islamic Period* (Jerusalem, 1987).

39. The latest survey is by M. Bates, "The Coinage of Syria under the Umayyads," *Fourth Bilad ab-Sham Conference, Proceedings* (Amman, 1989), pp. 195–228. See also Rachel Milstein, "A Hoard of Early Arab Figurative Coins," and Shraga Qedar, "Copper

Coinage of Syria in the Seventh and Eight Centuries," in *INJ* 10 (1988–89).

40. Kathleen M. Kenyon, *Jerusalem, Excavating 8000 Years of History* (London, 1967); A. Douglas Tushingham, *Excavations in Jerusalem 1961–1967*, I (Toronto, 1985).

41. Hamilton, *Aqsa*. Alternate interpretations are discussed below, pp. 119–20.

42. This is the proper place for me to record the many hours I spent in 1953 and 1954 poring over the big file boxes and albums that contained these documents. It is also proper to recall the gentle help of the late Yusuf Sa'ad. A study of some of these documents by Julian Raby is in preparation and will presumably appear in *Bayt al-Maqdis II*.

43. Charles Coüasnon, *The Church of the Holy Sepulchre in Jerusalem* (London, 1974); Virgilio C. Corbo, *Il Santo Sepolcro di Gerusalemme. Aspetti archeologici dalle origini al periodo crociato*, 3 vols. (Jerusalem, 1981). For alternate views see Ousterhout's review of the evidence.

44. Benjamin Mazar, *The Excavations in the Old City of Jerusalem near the Temple Mount. Preliminary Report of the Second and Third Seasons 1969–1970*; and especially Meyer Ben-Dov, *The Omayyad Structures near the Temple Mount* (Jerusalem, 1974), and *In the Shadow of the Temple: The Discovery of Ancient Jerusalem* (Jerusalem, 1985). The architectural finds from these excavations have been used to make a park. The idea is a good one, but the insertion of the excavated material into a place for relaxation in a historical setting is meaningless because the specific history of that area is not commonly known or properly explained. The park's failure to connect the ancient material with local history provides an instructive example for conservation projects in urban settings.

45. Nahman Avigad, *Discovering Jerusalem* (Nashville, 1983), is a statement for the general public, while learned versions are found in articles in *Eretz Israel* and *IEJ*, especially for 1970–1978.

46. This is not the place to deal with a full criticism of an architecturally admirable project, but the contrast between its cleanliness and almost deathly quiet and the messy but active real life in the streets farther south is striking.

47. A full list of these many discoveries would require a lengthy bibliographical appendix not appropriate to this book. Bieberstein-Bloedhorn can be consulted for more details as well as the excellent maps of the Tübingen Atlas des Vorderen Orients.

48. The full study of these walls has never, to my knowledge, been made. It would be a wonderful place to work out coherent masonry typologies for the creation of a dictionary of building techniques and eventually a history of these techniques. It should further be added that the simplified scheme I am providing does not take into account many topographical variations, especially in the area of Mount Sion, some of which may be found in Bieberstein-Bloedhorn, under "Haram," "Tor," "Umfassungmauer," etc.

49. For instance, as can be done with the western and northern edges of the Haram and with the Jewish quarter, which were certainly not comparable to what they are now. The present Jewish quarter is probably not in the same area as in early Islamic or Roman times.

50. There are, of course, the records kept the restorations carried out during the early 1960s by an Egyptian team sponsored by the League of Arab Nations. I simply do not know whether they are well kept somewhere and will eventually be available for scrutiny. Ernest T. Richmond's book, *The Dome of the Rock in Jerusalem* (Oxford, 1924), is a record of the building's physical shape, and important details are found in various notes by Charles Clermont-Ganneau, which will be quoted in my discussion below.

51. I have learned a lot in this respect from my long association on the steering committee for the Aga Khan Award for Architecture and especially from visiting so many different places in the lively company of William Porter, Charles Correa, and Nader Ardalan, architects of considerable verbal as well as visual imagination. Works like Kevin Lynch, *The Image of the City* (Cambridge, 1960) and many of the later studies by the much lamented Spiro Kostof provide examples of the new sophistication I have in mind.

52. For example, Jacob Schächter, *Jerusalem through the Ages* (Jerusalem, 1975), contains 194 pages of titles on the Temple site and on the water supply of the city. The prompt for "Jerusalem" on the keyboard of one large research library brought out nearly six hundred titles produced since 1975.

53. Bieberstein-Bloedhorn. The maps are dated 1992.

54. Charles W. Wilson and Charles Warren, *The Recovery of Jerusalem* (London, 1871); C. W. Warren, *Underground Jerusalem* (London, 1876); Claude R.

Conder and Horation H. Kitchner, *Survey of Western Palestine III* (London, 1884).

55. Since the issue is not important for this book, I did not try to investigate Ottoman military archives, but the ways in which the Ottomans would have kept track of their possessions is an interesting subject of enquiry.

56. Max van Berchem, *Matériaux pour un Corpus Inscriptionum Arabicarum: Jerusalem Ville et Haram* (Cairo, 1922–27). For a useful and moving account of van Berchem's work in Jerusalem, see Marguerite (Gautier-)van Berchem and Solange Ory, *La Jérusalem Musulmane dans l'oeuvre de Max van Berchem* (Lausanne, 1978). For an update on inscriptions, see Walls and Abul-Hajj, *Arabic Inscriptions*.

57. On the useful side are several books in Hebrew by Dan Bahat (on Jerusalem plans, 1969; the Aqsa Mosque, 1978; the Dome of the Rock, 1976; the whole city, 1983 and 1990) which serve as introductions to most of the major buildings of the city. For inventive schemes for the future, see Arthur Kutcher, *The New Jerusalem; Planning and Politics* (London, 1973), or Moshe Safdie, *The Harvard Jerusalem Studies* (Cambridge, 1986), among many others. Old picture books, often with incompetent texts, are too numerous to mention; a recent book, *Jerusalem Architecture* (New York, 1994), by David Kroyanker has excellent illustrations and a more scholarly text.

58. The main compendia based on texts are: Mednikoff, *Palestina*; Le Strange, *Palestine*; A. S. Marmarji, *Buldaniyah Filastin al-Arabiyah* (Beirut, 1948), trans. into French as *Textes Arabes sur la Palestine* (Paris, 1952); Kamel J. Assali, *Bayt al-Maqdis fi kutub al-Riblat* (Amman, 1992); Wilkinson, *Jerusalem Pilgrims*. One should mention, even though the texts have mostly been superceded, the old volumes of the Palestine Pilgrim Text Society. A recent, mostly photographic, second hand, catalogue is the *Kunuz al-Quds*, ed. Rauf Y. Nijim (Amman, 1983); and a special mention must be made of the admirably complete *A History of Palestine 634–1099* by Moshe Gil (Cambridge, 1992, from Hebrew edition of 1983) which is a well-documented and intelligently evaluated paraphrase of hundreds of texts.

59. I have not learned much about the author, but he belongs to the generation which produced scholarly giants like Caetani and Brockelman with the same passion for precision. The originality of Med-

nikoff has recently been recognized by A. Noth and L. Conrad in *The Early Arabic Tradition*, pp. 3–5.

60. Louis Hugues Vincent and A. M. Stève, *Jérusalem de l'Ancien Testament*, 3 vols. (Paris, 1954–56), a partial rewriting of his earlier (with F. M. Abel) *Jérusalem, Recherches de topographie d'archéologie et d'histoire* (Paris 1912–1914); Jan Josef Simons, *Jerusalem in the Old Testament* (Leiden, 1952); Theodor A. Busink, *Der Tempel von Jerusalem, von Salomo bis Herodes*, 2 vols. (Leiden, 1970–1980).

61. The most striking are in the books by Vincent and Busink in which Muslim constructions or buildings are discussed, sometimes quite accurately and imaginatively as Busink's description of the Haram, *only* in order to elucidate Jewish or Christian practices or monuments.

62. One exception is Alistair Duncan, *The Noble Sanctuary* (London, 1972), an attractive and simple booklet on the Haram. The work of the British School of Archaeology on Mamluk Jerusalem is partly connected to these political considerations in a most creative way. The reissue of an old classic, Arif al-Arif's *Al-Mufassal f ta'rikh al-Quds* (Jerusalem, 1986), is an instance of reviving traditional Muslim learning on the city, while Abdel-Aziz Duri's "Bait al-Maqdis in Islam" in Adnan Hadidi, ed., *Studies in the History and Archaeology of Jordan* (Amman, 1988) is an example of the new national scholarship at its best.

63. See, particularly, the always very learned and at times imaginative studies by Heribert Busse, from "The Sanctity of Jerusalem in Islam," *Judaism* 17 (1968) to (with Georg Kretschmar) *Jerusalemer frühislamischer zeit* (Wiesbaden, 1987); and the scholarly essays in Richard I. Cohen, ed., *Vision and Conflict in the Holy Land* (New York, 1985). A touching puzzlement about all these issues permeates the highly readable book by Thomas A. Idinopoulos, *Jerusalem Blessed, Jerusalem Cursed* (Chicago, 1991).

64. Some examples are: Eva Baer, "The Mihrab in the Cave of the Dome of the Rock," *Muqarnas* 3 (1985); Nasser Rabbat, "The Meaning of the Umayyad Dome of the Rock," *Muqarnas* 6 (1989); Nuha Khoury, "The Dome of the Rock, the Ka'ba, and Ghumdar," *Muqarnas* 10 (1993); Rabbat also in *Muqarnas* 10. In a sense the very recent volume with many brilliant essays edited by Julian Raby and Jeremy Hohsn, *Bayt al-Maqdis I*, illustrates this new tendency of trying to understand a moment of

Islamic history and of Muslim experience, discussing the past only when it elucidates that history and that experience. The several books and articles by Frank Peters are a one-man show on how Jerusalem became Muslim, with perhaps more concern for religious than visual issues: Francis E. Peters, *Jerusalem* (Princeton, 1985), an excellent introduction to the city; *Jerusalem and Mecca* (New York, 1986), a more ambitious effort at holy urbanism; "Why did Abd-al-Malik build the Dome of the Rock," *Graeco-Arabica* 2 (1983), an original and provocative explanation for a nearly forgotten question. Over the past few years, sophisticated historical arguments of national positions have begun to appear in a new literature which I did not fully survey, inasmuch as it sometimes occurs in the daily press, as happened with the discussion on the financial responsibilities for the refurbishing of the Dome of the Rock.

65. M. Halbwachs, *La Topographie légendaire des Evangiles en Terre Sainte* (rpr. Paris, 1971). This extraordinary investigation of holiness and sacredness was first published in the dark year of 1941. I owe my knowledge of it to the colleagues at the Ecole des Hautes Etudes en Sciences Sociales who attended a seminar I gave there in 1994. I am particularly pleased to thank Lucette Valensi and François Pouillon.

Chapter One

1. The whole issue and the arguments used are fully developed in P.W.L. Walker, *Holy City, Holy Places* (Oxford, 1990), whence come nearly all of my examples. For an important book with a wider objective around the same topic, see Robert L. Wilken, *The Land Called Holy* (New Haven, 1992).

2. The presentation of this visionary Jerusalem will be made in conjunction with an account of the Persian invasion of 614 and the subsequent occupation (or whatever it was) of Jerusalem. As it appears nearly fifteen centuries later, this invasion is an event that strikingly reflects the mixture of objective and lurid events with saintly or bizarre ones so typical of the Holy City at that time and through much of its history.

3. John Wilkinson, trans., *Jerusalem Pilgrims before the Crusades*, (Warminster, 1977) p. 53; see also pp. 3–4 for a discussion of the authenticity of Eucherius'

account, ultimately accepted by Wilkinson. For the archaeological record, see Vincent-Abel, pp. 441–72, and Yorem Tsafrir, "Jerusalem," *RBK*, pp. 601–2.

4. Vincent-Abel, pp. 909f.

5. The issue of visible and invisible boundaries between sacred and profane spaces has been identified by most sociologists and anthropologists of religion (see, for example, Mircea Eliade, *Traité d'Histoire des Religions* [Paris, 1949], pp. 315–31; and *The Myth of the Eternal Return* [Princeton, 1954], pp. 76ff.), but it extends to all attempts at defining spaces through means other than those of the natural landscape. Such are administrative and political boundaries, as in the gerrymandering of American electoral districts, the divisions of Irish cities, or the processes incorporating Jerusalem into Israel.

6. The Herodian Temple and all of its features have often been described and discussed. For the most thorough scholarly summary of all the issues, see Theodor Busink, *Der Tempel von Jerusalem, von Salomo bis Herodes* (Leiden, 1970–1980), esp. pp. 1017ff. Simpler descriptions are found in Kay Prag, *Jerusalem* (Blue Guide, London, 1989), pp. 77–81. For more popular reconstructions, see *Biblical Archaeology Review*, 15 (Nov./Dec. 1989). In a provocative article, "Who built the Dome of the Rock," *Graeco-Arabica* 2 (1989), pp. 125ff., Frank Peters argues that the Herodian Temple platform may have been square rather than rectangular. His hypothesis helps to explain several unusual features of the Golden Gate, but too much evidence, both archaeological and written, militates against it. It is, however, proper to acknowledge how refreshing it is to read new and constructive hypotheses, even if they are not acceptable in the end, in a field where political excitement is more prevalent than intellectual activity.

7. Cyril Mango in *Bayt al-Maqdis I*, and below, pp. 49–50.

8. The issue of what remained on the Haram from the Temple was discussed, with some interesting and many debatable suggestions, by Father Bellarmino Bogatti in *Recherches sur le Site du Temple de Jérusalem* (Jerusalem, 1979). The suggestion that imperial temples remained standing throughout the Christian period was made by Cyril Mango, *Bayt al-Maqdis I*, who argues provocatively that the word

templum in Arculf's text referred to a pagan temple, not the Temple of Solomon.

9. See Wilkinson, *Jerusalem Pilgrims*, p. 173, for a convenient summary of appropriate sources, but the exact interpretation of each one of them poses its own set of problems.

10. Michael Avi-Yonah, *The Jews under Roman and Byzantine Rule* (New York, 1976), esp. pp. 191ff.

11. Avi-Yonah, *Jews*, p. 214. Avi-Yonah, who was sensitive to the moods of Palestinian history, already seems to have had some doubts about the association of the pilgrim's story and the stone under the Dome of the Rock; see Avi-Yonah, *The Madaba Mosaic Map* (Jerusalem, 1954), p. 59, n. 79. It is, however, possible that special rites or practices had been developed for Jerusalem, since several later sources mention again that Jewish servants of the Muslim Haram anointed the Rock. See also, below, pp. 132–33, for discussion of a problem which requires further investigation.

12. Such an investigation will never be possible through traditional means, but this may well be a place where recent technologies of subterranean mapping through photography could be used.

13. Wilken, *The Land Called Holy*, pp. 207ff., for the *Book of Elijah* and the *Book of Zerubbabel* as two early seventh century messianic sources.

14. André Grabar, *Ampoules de Terre Sainte* (Paris, 1958); and Gary Vikan, *Byzantine Pilgrimage Art* (Washington, 1982), with the examples of ceramic versions of silver objects.

15. The Roman mosaics are listed and discussed briefly in Zev Vilnay, *The Holy Land in Old Prints and Maps* (Jerusalem, 1965), pp. 29ff.; Bianca Kühnel, *From the Earthly to the Heavenly Jerusalem* (Rome, 1987); and Moshe Catane, *Jérusalem à travers trois millénaires* (Freiburg, 1984) pp. 21–55. For manuscripts, see Carlo Ceccheli and others, *The Rabbula Gospels* (Olten, 1959), pl. III and appropriate commentaries. A subject for eventual investigation is the geographical spread of these images. Why were they so common in Rome and so rare in Constantinople?

16. The map is illustrated in Hubert Donner and Heinz Cüppers, *Die Mosaikkarte von Madeba I* (Wiesbaden, 1977). This publication has not superceded the older and much more learned studies by Father P. O'Callaghan in *Dictionnaire de Théologie Chrétienne*, and by Avi-Yonah, *The Madaba Mosaic Map*.

17. The Madaba map, as discussed below, has also influenced the schematic composition of the CAD reconstructions.

18. The presence and location of secular power is very difficult to identify in Jerusalem before the eleventh century.

19. Michele Piccirillo, *The Mosaics of Jordan* (Amman 1992), is a convenient introduction to the most characteristic examples of Jerash and Umm al-Rasas, with references to Antioch and eastern Mediterranean examples. For Italy, see Zev Vilnay, *The Holy Land in Old Prints and Maps* (Jerusalem, 1963), pp. 42–46. On a more general level, see André Grabar, "Quelques Notes sur les Psautiers byzantins," *Cahiers Archéologiques* 15 (1965) and I. Ehrensperges-Katz, "Les Representations de Villes fortifiées," *Cahiers Archéologiques* 19 (1969).

20. As a result, there never can be a definitive study of the Holy Sepulchre; see Yoram Tsafrir, ed., *Ancient Churches Revealed* (Jerusalem, 1993), pp. 101–22, for a good summary.

21. Our reconstruction follows Father Coüasnon and others in showing the central nave as higher than the side ones, following in this the traditional scheme for five-aisled basilicas. The Madaba map, on the other hand, clearly shows a single roof over the whole building. One could argue that the image closest in time to the period involved takes precedence for a historical reconstruction over parallels in Rome or even in Bethlehem. But the Madaba map is not a record of how things look, only of the hierarchy of their importance. This is why our computer-aided drawing has reconstructed the Holy Sepulchre with a higher central nave following the normal practice of buildings of this type. At issue here is the rather interesting point of the spirit of a document limiting or extending the value of its information.

22. Wilkinson, *Jerusalem Pilgrims*, pp. 196–97, pls. 5 and 6; Paul Horn and Ernest Born, *The Plan of St. Gall* (Berkeley, 1974), p. 54.

23. The list, a partial one, is culled from the *Breviarus* of ca. 500 and the account of the pilgrim from Piacenza of ca. 570; Wilkinson, *Jerusalem Pilgrims*, pp. 59–61, 83. Some of these items were found in more than one place, just as the location of sacred events moved from place to place, even from city to city.

24. Wilkinson, *Jerusalem Pilgrims*, pp. 91–92.

25. Nahman Avigad, in *IEJ*, 27 (1977), and 37 (1987); "Die Entstehung der Nea genannten Marienkirche," *Antike Welet* 10 (1979); *Discovering Jerusalem* (Nashville, 1983). Vincent-Abel, pp. 911ff., is still useful for its discussion of the sources, which are all given in the book; Tsafrir, *Ancient Churches*, pp. 128–35. A building inscription was found during Professor Avigad's excavations which can be dated either 534–535 or 549–550.

26. It is impossible to know whether the emperor and his advisors in Constantinople or Jerusalem made the distinction between Solomonic and Herodian buildings.

27. Wilkinson, *Jerusalem Pilgrims*, p. 83; Vincent-Abel, p. 821. For the tomb of the Virgin, see Creswell, *EMA²*, pp. 108–9.

28. See Vincent-Abel, pp. 421–81, 516–28, which contain the largest number of documents and much pertinent discussion; and Wilkinson, *Jerusalem Pilgrims*, pp. 171–72 for a chronological commentary on texts without concern for archaeological sources and without interpretation of the spaces involved.

29. In addition to earlier sources, the most important one is the account put together from Georgian, Arabic, Armenian, and Greek versions of the story told by one Strategios, a monk in St. Saba's monastery; see J. T. Milik, "La Topographie de Jérusalem vers la fin de l'époque byzantine," *Mélanges Université St. Joseph* 37 (1961). There are many lists of churches in Palestine; see, for example, Asher Ovadiah, *Corpus of the Byzantine Churches of the Holy Land* (Boston, 1970) and articles by H. Leclercq in *DACL* (Paris, 1971) and Y. Tsafrir in *RBK*. For a summary of summaries, see now Bieberstein-Bloedhorn, pp. 161–75. For a partial archaeological record, see Tsafrir, *Ancient Churches*, pp. 101ff.

30. Wilkinson, *Jerusalem Pilgrims*, pp. 83, 166–67.

31. Wilkinson, *Jerusalem Pilgrims*, p. 10.

32. Derward J. Chitty, *The Desert as a City* (London, 1960).

33. Glen W. Bowersock, *Hellenism in Late Antiquity* (Ann Arbor, 1990), especially chapter 6. For Armenian sources, there is the interesting list of monasteries allegedly found in the seventh century; the list is certainly later, but it is interesting that a later writer saw the sixth century as the appropriate time for increased ethnic diversity in Christian Je-

rusalem. See A. K. Sanjian, "Anastos Vardapet's Lis," *Le Museon*, 82 (1969).

34. Maurice Halbwachs, *La Topographie légendaire des Evangiles en Terre Sainte* (rpr. Paris 1971), p. 123.

35. A wonderful example occurs in the late medieval and pre-modern transformations of Mount Zion and the eventual "discovery" there of the tomb of David, now a Muslim prophet. Vincent-Abel, pp. 571 and ff., for parts of the story.

36. Seeing Jerusalem as a "focus of confrontation between Judaism and Christianity" has been stated by Amnon Linder, "Jerusalem as a focus of confrontation," in Richard I. Cohen, ed., *Vision and Conflict in the Holy Land* (New York, 1985).

37. Walker, *Holy City*, p. 317.

38. John F. Baldovin, *The Urban Character of Christian Worship in Jerusalem* (New Haven, 1982), and Peter Jeffery, "The Earliest Christian Chant Repertory Recovered," *Journal of the American Musicological Society*, 47 (1994).

39. Wilkinson, *Jerusalem Pilgrims*, p. 49.

40. Bernard Flusin, *Saint Athanase le Perse* (Paris, 1992), vol. 2, p. 34. In fact, both public and private ways of professing one's faith can still be seen in the Old City of today, if one learns to interpret the gestures, behavior, at times, the clothes of persons in the street.

41. Meyer Ben-Dov, *In the Shadow of the Temple* (New York, 1985), especially pp. 243ff. Many aspects of the reconstructions provided by Ben-Dov, especially the clusters of houses on p. 255, are really fantasy pushed a bit too far. Our own reconstructions of these spaces (figs. 12, 13) are also based on practically no information and this is why they were left as blank boxes rather than provided with people and trees. The question of how much detail to include in restorations remains unresolved.

42. A. Couret, *La Palestine sous les empereurs grecs* (Paris, 18).

43. Flusin, *Saint Athanase*, is a prime example of the wealth of information on all sorts of topics that can be gleaned from the life of a saint.

44. Avi-Yonah, *The Jews under Roman and Byzantine Rule*, p. 224.

45. In addition to Vilnay, *The Holy Land*, and Bianca Kühnel, *From the Earthly to the Heavenly Jerusalem*, mentioned earlier, see M. L. Gatti Perer, *Immagine della Gerusalemme Celeste dal III al XIV secolo* (Milan, 1983).

46. Wilkinson, *Jerusalem Pilgrims*, p. 91.

47. See André Grabar, *Ampoules*, esp. pp. 46ff., for an interpretation of their meaning; see also Gary Vikan, *Byzantine Pilgrimage Art*.

48. Much has been written about the Persian invasion since Alphonse Couret, *La Prise de Jérusalem* (Orléans, 1896). Wisely or not, I have followed the following sources and discussions: Gérard Garitte, *Expugnationes Hierosolymae A.D. 614* (Louvain, 1973–4); Paul Peeters, "La Prise de Jérusalem par les Perses," *Recherches d'Histoire et de Philologie Orientales* (Bruxelles, 1951); Sebeos, *Histoire d'Héraclius*, trans. Frédéric Macler (Paris, 1904); C.J.F. Dowsett, *The History of the Caucasian Albanians* (London, 1961); Cyril Mango, "Deux Etudes sur Byzance et la Perse," *MT* 9 (1985); Anatole Frolov, *La Relique de la Vraie Croix* (Paris, 1961); Flusin, *Athanase*; Cyril Mango, "The Temple Mount," in *Bayt al-Maqdis I*. I have also consulted Michael Morony, "Syria under the Persians 610–629," *Proceedings of the Second Symposium on the History of Bilad al-Sham*, ed. Muhammad A. Bakhit (Amman, 1987), which raises important issues, but may not have been sufficiently critical of sources.

49. Brannon M. Wheeler, "Imagining the Sasanian Capture of Jerusalem," *Orientalia Christiana Periodica*, 57 (1990).

50. See Bieberstein-Bloedhorn, pp. 175ff., for a bibliographical introduction.

51. Creswell, *EMA²*, pp. 124–25; Mango in *Bayt al-Maqdis*; Peters in *Graeco-Arabica*, with a provocative suggestion of an attempt by Heraclius to recapture the Temple begun anew by Jews. The suggestion cannot, I believe, be accepted, but it points in the right direction for an eventual explanation of what happened.

52. Flusin, *Anastase*, esp. pp. 329; Mango in *Bayt al-Maqdis*.

53. Flusin, *Anastase*, p. 315, with further references.

54. This complexity comes out strikingly in the volume of commentaries by Flusin, *Anastase*. His brilliantly detailed unraveling of the fabric which created a given narrative ends up by eliminating the fabric and the narrative.

55. Mednikoff, *Palestina*, I, pp. 502ff., and throughout vol. II; Leone Caetani, *Annali dell'Islam* (Turin, 1905–1926), 3, pp. 920ff.; Michael de Goeje, *Mémoire sur la Conquête de la Syrie* (Leiden, 1900); Sholomo Dov Goitein, "al-Kuds," *EI2*; Gil, *Palestine*

pp. 57ff.; Shafiq J. A. Mahmud, *Ta'rikh al-Quds* (Amman, 1984), pp. 83ff., and esp. after p. 95.

56. Michael Bates, "History, Geography and Numismatics in the first Century of Islamic Coinage," *Revue Suisse de Numismatique* 65 (1986); "The Coinage of Syria under the Umayyads," *Proceedings, Fourth Bilad al-Sham Conference* (Amman, 1989); and a few local studies mentioned later.

57. During his sermon of Christmas 636 he said that he was unable to go to Bethlehem because of roaming Arabs in the countryside, but the implication is that the city of Jerusalem was still controlled by him. He is alleged to have died in 639 (or 641, according to some) out of grief over the loss of the Holy City. The explanations are in both cases dubious, since nothing says that the warring Arabs were the new Muslims rather than old-fashioned brigands and the patriarch's sorrow may have been genuine, but not necessarily death-inducing.

58. As a typical example of the confusion, much discussion has surrounded the covenant the caliph Umar is alleged to have signed with the Christians of the city. But every version of this covenant contains anachronistic passages that throw doubt on the very existence of such a document.

59. An example of how this works in a small detail is shown by Patricia Crone, *Slaves on Horses, The Evolution of the Islamic Policy* (Cambridge, 1980), pp. 207–8, n. 60.

60. Sophronius was a poet in classical Greek verse as well as a liturgical poet. He was also a powerful ecclesiastical leader who was isolated among the other church leaders of his time because of his opposition to the monotheletic doctrine propagated by Heraclius and his entourage. Ch. von Schönborn, *Sophrone de Jérusalem* (Paris, 1972), pp. 89ff., and Sophronius, "Lettre à Arcadius de Chypre", ed. Micheline Albert and Christoph von Schönborn, in *PO* 39 (Turnhout, 1978).

61. In addition to the previous sources and studies, see Fred M. Donner, *The Early Islamic Conquests* (Princeton, 1981), pp. 151ff., expressing, among other things, some uncertainty as to whether the cities of the Palestinian coast had already been subdued; and Walter Kaegi, *Byzantium and the Early Islamic Conquests* (Cambridge, 1992).

62. There are, of course, numerous questions about the preserved texts of these agreements, but their large

number, their use in later litigations, and the fact that they often fit with broader patterns of agreements in the Arabian world indicate that some of their features may well have been typologically consistent; see Donald R. Hill, *The Termination of Hostilities in the Early Arab Conquests A.D. 634–656* (London, 1971).

63. Whether Umar really came cannot in fact be established, and on the whole, the arguments against his undertaking such a long voyage for the purpose of accepting the surrender of Jerusalem seem stronger to me than those in favor, mostly because all the accounts, without a single exception, contain anachronisms or biases that weaken their credibility. Since these accounts have all been discussed by most scholars since Le Strange and Mednikoff, I list only the main sources and a very important one unknown a century ago: al-Baladhuri, *Kitab Futuh al-Buldan* (Leiden, 1866), pp. 138–40, trans. Philip K. Hitti, as *The Origins of the Islamic State* (New York, 1916), pp. 213–15; Tabari, *Ta'rikh*, ed. Michael de Goeje and others (Leiden, 1879–1901), I, pp. 2403ff., and vol. 12 of translation (SUNY, 1992), pp. 189ff.; M. B. Abdallah al-Azdi al-Basri, *Ta'rikh futuh al-Sha'm* (Cairo, 1970), pp. 247ff., for a very interesting version with shi'ite overtones; Ahmad b. A'tham al-Kufi, *Kitab al-Futuh*, ed. M. A. M. Khan (Hyderbabud, 1968), I, pp. 289ff. in which Christians and Jews play a prominent role as people to be converted; Michael the Syrian, *Chronique*, trans. J.-B. Chabot (Paris, 1901), 2, p. 425, for one of several Christian versions; Gil, *Palestine*, pp. 68ff., for Jewish sources, mostly eschatological, on this topic. Recent discussions of these events are found in Heribert Busse "Omar as Conqueror," *BSOAS* 8 (1986) revised in "The Tower of David/Mihrab Dawud," *JSAI* 17 (1994).

64. Claude Cahen, "Note sur l'accueil des chrétiens d'Orient à l'Islam," *Revue de l'Histoire des Religions* 166 (1964). Whether the Greek clergy of Jerusalem in 638 would have reacted like Christian Arabs in later times is perhaps less certain, but one can assume that neither had any idea of what the new religion was about.

65. Tabari, *Ta'rikh*, I, p. 2403.

66. See article "Ka'b al-Ahbar," in *EI²*.

67. A lengthy discussion of the issues involved is found in the entry "mi'radj" in *EI²*.

68. Mednikoff, *Palestina*, II, pp. 614–15.

69. For instance, Pseudo-Methodius of Patara in Andrew Palmer, *The Seventh Century in the West-Syrian Chronicles* (Liverpool, 1993), pp. 222ff. Most of the messianic prophecies belong to the second half of the century, but they take into account the Persian invasion and the arrival of Muslim rule, especially in Jerusalem.

70. Al-Azdi, *Ta'rikh*, p. 247; and see below, pp. 72–73, for trees and eschatology.

71. I am aware of the problem involved in translating *khalifah* as "representative," but the usual translation of "viceroy" smacks too much of British rule in India.

72. I am not necessarily adopting the provocative position developed by Michael Cook and Patricia Crone, in *Hagarism The Making of the Islamic World* (Cambridge, 1977), but I am arguing that in the ill-focused and depressed Jewish world of Arabia, Palestine, and Syria, conversions to Islam were frequent and doctrinal differences had not yet become clear. The circumcised were winning. There are many different views on the topic of Jewish institutional and spiritual history at this time. See Avi-Yonah, *The Jews of Palestine*; and Andrew Sharf, *Byzantine Jewry from Justinian to the Fourth Crusade* (London, 1971). Jewish messianic texts usually portray the Muslim invasions as favorable to Jews.

73. Wilkinson, *Jerusalem Pilgrims*, pp. 95–106. The drawings have been mentioned earlier.

74. Wilkinson, *Jerusalem Pilgrims*, p. 95.

75. Creswell, *EMA²*, pp. 32–35.

76. Gérard Garitte, "La version géorgienne du 'Pré Spirituel'," in *Mélanges Eugène Tisserant*, vol. 2 (Vatican, 1964), p. 182. The text was retranslated with more comments by Bernard Flusin, in *Bayt al-Maqdis I*, pp. 17ff.

77. Gil, *Palestine*, pp. 70–73, gives sources and discusses various problems posed by them. See also Amikam Elad in *Bayt al-Maqdis I*, especially. p. 39, for another version of Jewish attendants on the Haram.

78. Goitein, "al-Kuds'"; see also all the texts in Mednikoff, *Palestina*, pp. 644ff. Oleg Grabar, "The Meaning of the Dome of the Rock," in Marilyn J. Chiat and Kathryn L. Reyerson eds., *The Medieval Mediterranean: Cross-Cultural Currents* (St. Cloud, 1988), develops the idea from a different point of view.

79. Peters in *Graeco-Arabica* 2 (1983), Flusin and Elad in *Bayt al-Maqdis I*.

80. Gil, *Palestine*, p. 751.

81. Arif al-Aref, *Al-Mufassah Ta'rikh al-Quds* (rpr. Jerusalem, 1986), pp. 102–4; Goitein, "al-Kuds."

82. Heribert Busse and Georg Kretschmar, *Jerusalemische Heiligstumstraditionen in altkirchlicher und frühislamischer Zeit* (Wiesbaden, 1987), pp. 24–27.

Chapter Two

1. Muqaddasi, text on p. 159; I have adapted the translation by Le Strange, *Palestine*, pp. 117–18, which is most complete; short excerpts from this text are found in many manuals on Islamic architecture.

2. Gil, *Palestine*, p. 92.

3. Bernard Flusin, "Démons et Sarrasins," *TM* 11 (1991), p. 386.

4. Andrew Palmer, *The Seventh Century in the West-Syrian Chronicles* (Liverpool, 1993), pp. 45–48.

5. Gil, *Palestine*, p. 92.

6. In the late twelfth century, John of Würzburg is one of several writers giving the lengthy texts of Latin inscriptions located somewhere in the building; see John Wilkinson, *Jerusalem Pilgrimage 1099–1185* (London, 1988), pp. 245–48, 289ff. One of those texts also alludes to older Arabic inscriptions which may have been covered up by the Latin ones.

7. Max van Berchem, *Matériaux: Haram*, pp. 225ff.; see also *RCEA*, no. 9.

8. Christel Kessler, "Abd al-Malik's Inscription in The Dome of the Rock, a Reconsideration," *JRAS*, 1970.

9. Sheila Blair, "What is the Date of the Dome of the Rock," *Bayt al-Maqdis I*, pp. 86–87. Heribert Busse, "Monotheismus und islamische Christologie in der Bauiuschrift der Felsendoms in Jerusalem," *Theologische Quartalschrift* 161 (1981), and "Die arabischen Inschriften im und am Felsendom," *Das Heilige Land*, 109 (1977).

10. The exact meaning of the word *al-samad* used in this celebrated surah, *al Ikhlas* ("Purity of Faith"), is difficult to determine; see Régis Blachère, *Le Coran Traduction* (Paris, 1949), vol. 2, pp. 122–24. I finally decided on "alone" rather than "eternal" or "incorporeal," because of the broader meaning I give to the inscription and because it seems to conform with a meaning clearly attested in early times.

11. Other readings of these words are possible, but the differences between them do not seem important to our understanding of the building.

12. There is a significant change here, as the Koran has Jesus speaking in the first person when referring to his birth, death, and Resurrection; or else the passage could be an earlier alternate version. This is also the location of three large dots set above each other, spandrel 98 (fig. 48), as though indicating a clear separation in value between quoted passages from the Holy Text.

13. Arthur Jeffery, *Materials for the History of the Text of the Quran* (Leiden, 1937), pp. 150ff.

14. Here as well, the Koranic model, if it is one, was adapted to the inscription by putting the text of the quote in third instead of first person.

15. For a recent summary of the situation see Yusuf Raghib, "L'Ecriture des Papyrus Arabes," *RMM* 58 (1991), pp. 17–18. A convenient survey of all the issues involved and of the pertinent documents is found in the chapter by various authors in Wolf-dietrich Fischer, *Grundriss der Arabischen Philologie I: Sprachwissenchaft* (Wiesbaden, 1982), esp. pp. 165ff.

16. Adrian Brockett, "The Value of the Hajs and Warsh Transmissions," in Andrew Rippin, ed., *Approaches to the History and Interpretation of the Qur'an* (Oxford, 1988); p. 45; S. Ory, "Aspects religieux des textes épigraphique," in *Un Début de l'Islam Les Premières Ecritures Islamiques*, vol. 58, *RMM* (1991); for milestones, see van Berchem, *Matériaux*, pl. I.

17. Any collection of early pages will make the point, for instance Paris, Bibliotèque Nationale, *Splendeur et Majesté, Korans de la Bibliotèque Nationale* (Paris, 1987), pp. 22–28

18. The old book of examples is Bernhard Moritz, *Arabic Palaeography* (Cairo, 1905) and the classical standard study is Adolf Grohmann, *Arabische Paläographie*, 2 vols. (Vienna 1967 and 1971). Access to more recent work can be found in François Déroche, *The Abbasid Tradition*, vol. I, *The Nasser D. Khalili Collection of Islamic Art* (Oxford, 1992), with references to his and other works. For the Yemen fragments only very partial accounts exist; see, for example, the Kuwait National Museum exhibit catalogue, *Masahif San'a* (1985).

19. Drafts of texts were written on marble and other materials used in building as we know from Umayyad palaces like Khirbat al-Mafjar, Robert W. Hamilton, *Khirbat al-Mafjar* (Oxford, 1959), pp. 41–44. Some lighter material must have been

used in Jerusalem, as one can hardly imagine marble plaques carried up a scaffolding with the text of the inscription. But the wider question is whether literacy in general or in the specific language of an inscription is needed to copy it.

20. A group of manuscripts remain which are either dated or datable between 843 and 911; François Déroche, *Les Manuscrits du Moyen Orient* (Paris, 1989), p. 102. It should be noted that this foremost expert on early Koranic manuscripts wrote that "colophons are . . . the least common type of inscriptions found in Quranic manuscripts . . . and a high proportion [of these colophons] . . . are fakes," in *Abbasid Tradition: Khalili Collection*, p. 13. For examples of these early manuscripts see also Salah al-Din al-Munajjed, *Le Manuscrit Arabe jusqu'au Xᵉ Siècle* (Cairo, 1960), pls. 13–16. To my knowledge the 40,000 parchment pages found in Yemen have not yielded a single date.

21. *RCEA*, nos. 6 (dated 652 with Koran 112, like the Dome of the Rock), 18 (mosque of Damascus, 705–715, in one of the two versions recorded by medieval chroniclers), 19 (Mosque of Amr in Cairo, restored in 711), 30 (a curious and slightly dubious example from a private house in Medinah with an inscription allegedly dated 735), 38, 46, 47 (the 758–778 work done in the Mosque of Medinah and reported by the geographer Ibn Rustah), and 40 (Mekkah in 758). An additional and very unusual example occurs in Ramlah, Myriam Rosen-Ayalon, "The first Mosaic discovered in Ramla," *IEJ*, 26 (1976). For an earlier discussion with useful insights, see Muhammad al-Hawary, "The Most Ancient Islamic Monument," *JRAS* 1970.

22. The classical studies are Theodor Nöldeke, Georg Bergstrasser, Otto Pretzl, Friedrich Schwally, *Geschichte des Qorans* (Leipzig, 1904–1938), and A. Jeffery, *Materials for the History of the Text of the Qur'an* (Leiden, 1937). A different approach using alternate techniques of literary criticism was developed by John Wansbaugh, *Quranic Studies* (Oxford, 1977), and John Burton, *The Collection of the Quran* (Cambridge, 1977), among others; see the thoughtful and complete summaries and discussions by Alford T. Welch, "al-Kur'an," *EI²*, and Andrew Rippin, ed., *Approaches*.

23. Adrian Brockett, "The Value of the Hajs and Warsh Transmissions," in Rippin, *Approaches*, p. 32, n. 5. It is curious that Brockett discusses the matter

only in a footnote and in fact his opinion is fairly reserved: "indeed the extent of the agreement of the inscriptions with the text of the Quran is far more impressive and strongly suggests that the text must, in fact, have been fixed. Nor can such inscriptions be considered to be actual copies of the Quran requiring strict adherence to the rules of transmission." I am not certain that I fully understand the reason for this last sentence except to illustrate once again the textual historian's unease with monumental sources.

24. Although they did not say so *expressis verbis*, such was, I believe, the implication of the remarks on the Dome of the Rock made by Michael Cook and Patricia Crone in *Hagarism* (Cambridge, 1977).

25. It is worth noting that Jeffery's list of Koranic passages (above, n. 13) with known alternate readings or modifications does not include the instances found in the Dome of the Rock, but he made no claim to completeness, and I did not seek out the literature that may have additional examples.

26. What is at issue in these remarks goes beyond the inscriptions of the Dome of the Rock. They question in fact a whole attitude, developed by positivist historians in the nineteenth century, among whom the great Max van Berchem was a shining light. The objectives of this approach were to date monuments properly and when necessary as in the case of objects, to describe their context, or else to set up evolutionary chronologies for everything from construction techniques to styles of writing. As a result, this approach often dismissed whole sections of written information that did not provide a name or a date by calling them "inscriptions banales" and interpreted anything vaguely connected with the faith as "inscription koranique." Inscriptions were indeed seen as collages, not to say pastiches, with sections of varying importance, rather than as documents. In fact dates and names of people or places always took precedence over the rest of an inscription. The only consistent exception to this attitude has come about in the various studies of medieval and pre-modern objects by Souren Melikian-Chirvani, who gave equal weight to all parts of inscriptions, although he too ends up by dating and localizing. As an example, see his *Islamic Metalwork from the Iranian World* (London, 1982).

27. Max van Berchem, *Matériaux: Haram*, p. 238. Positivist approaches could not understand the illogical statement which was composed by al Ma'mun.

28. *RCEA*, nos. 100, 116, 122; Hassan al-Hawary and Gaston Wiet, *Matériaux pour un Corpus Inscriptionum Arabicarum IV: Arabie*, vol. 1, ed. Nikita Elisséev (Cairo, 1985).

29. The main argument on this topic has been developed by Blair, *Bayt al-Maqdis*. See also Moshe Sharon, "An Inscription from the year 65 A.M. in the Dome of the Rock," *Studia Orientalia Memoriae D. H. Baneth Dedicata* (Jerusalem, 1979). I am not entirely convinced by Sharon's argument and feel that the dates of 65 or 66 for the beginning of the work on Dome of the Rock are much later accommodations to the existing date of 92.

30. Hubert Donner, *Die anakreontische Gechichte Nr. 18 und Nr. 20 des Patriarchen Sophronius* (Heidelberg, 1981), pp. 12, 23, and esp. 36–37. See also John Wilkinson, trans., *Jerusalem Pilgrims before the Crusades* (Warminster, 1977), p. 91, who anticipated my argument in his n. 2. The word could have reflected what has been identified as the special dialect of Palestinian Christian Aramaic (communication by Prof. Sydney Griffith at the 1995 symposium at Dumbarton Oaks).

31. The text is translated in Cyril Mango, *The Art of the Byzantium Empire* (New York, 1972), pp. 57–60, where a good bibliography can be found.

32. See Daniel Gimaret, *Les Noms Divins en Islam* (Paris, 1988), for a theological introduction to the subject.

33. Van Berchem, *Matériaux: Haram*, pp. 251ff.

34. There is some uncertainty about Jewish liturgical practices at the time, but there is later evidence for prayers on behalf of the non-Jewish rulers of the moment; S. D. Goitein, "Prayers from the Geniza for Fatimid Caliphs," *Studies . . . presented to Leon Nemoy* (Bar-Ilam, 1982).

35. Joseph Van Ess, *Theologie und Gesellschaft im 2, und 3. Jahrhundert Hidschra: Eine Geschichte des religiosen Denkens im frühen Islam* (Berlin/New York, 1991), pp. 29–30, for the very astute argument that the universality of the Muslim message derived from the establishment of Muhammad as the last prophet, as the seal of prophets.

36. There is a curious methodological problem here. Max van Berchem was probably right in pointing out that the passage in the inscription could be either a direct quotation of 2:139 or an alteration of 3:84 (rather than 78, as in *Matériaux: Haram*, p. 250). But why bother with a possible adaptation when the quotation has a direct antecedent or when these few words could have been chosen independently from the Koran? Did it matter at the time that no sign separates quotations from other passages? Altogether, while we are well aware of the pertinence of Koranic passages in inscriptions, the processes of selection and especially of reception are still unclear.

37. *RCEA*, no. 56, dated 795, is the earliest preserved epitaph from a long series.

38. Busse, "Monotheismus," p. 171, compares it to a *catena*, a sequence of patristic excerpts.

39. Oleg Grabar, "The Umayyad Dome of the Rock," *Ars Orientalis* 3 (1959), and *The Formation of Islamic Art* (New Haven, 1987, rev. ed.), pp. 400ff.; Busse, "Die arabischen Inschriften"; and others. The Christological emphasis of the inscription is generally accepted.

40. The passage, it is true, is a bit convoluted and traditional commentators like Tabari seem to have avoided dealing with it. The angels are explained as those of the second heaven, which, in later religious cosmology, will be the heaven of Jesus. See Tabari, *Commentaire du Coran*, trans. Pierre Godé (Paris, 1986), vol. 3, pp. 536–40.

41. In fact, only two topics with Christian associations are part of the long-range development of the Haram: the Cradle of Jesus, located in the passage leading to the Stables of Solomon in the southeastern corner of the esplanade and the "mihrab" of Zakariyah which had already been mentioned. The former is relatively late and the latter consistently confused. Below pp. 148–50.

42. See Geoffrey Parrinder, *Jesus in the Qur'an* (Oxford, 1977), and Alphonse Couret, *La Palestine sous les Empereurs Grecs* (Paris, 1864), among many books dealing with the subject.

43. Tabari, *Commentaire*, vol. 3, pp. 508–30.

44. The process is related to the *Formelschatz* described by Van Ess, *Theologie*, pp. 9–11.

45. The point is subsumed or expressed in most scholarly writing on early Islamic art and culture; the explanation is most forcefully established in Erica Dodd and Shereen Khairallah, *The Image of the Word* (Beirut, 1981), especially in the introductory chapter by Dodd which reproduces her earlier article

with the same title published in *Berytus 18* (1969). It is, of course, connected with theories and explanations of Muslim "iconoclasm" or "aniconism."

46. Oleg Grabar, *The Mediation of Ornament* (Princeton, 1992), pp. 47ff.

47. Oleg Grabar, *Formation*, pp. 128–29.

48. *RCEA*, no. 1758, for instance; Oleg Grabar "Notes sur le *mihrab* de la Grande Mosquée de Cordove," in Alexandre Papadopoulo, ed., *Le mihrab dans l'Architecture de la Religion Musulmane* (Leiden, 1988).

49. I am aware of the dangers involved in building up the central Iraq of the ninth century as a paradigm of cultural perfection. It was certainly not that, but as Van Ess' monumental studies suggest, it was a period for which enough good information exists to take stock of what was going on and to express it in terms meaningful for the whole culture.

50. *RCEA*, nos. 38, 40, 46–52; the Mekkan inscriptions come for the most part from Azraqi's description of the city and the ones from Medina are found in Ibn Rosteh's geography. For a discussion of the Mekkan examples, see Al-Hawary and Wiet, *Matériaux Arabie*, pp. 39–63.

51. From the eleventh century or so, these titles become almost automatic and appear quite frequently, as the most cursory perusal of the appropriate volumes of the *RCEA* shows. It would be useful to investigate the chronology of these attributes.

52. *RCEA*, no. 8. I am not aware of any recent discussion of these texts.

53. Al-Azraqi, *Akhbar Mekkah*, pp. 168–69 and 158–59, respectively. The text and a translation are also found in *RCEA*, nos. 110, 116. The objects themselves, which no longer exist but have been described, deserve a separate study.

54. *RCEA*, no. 19. The specific context of the French version of the inscription has not been worked out and some of its details need further investigation. Pending such investigation, I am leaving it out of my discussion.

55. *RCEA*, no. 55, is the earliest dated one. I am excluding no. 6, from a tomb in Cyprus dated 652 with K 112, as posing technical problems of authenticity which are beyond my concerns here. Many thousands of epitaphs exist besides those in the *RCEA* and some spectacular groups were found in Madinah which, to my knowledge, have not been published. For analyses of the cultural or so-cial content of these epitaphs, see Jonathan Bloom, "The Mosque of the Qarafah," *Muqarnas 4* (1987); and Richard Bulliet, *Conversion to Islam in the Medieval Period* (Cambridge, 1979). Both studies have been criticized for premature conclusions.

56. The elaboration of this system is one of the objectives of Van Ess, *Theologie*.

57. The identification of an "Islamic" language is rather important for the contemporary world, where considerable confusion rules in the overlapping discourses on nationality and Islam.

58. *RCEA*, no. 30.

59. Rosen-Ayalon, "The first Mosaic," has a lengthy and thorough discussion of the issues. I feel less certain than the author that we have here an actual mihrab in a private house, but I have no intelligent alternative to suggest.

60. The fundamental study on these inscriptions is by Louis Robert, "Epigrammes du Bas-Empire," *Hellenica 4* (1948). For many examples see *The Greek Anthology*, ed. William R. Paton (Cambridge, 1916), esp. vol. 1, pp. 10–17, 19ff, 106–7. For St. Polyeuktes see R. Martin Harrison, *Excavations at Saraçhane in Istanbul 1* (Princeton, 1986), esp. pp. 5–8. For comparative but different examples, see Henri Grégoire, *Recueil des Inscriptions greques chrétiennes: Asie Mineure* (Paris, 1922), pp. 22–24, 24–30, 109ff.

61. Mango, *The Art of the Byzantine Empire*, p. 184.

62. Creswell, *EMA²*, pls. 7–37; it should be noted that there are several errors in the identification of the location of the mosaics on the walls; cf. Blair, *Bayt al-Maqdis I*, notes on p. 73.

63. The book was part of the collection created by Albert Skira, a remarkable inventor of photographic processes and promoter of beautiful books with color pictures. The same three pictures were reproduced several times and were included as well in Creswell's second edition. Partial sets of color reproductions were made for commercial purposes after 1965 or thereabouts: see Rosen-Ayalon, *EIM*, pls. I–XVI, for the lower drum.

64. I must record here my gratitude to the Egyptian engineers in charge of the project, who in 1960 and 1961 allowed me to study the mosaics themselves and the photographs they had taken of them, all of this during a time of considerable political tension between Egyptian and Jordanian authorities. I was not allowed to take notes on the

spot and, therefore, my record of what I saw consists of later recollections. But the experience of walking face to face with the mosaics of the octagon and of touching them is unforgettable. Much of what I recorded at that time deals with technical details which have not always been included in the pages which follow, but which have contributed to my understanding of the mosaics.

65. Some of the plates consist of combinations of several separate negative transparencies. A book of photographs with introductory essays by Said Nuseibeh and myself is forthcoming (Rizzoli).

66. Byzantinists and historians of Late Antique Mediterranean art have frequently mentioned these mosaics in their surveys or, as in the case of J. Strzygouski, in their elaboration of sweeping historical and formal theories. For more specific discussions, see André Grabar *L'Iconoclasme Byzantin* (Paris, 1957), pp. 62–67, and Henri Stern, "Les Représentation des Conciles," *Byzantion* 11 (1936) and 13 (1938), where these mosaics are involved in various reasonings dealing with Iconoclasm.

67. There is no single introduction to this repertory, inasmuch as scholarship preferred to identify and study evolutions in the depiction of forms rather than to emphasize the continuous visibility, use, and impact of most examples; see esp. Alois Riegl, *Spätrömische Kunstindustrie* (Vienna, 1927). A sophisticated example of more recent approaches is Ernest Kitzinger, *Byzantine Art in the Making* (Cambridge, 1977). Many of Kitzinger's former students like Anna Gonosova and James Trilling have made significant contributions to the field of Late Antique decorative forms.

68. The issue of the craftsmen used in the major monuments of Umayyad art has been much discussed, usually fruitlessly because it involves contemporary nationalist and regionalist agendas which were not significant at the time and because a later Muslim tradition transformed the simple activity of craftsmen going from one place to another seeking employment (no doubt, common in the seventh and eighth centuries) into a reflection of political and ideological competitions. Hence the lengthy debates on whether Syrians, Palestinians, Byzantines, or others decorated Umayyad buildings; pertinent texts and references have been gathered by Marguerite van Berchem in Creswell *EMA*[1], pp. 222ff.,

321–22, pp. 367ff., although her preferred conclusion is certainly not mine. It should be noted, for instance, that the problem of the origins of craftsmen occurs most consistently in the context of wall mosaics, a particularly rare and expensive technique used in high visibility buildings like the mosques of Medinah, Damascus, and Jerusalem, and the Dome of the Rock (and later the Mosque of Cordova). It is never brought up by medieval chroniclers or by contemporaneous writers in relationship to mosaic pavement. The latter continued to be made as late as the end of the eighth century at several levels of quality corresponding to different financial investments, as can be easily demonstrated in Christian Palestine or Transjordan and in Umayyad palaces like Khirbat al-Minyah and Khirbat al-Mafjar. In Syria with a lesser tradition of mosaic pavements by the seventh century, Umayyad palaces like Qasr al-Hayr West have paintings instead of mosaics, and a settlement like Qasr al-Hayr East has mosaics of low quality. In short, neither the remaining archaeological evidence alone nor written sources allow, at this stage, for any general conclusion about the ways in which artists and craftsmen operated in early Islamic times. Each instance seems to be different and some yet unknown rules of the market must have operated.

69. There are examples of eastern themes in Byzantine art before the end of the seventh century in the Church of St. Polyeuktes in Constantinople, in textiles, maybe in ceramics. In a very perceptive way, Jean-Michel Spieser has argued that the appearance of Iranian themes in the sixth century was a way for that art to revitalize itself by searching for new ideas rather than to passively adopt the art of other lands; Jean-Michel Spieser, *Thessalonique et ses Monuments* (Paris, 1984), p. 140. Whether a similar interpretation can be given to the appearance of eastern themes under the Macedonians is an open question; see André Grabar, "Le Succès des Arts Orientaux," *Münchner Jarbuch der bildenden Kunst* 23 (1951).

70. For example, Moshe Sharon, "An Inscription from the year 65 A.M."

71. Marguerite van Berchem, in Creswell, *EMA*[2], pp. 321–22. This is the position taken, for instance, by most historians of Late Antique and Byzantine art. For a more complex statement of a

comparable view see Oleg Grabar, *Mediation*, pp. 37ff.

72. Such was the central thesis of Oleg Grabar, "Umayyad Dome of the Rock." The basic premise and some of the conclusions of that thesis were accepted by many and criticized by some, including the author, especially in more recent years.

73. Priscilla Soucek, "The Temple of Solomon in Islamic Legend and Art," Joseph Guttman, ed., *The Temple of Solomon* (Ann Arbor, 1976); Rosen-Ayalon, *EIM*; Janine Sourdel-Thomine, "Une image musulmane de Jérusalem," in D. Poirion ed., *Jérusalem, Rome, Constantinople* (Paris, 1986); and Nasir-i Khosro, *Sefer Nameh*, English trans. by Wheeler M. Thackston Jr., *Book of Travels* (Albany Press, 1985), p. 35. We have already noted a significant eschatological component in the inscriptions of the Dome of the Rock, and I shall return later to several instances around the Haram involving the end of time.

74. That trees and especially jewels were meant to be highlighted is illustrated by a small detail in the technique of decoration. Mother-of-pearl pieces and glass cubes associated with these motifs were set at an angle to the wall, so that they can catch light more strikingly than the rest of the mosaic cubes and thereby appear in relief.

75. This statement can be challenged on purely theoretical grounds as devoid of proof. But such a proof can, I believe, be found by recalling the hierarchy of visual prominence given in classical and early Christian art to people or to buildings compared to trees or jewels. The issue has been introduced with as yet insufficient theoretical support by Oleg Grabar, *Formation*, pp. 127–28, with respect to the mosque of Damascus.

76. These are important theoretical issues which are central to the practice of the history and criticism of the arts, yet rarely, if ever, brought up in scholarship. One is the nature of similarity between two designs or two motifs and its corollary, how the perception of similarity is interpreted by a viewer, since there is a range of positive and negative responses from soothing satisfaction to protest against a lack of imagination. Another issue is the viewer's reaction to seeing only a fragment of a design at one time. Is a segment sufficient to complete a form or interpret a motif. This problem of

what is called the synecdoche principle of artistic perception has been raised, in a very different way, by André Grabar, *Les voies de la Création en Iconographie Chrétienne* (Paris, 1994), pp. 380ff.

77. Rosen-Ayalon, *EIM*, especially through the drawings on pp. 18–19.

78. The little that remains of these mosaics is in apsidal niches of the parapet over the outer wall. See Charles Clermont-Ganneau, *Archaeological Researches in Palestine I* (London, 1889), pp. 187ff.; and Creswell, *EMA²*, p. 80. The fragments seen by Clermont-Ganneau were again uncovered in 1960, when I was able to see them.

79. We know little about the floor. It is, in theory, possible to imagine that it was covered with mosaics, since mosaic decoration was so common all over Palestine and Transjordan; see Michelle Piccirillo, *The Mosaics of Jordan* (Amman, 1994). It was used in one of the earlier floors of the Aqsa Mosque and appeared later in several Umayyad secular buildings. There is no evidence, however, for mosaic floors in the Dome of the Rock. It is possible to argue that floor and wall mosaics were rarely found together and are esthetically incompatible.

80. Studies of Roman art seem not to deal with the esthetic qualities of this type of decoration and to concentrate on archaeological issues of reconstruction; see, for example, M. L. Bruto and Giuseppi Vannicola, "Ricostruzione e tipologie," *Archaeologia Classica* 42 (1990); and Kristin Ann Kelly, *Motifs in Opus Sectile* (Diss. Columbia University, 1986), for a broader survey.

81. So it is today and the restorers of this century probably copied much earlier models whose dates cannot be determined with any degree of certainty, but the painting of reused capitals was a common feature of slightly later Umayyad secular art.

82. An argument for a decoration of carved and painted beams is supported by the beams with painted ornament discovered under the present ceiling. A few fragments were published by Christel Kessler "Above the Ceiling of the Outer Ambulatory," *JRAS* 1964, pls. I–IV. The practice of painting the carvings on beams that are hardly visible existed in the Mediterranean area from Late Antique times through the Middle Ages. Some doubt exists, however, about actual date of these

particular paintings, as the surviving date (ca. 301–310/903–912) is only valid for the specific beam on which it is found.

83. This does not eliminate the need for additional analysis of elements in the mosaics now possible because of the quality of available photographs, but such a detailed study is outside the concerns of this book. By organizing the discussion around units of composition I avoid dealing with a technical and archaeological problem of considerable importance: the identification of repairs, replacements, and restorations. These are numerous, and they vary enormously in quality. Most are easily recognizable in photographs, but it is not always easy to know how far the repairs in the lower drum carried out and recorded by the Fatimids in 418/1027–28 affect what is now there or what sequences of repairs occurred in the octagon. For instance, did the change of name from Abd al-Malik to al-Ma'mun accompany changes in the decorative mosaics? For an eventual history of the mosaics in the Dome of the Rock, such questions are important and the type of micro-analysis carried out both in San Marco in Venice and on certain floor mosaics ought to be extended to the mosaics of the Dome of the Rock; see Otto Demus, *The Mosaics of San Marco in Venice* (Washington, 1984) and Claudine Dauphin and Gershen Edelstein, *L'Eglise byzantine de Nahariya* (Thessaloniki, 1984) as an instance of studies culminating in Dauphin's unpublished dissertation. But in almost all instances the original model can be easily imagined, and for my purposes of explaining the creation of a specific time, a typological identification of the original compositional patterns suffices, even if the initial designs have been transformed in many details. The only issue is whether anything has been replaced by something totally different from the original. There are a few such examples, especially in the drums. On the whole, however, such replacements are rare and most repairs, even clumsy ones, have not obliterated the original model. An interesting example occurs in the outside octagon, 128°, where *Lilah al-hamd* has been put on either side of the stylized plant (fig. 41), written in nice lapidary script. Is it one instance contemporary with the earliest mosaics or the words of a later restorer? Why repeat these words there?

84. Such was the opinion of de Vogüé, followed by Max van Berchem, *Matériaux: Haram*, pp. 274ff.

85. The subject of Sasanian crowns was a "hot" topic in the 1930s and 1940s. It has now been relegated to the purpose of identifying rulers, for which see, as an example, Kurt Erdmann, "Die Entwicklung der sasanidischen Krone," *Ars Islamica* 15–16 (1952). Little has been done on the use of the motif as an ornament.

86. I do not exclude the possibility that this and other similar examples are later restorations and that there were originally fewer variations than exist now. But at this stage, I prefer to think of them as original.

87. Such is the argument developed by Marguerite van Berchem in Creswell, *EMA*[2], and she gives most of the appropriate parallels from Iran or Iraq.

88. Note that arches 22–67 have a much more recent pattern of a totally different nature from the usual patterns found in the building.

89. Trees are frequent on floor mosaics from Antioch and elsewhere. Doro Levi, *Antioch Mosaics* (Princeton, 1947), pls. XX–XX. They occur on walls as well, for example in the Great Mosque of Damascus; see Marguerite van Berchem and Etienne Clouzot, *Mosaïques Chrètiennes* (Geneva, 1924), pp. 68–70.

90. The panel on 158 left is an example of an overly repaired section in which individual motifs have consistently been misunderstood.

91. The octagon's mosaics are different from a design of repeated patterns like those found in a seventh-century Church of Sanulliana in Spain; see Helmut Schlunk, *La Pintura Mural Asturiana* (Madrid, 1957), pp. 84–105. It is closer to the mosaic decoration of St. George in Saloniki, which is of the sixth century, or to the nave mosaics of the Church of the Nativity in Bethlehem whose date is the subject of much controversy. In both these examples, significant variations occur within repeated designs, but the variations do not seem to be iconographically related and reflect some other concern or practice. For Saloniki, see Jean-Michel Speiser, *Thessalonique et ses Monuments* (Paris, 1984); and for Bethlehem, the articles by H. Stern in *Byzantium*.

92. Parallels were made by Marguerite van Berchem in Creswell, *EMA*[2], and Oleg Grabar in *Umayyad Dome of the Rock*. More specific comparisons with

intriguing implications are made by Julian Raby in a forthcoming article.

93. There is some question as to whether it is appropriate and possible to identify every one of the vegetal elements involved, but the illusionism of their representation is certain. Comparably clear images occur in some Tunisian mosaics; see Suzanne Gozlan, *La Maison du Triomphe de Neptune à Acholla* (Rome, 1992), pp. 55–56. I owe this reference to Dr. Christine Kondoleon.

94. It is also possible that some compositions copied or imitated each other, like 38 and 67.

95. The question of pattern books and other means of transmitting techniques, designs *and* the opportunity of choosing whatever one wanted is a recurring issue in the study of the arts of Late Antiquity and the early Middle Ages. It is a crucial one before the availability of paper.

96. The contrast is striking with two other celebrated buildings among many others in which very different styles exist. One is the Great Mosque of Damascus, in whose courtyard a very poor mosaic decoration has been added in recent years to the celebrated eighth-century ones; see Marguerite van Berchem in Creswell *EMA*², pp. 324ff. The other example is the Martorana in Palermo, where Byzantium mosaics were replaced in the Baroque period with paintings of lesser quality, but without the loss of authenticity so obvious in Damascus.

97. References to nearly all these buildings are found in Marguerite van Berchem and Etienne Clouzot, *Mosaïques Chrètiennes*, more specific parallels are in Cyril Mango, *Materials for the Study of The Mosaics of St. Sophia* (Washington, 1962), esp. pls. 5, 8, 12, 22; see also F. W. Deichmann, *Frühchristhide Bauten und Mosaiken von Ravenna* (Baden-Baden, 1958); Speiser, *Thessalonique*, pp. 165ff.; George H. Forsyth and Kurt Weitzmann, *The Monastery of St. Catherine at Mount Sinai* (Ann Arbor, 1973). For Gaza, see texts and bibliographies in Mango, *The Art of the Byzantine Empire*, pp. 60–68.

98. Reversing my own views of over thirty-five years ago, I no longer believe that it was to *represent* through the insignia of their power the defeated enemies of the early Muslims or simply the rulers and the lands that had entered into their realm. Nor do I believe it appropriate to understand the trees and the vegetation as images or even evocations of something as specific as Paradise or the gardens of Solomon's palace. Such iconographic interpretations would be possible if the major motifs on which they are based—specifically imperial Persian and Byzantine crowns and jewel-laden trees—had been shown only once, but the constant repetition weakens the charge of any possible meaning when there is no established outside referent.

99. But, even on this point, one may have to reserve judgment, as accounts exist of the transfer to Jerusalem of some of the treasures found in Mekkah and of the presence in Jerusalem of a unique pearl, the *Yatimah;* see Nasser Rabbat, "The Dome of the Rock Revisited," *Muqarnas* 10 (1993), pp. 71ff. For a list of the treasures in the Ka'bah in early Islamic times, the most accessible source is Mahmet Aga-Oglu, "Remarks on the character of Islamic art," *AB*, 36 (1954), p. 182, based primarily on al-Azraqi.

100. Although there is no way of establishing a historical filiation, this point is curiously comparable to the "iconographie du silence" discussed recently by Marc Fumaroli for the Baroque, *L'Ecole du Silence* (Paris, 1994). Behind these observations there lies a deeper truth about our interpretation of perception which needs philosophical discussion.

101. A striking small example of a mausoleum and several other parallels are found in E. Alföldi-Rosenbaum, "External Mosaic Decoration on Late Antique Buildings," *Frühmittelalterische Studien* 4 (1970). Otherwise there were mosaics on a few facades, for example, in Parenzo or St. Peter's in Rome; see Milan Prelog, *The Basilica of Euphrasius in Poreč* (Zagreb, 1986).

102. I am deliberately avoiding the kind of conclusions about representations of wings or trees and their relation to the Temple of Solomon that have been reviewed recently by some writers like Moshe Sharon. Too much is hypothetical in all these arguments and in fact the Crusaders are much more likely than the early Muslims to have put Solomonic symbols on the outside of the Dome of the Rock, since they believed that it *was* the Temple. But all of this is pure speculation inasmuch as the numerous descriptions by the Crusaders themselves fail to mention anything like wings.

103. See Creswell *EMA*², pp. 101–23; and Creswell, *A Short Account of Early Muslim Architecture*, rev. ed. by James Allen, pp. 39–40.

104. For the plan, Creswell, *EMA*², pp. 73–76, more or

less adopted an older theory developed in 1888 by C. Mauss whereby the position of the octagons were determined by the extension of two squares inscribed within the circle enclosing the rock. For the elevation, he picked up E. T. Richmond's calculations of 1:2, 1:2, and 1:3 proportions for most of the significant hinges between parts. Since Creswell's time, Michel Ecochard set the proportions of the Dome of the Rock within a historical and formal set defined, in part, by its manipulation of the Golden Mean (*Filiations des Monuments Greco, Byzantins et Islamique* [Paris, 1977], pp. 13–40). Most recently Doron Chen has developed a more sophisticated metrological analysis of the building and a more likely explanation of the ways in which the building's plan was evolved. He demonstrates a basic module of 0.31 meters and approximations of the Golden Mean as operational principles for the Dome's construction; see Doron Chen, "The Design of the Dome of the Rock," *PEQ*, 112 (1980), and "The Plan of the Dome of the Rock Reconsidered," *PEQ*, 117 (1985), in critical reaction to John Wilkinson, "Architectural Procedures in Byzantine Palestine," *Levant* 13 (1981).

105. The exact height of the Holy Sepulchre and of its surroundings can only be estimated and the computer generated drawings that accompany this section are hypothetical reconstructions.

106. There is an interesting, if minor, question of the fate of the architectural elements of the Nea, its capitals and columns, which various scholars have assumed to have contributed to the building, *after* the Dome of the Rock, of the Aqsa Mosque. Some had even argued that the Aqsa Mosque was the Nea. The point is simply that, when the Dome of the Rock was being built, the Nea was still quite visible, but it seems to have been forgotten relatively soon after being abandoned.

107. Creswell, *EMA²*, pl.1c, and pp. 84–85.

108. For Isfahan, Oleg Grabar, *The Great Mosque of Isfahan* (New York, 1992), pp. 21ff. For Rome, see William L. MacDonald *The Architecture of the Roman Empire* (New Haven, 1982), esp. pp. 112, 114, Fig. 8, and *The Pantheon* (London, 1976), pp. 62, 67.

109. This excludes, of course, casual tourists or esthetically inclined visitors, but both of these categories are for the most part contemporary. And, even today, as one observes visitors to the Dome of the Rock, those who know something about the interior seem always more eager in their anticipation and subsequent satisfaction than uninformed visitors, some of whom fail even to notice the mosaics.

110. Creswell, *EMA²*, pp. 68–69, following Richmond, p. 9.

111. The later history of the rock and the stories, legends, and images associated with it confirm the aura of partially visible mystery around it. They should some day be gathered in a study of the range of pious meanings and practices. For instance, for some time through the nineteenth century, there was a huge curtain hanging down over the rock. Why? When did this idea begin?

112. For all the buildings in Jerusalem, see the various studies by Creswell, Ecochard, and Chen. One should add Theodor Hauschild, "Das Mausoleum von Las Vegas de Pueblanueva," *MM* 19 (1978), on the large (22-meter) original mausoleum from Early Christian times, which does, however, contain an apse only apparent inside the building.

113. See J. Ebersolt, *Le Grand Palais de Constantinople* (Paris 1910), p. 78, for the *chrysotriclinos* with a dome over an octagon.

114. See Yoram Tsafrir, ed., *Ancient Churches Revealed* (Jerusalem, 1993); K. Holum et al., "Preliminary Report on the 1989–1990 Seasons," *Caesarea Papers*, ed. R. L. Vann (Ann Arbor, 1992), pp. 100–104. I am grateful to Professor Slobodan Ćurčić for letting me read a forthcoming paper of his dealing with this group of buildings from yet another point of view and to Professor Kenneth Holum for sending me information about his excavations. I regret that I could not digest it all as much as I should have done.

115. For the relations between ancient and Christian art, see Ernst Kitzinger, *Byzantine Art in the Making*; Judith Herrin, *The Formation of Christendom* (Princeton, 1987); Thomas Mathews, *The Clash of Gods* (Princeton, 1992) for various and not exclusive ways of dealing with the problem. For Buddhism see Hugo Buchtal, *The Western Aspects of Gandhara Sculpture* (Oxford, 1945). For Jewish art, it is enough to peruse the many volumes of W. Goodenough, *Jewish Symbols in the Greco-roman Period* (New York, 1953ff.).

116. Theodor A. Busink, *Der Tempel von Jerusalem, von Salomo bis Herodes*, 2 vols. (Leiden, 1970-80), pp. 904ff., has the most complete statement of opinions on that topic.

117. Gil, *Palestine*, pp. 65–68.

118. The issue of the nature of Umayyad power was first raised in the classical study by Julius Wellhausen, *The Arab Kingdom and its Fall*, trans. M. G. Weir (Calcutta, 1927). Much has been written since then; for a summary see Hugh Kennedy, *The Prophet and the Age of the Caliphate* (London, 1986).

119. Michael Morony, trans., vol. 18 of *The History of Al-Tabari* (SUNY Press, 1987), p. 6; Gil, *Palestine*, p. 78, gives a list of other texts.

120. Palmer, *The Seventh Century*, pp. 30–31.

121. Ibid., p. 47.

122. Gil, *Palestine*, p. 104.

123. Abu al-Faraj al-Isfahani, *Kitab al-Aghani* (Buluq, 1867–1869), vol. 19, p. 90; Wellhausen, *Arab Kingdom*, p. 214. Tabari *Ta'rikh*, 2, p. 1666, quotes a poem by another governor, Nasr ibn Sayyar, equating Mekkah and Jerusalem; vol. 25 of translation, p. 193.

124. The evidence has been assembled and discussed any number of times from Creswell, *EMA²*, pp. 65–67, to Elad in *Bayt al-Maqdis I*, or several articles by Busse. Objections to the theory begun by Goitein were developed by Grabar and others; see Goitein and Grabar, "al Kuds." The classical local, late medieval, tradition, as expressed in Mujir al-Din's *al-Uns al-Jalil*, fully accepts the theory and embroiders it.

125. Gil, *Palestine*, pp. 110–13. Goitein, "al-Kuds" (2d ed.).

126. Michael Cook and Patricia Crone, *Hagarism*, p. 32, which follows a reasoning totally different from mine.

127. The best summary is in the narrative *and* notes of Gil, *Palestine*, pp. 69–74.

128. J. Mann, *The Jews in Egypt*, pp. 44–45. Early in the eighth century, apparently at the time of the caliph Umar ibn Abd al-Aziz (717–720), slaves belonging to the collective Muslim treasury replaced these Jewish attendants.

129. There is a huge bibliography on the subject of what will become later the *Isra'iliyyat* and the *qisas al-Anbiyah*, "stories about Prophets." For examples of early documents, see Raif G. Khoury, *Wahb b. Munabbih* (Wiesbaden, 1972), with sources from the first century of the *hijrah*; Khoury, *Les Légendes Prophétiques dans l'Islam* (Wiesbaden, 1978), esp. pp. 167–76, on the building of Jerusalem and several other passages that deal with the city.

130. But the matter is far less certain than I had imagined many years ago; see Oleg Grabar, "The Umayyad Dome of the Rock; for major changes in our understanding of Abrahamic presence, see now René Dagorn, *La Geste d'Ismael* (Paris, 1981); Reuven Firestone, *Journeys in Holy Lands* (New York, 1990), esp. pp. 135ff.; and Garth Fowden, *Empire to Commonwealth* (Princeton, 1993), pp. 147–49. For other useful remarks see Heribert Busse, "Jerusalem and Mekkah," in Moshe Sharon, ed., *The Holy Land in History and Thought* (Leiden, 1988), pp. 236ff.; Francis E. Peters, *Jerusalem and Mecca* (New York, 1986); and Suleyman Bashear, "Abraham's Sacrifice of his Son," *Der Islam* 67 (1990).

131. A celebrated example is the account of the Pilgrim of Bordeaux and the *lapis pertusus* or "perforated stone" usually identified as the Rock and around which Jews came to lament; see John Wilkinson, *Egeria's Travels to the Holy Land* (Jerusalem, 1981), pp. 153–61.

132. For the latest statement on that subject, see Joseph van Ess, "Abd al-Malik and the Dome of the Rock," *Bayt al-Maqdis I*, p. 89. For earlier discussion on the confusion, see LeStrange, *Palestine*, pp. 96ff., and Busse, "Jerusalem in the Story of Muhammad's Night Journey," *JSAI* 14 (1991).

133. Van Ess, in *Bayt al-Maqdis I*, pp. 95–99.

134. Claude Gilliot, "Muqatil, Grand Exégète, Traditionniste et Théologien maudit," *Journal Asiatique* 279 (1991); and Joseph Van Ess, *The Youthful God: Anthropomorphism in Early Islam* (Tempe, Arizona, 1988).

135. The search for "signs" forecasting the end of time was a common preoccupation among Jews, Christians, and Muslims at the end of the seventh century. Jewish and Christian apocalyptic visions are well-known; for the Muslim ones, see Bashear, "Muslim Apocalypses and the Hour," *IOS* 13 (1993); and al-Wasiti, pp. 88–89, among other early references associated with Jerusalem.

136. See the latest statement in Busse, *JSAI* 14 (1991), with a complete analysis of most of the known evidence. I tend to agree with most, but not all, of Busse's conclusions.

137. See Ibn Ishaq, *Sirah al-Rusul*, ed. Ferdinand Wüstenfeld (Göttingen, 1858–1860), pp. 263ff.; and *The Life of Muhammed*, trans. by Alfred Guillaume (Oxford, 1955), p. 181.

138. For an introduction see "mi'radj" in *EJ²* and, as an

example of later use, Jamel Eddine Bencheikh, *Le Voyage Nocturne de Mahomet* (Paris, 1988).

139. Goitein, "al-Kuds"; and O. Grabar in "The Meaning of the Dome of the Rock".

140. Sheila Blair, in *Bayt al-Maqdis I.*

141. Creswell, *EMA²*, pp. 64ff., discusses the various statements of the story known to him. Its most direct expression for the classical Muslim tradition is found in Mujir al-Din, *Al-Uns al-Jalil* I, pp. 240ff.; and Sauvaire, *Histoire de Jérusalem*, pp. 48ff. For a more sophisticated version of this account see Amikam Elad, in *Bayt al-Maqdis I.*

142. I owe much to the interpretation provided by Nasser Rabbat in *Muqarnas* 10, but I feel that he took the text too literally.

143. Rosen-Ayalon, *EIM.*

Chapter Three

1. Actually there are also problems in the exact relationship of the building with the southern end of the Haram. The study of these, however, requires an analysis of masonries and the availability of drawings which do not exist. In the meantime, see Hamilton, *Aqsa*, pp. 66–70.

2. Texts and references are given in Creswell, *EMA²*, I, p. 373. But Creswell chose from available evidence, as there are more instances in Henry I. Bell, catalogue of *Greek Papryi in the British Museum* IV (London, 1910). The matter is most recently reviewed in Raby (*Aqsa Mosque*, forthcoming), and all the texts have been conveniently gathered by Max Küchler, "Moschee und Kalifenpaläste Jerusalems nach den Aphrodito Papyri," *ZDPV* 107 (1991).

3. There is an issue here which affects Jerusalem only indirectly, but which led many scholars, myself included, not so much into error as into a confusion. It is not necessary to assume, as most of us did, that the mosques in Damascus and Medinah were built from scratch and, therefore, that the mosque at Jerusalem and various modifications brought to the Mekkan sanctuary involved new buildings. In all these examples, we are dealing with various degrees of recomposition and modification to existing built spaces, not necessarily with new creations. For traditional statements, among many possible examples, see Jean Sauvaget, *La Mosquée Omeyyade de Médine* (Paris, 1947), and Oleg Grabar, *The Formation of Islamic Art*, 2d ed. (New Haven, 1987), pp. 104–5.

4. The text is translated in Le Strange, *Palestine*, pp. 98–100, and André Miquel, translation of al-Muqaddasi, *Ahsan al-Taqasim fi Ma'rifat ul-Aqalim*, pp. 190–92; significant excerpts are in Creswell, *EMA²*, p. 375, and nearly every discussion of the mosque mentioned in subsequent notes.

5. The text is actually rather confusing and the translations not very helpful. Literally what is said is that "all the ceilings (*suquf*) were covered with sheaths of lead except *al-mu'akhkhirah*, the "rear one"—I don't understand why Le Strange read this to mean the front ones to the north—which were covered with large mosaics (*al-fusayfisa al-kubar*)." Whatever Muqaddasi may have meant by "large" mosaics should probably be interpreted as some unusual decorative technique using inlaid colored pieces. We encounter here, as so often with medieval texts describing monuments that have disappeared, the problem of explaining terms that describe something seen, the technical character of which was probably not understood.

6. I am aware, of course, of the fact that other scholars have assumed the possibility of more reconstructions from written texts than I have. Since my purpose is not to provide an archaeological history but a visual reconstruction of a whole city, broad categories of analysis seemed preferable. For a full account of archaeological details, see Julian Raby's forthcoming study.

7. Hamilton, *Aqsa*, and see *Bayt al-Maqdis I* for some alterations in his conclusions. Examination of these repairs did not constitute a formal excavation, although trenches were dug to strengthen supports, and not all parts of the building were affected in the same manner. Little is said about small finds, except on pp. 65–66. The files kept in the former Palestine Archaeological Museum (now Rockefeller Museum) in Jerusalem contain hundreds of photographs of mosaics and carved stone or marble slabs from the excavations. They deserve to be studied and published in full.

8. Hamilton, *Aqsa*, pp. 22–27, 70–74, whose conclusions are not always clearly drawn; a better account is found in Creswell *EMA²*, pp. 374–80, and especially in Creswell-Allen, *A Short Account*, pp. 73–82, which is remarkable for its clarity. All of my references to the woodwork will be found there.

9. This, in a simplified form, is the position defended by Creswell and Hamilton.

10. This, again with simplifications and without taking into considerations variations between proponents, is the position first argued by Henri Stern, "Recherches sur la Mosquée al-Aqsa et ses Mosaiques," *Ars Orientalis* 5 (1963), and Rosen-Ayalon, *EMI*, pp. 4–7.

11. See Allen in Creswell-Allen, *A Short Account*, pp. 79–82.

12. See the readings and comments by M. Schwab in Hamilton, *Aqsa*, pp. 92–95. Their methodological importance is also noted in Raby's forthcoming article in *Bayt al-Maqdis II*.

13. Hamilton, *Aqsa*, pp. 83ff., and fig. 6; Marçais in Creswell, *EMA*², pp. It is curious that no new discussion of the style of these easily accessible fragments has been undertaken.

14. I am referring to the so-called third Samarra style in which pan-Islamic influence was demonstrated by Richard Ettinghausen, "The 'Beveled Style' in the post-Samarra Period," in G. C. Miles, ed., *Archaeologica Orientalia in Memoriam E. Herzfeld* (Locust Valley, 1952).

15. Creswell-Allen, *A Short Account* pp. 237–41 and 196–97, respectively.

16. These mosaics, mostly unpublished, have extremely simple designs, usually of diagonal lines creating diamonds with a flower or something small in the middle of the diamonds. It is possible that there were spolia from some earlier, classical or Herodian, building.

17. The latest to emphasize this point are Busse, "Tempel, Grabes kirche, und Haram al-Sharif," and G. Kretschmer, *Jerusalema Heiligtrumstraditimen* (Weisbaden, 1987), and Rosen-Ayalon, *EIM*, p. 6. For an earlier statement, see Theodor A. Busink, *Der Tempel von Jerusalem, von Salomo bis Herodes* (Leiden, 1970-80)Busink, pp. 911–12, 921ff.

18. Rosen-Ayalon has already pointed out, in *EIM*, p. 6, that the number of workers and the amount of funds involved are actually very small.

19. Even if excavations were possible and a masonry catalogue were available, I suspect that centuries of unrecorded repairs and transformations have eradicated much original data. But it does not take a seasoned archaeologist to see that masonry technique is the only accessible body of relatively neutral data that could be tapped for further work.

20. In addition to the often quoted arguments developed simultaneously and partly independently of each other by Rosen-Ayalon, Chen, and Busse, see Spencer Corbett in "Some observations on the gateways to the Herodian Temple in Jerusalem," *PEQ* (1952), and Ugo Monneret de Villard, *Introduzione allo Studio dell'archeologia Islamica* (Venice, 1966), pp. 181ff., who were the first to think along these lines.

21. Rosen-Ayalon, *EIM*, p. 33.

22. I tried to argue that the *stoa* was preserved in the early ninth century based on some unusual illustrations in the marginal manuscript known as the Chludoff Psalter; see "A note on the Chludoff Psalter," *Okeanos (Harvard Ukraininan Studies)*, 7 (1983). My argument has not generally been accepted; see Rosen-Ayalon, *EIM*, p. 4, n. 1. This is not the place to respond, but in fact the criticisms have convinced me of the probable correctness of my interpretation. Yet enough uncertainty remains that I decided not to incorporate a standing *stoa* in the computer reconstructions of the Haram.

23. The elaborate proportions worked out by Chen are certainly true, but they reflect, I believe, the automatic competence of local builders rather than a formal system especially elaborated for this building. Chen, "On the Golden Gate in Jerusalem," *ZDPV* 97 (1981); and Rosen-Ayalon, *EIM*, pp. 33ff.

24. Rosen-Ayalon, "The Facade of the Holy Sepulchre," *RSO* 59 (1985).

25. Busink, *Tempel*, pp. 968–71.

26. The area was partly described by Warren and Wilson; see Busink, *Tempel*, pp. 971–74. It has recently been the object of highly controversial occupations and reuses.

27. This is the argument made by Burgoyne, *The Architectural Development of the Haram in Jerusalem under the Bahri Mamluks* (D.Phil. thesis, Oxford, 1979), p. 43. I am grateful to Dr. Burgoyne for several letters on this subject.

28. These sources are all summarized and partly evaluated by Gil, *Palestine*, pp. 75–278; his lengthy text does not read easily, as it does not form a coherent whole, but it contains references to all the appropriate sources and to a few original documents like the milestones of Abd al-Malik (p. 109), the coinage, pp. 109–10, and such Geniza fragments as seem relevant for the early period (pp. 140ff.). A simpler, but incomplete, survey of sources is found

in Ibrahim M. al-Arif, *Al-Mufassal f: Ta'rikh al-Quds* (rpr. Jerusalem, 1986). Goitein in *EI* ² (1978) provides much more coherent reading, but does not always indicate his sources.

29. There may have been one Christian branch of the Ghassanids among them: see Gil, *Palestine*, p. 132.

30. Ibid., p. 108.

31. Ibid., p. 119, where there are a few other possible examples of settlers whose names have been preserved.

32. Al-Wasiti, *Fada'il al-Bayt al-Muqaddas*, ed. Isaac Hassoun (Jerusalem, 1979), p. 87; A. A. Duri, "Jerusalem in the Early Islamic Period," in K. J. Assali, ed., *Jerusalem in History* (London, 1989), p. 110. More complex and sophisticated discussion can be found in Richard Eisener, *Zwischen Faktum und Fiktion* (Wiesbaden, 1987), pp. 39–41.

33. All earlier accounts and publications are assumed in Meir Ben-Dov, *In the Shadow of the Temple: The Discovery of Ancient Jerusalem* (New York, 1985), pp. 193ff.; see also Rosen-Ayalon, *EMA* ², pp. 8–10. Ben-Dov's reconstructions are very imaginative and very persuasive. They have often been reproduced—they were used as well in our computer-generated models—but they are based on minimal information, and the true archaeological record of these excavations has not been published.

34. For example, both Ben-Dov and Rosen-Ayalon use the papyri from Aphrodito in Egypt which mention workers sent to built the "mosque in Jerusalem and the palace of the Commander of the Faithful." In fact, there is no necessity, only a probably assumption, to conclude that the palace was also in Jerusalem, as many other papyri of the same time and also from Aphrodito mention a palace for the Commander of the Faithful being built in Egypt itself, in Fustat. But the most important point is that the word which has been translated as "palace" is *aula* which means a court or an official hall and, at least at this time, not a separate royal building. See Henry I. Bell, "Translations of the Greek Aptheolato Papyri," *Der Islam* 1 (1911), p. 383; 3 (1912), pp. 137, 370; 17 (1928), p. 6. A second example concerns the mural paintings discovered during the excavations, described as simply "colored Early Islamic paintings" in an early report and "frescoes and other luxurious items" in a later one. The published ones in Ben Dov, *In the Shadow*, pp. 294–95, are hardly spectacular. In short, there is much

left to be desired in what we know of these excavations.

35. Donner, Frederic M., *The Early Islamic Conquests* (Princeton 1981), provides the most accessible survey, but much work is still needed on such items as the architectural vocabulary for settlements. A few terms and their relationship to one early settlement are discussed in Grabar et al., *City in the Desert* (Cambridge, 1978), pp. 80–81. A very provocative article on migrations in early Islamic times is Patricia Crone, "The First-Century Concept of Higra," *Arabica* 41 (1994).

36. Basic information on the building can be found in M. Van Berchem, *Matériaux: Haram*, pp. 178ff., and Rosen-Ayalon, *EIM*, pp. 25–29. There is no recent architectural description and analysis of the building and its components, nor, to my knowledge, published dimensions.

37. The Holy Sepulchre had an altar on nine columns where the Holy Cross would have been found. There may be a connection between buildings with unusual geometric dimensions. See John Wilkinson, trans., *Jerusalem Pilgrims before the Crusades* (Warminster, 1977) p. 59.

38. Examples are: a large wall found by the Golden Gate (see Yoram Tsafrir, "The Massive Wall East of the Golden Gate," *IEJ* 40 [1990]); a cistern near the Damascus Gate (G. J. Wightman, *The Damascus Gate, Jerusalem* [Oxford, 1989], pp. 99ff.); a wall modified by the Umayyads located somewhere to the southwest of the Haram (see "Chronique Archéologique," *RBi*, 69 [1962], p. 82), which may have been rediscovered later by the excavations carried out in that area by Professor Mazar.

39. Josef T. Milik, "Notes d'Epigraphie et de Topographie Palestiniennes," *RBi*, 67 (1960), esp. pp. 552–54.

40. Theophanes, *Chronicle*, trans. L. Breyer (Bonn, 1957), p. 48. See also Charles Diehl, *Choses et Gens de Byzance* (Paris, 1926), pp. 190ff.; and Ilse Rochow, *Byzanz im 8. Jahrhundert in der Sicht des Theophanes* (Berlin, 1991), p. 134.

41. G. J. Reininck, "Ps.-Methodius: A Concept of History in Response to the Rise of Islam," in Averil Cameron and Lawrence Conrad, eds., *The Byzantine and Early Islamic Near East* (Princeton, 1992), esp. pp. 170–71, 182ff.

42. Bashear in *IOS* 13 (1993) and any corpus of Traditions under concepts such as *isra'* or "Jerusalem."

43. Christian Décobert, *Le Mendiant et le Combattant* (Paris, 1991), esp. p. 31.

Chapter Four

1. Van Berchem, *Matériaux: Haram*, no. 144, pp. 7–9, 11–19, 257–305, whose interpretations I do not entirely share.

2. The question is not as vacuous as it seems, for the evolution of the Mekkan and Medinese sanctuaries clearly shows that the idea of a visually composed rather than simply additive architectural program is already present in the second half of the eighth century for Mekkah; see Oleg Grabar, "Upon Reading al-Azraqi," *Muqarnas* 3 (1985), and Jonathan Bloom, *The Minaret* (Oxford, 1989), pp. 50–53, for a plausible visual reconstruction. For Medinah the classic study is still Jean Sauvaget, *La Mosqué Omeyyade de Médine* (Paris, 1941). More accurate plans and some novel observations can be found in S. Lamei Mustafa, *Madinah al-Munawwarah* (Beirut, 1981).

3. See Gil, *Palestine*, pp. 398–400, among several examples.

4. Ibid., pp. 279ff. Once again, I want to pay special homage to Moshe Gil's amazing coverage of people and events, in spite of his failure to propose any sort of clearly understandable overview.

5. For a discussion of Nasir-i Khosraw's philosophy, see Henry Corbin, "Nasir-i Khosraw and Iranian Ismailism," in Richard N. Frye, ed., *The Cambridge History of Iran*, 4 (Cambridge, 1975). There is a fairly recent literature on the subject in Persian, which I have not consulted; it is summarized by Azim Nanji in *EI*². The *Sefername* has been edited and translated into French by Charles Schefer, *Sefer-nameh* (Paris, 1881; repr. Amsterdam, 1970) and translated into English by Wheeler M. Thackston Jr. as *Book of Travels* (New York, 1986).

6. A full study of Nasir-i Khosraw's motivation in making and recording his trip still remains to be written, as well as a detailed analysis of his observations and descriptive vocabulary. The editors and translators of the *Sefernameh* have all alluded to the possibility that his sectarian allegiances explain his avoidance of a great Muslim center like Baghdad, but it could also be argued that he only became a full-fledged convert to Isma'ilism after his visit to Egypt. For various opinions on Nasir-i Khosraw, see Thierry Bianquis, *Damas et la Syrie sous les Fatimides* (Damascus, 1989), pp. 527–47; or A. G. Sayyid, "Lumières sur quelques sources de l'histoire Fatimide," *Annales Islamologiques* 13 (1977). As a preliminary assessment, see Vladimir Ivanov, *Nasir-i Khosraw and Isma'ilism* (Bombay, 1940).

7. For Arculf, see Azraqi, *Ta'rikh Makkah*, p. 112. For more examples of drawings of Jerusalem from the time of the Crusades and from the later Middle Ages in the Christian world, see Zev Vilnay, *The Holy Land in Old Prints and Maps* (Jerusalem, 1965), pp. 10–35; and Walter Horn and E. Born, *The Plan of St. Gall* (Berkeley, 1979). There are fewer Muslim examples and the ones that exist are fourteenth-century or later; see, for example, Paolo Cuneo, *Storia dell'urbanistica: Il Mondo Islamico* (Bari-Rome, 1986), pp. 9–37.

8. One story, a standard topos of imperial legend, is pertinent to the theme developed by the Persian traveler: the Byzantine emperor is alleged to have visited Jerusalem in secret, but the caliph al-Hakim sent an emissary from Cairo to tell the emperor that he, al-Hakim, knew all about his presence in the holy city, but that he should not fear for his safety. The assumption of dynastic control was an essential feature of the Fatimid presence in Jerusalem, and elsewhere in their realm.

9. I assume that this includes all religious affiliations, which would give it a total population of some eighty thousand people, a high but not unreasonable figure.

10. Nasir-i Khosraw notes that the artisans were grouped according to their specialities (*karuh*) or some other ordering system. The two translators have interpreted differently the Persian word *karuh*, thus once again pointing up the regrettable absence of a lexicographic study of the traveler's vocabulary.

11. Some scholars have argued for a southern location of the Gate of Jeremiah's pit, as in Amikam Elad, *Medieval Jerusalem and Islamic Worship* (Leiden, 1995), pp. xxii–xxiii, based on Dan Bahkat's publication. The answer hinges on whether Herod's Gate existed before 1100.

12. See al-Muqaddasi, *Ahsan al-Taqasim fi Ma'rifat ul-Aqalim*, trans. André Miquel, pp. 189, 267; Le Strange, *Palestine*, p. 213; and Bieberstein-Bloedhorn, 2, pp. 68, 95.

13. I fully accept the reading of *niyah* instead of *tih* in Muqaddasi's text, made by Miquel among others.

14. Gil, *Palestine*, pp. 407–08.

15. Ibid., pp. 636–53. On the whole, however, little is clear about trade, and it is for this reason that we left the bazaars out of the information provided in our drawings.

16. See, for instance, Yahya b. Sa'id al-Antaki, *Annales*, ed. J. Cheikho (Beirut, 1909), p. 272. The statement was accepted by Vincent-Abel, p. 942, and by Joshua Prawer, "The Jerusalem the Crusaders captured," in P. W. Edbury, *Crusade and Settlement* (Cardiff, 1985), p. 2. For small pertinent archaeological details and a monumental but illegible Fatimid inscription, see Moshe Sharon, "Arabic Inscriptions," *IEJ* 23 (1973); and J. W. Crowfoot, "Ophel Again," *PEQ*, 77 (1945).

17. See Gil, *Palestine*, p. 400, n. 53.

18. Marius Canard, "La destruction de l'Eglise de la Résurrection," *Byzantion* 35 (1955), repr. in *Byzance et les Musulmans au Proche-Orient* (London, 1973), is the most clearheaded account of an event which is also described in Mednikoff, *Palestina*, pp. 853ff.; Vincent-Abel, pp. 248ff.; LeStrange, *Palestine*, pp. 204–9; Gil, *Palestine*, pp. 373–75, and many other places.

19. It is interesting that a remote and rational scholar like al-Biruni, living in northeastern Iran, wrote about the "miracle" of the sacred fire and tried to explain it.

20. Van Berchem, *Matériaux: Ville*, pp. 53–67, with an admirable commentary.

21. See Archibald Wells, "Two Minarets flanking the church of the Holy Sepulchre," *Levant* 8 (1976).

22. See the summary and long bibliography in Bieberstein-Bloedhorn, vol. 2, pp. 183–216; see also Virgilio C. Corbo, *Il Santo Sepolcro di Gerusalemme. Aspetti archeologici dalle origini al periodo crociato*, (Jerusalem, 1981), pp. 139ff. and pls. 4–5.

23. Ibn al-Zubayr, *Kitab al-Dhakha'ir wa al-Tuhaf*, ed. M. Hamidullah (Kuwait, 1959), no. 86; trans. Ghada H. Qaddumi as *A Medieval Islamic Book of Gifts* (Ph.D. thesis, Harvard University, Cambridge, 1990), pp. 85–86. See also Robert Ousterhout, "Rebuilding the temple," *JSAH* 48 (1989).

24. See Moshe Rosen-Ayalon, "Une Mosaique Médiévale au Saint-Sépulcre," *RBi* 83 (1976).

25. See Vincent-Abel, pp. 942–43; Gil, *Palestine*, pp. 431–89; T.V. Virsaladze, *Rospis Ierusalimskogo Monastyria* (Tiblisi, 1973). The monastery still exists, today under the Greek Orthodox Church.

26. Vincent-Abel, p. 943.

27. There may, however, have been considerable fluctuation in their number. See Titus Tobler and Augustus Molinier, *Itinera Hierosolymitana Yana* (Geneva, 1879), pp. 301–5. The calculations and assorted interpretations were made in a paper read by Prof. Michael McCormick, who is preparing a new edition of the text and to whom I am grateful for his generosity in sharing with me his knowledge of Latin sources on Jerusalem.

28. See Gil, *Palestine*, pp. 481–82, but there are some uncertainties as to what was really involved.

29. Ibid., p. 486–89.

30. Gil devoted nearly half of his book on Palestine (pp. 490–837) to Jews, mostly in Jerusalem. The early classic on the subject is Jacob Mann, *The Jews in Egypt and Palestine under the Fatimid Caliphs* (Oxford, 1920; repr. with an important introduction by S. D. Goitein, New York, 1970). A clear summary is provided by Joshua Prawer, *The History of the Jews in the Latin Kingdom of Jerusalem* (Oxford, 1988). Thoughtful appraisals can be found in the six volumes of S. D. Goitein, *A Mediterranean Society* (Berkeley, 1967–1988), which has a volume of indices completed by Paula Sanders (Berkeley, 1993).

31. Gil, *Palestine*, pp. 648–49.

32. Ibid., pp. 635–43; for synagogue, pp. 647–49.

33. The story is recounted in ibid., pp. 376–77, 649–50.

34. See Van Berchem, *Matériaux: Haram*, pp. 84–97, for a discussion of the issue and of the general matter of inscribing dimensions as part of the record of a space.

35. The expression *mihrab-i Khoda*, literally "the mihrab of God," is not translated that way by either Scheffer or Thackston, but it is interesting in that it gives to the word *mihrab* a particularly broad meaning and associates it with pre-Islamic sanctity.

36. There is no way of estimating the height of the debris that would have existed in the early eleventh century. Recently (1994), a passage level has been excavated just below the present gate. It may correspond to the level of the Fatimid gate, but much more has to be done about its context before one can reasonably draw that conclusion.

37. The Fatimids were the first rulers within the Islamic world to proclaim and assert their power and

their legitimacy through monumental inscriptions on the facades of buildings, or in any way that would make them visible to a large public. The point has been argued and elaborated in a series of, to my knowledge unpublished, studies by Professor Irene Bierman of the University of California at Los Angeles. I am grateful to her for having over the years shown me her doctoral dissertation and some of her papers on that subject. The earliest instance of external formal inscriptions is the strange mosque of the Three Gates in Kairouan dated to the early ninth century; Bernard Roy and Paul Poinssot, *Inscriptions Arabes de Kairouan* (Paris, 1950), pp. 61–64.

38. The term used is *dârvizah* and I am not certain whether it refers to a function—begging—or to a form. Both Thackston and Schefer appear to have been baffled by many details in this section of the text, as their translations, pp. 25 and 75 respectively, do not seem quite accurate to me, but I fail to come up with a satisfactory one.

39. LeStrange, *Palestine*, pp. 96–97, is only the first of several scholars to mention the confusion of the terms—*masjid, mughatta, masjid al-Aqsa, jami*—used for the large covered building to the south of the Haram, but Nasir-i Khosraw states very clearly "and it is called the *masjid al-Aqsa*."

40. LeStrange, *Palestine*, pp. 101ff.; Creswell, *EMA*, pp. 373–80; and Creswell-Allen, pp. 73–82; see also Henri Stern, "Recherches sur la Mosquée al-Aqsa et ses mosaiques," *Ars Orientalis* 5 (1963).

41. Such are the mosques of Madinah and Cordova, both of which were organized, like the Aqsa Mosque, according to parallel naves. For a most cogent argument, see Busink, *Tempel*, pp. 904–1011.

42. The inscription was unknown to Max van Berchem, but photographs of it were seen by Gaston Wiet, who, as editor of van Berchem's work on Jerusalem, added a rapid reading based on the photographs of an inscription he thought had been destroyed; see van Berchem, *Matériaux: Haram*, pp. 452–53; his reading is correct, but the estimates of lacunae faulty. The archives of the Palestine Archaeological Museum (now the Rockefeller Museum) contain other photographs taken during the restorations of the 1920s and line drawings showing the numerous areas of repairs. The repairs were well done and do not seem to

have altered the sense of the inscription. See also Hamilton, *Aqsa*, p. 9.

43. The words *jaddada* and *'imârah* have a wide range of possible meanings in inscriptions which have often troubled Max van Berchem; cf. the indices to his various volumes. What can always be assumed with *jaddada* is that there was something before whatever is commemorated; the new work could be a small repair or a total reconstruction. The second word, *'imârah*, can refer to any type of building and to almost anything done to an existing one. But clearly these two words, like so many others dealing with construction, need fuller investigation than I am competent to provide.

44. It could be a name or a title.

45. The last two words meaning "may God help him" seem to have been added as an afterthought below the main two lines of the inscription. Since they cut into the ornamental pattern, they must be later, especially as the letters are also smaller in size. But when would someone have added these two words? I should note that the photographs taken in the 1920s and those made in the 1960s show different arrangements for the last letters of the second line of the inscription as well. It is easiest to imagine that some later restorer tried to reproduce an original text but became confused by something he did not quite understand.

46. A triumphal arch inside a building is unusual in Islamic architecture, at least at first glance. But it can be argued that the same sort of statement was made by the facade of the axial nave in the Great Mosque of Damascus, whose original decoration is unclear, and by the position facing the court of the large dome in the Great Mosque of Isfahan, which was built later in the eleventh century, where an inscription also served to make a political message; see Oleg Grabar, *The Great Mosque of Isfahan* (New York, 1990), pp. 49ff.

47. See van Berchem, *Matériaux: Haram*, pp. 381–92, with very important comments. See also Janine Sourdel-Thomine, *Guide des Lieux de Pélerinage* (Damascus, 1957), pp. 64–65, for additional comments.

48. Inasmuch as the inscription copied by al-Harawi also contains the Koranic passage dealing with the *masjid al-Aqsa*, which would be an unusual repetition in the same building, it is tempting to argue that the twelfth-century traveler conflated several

inscriptions. But it is also possible that the Fatimids repeated in their inscriptions the main message they were trying to broadcast.

49. Although they must exist somewhere, I have not found any scaled drawings showing the exact structure of the presumably plaster form in which the mosaics are set and its relationship to the square that supports it.

50. The artisan in charge of that job had the curious nickname of *al-Ajwaf*, the "big but hollow one"; see S.A.S. Husaini, "An Inscription of the caliph al-Mustansir billah," *QDAP* 9 (1939).

51. The word usually means "shop," but its original meaning, was of a "flattened area." It is more frequently *dikak* in Arabic,

52. See Lisa Golombek, *The Timurid Shrine at Gazur Gah* (Toronto, 1969), pp. 109ff.; and Lamei Mustafa, *Al-Madinah al-Munawwarah* (Beirut, 1981), for the shape of the Prophet's mosque. It is interesting to note that already in 985, Muqaddasi compared this upper platform on the Haram with the *rowdah* around the Prophet's tomb in Medinah; see Arabic text, p. 169.

53. Van Berchem, *Matériaux: Haram*, pp. 275ff.

54. See van Berchem, *Matériaux: Haram*, pp. 261–74, with a truly brilliant commentary.

55. This is a most common inscription in mosques, inasmuch as it continues with a list of the main duties imposed on the faithful. Melchior de Vogüé, *Le Temple de Jérusalem* (Paris, 1864), p. 93 and pl. XXVII, has a slightly different reading of two of the inscription's words, but van Berchem's is probably more accurate.

56. One flat *mihrab* for private devotions is still preserved; Eva Baer, "The Mihrab in the Cave of the Dome of the Rock," *Muqarnas* 3 (1985).

57. Van Berchem, *Matériaux: Haram*, no. 145, as corrected by Leo Mayer, *Islamic Architects* (Geneva, 1956), p. 40, n. 1.

58. The best discussion is in van Berchem, *Matériaux: Haram*, pp. 73–84. For a different interpretation, see Rosen-Ayalon, *EIM*, pp. 30–32.

59. See Alexandre Papadopoulo, ed., *Le Mihrab* (Leiden, 1988).

60. See E. Baldwin Smith, *The Dome* (Princeton, 1950), pp. 72–74; and Henri Lammens, "Le Culte des bétyles," *Bulletin de l'Institut Français d'Archéologie au Caire* 17 (1920).

61. An intriguing possibility for a Byzantine parallel exists if the *tropiké* of the *Book of Ceremonies* by Constantine Porphyrogenetes are indeed "arches supported by columns," as they were interpreted by Jean Ebersolt, in *Le Grand Palais de Constantinople* (Paris, 1910), p. 112 (Vogt edition, I, p. 205). The matter may be worth pursuing in light of the present concern for *spolia* in medieval art.

62. Oleg Grabar, "The Earliest Islamic Commemorative Monuments," *Ars Orientalis*, 6 (1966); much has been written on the subject since then, among others by Jonathan Bloom, Caroline Williams, Thomas Leisten, and Yusuf Ragheb. See also Christopher Taylor, "The Shi'i Role in the development of Funerary Architecture," *Muqarnas* 9 (1992), where many appropriate references can be found. I agree with some but not with all of the corrections brought to my own study of thirty years ago. For a very broad survey, excellent in dealing with the monuments, more debatable in historical interpretation, see the chapter on mausoleums in Robert Hillenbrand, *Islamic Architecture* (Edinburgh, 1994). In general, the pious landscape of Islam needs mor detailed study.

63. See above, pp. 48–49; the fundamental work is by Nuha Khoury, partially published in "The Mihrab Image," *Muqarnas* 9 (1992).

64. See Paula Sanders, *Ritual, Politics, and the City in Fatimid Cairo* (New York, 1994).

65. Much less has been written in recent years on Fatimid art than was true a generation ago. For the theme of Late Antique revivals or continuation, see Eva Hoffman, "The Author Portrait," *Muqarnas* 10 (1993), and compare it with Terry Allen, *A Classical Revival in Islamic Architecture* (Wiesbaden, 1986).

66. All these documents are mentioned in Gil, *Palestine*, pp. 279–306; a more accessible summary is in Goitein, "al-Kuds," *EI2*, while the relationship to the monuments is discussed by LeStrange, *Palestine*, pp. 90ff., and in Creswell-Allen.

67. Van Berchem, *Matériaux: Haram*, nos. 144, 145, 146, 219.

68. Van Berchem, *Matériaux: Ville*, nos. 25, 26 29.

69. See Gil, *Palestine*, the pages identified in note 6, which gives several examples of these troubles as reported from remote Constantinople. Theophanes always mentions how Christians were made to suffer from plunders or other exactions (*Weltchronik:*

Bilderstreit und Arabersturm, trans. Leopold Beyer [Graz, 1957], pp. 74, 97, 149), while nothing of the sort is reported by Baghdad sources.

70. For example, an inscription of 1053–54 refers to the endowment of houses for pilgrims from Diyarbakr in the upper Euphrates valley, today in Turkey; Michael H. Burgoyne, "A recently discovered Marwanid inscription in Jerusalem," *Levant*, 14 (1982).

71. Maqrizi, *Khitat* (Cairo, 1853–54), II, p. 250, mentions a *mutawalli* or "supervisor" of the mosque in Jerusalem for the year 988–89, but what the reference really means is not clear; see also Gil, *Palestine*, p. 315.

72. Ibid., p. 301, suggests that this mix may have included the founder of the Karrami sect.

73. Van Berchem, *Matériaux: Haram*, no. 274; Gil, *Palestine*, pp. 294–95; there is no need, in my opinion, to assume, as Gil does on p. 299, that al-Ma'mun visited the city, just because he sponsored a lot of work there.

74. Van Ess, Joseph, *Theologie und Gesellschaft im 2, und 3. Jahrhundert Hidschra: Eine Geschichte des religiosen Denkens im frühen Islam* (Berlin/New York, 1991), pp. 200ff.

75. The very peculiar political condition of Jerusalem after 1183 explains, in part, the absence of visible evidence of the reconquest.

76. See articles on "Makkah" and "Madinah" in *EI2*.

77. Muqaddasi, *Ahsan*, trans. Miquel, p. 198.

78. Severus b. al-Muqaffa, II, p. 364.

79. See Ibn al-Faqih in *BGA*, 5: 93ff., trans. Henri Massé, *Abrégé du Livres des Pays* (Damascus, 1973), pp. 114ff., where mention is made of the celebrated Meshed manuscript of the text with many variants and additions. That text has, to my knowledge, not been edited. See André Miquel, *La géographie humaine du monde musulman jusqu'au milieu du 11e siècle*, (Paris 1967–1988), vol. 1, pp. 153–89, for a good analysis of this passage and of the whole text.

80. Ibn Abd Rabbih, Ahmad Ibn Mohammad *Al-'Iqd al-Farid*, ed. M. al-Ariyan (Cairo, 1940) or Kh. Sharaf al-Din (Beirut, 1986), 7, p. 297.

81. I give only two examples. Muqaddasi describes the Dome of the Rock as consisting of three concentric arcades, *riwaq*, thus implying a perception of the building in terms of volumes of space rather than as systems of construction, but the terminology he uses seems to be mostly that of construc-

tion. There is also a distinction between *taq* and *qantarah* for arches which does not make very good sense; see Arabic text, pp. 170–72; Miquel trans., pp. 193–95.

82. My paraphrase interprets, I believe correctly, a text that simply says "to the left"; cf. Miquel's comments on p. 196, n. 202.

83. The first instance known to me occurs in Azraqi's description of the changes made in the Mekkan sanctuary during the eighth and ninth centuries; O. Grabar in *Muqarnas* 5.

84. I dealt with this topic some thirty years ago in "A New Inscription from the Haram al-Sharif," *Studies in Honour of K.A.C. Creswell* (Cairo, 1965) and simply summarize here my own earlier investigations which may need modification on the archaeological level but which seem to me to have withstood the test of time in conceptual terms.

85. This is apparently the earliest reference to this name; see Simons, *Jerusalem*, p. 417, n. 2.

86. The latest attempt is in Elad, *Jerusalem*, especially map 3.

87. Elad, *Jerusalem*, is based primarily on the unpublished texts of al-Musharraf and al-Murajja and on the wonderful collective accomplishments of the Hebrew University in Jerusalem which sponsored the edition of al-Wasiti's text.

88. On this "micro" level of analyzing a specific issue posed by some passage of the *fada'il*, one of the rare instances is N. Rabbat in *Muqarnas* 6 (1989) and 19 (1993).

89. Al-Musharraf, Tübingen ms., fol. 13.

90. The role played in Islamic culture at that time by the genre known as "Israiliyat," stories about Jewish topics, has been studied by others; see G. Vajda, "Israiliyat," in *EI*.

91. It is perhaps for these reasons of control over the emotional content of the city that the story of Jewish servants in the Haram, possibly based on actual practices in the late seventh century, entered into several accounts.

92. Al-Musharraf, fols. 29–30.

93. Ibid., fols. 3v–4.

94. See above, p. 162, and below, p. 169, for the cemeteries which offer some curious evidence.

95. See Mednikoff, *Palestina*, I, pp. 138–57, for a very thoughtful analysis of Christian sources. More recently, Robert Schick, "Christianity in the patriar-

cate of Jerusalem in the early Abbasid Period," in M.A. al-Bakhit and R. Schick eds., *Bilad al-Sham during the Abbasid Period* (Amman, 1991); Sidney H. Griffith, *Arabic Christianity in the Monasteries of Ninth-Century Palestine* (London, 1992). The literature in Arabic has only begun to be investigated.

96. Griffith, *Arabic Christianity*, p. 166. It may be worth noting that the earliest dated manuscript (868 C.E.) in the so-called "kufic" script is a manuscript of the Gospels preserved in the monastery of St. Catherine on Mount Sinai; I. E. Maimare, *Katalogos ton neon arabikon kheirografon* (Athens, 1985), no. 1.

97. Griffith, *Arabic Christianity*, VIII, p. 118.

98. Marius Canard, *Byzance et les Musulmans du Proche-Orient* (London, 1973), p. 42.

99. Much has been written on these topics. For directions to the literature, see Michael Borgolte, *Der Gesandtenaustausch der Karolingen mit den Abbasiden* (Munich, 1976); Ariyeh Grabois, "Charlemagne, Rome, and Jerusalem," *Revue Belge de Philologie et d'Histoire*, 59 (1981); Gil, *Palestine*, pp. 285ff.; Schick, in *Bilad al-Sha'm*, pp. 71–72.

100. Titus Tobler and Alfred Molinier, eds., *Itinera Hierosolymitana* (Geneva, 1880), pp. 301–5; Wilkinson, *Pilgrims*, pp. 137–38.; Gil, *Palestine*, pp. 435ff. I am very grateful to Professor Michael MacCormick of Harvard University for enlightening me on the issue and look forward to his new edition of the original text.

101. Kühnel, *Wall-Painting*, pp. 118ff., for an account of King Olaf I in 990–992; and Sven B. F. Jansson, *Runes in Sweden* (Värnamö, 1987), for a runic stone mentioning one Osten who went out to Jerusalem and died in Greece in 1027. See also Bernard F. Reilly, *The Contest of Christian and Muslim Spain, 1031–1157* (Cambridge, 1992), pp. 121, 238, for Christian and Jewish pilgrims.

102. F. W. Buckler, *Harun al-Rashid and Charles the Great* (Cambridge, 1931), p. 36.

103. See Tobler and Molinier, *Itineraria*, p. 31; and Vincent-Abel, *Jérusalem Nouvelle*, pp. 455–59, whose documentation disappears after the middle of the tenth century.

104. Many scholars have already dealt and are still dealing with the masses of information found in these fragments and, even though new information may still be found, various summaries of the state of Jews in Jerusalem, mostly in the eleventh century,

are available. Gil, *Palestine*, pp. 490–770, is the most complete survey available at this stage, but much profit can be derived from earlier works by J. Mann and S.D. Goitein.

105. Gil, *Palestine*, pp. 647–53. I fail to see why Gil interprets Muqaddasi's depiction of a cavern under a rock as a reference to a synagogue rather than to the cave under the Dome of the Rock.

106. Gil, *Palestine*, pp. 626–29.

107. The Karaites even manufactured a special cheese on the mountain; Gil, , pp. 628–29.

108. A very interesting document about Jewish prayers for the Fatimid caliph has been published by S. D. Goitein, "Prayers from the Geniza for Fatimid Caliphs, the head of the Jerusalem Yeshiva, the Jewish community, and the local congregation," Sheldon R. Brunswick, ed., *Studies in Judaica, Karaitica, and Islamica to Leon Nemoy* (Bar-Ilan, 1982).

109. The late eleventh century is, on the whole, a rather confusing time and it is difficult to know how much insecurity there really was, since western pilgrims appear to have been coming and going with relative ease. See Bianquis, *Fatimides*, pp. 411, 464, 527ff.; and Gil, *Palestine*, pp. 414–17.

110. The eschatological concerns of the city have always been present, even if held somewhat in abeyance in the sources of the tenth to the eleventh centuries. As a curious, slightly later, example, there is the representation of Jerusalem next to Mekkah and Medinah on a pilgrimage certificate of the thirteenth century; Janine Sourdel-Thomine, "Une image musulmane de Jérusalem," in D. Poirion, ed., *Jérusalem, Rome, Constantinople* (Paris, 1986).

111. Van Berchem, *Matériaux: Ville*, nos. 7, 8, 10, 12, 29.

Conclusion

1. See, for example, Raymond E. Brown, Joseph A. Fitzmayer, and Roland Murphy, *The New Jerome Biblical Commentary* (Englewood Cliffs, 1990), pp. 731–32.

2. The "greening" of the Haram is a relatively recent phenomenon and certainly a welcome one for visitors and probably for the protection of the space. I have not been able to figure out whether there were more trees and other forms of vegetation in the Middle Ages than in the Jerusalem I first knew in 1953.

Appendix A

1. The participants in this project would like to thank Kirk Alexander, Manager, Interactive Computer Graphics Laboratory (ICGL) at Princeton University, and ICGL personnel, Carlo Balestri and Kevin Perry, for the invaluable help they offered us concerning the use of computer-aided design technologies for the reconstruction of early Islamic Jerusalem. We are also indebted to Harrison Eiteljorg II, Director, Center for the Study of Architecture, for the valuable advice he gave us during different phases of the project. Parts of this essay previously appeared in Mohammad al-Asad, "Computer-Aided Design Programs and the Study of Architectural History: The Case of Early Islamic Jerusalem," *Newsletter of the Center for the Study of Architecture* 6 (August 1993): pp. 5–10.

2. Definitions of the computer terms used in this essay are available in computer dictionaries such as *Microsoft Press Computer Dictionary: The Comprehensive Standard for Business, School, Library, and Home* (Redmond, Washington, 1991). For an introduction to the principles and applications of computer-aided design technologies, see Malcolm McCullough and William J. Mitchell, *Digital Design Media: A Handbook for Architects and Design Professionals* (New York: Van Nostrand Reinhold, 1991).

3. See *Jerusalem: 600–1100*. Produced by Intermedia Communications for the Institute for Advanced Study, Princeton, New Jersey. (Authored by Mohammad al-Asad, Abeer Audeh, and Oleg Grabar. Produced in conjunction with Kirk Alexander, Manager, Interactive Computers Graphics Laboratory, Princeton University, 1993).

BIBLIOGRAPHY

A'tham al-Kufi, Ahmad B., *Kitab al-Futuh*, ed. M.A.M. Khan (Hyderabad, 1968)

Aga-Oglu, M., "Remarks on the character of Islamic art," *AB*, 36 (1954)

Alexander, Paul J., "Medieval Apocalypses as Historical Sources," *American Historical Review* 73 (1968)

Alexander, Paul J., *The Byzantine Apocalyptic Tradition* (Berkeley, 1985)

Alföldi-Rosenbaum, E., "External Mosaic Decoration on Late Antique Buildings," *Frühmittelalterische Studien* 4 (1970)

al-Arif, Ibrahim M., *Al-Mufassal f: Ta'rikh al-Quds* (rpr. Jerusalem, 1986)

al-Asad, Mohammad, Abeer Audeh, and Oleg Grabar, *Jerusalem: 600-1100*. Produced by Intermedia Communications for the Institute for Advanced Study, Princeton, New Jersey. Produced in conjunction with Kirk Alexander, Manager, Interactive Computers Graphics Laboratory, Princeton University, 1993)

Asad, Mohammad Al-, "Computer-Aided Design Programs and the Study of Architectural History: The Case of Early Islamic Jerusalem," *Newsletter of the Center for the Study of Architecture* 6 (August 1993)

Assali, Kamel J., *Bayt al-Maqdis fi kutub al-Rihlat* (Amman, 1992)

Assali, Kamel J., ed., *Jerusalem in History* (London, 1989)

Avi-Yonah, Michael, *The Madaba Mosaic Map* (Jerusalem, 1954)

Avi-Yonah, Michael, *The Jews under Roman and Byzantine Rule* (New York, 1976)

Avigad, Nahman, in *IEJ*, 27 (1977) and 37 (1987); "Die Entstehung der Nea genannten Marienkirche," *Antike Welet* 10 (1979).

Avigad, Nahman, *Discovering Jerusalem* (Nashville, 1983)

al-Azdi al-Basri, Abdallah, *Ta'rikh futuh al-Sha'm* (Cairo, 1970)

al-Azraqi, *Akhbar Mekkah*, ed. F. Wüstenfeld (Leipzig, 1858; rpr. Beirut, 1964)

Baer, Eva, "The Mihrab in the Cave of the Dome of the Rock," *Muqarnas* 3 (1985)

Bahat, Dan, *Historical Atlas of Jerusalem* (Jerusalem)

Bahat, Dan *Jerusalem, Selected Plans* (Jerusalem, 1969)

al-Bakhit, M., and Robert Schick, *Bilad al-Sham During the Abbassid Period* (Amman, 1991)

Baladhuri, Ahmad Ibn Yahya, *Futuh al-Buldan* (Leiden, 1866), trans. P.K. Hitti (New York, 1916)

Baldovin, John F., *The Urban Character of Christian Worship in Jerusalem* (Ph.D. thesis, Yale University, New Haven, 1982)

Bashear, Suleyman, "Abraham's Sacrifice of his Son," *Der Islam* 67 (1990)

Bates, Michael, "The Coinage of Syria under the Umayyads," *Fourth Bilad ab-Sham Conference, Proceedings* (Amman, 1989)

Bell, Henry I., ed., *Greek Papyri in the British Museum*, vol. IV (London, 1910)

Bell, Henry I., "Translations of the Greek Papyri," *Der Islam*, vols. 2 (1912), 3 (1913), 4 (1914), and 17 (1927)

Ben-Dov, Meyer, *The Omayyad Structures near the Temple Mount* (Jerusalem, 1974)

Ben-Dov, Meyer, *In the Shadow of the Temple: The Discovery of Ancient Jerusalem* (Jerusalem, 1985)

Bianquis, Thierry, *Damas et la Syrie sous les Fatimides* (Damascus, 1989)

Bieberstein, Klaus, and Hanswulf Bloedhorn, *Jerusalem, Grundzüge der Baugeschichte*, 3 vols. (Wiesbaden, 1994)

Blair, Sheila, "What is the Date of the Dome of the Rock," in *Bayt al-Maqdis I* (Oxford, 1992)

Blake, Robert P., "La Littérature grecque en Palestine," *Le Museon* 78 (1965)

Bloom, Jonathan, "The Mosque of the Qarafah," *Muqarnas* 4 (1987)

Bloom, Jonathan, *The Minaret, Symbol of Islam* (Oxford, 1989)

Borgolte, Michael, *Der Gesandtenaustausch der Karolinger mit den Abbasiden* (Munich, 1976)

Bowersock, Glen W., *Hellenism in Late Antiquity* (Ann Arbor, 1990)

Brockett, Adrian, "Value of *Hafs* and *Warsh* Transmissions for the Textual History of the Qur'an," in Andrew Rippin, *Approaches to the History and Interpretation of the Qur'an* (Oxford, 1988)

Buckler, F. W., *Harun al-Rashid and Charles the Great* (Cambridge, 1931)

Burgoyne, Michael H., "A Recently Discovered Marwanid Inscription," *Levant* 14 (1982)

Burgoyne, Michael H., *The Architectural Development of the Haram in Jerusalem under the Bahri Mamluks*, D.Phil. thesis (Oxford, 1979)

Burgoyne, Michael H., *Mamluk Jerusalem* (Buckhurst Hill, 1987)

Burton, John, *The Collection of the Quran* (Cambridge, 1977)

Busink, Theodor A., *Der Tempel von Jerusalem, von Salomo bis Herodes*, 2 vols. (Leiden, 1970-80)

Busse, Heribert, "The Sanctity of Jerusalem in Islam," *Judaism* 17 (1968)

Busse, Heribert, "Die arabischen Inschriften im und am Felsendom," *Das Heilige Land*, 109 (1977)

Busse, Heribert, "Monotheismus und islamische Christologie in der Bauiuschrift der Felsendoms in Jerusalem," *Theologische Quartalschrift* 161 (1981)

Busse, Heribert, and G. Kretschmar, *Jerusalemische Heiligstumstraditionen* (Wiesbaden, 1987)

Busse, Heribert, "Jerusalem and Mekkah," in Moshe Sharon, ed., *The Holy Land in History and Thought* (Leiden, 1988)

Busse, Heribert, "Jerusalem in the Story of Muhammad's Night Journey," *Jerusalem Studies in Arabic and Islam* 14 (1991)

Caetani, Leonie, *Annali dell'Islam* (Milan, 1905–1926)

Cahen, Claude, "Note sur l'accueil des chrétiens d'Orient à l'Islam," *Revue de l'Histoire des Religions* 166 (1964)

Canard, Marius, "La destruction de l'Eglise de la Résurrection," *Byzantion* 35 (1955)

Canard, Marius, *Byzance et les Musulmans du Proche-Orient* (Variorum, London, 1973)

Catane, Moshe, *Jérusalem á travers trois millénaires* (Freiburg, 1984)

Chen, Doron, "The Plan of the Dome of the Rock reconsidered," *Palestine Exploration Quarterly* 117 (1985)

Chen, Doron, "The Design of the Dome of the Rock," *Palestine Exploration Quarterly*, 112 (1980)

Chiat, Marilyn Joyce Segal, and Kathryn L. Reyerson, eds., *The Medieval Mediterranean* (St. Cloud, 1988)

Chitty, Derward J., *The Desert as a City* (London, 1960)

Clermont-Ganneau, Charles, *Archaeological Researchesin Palestine* (London, 1889)

Cohen, Richard I., ed., *Vision and Conflict in the Holy Land* (New York, 1985)

Cohn, Norman, *The Pursuit of the Millennium* (London, 1957)

Conder, Claude R., and Horatio H. Kitchner, *Survey of Western Palestine III* (London, 1884)

Cook, Michael, and Patricia Crone, *Hagarism* (Cambridge, 1977)

Corbett, "Some observations on the gateways to the Herodian Temple in Jerusalem," *PEQ* 1952

Corbo, Virgilio C., *Il Santo Sepolcro di Gerusalemme. Aspetti archeologici dalle origini al periodo crociato*, 3 vols. (Jerusalem, 1981)

Coüasnon, Charles, *The Church of the Holy Sepulchre in Jerusalem* (London, 1974)

Couret, Alphonse, *La Palestine sous les Empereurs Grecs* (Paris, 1864)

Creswell, Keppel Archibald Cameron, *Early Muslim Architecture*, 2d ed. (Oxford, Clarendon, 1969)

Crone, Patricia, *Slaves on Horses* (Cambridge, 1980)

Crone, Patricia, "The first-century concept of Higra," *Arabica* 41 (1994)

Crowfoot, J. W. "Ophel Again," *PEQ* 77 (1945)

Dagorn, René, *La Geste d'Ismael* (Paris, 1981)

Dagron, Gilbert, and Vincent Déroche, "Juifs et Chrétiens dan l'Orient du VIIᵉ siècle," *TM*, 19, (1991)

Dagron, Gilbert, *Naissance d'une Capitale, Constantinople et ses institutions de 330 à 452*, 2d ed. (Paris, 1984)

Davies, Hugh Williams, *Bernhard von Breytenbah* (London, 1911)

Décobert, Christian, *Le Mendiant et le Combattant* (Paris, 1991)

Deichmann, Frederich Wilhelm, *Frühchristliche Bauten und Mosaiken von Ravenna* (Baden-Baden, 1958)

Demus, Otto, *The Mosaics of San Marco* (Washington, 1988)

Déroche, François, *Les Manuscrits du Moyen Orient* (Istanbul-Paris, 1989)

Déroche, François, *The Abbasid Tradition*, vol. I of *The Nasser D. Khalili Collection of Islamic Art* (Oxford, 1992)

de Vogüé, Melchior, *Le Temple de Jérusalem* (Paris, 1864)

Diehl, Charles, *Choses et Gens de Byzance* (Paris, 1926)

Dodd, Erica Cruikshank, and Shereen Khairallah, *The Image of the Word* (Beirut, 1981)

Donner, Frederic M., *The Early Islamic Conquests* (Princeton, 1981)

Donner, Hubert, *Die anakreontische . . .* (Heidelberg, 1981)

Donner, Hubert, and Heinz Cüppers, *Die Mosaikkarte von Madeba I* (Wiesbaden, 1977), Eng. version (Kampen, 1992)

Duncan, Alistair, *The Noble Sanctuary* (London, 1972)

Duri, Abd al-Aziz, "Bait al-Maqdis in Islam" in Adnan Hadidi ed., *Studies in the History and Archaeology of Jordan* (Amman, 198X)

Duri, Abd al-Aziz, *The Rise of Historical Writing among the Arabs*, ed. and trans. Lawrence Conrad (Princeton, 1983)

Duri, Abd al-'Aziz, "Baghdad" in *The Encyclopedia of Islam*, 2nd edition

Ebersolt, Jean, *Le Grand Palais de Constantinople*

Ecochard, Michel, *Filiation de Monuments Grecs, Byzantins et Islamiques* (Paris, 1977)

Ehrensperger-Katz, "Les représentations de Villes fortifiées," *Cahiers Archéologiques* 19 (1969)

Elad, Amikam, "Why did Abd al-Malik build the Dome of the Rock," *Bayt al-Maqdis I*

Elad, Amikam, *Medieval Jerusalem and Islamic Worship* (Leiden, 1995)

Ettinghausen, Richard, "The 'Beveled Style' in the post-Samarra Period", in G. C. Miles, ed., *Archaeologica Orientalia in Memoriam E. Herzfeld* (Locust Valley, 1952)

Ettinghausen, Richard, *Arab Painting* (Geneva, 1962)

Fischer, Wolfram, *Grundriss der Arabischen Philologie I: Sprachwissenschaft* (Wiesbaden, 1982)

Flusin, Bernard "L'Esplanade du Temple," in *Bayt al-Makdis* I

Flusin, Bernard, "Démons et Sarrasins," *Travaux et Mémoires* 11 (1991)

Flusin, Bernard, *Saint Athanase le Perse* (Paris, 1993)

Fowden, Garth, *Empire to Commonwealth* (Princeton, 1993)

Garitte, Gerard, "La version géorgienne du 'Pré Spirituel'," *Mélanges Eugène Tisserant*, vol. 2 (Vatican, 1964)

Gil, Moshe, *Documents of the Jewish Pious Foundations* (Leiden, 1976)

Gil, Moshe, *A History of Palestine 634-1099* (Cambridge, 1992, from Hebrew edition in 1983)

Gilliot, Claude, "Ibn II Muqatil, Grand Exégète, Traditionniste et Théologien maudit," *Journal Asiatique* 279 (1991)

Goeje, Michael de, *Mémoire sur la Conquête de la Syrie* (Leiden, 1864)

Goitein, Shelomoh Dov, *A Mediterranean Society*, 5 vols. (Berkeley, 1967-88)

Goitein, Shelomoh Dov, "Prayers from the Geniza," *Studies in Judaica to Leon Nemoy* (Bar-Ilan, 1982)

Goitein, Shelomoh Dov, "al-Kuds," *Encyclopedia of Islam*, 2nd ed.

Golombek, Lisa, *The Timurid Shrine at Gazur Gak* (Toronto, 1969)

Gousset, Marie-Thérèse, *Iconographie de la Jérusalem Céleste* (Thèse Univ. de Paris IV, 1978)

Gozlan, Suzanne, *La Maison du Triomphe de Neptune à Acholla* (Rome, 1991), no. 12

Grabar, André, *L'Iconoclasme Byzantin* (Paris, 1957)

Grabar, André, *Ampoules de Terre Sainte* (Paris, 1958)

Grabar, André, "Quelques Notes sur les Psautiers Byzantines," *Cahiers Archéologiques* 15 (1965)

Grabar, Oleg, "The Umayyad Dome of the Rock," *Ars Orientalis* 3 (1957)

Grabar, Oleg, "A New Inscription from the Haram al-Sharif," *Studies in Honour of K.A.C. Creswell* (Cairo, 1965)

Grabar, Oleg et al., *City in the Desert* (Cambridge, 1979)

Grabar, Oleg, "A Note on the Chludoff Psalter," *Okeanos* (Harvard Ukrainian Studies 7, 1983)

Grabar, Oleg, "Upon Reading al-Azraqi," *Muqarnas* 3 (1985)

Grabar, Oleg, *The Formation of Islamic Art*, 2d ed. (New Haven, 1987)

Grabar, Oleg, "The Meaning of the Dome of the Rock," in M. J. Chiat and K. Reyerson, eds., *The Medieval Mediterranean* (St. Cloud, Minn., 1988)

Grabar, Oleg, *The Great Mosque of Isfahan* (New York, 1992)

Grabar, Oleg, *The Mediation of Ornament* (Princeton, 1992)

Grabois, H., "Charlemagne, Rome and Jerusalem," *Revue Belge de Philologie et d'Histoire* 59 (1981)

Grégoire, Henri *Inscriptions greques chrétiennes: Asie Mineure* (Paris, 1922)

Griffith, Sidney, *Arabic Christianity of Ninth Century Palestine* (London, 1992)

Grohmann, Adolph, *Arabische Paläographie*, 2 vols. (Vienna 1967 and 1971)

Gruber, Ernst A., *Verdienst und Rang; die Fada'il als literarisches und gesellschafficshes Problem im Islam* (Freiburg, 1975)

Guillaume, Alfred, trans. *The Life of Muhammed* (Oxford, 1955)

Halbwachs, Maurice, *La Topographie légendaire des Evangiles en Terre Sainte* (rpr. Paris, 1971)

Hamilton, Robert W., *The Structural History of the Aqsa Mosque* (Jerusalem, 1949)

Hamilton, Robert W., *Khirbat al-Mafjar* (Oxford, 1959)

Harrison, R. Martin, *Excavations at Saraçhane in Istanbul 1* (Princeton, 1988)

Hauschild, Theodor, "Das Mausoleum von Las Vegas de Pueblanueva," *Madrider Mitteilungen* 19 (1978)

al-Hawary, Hassan, and Gaston Wiet, *Matériaux pour un Corpus Inscriptionum Arabicarum IV: Arabie*, ed. N. Elisséev (Cairo, 1985)

Hill, Donald Routledge, *The Termination of Hostilities in the Early Arab Conquests* (London, 1971)

Hirschberg, S. W., "The Sources of Moslem Traditions Concerning Jerusalem," *Rocznik Orientalistyny* 17 (1951-52)

Hirschfeld, Y. *The Judean Monasteries in the Byzantine Period* (New Haven, 1992)

Holum, Kenneth, *Theodosian Empresses* (Berkeley, 1982)

Holum, Kenneth, Avner Ruban, et al., *The Combined Caesarea Expedition* (Haifa, 1993)

Horn, Walter, and Ernest Born, *The Plan of St. Gall*, 2 vols. (Berkeley, 1974)

Humphreys, R. Stephen, *Islamic History, A Framework for Inquiry* (Princeton, 1991)

Husaini, S.A.S., "An inscription of the caliph al-Mustansir billah," *QDAP* 9 (1939)

Ibn Abd al-Rabbih, Ahmad Ibn Mohammad, *Al-'Iqd al-Farid*, ed. M. al-Ariyan (Cairo, 1940) or Kh. Sharaf al-Din (Beirut, 1986)

Ibn al-Zubayr, *Kitab al-Dhakha'ir wa al-Tuhaf*, ed. M. Hamidullah (Kuwait, 1959)

Ibn Ishaq, Muhammad, *Sirah al-Rusul*, ed. F. Wüstenfeld (Göttingen, 1859)

Idinopulos, Thomas A., *Jerusalem Blessed, Jerusalem Cursed* (Chicago, 1991)

Ivanov, Vladimir, *Nasir-i Khosraw and Ismailism* (Bombay, 1940)

Jeffery, Arthur, *Materials for the History of the Text of the Qur'an* (Leiden, 1937)

Jeffery, Peter, "The Earliest Christian Chant Repertory Recovered: The Georgian Witnesses to Jerusalem Chant," *Journal of the American Musicological Society*, 47 (1994)

Kenyon, Kathleen M., *Jerusalem, Excavating 8000 Years of History* (London, 1967)

Kessler, Christel, "Above the Ceiling of the Outer Ambulatory," *Journal of the Royal Asiatic Society* 1964

Kessler, Christel, "Abd al-Malik's Inscription in The Dome of the Rock, a Reconsideration," *Journal of the Royal Asiatic Society*, 1970

Kevran, Monik, Solange Ory, and Madeline Schneider, *Index Géographique du Répertoire Chronologique d'Epigraphie Arabe*, vols. 1–16 (Cairo, 1975)

Khalidi, Tarif, *Islamic Historiography: The Histories of Mas'udi* (Albany Press, 1975)

Khoury, Rawf George, *Wahb b. Munabbih* (Wiesbaden, 1972)

Khoury, Nuha, "The Dome of the Rock, the Ka'ba, and Ghumdan," *Muqarnas* 10 (1993)

Kister, M. J., *Studies in Jahiliyya and Early Islam* (London, Variorum, 1980)

Krautheimer, Richard, "Introduction to an 'Iconography of Medieval Architecture,'" *Journal of the Warburg and Courtauld Institutes* 5 (1942)

Krautheimer, Richard, *Rome, Profile of a City 312-1308* (Princeton, 1982)

Küchler, Max, "Moschee und Kalifenpaläste Jerusalems nach den Aphrodito-Papyri," *ZDPV* 107 (1991)

Kühnel, Bianca, *From the Earthly to the Heavenly Jerusalem: Representations of the Holy City in Christian Art of the First Millenium* (Rome, 1987) [*Röm Q Schr* suppl. 42]

Kühnel, Gustav, *Wall Painting in the Latin Kingdom of Jerusalem* (Berlin, 1988)

Kutcher, Arthur, *The New Jerusalem; Planning and Politics* (London, 1973)

Lammens, Henri, "Le culte des bétyles," *Bulletin de l'Institut Français d'Archéologie au Caire* 17 (1920)

Lapidus, Ira M., *Muslim Cities in the Later Middle Age* (Cambridge, 1967)

Lassner, Jacob, *The Shaping of Abbasid Rule* (Princeton, 1980)

Le Strange, Guy, *Palestine under the Moslems* (London, 1890)

Leclercq, H. in *DACL* (Paris, 1971)

Lewis, Bernard, "An Apocalyptic Vision of Islamic History," *BSOAS* 13 (1950)

Lewis, Bernard, and Peter M. Holt, eds., *Historians of the Middle East* (London, 1962)

Lewis, Bernard, "On that day. A Jewish apocalyptic poem on the Arab conquests," in: *Mélanges d'Islamologie: Volume dédié à la memoire de Armand Abel*, ed. Pierre Salmon (Leiden, 1974)

Linder, Amnon, "Jerusalem as a focus of confrontation," Richard I. Cohen, ed., *Vision and Conflict in the Holy Land* (New York, 1985).

Little, Donald P., "The Significance of the Haram Documents," *Der Islam* 57 (1980)

Lufti, Huda, *Al-Quds al-Mamlukiyya: A History of Mamluk Jerusalem based on the Haram documents* (Berlin, 1985)

Lynch, Kevin, *The Image of the City* (Cambridge, 1960)

Mahmud, Sayyid Fayyaz, *Ta'rikh al-Quds* (Amman, 1984)

Mango, Cyril, *The Mosaics of St. Sophia* (Washington, 1962)

Mango, Cyril, "The Temple Mount, A.D. 614-636," in *Bayt al-Maqdis*

Mango, Cyril, *The Art of the Byzantine Empire* (Englewood Cliffs, 1972)

Mann, Jacob, *The Jews in Egypt and in Palestine under the Fatimid Caliphs* (New York, 1920, rpr. 1970)

Marmarji, A. S. *Buldaniyah Filastin al-Arabiyah* (Beirut, 1948), trans. into French is *Textes Arabes sur la Palestine* (Paris, 1952)

Mazar, Benjamin, *The Excavations in the Old City of Jerusalem near the Temple Mount. Preliminary Report of the Second and Third Seasons* (Jerusalem, 1969–1970)

McClung, William Alexander, *The Architecture of Paradise: Survivals of Eden and Jerusalem* (Berkeley, 1983)

McCullough, Malcolm, and William J. Mitchell, *Digital Design Media: A Handbook for Architects and Design Professionals* (New York: Van Nostrand Reinhold, 1991)

Mednikoff, Nikolai A., *Palestina ot Zavoevaniya ea Arabami do Krestovykh Pohodah*, 2 vols. (St. Petersburg, 1902)

Meinecke, Michael, *Die Mamlukische Architektur in Agypten und Syrien*, 2 vols. (Berlin, 1992)

Melikian-Chirvani, Souren, *Islamic Metalwork from the Iranian World* (London, 1982)

Meshorer, Yacov, "Coins of Jerusalem under the Umayyads and Abbasids," Joshua Prawer, ed., *The History of Jerusalem; the Early Islamic Period* (Jerusalem, 1987)

Michael the Syrian, *Chronique*, trans. J.-B. Chabot (Paris, 1901)

Milik, Jozef Tadeusz, "La Topographie de Jérusalem vers la fin de l'époque byzantine," *Mélanges Université St. Joseph* 37 (1961)

Milstein, Rachel, "A Hoard of Early Arab Figurative Coins," *INJ* 10 (1988–89)

Miquel, André, *La géographie humaine du monde musulman jusqu'au milieu du 11e siècle*, 4 vols. (Paris 1967–1988)

Monneret de Villard, U., *Introduzione allo Studio dell'archeologia Islamica* (Venice, 1966)

Moritz, Bernhard, *Arabic Palaeography* (Cairo, 1974)

Mujir Al-Din, *Al-'Uns al-Jalil fi ta'rikh al-Quds wa al-Khalil*, (Cairo, undated original edition in two volumes, subsequent editions in 1968, 1973, and 1992)

al-Munajjad, Salah al-Din, "Qit'ah min kitab. . . .al-Muhallabi," *Majallat Ma'ahad al-Makhtutat al-Arabiyah*, 4 (1958)

al-Muqaddasi, *Ahsan al-Taqasim fi Ma'rifat ul-Aqalim*, ed. Michael Jan de Goeje, *BGA*, vol. 3 (Leiden, 1906); partial translation by André Miquel (Damascus, 1963)

Mustafa, Lamei, *Al-Madinah al-Munawwarah* (Beirut, 1981)

Nasir-i Khosro, *Sefer Nameh*, ed. and trans. Schefer, Charles H. A. (Paris, 1881; rpr. Amsterdam, 1970), English trans. by Wheeler M. Thackston Jr., *Book of Travels* (Albany Press, 1985)

Nijim, Rauf Y., ed., *Kunuz al-Quds* (Amman, 1983)

Nöldeke, Theodor, Bergstrasser, Gotthelf, Pretzl, O., Schwally, Friedrich, *Geschichte des Qorans* (Leipzig, 1904-38)

North, Albrecht, and Lawrence Conrad, *The Early Arabic Historical Tradition* (Princeton, 1994)

O'Callaghan, R. T., "Madaba, Carte de," in *Dictionnaire de la Bible, Suppl. V* (Paris, 1951)

Ory, Solange, "Aspects religieux des textes épigraphique," *Les Premieres Ecritures Islamiques*, vol. 58 of *Revue du Monde Musulman et de la Mediterraneé* (1991)

Ousterhout, Robert G., "Rebuilding the Temple," *JSAH* 48 (1989)

Ovadiah, Asher, *Corpus of the Byzantine Churches of the Holy Land* (Boston, 1970)

Palmer, Andrew, *The Seventh Century in the West-Syrian Chronicles* (Liverpool, 1993)

Papadopoulo, Alexandre, ed., *Le Mihrab* (Paris, 1988)

Parrinder, Geoffrey, *Jesus in the Qur'an* (Oxford, 1977)

Patai, Raphael, *The Messiah Texts* (Detroit, 1979)

Paton, William Roger ed., *The Greek Anthology* (Cambridge, 1916)

Peters, Francis E., "Why did Abd-al-Malik build the Dome of the Rock," *Graeco-Arabica* 2 (1983)

Peters, Francis E., *Jerusalem and Mecca, The Typology of the Holy City in the Near East* (New York, 1986)

Peters, Francis E., *The Hajj* (Princeton, 1994)

Piccirillo, Michele, *The Mosaics of Jordan* (Amman, 1993)

Prag, Kay, *Jerusalem* (Blue Guide, London, 1989), pp. 77-81.

Prawer, Joshua, ed., *The History of Jerusalem: The Early Islamic Period* (Jerusalem, 1987)

Prawer, Joshua, "The Jerusalem the Crusaders Captured," in P. W. Edbury, *Crusade and Settlement* (Cardiff, 1985)

Qedar, Shraga, "Copper Coinage of Syria in the Seventh and Eight Centuries," *Israel Numismatic Journal*, vol. 10 (1988)

Qaddumi, Ghada H., *A Medieval Islamic Book of Gifts* (Ph.D. thesis, Harvard University, Cambridge, 1990)

Rabbat, Nasser, "The Meaning of the Umayyad Dome of the Rock," *Muqarnas* 6 (1989)

Rabbat, Nasser, "The Dome of the Rock Revisited," *Muqarnas* 10 (1993)

Raby, Julian, and Jeremy Johns, eds., *Bayt al-Maqdis I, 'Abd al-Malik's Jerusalem* (Oxford, 1992)

Ragheb, Yusuf, "L'Ecriture des Papyrus Arabes," *Revue du Monde Musulman et de la Méditerranée* 58 (1991)

Reininck, G. J., "Ps.-Methodius: A Concept of History in Response to the Rise of Islam," in Averil Cameron and Lawrence Conrad, eds., *The Byzantine and Early Islamic Near East* (Princeton, 1992)

Richmond, Ernest T., *The Dome of the Rock in Jerusalem* (Oxford, 1924)

Rippin, Andrew, *Approaches to the History and Interpretation of the Qur'an* (Oxford, 1988)

Robert, Louis, "Epigrammes du Bas-Empire," *Hellenica* 4 (1948)

Rochow, Ilse, *Byzanz im 8. Jahrhundert in der Sicht des Theophanes* (Berlin, 1991)

Rosen-Ayalon, Myriam, "The first Mosaic discovered in Ramla," *Israel Exploration Journal* 26 (1976)

Rosen-Ayalon, Myriam, "The Facade of the Holy Sepulchre," *Rivista di Studi Orientali* 59 (1985)

Rosen-Ayalon, Myriam, *The Early Islamic Monuments of al-Haram al-Sharif* (Jerusalem, 1989)

Rosen-Ayalon, Myriam, "Une Mosaique Médiévale au Saint-Sépulcre," *Revue biblique* 83 (1976)

Runciman, Steven, *A History of the Crusades*, vol. I (Cambridge, 1953)

Sadan, Joseph, "A Legal Opinion Regarding the Sanctity of Jerusalem," *IOS* 13 (1993)

Sadek, Mohammed-Moin, *Die Mamlukische Architecktur der Stadt Gaza* (Berlin, 1991)

Safdie, Moshe, *The Harvard Jerusalem Studies* (Cambridge, 1986)

Salem-Liebich, Hayat, *The Architecture of the Mamluk City of Tripoli* (Aga Khan Program, Cambridge, 1983)

Sanders, Paula, *Ritual, Politics, and the City in Fatimid Cairo* (New York, 1994)

Sanjian, Avedis Krikor, "Anastos Vardapet's Lis," *Le Museon*, 82 (1969).

Sauvaget, Jean, *La Mosquée Omeyyade de Médine* (Paris, 1947)

Sauvaire, Henri, trans., *Histoire de Jérusalem et d'Hébron* (Paris, 1876)

Sayyid, A. G., "Lumières sur quelques sources de l'histoire Fatimide," *Annales Islamologiques* 13 (1977)

Schächter, Jacob, *Jerusalem through the Ages* (Jerusalem, 1975)

Schick, Robert, "Christianity in the Patriarchate of Jerusalem," in M. al-Bakhit and R. Schick, *Bilad al-Sham* (Amman, 1991)

Schrieke, B., "mi'radj" in *Encyclopedia of Islam* 2

Setton, Kenneth M., ed., *A History of the Crusades*, vol. I (Philadelphia, 1958)

Sharf, A., *Byzantine Jewry* (London, 1971)

Sharon, Moshe, "An Inscription from the year 65 A.M. in the Dome of the Rock," *Studia Orientalia Memoriae D. H. Baneth Dedicata* (Jerusalem, 1979)

Sharon, Moshe, "Arabic Inscriptions," *IEJ* 23 (1973)

Sharon, Moshe, "The Praise of Jerusalem," *Bibliotheca Orientalis* 49 (1992)

Simons, Jan Josef, *Jerusalem in the Old Testament* (Leiden, 1952)

Sivan, Emmanuel, "The Beginnings of the Fada'il al-Quds Literature," *Der Islam* 94 (1971)

Smith, E. Baldwin, *The Dome* (Princeton, 1950)

Sophronius, *Lettre à Arcadius de Chypre*, ed. M. Albert and Ch. von Schönborn in *Patrologia Orientalis* 39 (Turnhout, 1978)

Soucek, Priscilla, "The Temple of Solomon in Islamic Legend and Art," in Joseph Guttman ed., *The Temple of Solomon* (Ann Arbor, 1976)

Sourdel-Thomine, Janine, *Guide des Lieux de Pélerinage* (Damascus, 1957)

Sourdel-Thomine, Janine, "Une image musulmane de Jérusalem," in D. Poirion ed., *Jérusalem, Rome, Constantinople* (Paris, 1986)

Spieser, M.-J., *Thessalonique et ses Monuments* (Paris, 1984)

Stern, Henri, "Les Représentatives des Conciles," *Byzantion* 11 (1936)

Stern, Henri, "Recherches sur la Mosquée al-Aqsa et ses mosaiques," *Ars Orientalis* 5 (1963)

Tabari, *History*, 31 volumes published to date (SUNY Press, 1984–)

Tabari, *Commentaire du Coran*, trans. Pierre Godé (Paris, 1986), vol. 3, (Paris, 1986)

Theophanes, *Chronicle*, trans. L. Beyer (Bonn, 1957)

Tobler, Titus, and Augustus Molinier, *Itinera Hierosolymitana* (Geneva, 1880)

Tsafrir, Yoram, ed., *Ancient Churches Revealed* (Jerusalem, 1993)

Tsafrir, Yoram, "Jerusalem" *RBK* (Stuttgart, 1978)

Tsafrir, Yoram, "The Maps used by Theodosius," *DOP* 40 (1986)

Tsafrir, Yoram, "The Massive Wall East of the Golden Gate," *IEJ* 40 (1990)

Tushingham, Douglas A., *Excavations in Jerusalem 1961-1967, I* (Toronto, 1985)

Vajda, Georges, "La Description du Temple de Jérusalem," *Journal Asiatique* (1959)

Van Berchem, Marguerite, and Etienne Clouzot, *Mosaïques Chrètiennes* (Geneva, 1924)

Van Berchem, Marguerite, and Solange Ory, *La Jérusalem Musulmane dans l'oeuvre de Max van Berchem* (Lausanne, 1978)

Van Berchem, Max, *Matériaux pour un Corpus Inscriptionum Arabicarum: Jerusalem Ville et Haram* (Cairo, 1922–27)

Van Ess, Joseph, "Abd al-Malik and the Dome of the Rock," in J. Raby, ed., *Bayt al-Maqdis* I

Van Ess, Joseph, *The Youthful God: Anthropomorphism in Early Islam* (Arizona State University, 1988)

Van Ess, Joseph, *Theologie und Gesellschaft im 2, und 3. Jahrhundert Hidschra: Eine Geschichte des religiosen Denkens im frühen Islam* (Berlin/New York, 1991)

Vikan, Gary, *Byzantine Pilgrimage Art* (Washington, 1982)

Vilnay, Zev, *The Holy Land in Old Prints and Maps* (Jerusalem, 1965)

Vincent, Louis Hugues (with F. M. Abel) *Jérusalem, Recherches de topographie d'archéologie et d'histoire II: Jerusalem Nouvelle* (Paris, 1922–26)

Vincent, Louis Hugues, and A. M. Stève, *Jérusalem de l'Ancien Testament*, 3 vols. (Paris, 1954–56)

Virsaladze, *Rospis Jerusalimskogo Monastyria* (Tiblisi, 1973)

Von Schönborn, Charles, *Sophrone de Jérusalem* (Paris, 1972)

Walker, P.W.L., *Holy City, Holy Places* (Oxford, 1990)

Walls, Archibald G., "Two Minarets flanking the church of the Holy Sepulchre," *Levant* 8 (1976)

Walls, Archibald G., and Amal Abul-Hajj, *Arabic Inscriptions in Jerusalem: A Handlist and Maps* (London, 1980)

Walls, Archibald G., *Geometry and Architecture in Islamic Jerusalem, A Study of the Ashrafiyya* (Buckhurst Hill, 1990)

Wansbaugh, J., *Quranic Studies* (Oxford, 1977)

Warren, C. W., *Underground Jerusalem* (London, 1876)

al-Wasiti, *Fada'il al-Bayt al-Muqaddas*, ed. Isaac Hassoun (Jerusalem, 1979)

Welch, A. T., "al-Kur'an," *Encyclopedia of Islam*, 2nd. ed.

Wellhausen, J., *The Arab Kingdom and its Fall* (Beirut rpr. ed. of 1965)

Werkmeister, Walker, *Quellenuntersuchungen zum Kitab al-'Iqd al Farid* (Berlin, 1983)

Wightsman, G. J., *The Damascus Gate, Jerusalem* (Oxford, 1989)

Wilken, Robert L., *The Land Called Holy* (New Haven, 1992)

Wilkinson, John, "The Streets of Jerusalem," *Levant* 7 (1975)

Wilkinson, John, *Egeria's Travels to the Holy Land* (Jerusalem, 1981)

Wilkinson, John, *Jerusalem Pilgrimage 1099-1185* (London, 1988)

Wilkinson, John, "Architectural Procedures in Byzantine Palestine," *Levant* 13 (1981)

John Wilkinson, trans., *Jerusalem Pilgrims before the Crusades* (Warminster, 1977).

Wilson, Charles W., and Charles Warren, *The Recovery of Jerusalem* (London, 1871)

Yahya b. Sa'id al-Antaki, *Annales*, ed. J. Cheikho (Beirut, 1909)

INDEX

CAD (computer-aided design) programs, 175–83
Caetani, Leone, 45
Caiphas, house of, 36
Cairo: during the Abbasid period, 136; during the Mamluk period, 6; sources concerning, 8, 12
Charlemagne (king of the Franks), 167
Chen, Doron, 108
Christianity, 6, 21–44, 32–38, 39–40; coexisting with Islam and Judaism, 166–69, 171–72, 173; in Dome of the Rock inscription, 68; during the Fatimid period, 143–44; significance of Church of the Ascension (Mount of Olives) for, 37; significance of Church of the Holy Sepulchre for, 32; significance of Herod's Temple for, 28; during the Umayyad period, 132
Christian population in Jerusalem: during the Fatimid period, 166–67; during the Mamluk period, 3
Chrysostom, John (saint), 67
Church of Golgotha, 32
Church of St. Catherine (Mt. Sinai), 101
Church of St. George (Saloniki), 101
Church of St. John (Ephesus), 101
Church of St. Polyeuktes (Constantinople), 71
Church of Sts. Sergius and Bacchus (Constantinople), 71
Church of the Ascension, Mount of Olives, 37, 50, 107, 108, 109
Church of the Eleona, 37
Church of the Holy Sepulchre, 33; Anastasis dome of, 32, 40, 142; caliph visits to, 46–47, 50; compared to Dome of the Rock, 104, 105, 107, 108, 109; destruction of, 138, 142, 143; during the Fatimid period, 138, 142–43, 160, 168; inscriptions in, 142; during the Mamluk period, 17; mosaics in, 101; reconstruction of, 167; religious significance of, 29, 32, 131; sources concerning, 13, 18; during the Umayyad period, 64–65, 126, 132; in writings by Piacenza Pilgrim, 29
Church of the Virgin (Mount Gerizim, Palestine), 108
Commemoratio de Casis Dei, 167
Constantine I (Roman emperor, "the Great"), 6, 114, 115, 162
Constantinople: attempts at conquest of, 129; craftsmen for mosaics from, 72, 100; sources concerning, 7
Corbo, Virgilio, 13
Cordova: mosque of, 69; sources concerning, 8
Couäsnon, Charles, 13, 33
Creswell, Keppel Archibald Cameron, 71, 72, 106, 115
Crusaders, 3, 4, 148
Cyril (bishop of Jerusalem), 21, 38

Damascus: inscriptions in mosque of, 69–70; sources concerning, 8
Damascus Gate (Gate of the Column), 14, 25, 31, 139
David (king of Judah and Israel): artifacts in Church of the Holy Sepulchre, 32; association with Christian Jerusalem, 38, 48–49, 114, 165; association with Dome of the Chain, 158; association with Haram al-Sharif, 148, 159; gates named for, 139; mihrab of, 163

de Vogüé, Melchior, 57, 64, 71, 72
Dome of the Chain: construction of, 130; dating of, 51; religious significance of, 157–58, 172; during the Umayyad period, 130–32; in writings by Ibn al-Faqih, 163
Dome of the Prophet, 157
Dome of the Rock: construction of, 44, 53, 54–55; dating of, 64; during the Fatimid period, 149, 156–57, 161, 162; history of, 172; inscriptions in, 11, 56–71, 136, 156, 162; location of, 28–29, 110–14; mosaics in, 58, 59, 71–104, 149; religious significance of, 7, 52–55, 110–11, 112, 114–16, 133, 163, 172; shape of, 104–10; sources concerning, 14, 18; during the Umayyad period, 52–55
Double Gate, 27, 123–24, 126, 172
Dung Gate, 31

Ecochard, Michel, 108
Egypt, during the Abbasid period, 136
Entry into Jerusalem (Church of the Holy Sepulchre), 143
Ettinghausen, Richard, 71–72
Eucherius (bishop of Lyon), 25
Eudocia (Eastern Roman empress), 25
Eusebius of Caesarea (bishop), 21

Fada'il al-Bayt al-Muqaddas (al-Wasiti), 11, 115
Fada'il Bayt al-Muqaddis wa al-Khalil wa Fada'il al-Sham ("The Merits of Jerusalem and Hebron and the merits of Syria") (al-Musharraf), 11
Fatimid period: Aqsa Mosque during, 120, 122, 148–52, 161–62; Christian population during, 166–67; Church of the Holy Sepulchre during, 138, 142–43, 160, 168; Dome of the Rock during, 149, 156–57, 161, 162; Haram al-Sharif during, 153–56, 158–59, 160–61, 162, 163, 164; Islam during, 160; Jerusalem during, 135–69; leadership of, 173; sources concerning, 11
Franciscan monks, during the Mamluk period, 3
Fustat, during the Abbasid period, 136

Gabriel, mihrabs for in Haram al-Sharif, 164
Gabriel's Dome, 157
Gate of Darkness, 27
Gate of Forgiveness, 153
Gate of Gates, 148
Gate of Hell, 148
Gate of Mercy, 146–48
Gate of Repentance, 146–48
Gate of St. Stephen (Jericho Gate), 25, 139
Gate of Siloam, 139
Gate of the Chain, 146–47
Gate of the Nea, 139
Gate of the Palace (Gate of the Court), 139
Gate of the Prophet (bab al-Nabi), 48, 66, 123, 152–53
Gate of the Prophet David (Zion Gate), 139
Gate of the Spring, 153
Gate of the Tribes, 148